Education & Society

Education & Society

Canadian Perspectives

Edited by

Wolfgang Lehmann

OXFORD

UNIVERSITY PRESS

OXFORD
UNIVERSITY PRESS

Oxford University Press is a department of the University of Oxford.
It furthers the University's objective of excellence in research, scholarship,
and education by publishing worldwide. Oxford is a registered trade mark of
Oxford University Press in the UK and in certain other countries.

Published in Canada by
Oxford University Press
8 Sampson Mews, Suite 204,
Don Mills, Ontario M3C 0H5 Canada

www.oupcanada.com

Library and Archives Canada Cataloguing in Publication
Education & society : Canadian perspectives / edited
by Wolfgang Lehmann.

Includes bibliographical references and index.
ISBN 978–0–19–901430–9 (paperback)

1. Education—Social aspects—Canada. I. Lehmann,
Wolfgang, 1965-, author, editor II. Title: Education and
society.

LC191.8.C2E38 2016   306.430971   C2015-908508-X

Cover image: © iStock/iofoto

Oxford University Press is committed to our environment.
This book is printed on Forest Stewardship Council® certified paper
and comes from responsible sources.

Printed and bound in the United States of America

1 2 3 4 — 19 18 17 16

Table of Contents

Part III • Reform Pressures and Alternative Visions 169

Acknowledgements

I thank all contributors to this volume for their time and dedication to the book. At Oxford University Press Canada, I thank Tanuja Weerasooriya, Suzanne Clark, and Steven Hall for bringing the book to life. Also, many thanks to J. Lynn Fraser for copyediting its final version. I thank all the undergraduate and graduate students at Western University who I have had the privilege to teach and supervise and who have in many ways inspired this book.

Many thanks to my parents, Lothar and Franziska Lehmann, to Petra, Paul, Carla and Anna Lucas, and most of all Audrey, for your love and support.

Wolfgang Lehmann
August 2015

To Audrey

Contributors

The Editor

Wolfgang Lehmann is an Associate Professor in the Department of Sociology, at the University of Western Ontario. He recently completed a study of the experiences of working-class, first-generation university students, supported by a SSHRC grant. He has also published on young people's school-work transitions and vocational education. His work has appeared internationally in journals like *Sociology of Education*, the *British Journal of Sociology of Education*, and *Sociology*. His book *Choosing to Labour? School-Work Transitions and Social Class* was published in 2007 by McGill-Queen's University Press.

Chapter Authors

Paul Anisef is a Professor (retired) of sociology at York University. His research agenda includes the settlement and integration of immigrant youth; an examination of the post-secondary (PSE) pathways of native born and immigrant youth; a social inclusion analysis of the role played by institutions in facilitating the integration of recent immigrants to Toronto; an examination of vulnerable populations (immigrants, seniors, low-income) living in York Region; the family-school-child nexus with relation to children's learning experiences and academic outcomes; school-to-work transitions at the secondary and post-secondary levels of education; and accessibility to higher education and careers for Canadian youth.

Janice Aurini is an Associate Professor in the Department of Sociology and Legal Studies at the University of Waterloo. She received her PhD at McMaster University and was a post-doctoral fellow at Harvard University. Her research primarily examines education policy, education inequality, and parenting. Articles on these topics can be found in *Sociology of Education,* the *Canadian Journal of Sociology*, and *Canadian Public Policy*. She is currently the primary investigator on a five-year SSHRC-funded project on summer learning inequality and is co-authoring an advanced qualitative methods book.

Jayne Baker has had an interest in education since her undergraduate studies. Her current research centres on two different aspects of education. First, she contributes to the *Sociology of Education* and is particularly interested in transitions to higher education and stratification among Canadian institutions. Second, she contributes to the Scholarship of Teaching and Learning, where she is particularly interested in researching how best to balance the quality of the student experience with large class sizes and a move toward technological efficiencies.

Gary R.S. Barron is a Doctoral candidate in Sociology at the University of Alberta. His research interests include the organization of knowledge, education, health and illness, and governance. His doctoral research examines the organization, work, and consequences of university rankings and performance metrics in governing universities.

Ryan Broll is an Assistant Professor in the Department of Sociology and Anthropology at the University of Guelph. His research interests include security, surveillance, social regulation, and victimization, particularly in relation to youth and cyberspace. His recent research has examined the ways in which parents, police officers, and educators prevent and respond to youth cyberbullying.

Robert S. Brown (Toronto District School Board) has worked in applied research for over 30 years, in media research, market research, and education research. After a Master's degree in Communication Studies at the University of Windsor, he completed his doctorate in education at the University of Toronto. A past President of the Association of Educational Researchers of Ontario, he is a Research Coordinator in the Toronto Board of Education and Adjunct Professor at York University, in the Faculty of Education and in Critical Disability Studies. His areas of study include the time structures of schools, including absenteeism; secondary achievement; special education needs; post-secondary student pathways; longitudinal tracking studies; and socio-economic and demographic patterns. He has authored or co-authored works in a number of fields including education, psychology, sociology, and medicine.

Darren Cyr has worked on a number of innovative education and community-based research projects, such as engaging community members about the effects that neighbourhoods have on students' learning opportunities and developing methods for understanding and measuring the cultural vibrancy of neighbourhoods. He holds Bachelor's degrees in Psychology and Sociology, a Master's in Sociology, and a PhD in Sociology from McMaster University.

Scott Davies is a Professor of Educational Policy and Leadership at the University of Toronto. He taught Sociology for 20 years at McMaster University, where he was Ontario Research Chair in Educational Achievement and At-Risk Students. He has published many articles on educational inequality, politics and organizations in journals such as the *American Journal of Sociology*, *Social Forces*, *Sociology of Education*, *Social Problems*, *European Sociological Review*, and *Research in Stratification and Mobility*. He is currently studying children's learning and attainment trajectories over lengthy spans of time.

George J. Sefa Dei is a Professor of Social Justice Education and the Director of the Centre for Integrative Anti-Racism Studies at the Ontario Institute for Studies in Education of the University of Toronto (OISE/UT). He is also the 2015 Carnegie African Diasporan Fellow. His teaching and research interests are in the areas of anti-racism, minority schooling, international development, anti-colonial thought and Indigenous knowledges systems. In June 2007, Professor Dei was installed as a traditional chief in Ghana, specifically, as the Gyaasehene of the town of Asokore, Koforidua in the New Juaben Traditional Area of Ghana. His stool name is Nana Adusei Sefa Atweneboah I.

Delia Dumitrica is an Assistant Professor in Political Communication at Erasmus University in the Netherlands. Her research focuses on mapping the social imaginary around digital technologies. She has an interest in social media and politics, and is currently working on an SSHRC-funded research project examining the role of new media in the communication ecosystem of civic engagement in Canada.

Catherine Gordon holds a PhD in Sociology and is Research Associate at Sarnia Lambton Workforce Development Board. She holds an Adjunct Professorship with the Aboriginal Policy Research Consortium (International). Her most recent publication is "Aboriginal Educational Attainment in Canada" co-authored with Jerry White, which appeared in the *International Indigenous Policy Journal* in 2014.

Cathlene Hillier is a PhD student in the Department of Sociology and Legal Studies at the University of Waterloo. Her earlier research examined teachers' responses to policies on religious inclusion and religious accommodation. Her doctoral research explores how lower-SES parents and children engage teachers and schooling processes in developing children's early literacy skills.

Magdalena Janus is an Associate Professor at the McMaster University's Department of Psychiatry and Behavioural Neurosciences and Offord Centre for Child Studies where she holds the Ontario Chair in Early Child Development. Her research interests focus on population-based indicators of children's developmental health, how to use them to provide communities with information about the state of early development of their children and enable mobilization of resources. While her particular focus is on children at school entry, and the Early Development Instrument, her interests encompass trajectories of child development from infancy to adolescence.

Michael Kehler is an Associate Professor in the Faculty of Education, University of Western Ontario. He examines gender, literacies, body image, health, masculinities, and the counterhegemonic practices of adolescent men. His nationally funded research addresses adolescent reluctance to participate in Health and Physical Education. He is co-editor (with Michael Atkinson) of *Boys' Bodies: Speaking the Unspoken*, and co-editor of *The Problem with Boys' Education: Beyond the Backlash* with Drs W. Martino and M. Weaver-Hightower. He is published in the *McGill Journal of Education*, the *Canadian Journal of Education*, the *International Journal of Men's Health*, *Thymos: Journal of Boyhood Studies*, *Discourse: Studies in the Cultural Politics of Education*, the *Journal of Adolescent and Adult Literacies*, and the *Journal of Curriculum Theorizing*.

Harvey Krahn is a Professor of Sociology at the University of Alberta. His research interests include social inequality, work, education, immigration, sustainable consumption, and political sociology. He is the lead author of *Work, Industry, and Canadian Society* (seventh edition) and has published research findings in a wide range of scholarly journals.

Shadi Mehrabi is a Doctoral student in Educational Policy Studies at the University of Alberta. As an Iranian student in Canada, her research mainly centres on academic/social life of racialized immigrants and international students in Canada. Focusing on the Middle Eastern Diaspora in Canada, she has tackled different areas in education including educational policy, citizenship education, social justice, and place and identity. She is the former Vice President of the Educational Policy Studies Graduate Students' Association (EPSGSA) at the University of Alberta.

Emily Milne is a PhD candidate in the Department of Sociology and Legal Studies at the University of Waterloo. Her Master's research explored the dynamics of inequality within school discipline policies and practices. Her doctoral thesis examines family-school relationships and educational inequality among Canada's Aboriginal peoples.

Thashika Pillay is a Doctoral candidate at the University of Alberta. Her scholarship focuses on issues related to educational policy, migration studies, critical and anti-colonial feminisms, and interlocking systems analysis. In her doctoral research, she uses critical, anti-colonial, and radical feminisms to examine political and community engagement among African-Canadian women. Her work engages issues of social justice, critical global citizenship, and Indigenous knowledge systems and aims to re-centre marginalized onto-epistemological perspectives.

Linda Quirke is an Associate Professor in the Department of Sociology at Wilfrid Laurier University. She has researched organizations, families, schooling, and teacher professionalism. Her most recent work explores parenting advice from mainstream Canadian and American parenting magazines.

Jessica Rizk is a Doctoral student in the Department of Sociology at McMaster University. Her research interests include the sociology of education, gender, families, and childhood and adolescence. She holds an MEd (2013), BEd, and a BA (2011) from York University. Her research is supported by the Social Sciences and Humanities Research Council (SSHRC).

Karen Robson is Associate Professor of Sociology at York University. Her research areas include the barriers to post-secondary education for marginalized youth, intersectionality as a policy framework, and critical race theory. She also has a strong interest in the analysis of large longitudinal data sets to examine issues around social mobility. She also has key textbooks in the area of social research methods and the sociology of education.

Brad Seward is a Doctoral student in the Department of Sociology and Anthropology at the University of Guelph. His research interests involve education and the labour market outcomes of disadvantaged youth, with specific focus on understanding the inequalities within social institutions. His past work has looked at the labour market transitions of recent university graduates and how different fields of study translate to the labour market; focusing specifically on students' ability to repay the loans accrued over the course of their degrees. More recently he has become involved in the issues of gender segregation within university fields of study and the labour market outcomes for graduates with disabilities.

Alison Taylor is an Associate Professor in the Educational Studies Department at the University of British Columbia. She has written several articles on the topic of school-to-work transitions. Her recent funded research projects address the topics of high school apprenticeship programs in Canada, temporary foreign workers, and community service-learning in higher education. Recent publications appear in *Work, Employment and Society*, the *Journal of International Migration and Integration*, and the *Journal of Education and Work*.

David Walters is an Associate Professor in the Department of Sociology and Anthropology at the University of Guelph. His primary areas of specialization include research methodology and the sociology of education. He has received several large grants to explore the labour market outcomes of recent immigrants, as well as school-to-work transitions of post-secondary graduates in Canada and the United States. He is currently investigating the employment prospects of university graduates with disabilities. His research is published in prominent international peer-reviewed journals and is regularly covered by the media.

Jerry White is Director of the Aboriginal Policy Research Consortium (International) and Editor-in-Chief of the *International Indigenous Policy Journal*. As a Professor and former Chair of the Department of Sociology, he has held many posts at the University of Western Ontario, including Acting Director of First Nation Studies, Senior Advisor to the Vice President and Senior Associate Dean of the Faculty of Social Science. He has won several teaching awards, including the Pleva Professorship, and has authored, co-authored, and edited 21 books including *Aboriginal Conditions: Research as a Foundation for Policy* (UBC Press, 2003), *Aboriginal Well-Being: Canada's Continuing Challenge* (TEP, 2007), *Aboriginal Education: Current Crisis, Future Alternatives* (TEP, 2009), and the 10-volume set *Aboriginal Policy Research: Moving Forward, Making a Difference*.

Amanda Williams is an Adjunct Associate Professor for the Faculty of Communication Studies at Mount Royal University in Calgary, Alberta. She teaches theory, research methods, and organizational communication for the Journalism, Information Design, and Public Relations programs. Her previous and current research projects include topics such as the role of metaphor in broadband policy, Massive Open Online Courses (MOOCs), discourses of sustainability and the Alberta Oil Sands, and research literacy learning and student identity. Her refereed publications have appeared in the *International Journal of Technology, Knowledge and Society*, the *International Electronic Journal for Leadership in Learning*, and the *Journal of Computer-Assisted Learning*.

David Zarifa is an Associate Professor of Sociology and a Canada Research Chair in Life Course Transitions in Northern and Rural Communities at Nipissing University. His research interests are in stratification, sociology of education, sociology of work, and quantitative methods and social statistics. His previous work has examined inequalities relating to post-secondary access, school-to-work transitions, workforce outcomes, literacy and skills, and the institutional stratification of post-secondary systems. He is currently working on a SSHRC Insight Development Grant that compares the education and employment outcomes of disadvantaged youth in Canada and the United States.

Introduction

There are no other social institutions of which we expect as much as we do of schools: Teach literacy and numeracy to produce a globally competitive workforce, socialize young people into responsible adult citizens, keep them out of trouble and harm's way, integrate newcomers into the social order, or help those less fortunate to achieve mobility. Schools also reflect the social and political climate of an era more immediately than other institutions. During the Cold War, school systems in the Western industrialized world were expanded in response to the Soviet Union's launch of the Sputnik satellite. Anti-authoritarian movements of the 1970s paved the way for more holistic, democratic ways to organize schools and led to curriculum changes to reflect, for instance, changing racial and gender relations. More recently, globalization and a shift toward neoliberal solutions to economic and political pressures have been accompanied by efforts to return curriculum "back to the basics" and make schools more accountable for what they do. Not surprisingly, then, sociologists have always had a keen interest in the study of education.

As I will outline in more detail in Chapter 1, functionalist thinkers discussed the role of education and schooling for the development of moral, social, and technical competence in increasingly complex and individualistic societies. At the same time, schools have to impart the skills necessary to succeed in a modern economy. To this day, this functionalist perspective remains what parents and policy-makers hope education to be: a system that prepares all young people for adulthood, citizenship, and economic participation, but achieves this in a manner that is free of discriminatory biases and where success is based on talent and effort.

Most contemporary research in the area of the sociology of education, and the chapters in this book are no exception, respond to this optimistic view of what education can achieve by looking at schooling as a key institution in the reproduction of social inequality, rather than a mechanism to level the playing field. Many of the seminal texts of the 1970s, which will be discussed in greater detail in Chapter 1, have investigated how school systems, teacher behaviour, or curriculum disadvantage those from low socio-economic status (SES) backgrounds. A number of chapters in this book offer useful updates on these debates using current, empirical data. Scott Davies, Darren Cyr, Jessica Rizk, and Magdalena Janus contribute a meta-analysis of current empirical studies in Canada, the United States, the United Kingdom, and elsewhere, suggesting that persistent patterns of educational achievement gaps cannot be reduced to single theoretical statements but are multifaceted and complex. Janice Aurini, Emily Milne, and Cathlene Hillier investigate the role parents play in the success of their children at school and how this may be related to social class. Karen Robson, Robert Brown, and Paul Anisef, using data from the Toronto District School Board, shed light on factors that predict why young people and their parents choose specific post-secondary options. These are important studies that empirically advance theoretical perspectives on educational inequality. The book closes with a chapter that may appear, at first sight, completely unrelated to the debates and studies that open it but in many ways brings arguments full circle nonetheless. Delia Dumitrica and Amanda Williams' chapter on Massive Online Open Courses (MOOCs) is not explicitly concerned with issues of educational inequality. Instead, it is focused on the experiences of university staff who develop and teach such courses. Yet MOOCs, which started as university courses, delivered free of charge to anybody in the world with Internet access, offered by renowned academic experts at the world's most prestigious universities, can be interpreted as attempts to overcome structural barriers that have kept many of the most disadvantaged from accessing university-level learning. Yet the authors show that the reach of these courses has been far less impressive than anticipated and that they create unique and troubling challenges about, among others, ownership of intellectual property.

One of the key concerns of both functionalists and critical sociologists is the extent to which education either promotes or hinders social mobility. Although achieving higher levels of educational attainment than one's parents is an important marker of mobility, whether this higher level of education is rewarded in the labour market is equally important. The inter-relationship between education and employment is especially important in what we have come to call knowledge economies. Schooling plays a central role in the transformation of most Western nations into post-industrial economies, by creating conditions for employment and innovation. A highly, formally educated population is not only more employable but also has the skills and the motivation to constantly innovate and thus develop global, competitive advantages. Yet we do know that occupational hierarchies have remained stubbornly unchanged over the past decade, despite massive increases in the educational attainment of Canadians. In other words, in order to break into high-status professional careers, it is as important today to come from a privileged background as it was decades ago; a finding that is confirmed by Harvey Krahn and Gary Barron in Chapter 3, who show that having university-educated (and thus more likely privileged) parents is of paramount importance for entering professional occupations.

One aspect that has been overlooked in research and in policy discourses are the employment prospects of Canadians with disabilities. In Chapter 5, Brad Seward, David Walters, and David Zarifa, use the National Graduate Survey to provide evidence that education–job mismatch, especially in the form of underemployment, is even more evident in the post-graduation trajectories of young Canadians with a disability.

Whereas early conflict sociologists focused on social class, debates have shifted toward the study of gender, race, and ethnicity. In Canada, the educational achievement of ethnic minorities offers very interesting patterns. Some ethnic minority groups significantly outperform white Canadians (of Caucasian descent), whereas other minority groups have been shown to struggle. Looking at the phenomenon of high educational achievement of minorities in Canada, Alison Taylor, Shadi Mehrabi, and Thashika Pillay, in Chapter 7, draw on interview data with racialized immigrant youth to investigate why their educational aspirations are noticeably higher than those of Canadian-born white youth. Yet there remain serious concerns about the educational experiences and attainment of some ethnic minority groups. Whereas Canadians of Asian descent perform well above average, African-Canadians and especially Aboriginal Canadians have been shown to struggle in the school system. George S. Dei (Chapter 12) and Catherine Gordon and Jerry White (Chapter 8) address these issues in different ways. Dei looks at curriculum and pedagogical reforms to address the struggles of minority groups, whereas Gordon and White chronicle First Nations education in an effort to point to future directions.

Scholarship on gender has seen a fascinating reversal in recent years, in which boys have become the focus of research and policy debates. Some have argued that this boy crisis may best be addressed through all-boys classes or schools. Separating boys and girls, proponents of such schools argue, allows teachers to tailor pedagogical strategies to the unique learning styles and needs of boys and girls, thus improving educational outcomes. Jayne Baker in Chapter 9 critically explores these claims in a study of All Boys and All Girls High, two private, exclusive single-gender schools, explaining that such claims generally conflate social class and gender, given the fact that most single-gender schools in Canada (and elsewhere) are exclusive, private schools.

More recently, researchers have extended their concerns beyond the structural constraints associated with class, gender, race, and ethnicity by researching, for instance, the role of ability, disability, and sexuality. As we have become more aware of the diversity students bring to the classroom and campuses, educational institutions also need to gain a better understanding of how diversity can be respectfully accommodated. Michael Kehler, in Chapter 10, shows how boys negotiate body image (something heretofore considered unique to the experience of being a girl) and physical education, and how their experiences are situated in a larger context of gender norms and school hierarchies.

Unfortunately, those who exhibit gender non-conforming behaviour, and those with visible and invisible disabilities are more likely to become victims of bullying. Getting a handle on and addressing bullying has become even more complicated in the digital age. As Ryan Broll shows in Chapter 13, bullying in its digital form, or cyberbullying as it is called, blurs the line of responsibility and expands the extent to which individuals can be objected to bullying. Unlike fighting in the schoolyard, for instance, cyberbullying can take place anywhere, anytime, which creates problems about whose responsibility it becomes to police it.

I opened this introduction arguing that there are no other social institutions of which we expect as much as we do of educational institutions. It is worth repeating this statement here. When we were concerned about losing the Cold War in the 1960s and 1970, the reach of schools was expanded. During the 1970s, learning was to become more holistic. Recently, emphasis has shifted back to competitiveness, individualism, and learning basic skills.

Some of these pressures serve as contexts of chapters in this book, even if they are not explicitly about reform. The work of Kehler emerges from the debate on childhood obesity; that of Taylor et al. and Dei from the need to integrate members of minority groups into a multicultural society. The chapters that open the book take a critical perspective on the demand that we become globally competitive and look at who succeeds at this game more so than others.

More directly addressing reform pressures, Linda Quirke and Janice Aurini in Chapter 11 discuss the effects of privatization on the professional status of teachers. We generally associate private education with elite education, forgetting that its proliferation is not tied to elite schooling but to schools with often precarious funding structures. Privatizing education, and thus introducing choice and competition into the "education market," is a hallmark of neoliberal reform pressures. Schools in a private system would be required to compete with each other for students, which, it is argued, would push them to offer ever better facilities, pedagogies, and teachers. Quirke and Aurini, however show that teachers experience a decline in their professional autonomy and capacity in private schools and tutoring centres.

Structure of the Book

Thematically, the chapters have been grouped into three parts, which only loosely correspond to this introduction. Given the diversity of research that can broadly be described as "sociology of education," organizing a book like this is never an easy task. I have taken the liberty of presenting the chapters in an order that benefits my very own approach to teaching courses in the area. My goal for this book was to introduce readers to the impressive range of topics currently studied by sociologists of education in Canada in various career stages, and the diversity in theoretical and methodological approaches they use to carry out their research. Such an effort cannot ever be representative of the state of the field in Canada, and I do apologize to all those excellent scholars whose work is not reflected in this volume. Yet I do hope that the book provides a stimulating snapshot of debates and developments in the sociology of education in this country in the second decade of the new millennium.

Part I is entitled Processes, Practices, and Outcomes. Its chapters are fundamentally concerned with the outcomes of schooling in relatively general terms. Lehmann opens the book with a review of theoretical debates in the Sociology of Education and how these can be applied to historical developments in education in Canada. Scott Davies, Darren Cyr, Jessica Rizk, and Magdalena Janus offer a meta-analysis of the various explanations and empirical evidence for persistently observable achievement gaps in secondary education. These first two chapters are followed by two empirical studies, one using data from Alberta and one from Ontario, that analyse how various structural factors affect educational and occupational decisions and outcomes. Harvey Krahn and Garry Barron draw on a unique longitudinal data set that followed a cohort of Edmonton high school students from their final year in high school to young adult life to analyse intergenerational reproduction of educational advantage and disadvantage. Karen Robson, Robert Brown, and Paul Anisef use data from the Toronto District School Board to determine what socio-demographic background characteristics of young people influence their choices for post-secondary education. Analysing data from Canada's National Graduate Survey, Brad Seward, David Walters, and David Zarifa bring to our attention the labour market challenges faced by young post-secondary graduates with disabilities.

Although the chapters in Part I deal with issues of inequality, they do so on a relatively broad level. Part II comprises chapters that investigate very specific dimensions of inequality. Janice Aurini, Emily Milne, and Cathlene Hillier look at the role social class plays in parents' engagement with teachers and the school system. This chapter continues a number of debates already raised in Part I of this book. Alison Taylor, Shadi Mehrabi, and Thashika Pillay shift our attention to the questions of race and ethnicity in a study of the aspirations of young racialized immigrant youth in Canada. Catherine Gordon and Jerry White analyse data from three Canadian Censuses and the 2011 National Household Survey to provide a profile of the state of Indigenous educational attainment in Canada and offer suggestions for reform. Jayne Baker engaged in ethnographic research in two elite private schools, one for boys and one for girls, to understand better whether single-gender schools reinforce or in fact challenge gender stereotypes. Michael Kehler, in Chapter 10 asks how changing masculinities affect young boys and their participation in physical education in schools.

Finally, Part III contains four chapters that each discuss various aspects of educational reforms and the effects of reforms on those in the school system. Linda Quirke and Janice Aurini analyse interviews with private school principals and owners of private tutoring business and franchises to find out whether private education impacts the professional status of those teaching in these institutions. George Dei, in Chapter 12, shows how teachers can use Indigenous proverbs and stories to enrich learning with the type of ethno-centric pedagogy often demanded by those concerned with anti-racist schooling practices. Ryan Broll addresses the roles of schools, the police, and parents in dealing with the problems of cyberbullying. Finally, Delia Dumitrica and Amanda Williams use interviews with educators in post-secondary education institutions who have first-hand experience using Massive Open Online Courses (MOOCs) to shed light on the potentials and pitfalls associated with this type of educational strategy.

All these chapters present research that is at the forefront of educational debates, controversies and reform trends. I hope that readers will find the work of these scholars useful in developing their understanding of schools as a social institution and schooling as a process that affects us all so profoundly.

Education & Society

Part I

Processes, Practices, and Outcomes

Introduction

Schools are expected to socialize young people into becoming responsible and active citizens, while also giving them the skills needed to participate in a complex modern economy. Moreover, this has to be done in a way that rewards individual merit and keeps children out of harm's way. The five chapters assembled in the first part of this book engage with the impossibility of these demands.

In Chapter 1, Wolfgang Lehmann introduces us to the theoretical debates that have shaped sociology of education as a discipline, from early functionalist statements concerned with the moral functions of school as socialization institutions, to conflict perspectives emerging prominently in the 1970s that saw schools as key institutions in the reproduction of unequal power relations, to more recent concerns with the roles of gender, race, and sexuality (among others) in the experiences of schooling. These theoretical debates are further linked to discussions of historical developments in schooling in Canada.

Some of the classic critical statements in the sociology of education have made a case that schools (and other educational institutions) are explicitly involved in sabotaging their own goals (Bowles and Gintis, 1976). Rather than rewarding merit, for instance, curriculum and teacher-student relationships favour those whose cultural capital and social background is aligned with the middle-class norms and expectations of schools, teachers, and curriculum (Bernstein, 1977; Bourdieu and Passeron, 1990; Rist, 1977). More importantly, these biases are seen as intentional, as powerful interests shape education and curriculum in ways that maintain existing inequalities. By emphasising the abstract and theoretical over applied knowledge, or Eurocentric over Indigenous forms of learning, schools make it easier for some students to succeed, while cooling out others who do not see their culture reflected in what and how they learn. As well, paying industrial or craft employment is disappearing in most post-industrial countries, disadvantages that begin in the school system reach far into adult lives. Increasingly, employers demand higher post-secondary credentials, even for jobs in which they are not required to do the work.

Yet this notion of a rigged system does not always reflect our own schooling experiences. Teachers, administrators, curriculum developers, and policy-makers, surely, work toward a system that is fair and meaningful to all. In Chapter 2, Scott Davies, Darren Cyr, Jessica Rizk, and Magdalena Janus review an extensive range of recent empirical research that has investigated the often unintended negative consequences of educational structures and processes. They argue that schools are no longer shaped by elite cultures and elite needs. Instead, schools have become more accommodating to a larger range of students than ever before. Yet achievement gaps persist. The authors argue that at least partly, this is explained by growing inequality between families (and neighbourhoods), while at the same time the influence of advantaged parents in advocating for their children's success has increased.

Shifting their attention to outcomes rather than processes, Harvey Krahn and Gary Barron in Chapter 3 draw on a unique longitudinal data set to show that parental educa-tion remains a key aspect of the intergenerational transfer of advantage and disadvantage: having university-educated parents pays off in terms of one's long-term educational and occupational attainment, and, consequently, income. As this data was collected in Alberta, the province's strong resource extraction economy also shows that entering technical edu-cation (for example, through apprenticeships) has positive income effects. This is an out-come less likely to be observed in service-driven economies like that of Ontario. Most worrisome, the authors document that Aboriginal youth were substantially less likely to acquire a university or technical post-secondary education, putting them at great disad-vantage in the labour market.

In Chapter 4, Karen Robson, Robert Brown, and Paul Anisef analyse data from the so-called 2006 "Student Census" in the Toronto District School Board (TDSB). Their research reveals that social class, gender, race, and special education needs have profound effects on young people's post-secondary choices. Importantly, they further argue that we cannot treat these characteristics individually but need to see them as intersecting. That means, there is no one-fits-all solution for disadvantaged students. The struggles of a poor African-Canadian student will be different from those of an affluent African-Canadian student or a poor Caucasian student. The authors argue that such an intersectional approach provides a fresh perspective on policy and support for successful transitions to further education and employment. It also increases the complexity of the policy environment in a world in which politicians look for simple solutions.

Finally, in Chapter 5, Brad Seward, David Walters, and David Zarifa analyse the Nation-al Graduate Survey (NGS) to investigate the labour market outcomes of university grad-uates with a disability. Their chapter begins with the observation that a growing number of students are self-identifying with a disability but that their experiences have remained largely under-researched. In recent years, universities (and other educational institutions) have made substantial efforts to integrate students with disabilities into the educational mainstream, either through relatively minor accommodations for those with less serious learning disabilities or through adaptive technologies for those whose disabilities are more severe or of a physical nature. The little research we do have shows that such efforts have mixed outcomes and that many students, especially those with invisible disabilities, con-tinue to struggle with the stigma of their disability (Mullins and Preyde, 2013). Seward, Walters, and Zarifa move this debate beyond the classroom and into the labour market. Their findings provide clear evidence that university graduates with a disability are far more likely to find themselves in employment below the level for which they are qualified, regard-less of their social background characteristics.

Taken together, the five chapters in Part I offer important insights into current research on issues that affect the schooling experience and outcomes of students in Canada.

References

Bernstein, B. "Social class, language and socialisation." In *Power and Ideology in Education*, J. Karabel and A.H. Halsey (eds.), (473–86). New York: Oxford University Press, 1977.

Bourdieu, P., and Passeron, J.C. *Reproduction in Education, Society and Culture*. Second edition. London: Sage, 1990.

Bowles, S., and Gintis, H. *Schooling in Capitalist America*. New York: Basic Books, 1976.

Mullins, L., and Preyde, M. "The lived experience of students with an invisible disability at a Canadian university." *Disability and Society* 28(2) (2013): 147–60.

Rist, R.C. "On understanding the processes of schooling: The contributions of labeling theory. In *Power and Ideology in Education*, J. Karabel and A.H. Halsey (eds.), (292–306). New York: Oxford University Press, 1977.

1

Sociology of Education in Canada
History, Theory, and Research

Wolfgang Lehmann

Introduction

In early 2015, the Province of Ontario announced to the public a new sex education curriculum. The curriculum is meant to bring sex education in Ontario schools into the twenty-first century, not only by introducing the discussion of sexual diversity to younger students but also by addressing online behaviour of a sexual nature (such as bullying or posting and sharing explicit images). To many observers this reflects a much needed update of a curriculum that has been out of touch with the growing acceptance of alternative sexualities and the easy and widespread access to sexually explicit material on the Internet. Yet it also has been vehemently opposed by many parents, as they feel that it infringes on their parental rights to instruct their children about something as personal as their sexuality, or because they feel it is incompatible with their moral values. This serves as an instructive example of the importance of education in all of our lives. In a country like Canada, education is one of the few shared experiences, as all children and young people attend school and most do so in institutions that are publicly funded. What we are taught in school, and how we are taught, profoundly affects us as individuals but also as social groups.

Functionalism and Education

The example of Ontario's new sex education curriculum highlights the continued importance of **functionalism** to our understanding of education and educational reform. Although changes to the curriculum do include "technical" aspects, such as earlier (but age-appropriate) discussion of body parts, biological changes during puberty, or what happens during intercourse and how diseases can be transmitted sexually, greater emphasis is arguably put on affecting attitudes and perceptions. Respect for sexual diversity is a key theme. This is functionalist in as much as it responds to larger social changes and needs. As more Ontarians openly express different sexual identities and preferences, schools are tasked with helping young people understand these differences, respect them, and also safely express them. Overall, the hope is that this will lead to less bullying, less discrimination, safer schools, more mutual respect, and healthier lives. Despite its modern and progressive concerns, the emphasis on cohesion and the need of the social whole is deeply rooted in functionalist thought, as is the emphasis on the moral development of children and young people.

Emile Durkheim (1858–1917) and later Talcott Parsons (1902–79) have offered key functionalist statements about the role of education in an industrial society. Witnessing the declining influence of the Catholic Church, and the rise of individualism, Durkheim (1961) emphasised the important moral role schools play as socialization agents. For Durkheim, trust was an essential element of social cohesion, especially in a society in which a complex division of labour leads to a decline in the role of the collective, yet makes us more dependent on others. Trust that is developed through a shared moral framework and norms of behaviour and interaction, therefore, becomes a central aspect of social life. Children and young people need to learn a set of rules that ultimately benefit collective (or social) interest. Moreover, students also need to learn the meaning and importance of these rules, rather than following them blindly (Davies and Guppy, 2014). In modern societies, the role of providing this kind of moral education falls to the education system and schools.

Whereas Durkheim was largely concerned with social cohesion through moral competence and the development of scientific and rational thought, Parsons, the most influential functionalist sociologist of the twentieth century, also looked at the role of the school system in this process. In 1959 he published a key functionalist statement entitled *The School Class as a Social System: Some of Its Functions in American Society* (Parsons, 1959). The text describes the roles schools play in socializing young people into adult roles and establishing an acceptable social hierarchy based on a meritocratic process that ultimately supports social stability. According to Parsons, schools socialize us to know, understand, and act according to social expectations, rules, and norms. After initially redirecting young people from the emotional and person-centred demands of home and family life toward accepting the universalistic rules of the elementary school classroom, emphasis eventually shifts to competitiveness, performance, testing, and streaming in middle and high school. Fundamentally, students learn to see achievement differences as reflective of their natural talent and effort. Passing through the school system thus not only prepares individuals for different roles in the workplace and the nature of social life more generally, it also creates conditions by which this role differentiation is accepted as being based on fair and meritocratic principles. The latter is particularly important for the maintenance of social stability.

Parson's work thus represents a crucial extension of Durkheim's concerns with moral education and stability. Writing at a time of economic expansion and optimism, sorting people into adult roles that best suit their abilities becomes essential. Furthermore, Parsons needed to reconcile the fact that, especially in modern immigrant nations like the United States and Canada, life chances should be based on achievement, not ascribed characteristics such as ethnic origin, status, or wealth of the family to which one happens to be born. Schools emerge as the most qualified institutions to achieve these goals.

Erwin and MacLennan (1994) offer an excellent and concise summary of how this optimistic functionalist view of self-fulfillment and learning for social cohesion has affected much of the history of education in Canada during the latter half of the twentieth century. A watershed moment in scholarship and policy was the publication of *The Vertical Mosaic*, a key text in Canadian sociology, in which John Porter (1965) argued that an outdated, elitist school system, coupled with the preference of the corporate class to use immigrants as the source for skilled labour rather than training and educating locally, led to entrenched forms of stratification. Expanding access to education is one of the mechanisms by which Canada could become less stratified and more meritocratic, and by which equality of opportunity can be achieved. Erwin and MacLennan (1994) argue that *The Vertical Mosaic* and subsequent policy documents, such as the report of the *Royal Commission on Bilingualism and Biculturalism* (1968) had significant effects on the expansion and reform of education in Canada in the 1960s and 1970s. These reforms were most spectacularly realized in Quebec, which completely overhauled its heretofore elite and church-run schools during the Quiet Revolution. Although not reforming their school systems as radically, other provinces embarked on massive expansions of their education systems, especially in the post-secondary sector, as new universities were founded and the community college system was established throughout the 1960s and 1970s.

In 1968, the seminal report *Living and Learning: The Report of the Provincial Committee on Aims and Objectives of Education in the Schools of Ontario* (Hall and Dennis, 1968) moved the debate from equality-of-opportunity issues toward individual growth and self-fulfillment as key goals of pedagogy, curriculum, and school governance. The report emphasised individual growth, which was to be achieved through child-centred learning, open-concept classrooms, more opportunities for experiential learning, more choices of subject, and greater flexibility in the allocation of educational credits (Erwin and MacLennan, 1994). As a consequence of these reforms, high school graduation rates increased substantially, as did enrolment in post-secondary education.

Canada today has one of the most highly educated workforces in the world (OECD, 2014). There are now more women, members of visible minorities, children of immigrants, and young people from working-class backgrounds in higher education than ever before. It could, therefore, be argued that reforms of education, rooted in the kind of technocratic belief in a just, merit-based society that informs functionalist thought, did fulfill their goals. As students, parents, educators, and policy-makers, we still hope that education is a system that prepares all young people for adulthood, citizenship, and economic participation on the basis of talent and effort, and without discriminatory biases. Yet Canada remains a stratified society in which advantage is still rather effectively reproduced. We need to turn to sociological **conflict perspectives** to understand why this is the case.

Conflict Perspectives

Most research in *Education and Society: Canadian Perspectives* responds to this optimistic view of what education can achieve by looking at schooling as a key institution in the reproduction of social inequality, rather than a mechanism to level the playing field. The famous *Coleman Report* (Coleman et al., 1966) was an early milestone in bringing to the forefront the important role of socio-economic status. The report found that parental socio-economic status (SES) was the strongest predictor of student achievement. Many of the seminal sociological texts of the 1970s have tried to explain these socio-economic differences by investigating how school systems, teacher behaviour, or curriculum disadvantage those from low-SES backgrounds. Bowles and Gintis (1976) have argued that organizational hierarchies in schools, streaming practices, and pedagogical approaches in different streams reproduce existing social inequalities. The majority of working-class children, placed in vocational streams, encounter restrictive pedagogies that ultimately instill in them an acceptance of their subservient and exploited future position in the capitalist labour market. Around the same time Bowles and Gintis published their structural critique of schooling in America, other scholars provided more cultural explanation for the lower educational attainment rates of working-class and low-SES students. In the United States, Rist (1977) described subtle, yet powerful ways in which teachers treat students differently, thus setting in motion self-fulfilling prophecies. Students' appearance, for example, is shown to be used by teachers as a marker of educational potential. This disadvantages students whose appearances do not conform to middle-class educational ideals. In the United Kingdom, Bernstein (1977) argued that middle- and working-class families have very different communication practices and patterns of speech. As school success is dependent on mastering elaborative patterns of speech, which are more likely found in the middle class, working-class students are at a distinct disadvantage. Willis (1977), in contrast, ascribes a more active role to working-class students, who, he argues, resist the middle-class values of formal education and instead embrace the applied and masculine culture of the British working class at the time.

Although social conditions may have changed since the 1970s, what has remained is a very strong association between family socio-economic status and educational attainment. Whether we look at standardized test scores of reading comprehension ability, or whether we take university participation as a measure of educational success, we do observe very clear patterns of socio-economic differences (Canadian Education Statistics Council, 2010; Finnie, Lascelles, and Sweetman, 2005). The higher the socio-economic status of the family (whether measured by family income or by parental level of education), the higher the scores children achieve on standardized tests and the more likely they are to attend university. For instance, drawing on Statistics Canada's *Survey of Income and Labour Dynamics*, the Canadian Council on Learning (2009) estimates that the proportion of young people attending university without university-educated parents is just over 15 per cent, compared to more than 50 per cent of those who have at least one parent with a university degree. Canadian longitudinal research by Harvey Krahn (forthcoming) at the University of Alberta and Paul Anisef and colleagues (2000) at York University further shows that students from lower-SES backgrounds are disproportionately more likely to be in vocational streams in high school and less likely to attend and complete university.

Rather than being the outcome of structurally determined disadvantages, Goldthorpe (1996) has argued that young adults and their parents from working-class backgrounds make, in fact, very rational decisions about the educational pathway, but that their assessment of the relative costs, benefits, and risks associated with educational options is very different from that of more privileged families. Put simply, in Goldthorpe's rational choice framework, a working-class family with low levels of financial resources will consider higher education relatively costly. If no one in the family has prior experience with higher education, the risk of failing may also be seen as relatively high. Finally, the benefits, in relation to the cost and risk involved, may be considered questionable, as social stability or perhaps even mobility may be achievable with less costly and risky options (such as apprenticeships or community college). In contrast, the same tuition maybe considered affordable by a more affluent family. Participation may be considered far less risky if others have graduated before. Thus, the option of not participating is actually what puts members of such families at risk of social demotion. Rational choice approaches can be criticized for over-emphasising individuals' capacity to make informed decisions and for under-estimating the reproductive dimension of institutional arrangements. Yet these very shortcomings can be seen as part of the explanatory strength in Goldthorpe's approach. Families do indeed have perceptions, rightly or wrongly, about whether or not the system is stacked against them. These perceptions filter into their relative assessments of the costs, risks, and benefits associated with education. For instance, Goldthorpe himself has argued that for working-class youths and their parents to consider higher education, their actual achievement in secondary schooling has to be exceptionally high (much higher then what more privileged families consider sufficient proof of educational ability). Furthermore, Usher (2005) has shown that Canadian low-income parents tend to over-estimate the costs and under-estimate the benefits associated with higher education for their children; an understandable misjudgement, considering that university tuition in Canada has indeed more than doubled in the past two decades, whereas lower incomes have remained relatively stagnant.

Financial concerns, rational choices, and academic ability, however, are only part of this story. Lehmann's (2007) research with Canadian high school students suggests that working and middle-class students are most comfortable with educational and occupational plans that remain within a range of options that is familiar to them. That is, working-class students gravitated toward applied and vocational courses, while middle-class students never considered anything other than courses and streams that set them on a path toward university. His work is part of an extensive body of research that has used the work of French theorist Pierre Bourdieu to explain educational inequalities.

Bourdieu's (1977, 1990) work has attempted to bridge the structure-agency divide present in the above approaches, by suggesting that the essentially middle-class field of education fundamentally clashes with the working-class habitus of low-SES students and their families (Bourdieu and Passeron, 1990). Although too complex to do justice in a few sentences, Bourdieu's key concepts revolve around the relationship between what he calls habitus, forms of capital, and field. Put simply, Bourdieu defined *habitus* as a set of acquired patterns of thought, behaviour, and taste, informed by one's social milieu (mostly class), that constitutes the individual's sense of self within the social structure. In addition, habitus creates dispositions to understand the world, and hence to behave, in certain ways. This means, for instance, that your own dispositions toward education, schools, and learning are fundamentally informed by attitudes in your family and your immediate social environment (for example, your friends, neighbours). Very important here is whether or not your parents have been successful at school, believe in the value of formal education, or have been to university.

Habitus is strongly related to different forms of *capital*. For instance, a middle-class habitus likely means support for education, which in turn affects acquisition of human capital (for example, having achieved a university degree), economic capital (for example, a university degree will likely give you a job with higher income potential), social capital (for example, having achieved a career in the professions gives you access to a different social network), and cultural capital (having a higher education and a job with a good income allows you to travel, go to the theatre, buy books, and so forth).

The final concept of importance is *field*. A certain habitus and certain forms of capital will have different values in different fields. For instance, to be successful as an electrician will require a different habitus and different forms of social and cultural capital than to be successful as a lawyer. It is often assumed that schools, colleges, and universities are essentially middle-class institutions in which middle-class teachers and professor teach a middle-class curriculum that prepares largely middle-class children and young people for middle-class careers. A middle-class habitus would, therefore, be an advantage in these fields, as are middle-class forms of cultural capital, which are rewarded in curriculum and pedagogy that value the abstract and theoretical over the applied.

Bourdieu's work continues to inform much of the recent research on educational inequality. For instance, focusing on experiences of childhood and parenting in the United States, Lareau (2003) has used the work of Bourdieu to great effect, showing that families' parenting practices and engagement with teachers and the school system lead to class-based differences in which middle-class children develop important forms of cultural capital and a sense of entitlement vis-à-vis their schooling, which is not the case for working-class families. This in turn reduces the likelihood that working-class children develop the kinds of educational dispositions necessary to consider higher education and do well in it. Leaning on the work of Bourdieu and Lareau, Calarco (2011) asked how children themselves, through their classroom help-seeking behaviour and their interaction with teachers, affect their learning experience and outcome. She found that middle-class children were significantly more likely to ask for help and seek teachers' attention, whereas working-class children were more likely to muddle through on their own, thus receiving less attention and support from teachers and often being viewed as less capable as a consequence. Calarco related this finding to differences in cultural capital. Middle-class children learn to ask for help at home and in the many extra-curricular activities in which they participate and bring these skills with them to school. As Rist (1977) has shown decades earlier, being able to interact with teachers, being noticed by them, and being treated differently as a consequence can profoundly change educational experiences.

The overwhelming evidence about social reproduction of educational decisions notwithstanding, the number of young men and women attending university from working-class backgrounds (and other backgrounds traditionally under-represented at university) has been increasing, as has the number of studies that have documented their experiences in higher education. Most apply Bourdieu's concepts of habitus, cultural capital, and field to show how even academically successful low-SES students may experience continued struggles, as they enter universities as cultural outsiders (Baxter and Britton, 2001; Lehmann, 2009, 2012; Reay, Crozier, and Clayton, 2010). For many university students from low socio-economic or working-class backgrounds, entering university can be a time of profound culture shock (Aries and Seider, 2005; Lehmann, 2007). Even experiences of personal growth are often balanced with accounts of feeling like outsiders or losing touch with their families and working-class roots (Lehmann, 2014). Finally, academic success at university has become less of a guarantee for employment outcomes.

Conflict Perspectives and the Transition to Employment

One of the key concerns of both functionalists and critical sociologists is the extent to which education either promotes or hinders social mobility. Although achieving higher levels of educational attainment than one's parents is an important marker of mobility, whether this higher level of education is rewarded on the labour market is equally important. The interrelationship between education and employment is especially important in what we have come to call knowledge economies.

Schooling plays a central role in the transformation of most Western nations into post-industrial economies. A highly, formally educated population is not only more employable but also has the skills and the motivation to constantly innovate and thus develop global, competitive advantages. In many respects, these modern-day discourses are reminiscent of the Cold War urgency about the need for a more highly educated population that followed the Soviet Sputnik launch in 1957. Concerns about military potential have been replaced by economic capacity, but most everything else about competitive advantage and disadvantage has remained. At an individual level, however, there is a world of difference. While the response to Sputnik and the resulting expansion of secondary and higher education was mostly driven by collective concerns, global economic competitiveness requires an individualized response tied to a collective outcome. In other words, individuals have to choose to participate in higher education and, moreover, study the right subject in order to make themselves more marketable and ultimately contribute to a national economic benefit. It is this emphasis on individual agency that is seen as the key to overcoming "old" structural inequalities, while those critical of individualistic approaches worry that it leads to a "blame-the-victim" mentality.

Brown (2013) is a conflict sociologist who criticizes this individualistic view. He argues that any social mobility we have seen in the past decades is the result of what he calls absolute mobility. Absolute mobility occurs when new employment is created at a level that benefits all who are looking for work. In such a situation, individuals from lower SES backgrounds can achieve upward mobility without those from upper-SES backgrounds being socially demoted. Relative mobility, in contrast, describes a situation in which there are not enough good jobs for all and in which the upward mobility of one person means the social demotion of somebody else. Only relative mobility, Brown argues, is mobility in the truest functionalist sense, as it would mean that in the competition for scarce resources, the most qualified succeed (and social background no longer matters). Yet relative mobility does not happen. For instance, there is no shortage of evidence that there has been relatively little change in occupational status hierarchies, despite the massive expansion of secondary and higher education over the past decades. In Canada, Wanner (2004) has shown that coming from a low-SES background makes you no more likely to enter high-status professional careers today than you were 40 years ago. The *Panel on Fair Access to the Professions* (2009) in the United Kingdom has shown that it was in fact easier for individuals from low-income backgrounds to break into the law profession in the 1970s than it is today.

These are sobering findings, especially considering that the number of university students from low-income and other non-traditional backgrounds has increased. Collins (1979) explained this stubborn persistence of occupational inequality despite educational expansion through the concept of *credential inflation*. Collins showed that educational requirements for professional occupations have steadily increased. Rather than indicating an increase in the complexity of skills required to work in high-status professional occupations, he argues that credential requirements have increased to maintain the exclusivity of such professions (and professional programs). Partly, this social closure is explained by the exponential increase in tuition for such programs, which puts studying law or medicine out of reach for many low-SES students. Moreover, access to professional programs such as law or medicine now also depends on applicants' ability to demonstrate extra-curricular excellence, for instance by having studied abroad and having career-relevant work or volunteer experience. All these require substantial amounts of economic capital, as well as the "right" kind of social capital, which many low-SES students do not have. For instance, low-SES students who need to work their summer months in typical student jobs to afford to come back to university in the fall cannot volunteer in hospitals or law firms to the same extent as those who do not have to worry about how to finance their university education. Similarly, access to volunteer or internship opportunities in law firms, doctors' offices, or newspapers often requires social networks that reach into these careers, which low-SES students are less likely to have. As the pool of qualified applicants has grown (due to an increase in young people with Bachelor's degrees), professional school admission committees increasingly are looking at extra-credential experiences to identify the best-suited applicants, thus (unwittingly) disadvantaging many highly qualified but low-SES applicants (Lehmann, 2011).

Also of note in this context is the concern of many education and labour market scholars that the transformation of formerly industrial nations into knowledge-economies is vastly overstated (Brown, Laurder, and Ashton, 2011) and, moreover, that an increasing number of knowledge-intensive jobs are off-shored to developing nations like India and China, where labour costs are low and skill supply is large. These critical perspectives are borne out in data that have documented an increase in underemployment (or overqualification) in Canada, according to which a growing number of university graduates find themselves in employment which requires no more than a high school diploma (Li et al., 2006).

Race and Ethnicity in Schools

The key texts in the conflict tradition emerging in the 1970s were mostly concerned with educational inequalities based on social class. Although class inequalities have hardly diminished, research and scholarship in the sociology of education have shifted emphasis toward issues of gender, sexuality, and race in the past three decades. Racial or ethnic differences in educational experiences and attainment are of great importance in multi-ethnic immigrant nations like Canada. Debates on race and ethnicity are often framed by a country's perspectives on immigrant integration, such that Canada's formal commitment to **multiculturalism** creates very different concerns from those in the United States, which prefers assimilation in its approach to immigration. Furthermore, the experiences of immigrants differ fundamentally from those of Indigenous populations (such as First Nations groups in Canada) or groups that have been historically oppressed (such as African Americans).

In that respect, the educational achievement of ethnic minorities in Canada offers very interesting patterns. Some ethnic minority groups significantly outperform white Canadians (of Caucasian descent), whereas other minority groups have been shown to struggle. It is generally argued that the high educational aspirations and achievement of some racial minority groups is the result of Canada's formal commitment to integrate a multicultural perspective into school curriculum. Canadian Census data show evidence these efforts pay off in the classroom (Abada, Hou, and Ram, 2009). Yet there remain serious concerns about the educational experiences and attainment of some ethnic minority groups. Despite a formal commitment to multiculturalism, it has been argued that Canada continues to rely on a largely Eurocentric approach to teaching and curriculum, which in turn is cited as a reason why many ethnic and racial minority students find themselves excluded. George S. Dei has shown that a lack of African-Canadian teachers and administrators as role models and the denial of African history and literature in curriculum create an atmosphere in which African-Canadian students see themselves as outsiders (Dei, 1996). In order to address the very root of these problems, Dei (1999) asks that Canada's focus on multiculturalism be extended to include **anti-racism** as part of educational practices. He argues that multiculturalism is focused on the celebration of cultural differences but does little to help students understand the political and historical dimensions that have shaped racial and ethnic oppression.

A different explanation for differences in educational attainment is offered by Ogbu (1992), who urges us to distinguish school performance by students' minority status. He argues that voluntary minorities, that is, those who have become minorities through voluntary migration, tend to perform better in schools as their ethnic cultures are not in conflict with mainstream society. In contrast, involuntary minorities are minorities against their will. This includes African Americans who were brought to the United States as slaves and who have suffered a long history of oppression and discrimination that makes them, at the very least, suspicious (if not hostile) to the mainstream expectations of schooling. The same can be said for the experiences of First Nations groups in Canada, whose involuntary minority status is tied to the fact that they did not choose to have their way of life disrupted by European settlers and whose negative schooling experiences have been exacerbated by a history of oppression and the trauma of residential schools. Residential schools are one of the darkest chapters in Canadian history. Founded on Euro-Canadian principles and run by both churches and the government, residential schools in Canada were introduced to socialize (or rather assimilate) Aboriginal children. These children were taken from their homes and communities and forced to abandon all that defined their culture (for example, their language, their songs, their games, and their connections to their home communities). We now know that his was a disastrous "social experiment" which not only stripped generations of Aboriginal children off their cultural identity but also exposed them to harrowing mental, physical and sexual abuse, the consequences of which are still felt in Aboriginal communities today (Bougie and Senécal, 2010).

It has, therefore, been argued that the educational needs of some minority groups would be addressed better in schools that more directly reflect the culture of the group (see, for example, Gordon and White [2014]). Different First Nations in Canada have long sought greater control over schools on reserves in order to connect young people with their cultural traditions and to redress the trauma of residential schools, which continues to haunt Aboriginal Canadians' ability to trust formal schooling with the safekeeping of their children and the transmission of valuable knowledge.

Leaders in the African-Canadian community have also looked at the potential of Africentric schools to improve educational experiences in their communities. Amid much controversy, the Toronto District School Board opened its first Africentric Alternative School in 2009. As with schools under the control of First Nations, it hopes to be respectful of differences in interests and learning styles, provide leadership opportunities that might not be accessible to minority students in regular schools, and create safer and more comfortable environments in which students can learn about the accomplishments of ethnic minority members and thus increase ethnic pride and self-confidence in ethnic minority students. Toronto's plan for an Africentric Alternative School was met with considerable resistance, including from members within the city's African-Canadian community, who worried that such schools constitute a form of re-segregation, albeit voluntarily. These concerns notwithstanding, the schools have been popular with parents. Enrolment has grown since its inception and early results from the Education Quality and Accountability Office (EQAO), which administers Ontario's provincial testing programs, has shown that students at the school indeed perform above average on province-wide tests[1]. Whether this is the outcome of anti-racist and/or Africentric pedagogy or related to the possibility that higher-SES parents actively choose to enroll their children at the school is not yet known, but the findings nonetheless suggest benefits to ethnocentric schooling.

Gender Issues

Scholarship on gender has seen a fascinating reversal in recent years; while early debates expressed concern about the educational attainment of girls and oppressive classroom atmospheres in which their unique learning needs are stifled (Buchman, DiPrete, McDaniel, 2008), focus has recently shifted to a discussion of a boy crisis supposedly brought on by the extraordinary success of girls and a feminization of teaching and curriculum (for a critique of this argument, see Ringrose [2009]). The boy crisis, it has been argued, is evident in boys' lower level of achievement at all levels of education, lower scores on provincial, national, and international tests, higher dropout out rates from high school, and overall lower participation in post-secondary education.

Given the importance of formal education in a modern knowledge-based economy, many are concerned about a lost generation of boys who are permanently unemployable, economically disadvantaged, and socially destructive. McDowell (2003) has argued that the decline of manufacturing and other traditionally male industries and the parallel rise of the service economy create conditions in which young men without education and less developed social skills are the main losers. As is usually the case, solutions are sought in the education system. Has curriculum become too feminized and if so, what needs to be changed? Do boys require male teachers in elementary school who can role model behaviour that embraces the value of learning, co-operation, and other social skills considered essential in a modern economy? At a more basic level, many educators ask: how can we get boys to read? In response, young men are encouraged to become elementary school teachers and provincial curricula are introducing reading programs especially designed to interest boys in reading at an earlier age.

These claims about a boy crisis are contested by feminist scholars who caution us not to confuse the success of girls as the cause for a decline in boy's attainment (Ringrose, 2009). There is sufficient evidence to suggest that boys' educational achievement has in fact not declined over time, but that of girls has risen more steeply. Why then should the success of girls be constructed as a social problem? Secondly, the decline of industrial employment opportunities and the parallel rise of mandatory school age has led to a situation in which many more boys are still in school at an age at which they would have had already left a few decades ago. Their struggles at school are likely not related to any claims about the feminization of schools or curriculum, but about economic conditions, over which school reform has little influence. Young men who see job opportunities disappear likely will not consider school an important aspect of their current and future lives.

Whereas the concerns about gender equity and educational outcomes could be considered mostly functionalist in nature (as the issue is centrally about rewarding merit and giving equal opportunity to demonstrate it), there is a separate branch of research about gender and sexuality that questions the very nature of how we perceive gender. Gender, it is argued, is socially and culturally constructed. Important for the study of education and schooling, gender is also something that we learn how to perform, be that at home, in our peer groups, or at school. These debates rest heavily on the theoretical work of Judith Butler (1990), who argues that social norms and conventions create strong pressures to perform gender accordingly. Through what she calls stylized repetition of acts and the body, we create the illusion of a natural state of gender. Performing gender correctly (according to these norms and conventions) is rewarded, whereas performing it incorrectly is sanctioned. Schools reinforce these culturally sanctioned **gender norms** in a number of different ways. Teachers have been shown to have different expectations of boys and girls, and, therefore, treat them differently. This reinforces gendered expectations, such as the ideas that girls are compliant, better at group work, and easier to manage in a classroom, whereas boys are naturally more inquisitive but also more unruly (Jones and Myhill, 2004). Curriculum, children's books, and textbooks have also been identified as sources in which traditional gender roles persist. As these are formally sanctioned sources of knowledge, they carry with them authority in their gender representation, thus convincing children of the right way to be a boy or a girl (Jackson and Gee, 2005).

These cultural scripts about gender roles equally apply to sexuality, as schools have been taken to task for being heteronormatively biased and for being inhospitable places for non-heterosexual young people. There has, however, been a subtle shift in scholarship and policy on these issues. Whereas most of the scholarship on sexuality in schools chronicled incidences of homophobia, bullying, and oppression (see for example Smith (1998) for a landmark Canadian study on this issue), more recent research has looked at the increased acceptance of homosexuality (and other forms of sexuality) among peers (McCormack and Anderson, 2010) and in pedagogy and curriculum. Ontario's new sex education curriculum is a piece of policy that reflects this change in attitudes, although it remains to be seen if it is successful or whether public resistance will persist.

Neoliberalism and Education

Any history of education is a reflection of broader social debates and concerns. The optimism about limitless economic growth of the post–Second World War era is evident in the massive expansion of educational institutions at the secondary and post-secondary level. Educational reformers and activists of the 1960s and 1970s, in contrast, tried to imagine a future education that was at once democratic and liberating. Reform efforts during this period were strongly influenced by countercultural movements (for example, the student, anti-authoritarian, and ecological movements), the emergence of feminism and anti-racism as serious challenges to orthodox knowledge, and debates around critical and liberation pedagogy. Alternative schools experimented with collective decision making about all school matters. Pedagogical strategies became increasingly focused on exploration, open learning, intrinsic motivation, and students having a measure of control over what and how they learned.

In the prolonged period of **neoliberalism** that began in the Thatcher/Reagan/Mulroney era, emphasis has shifted back to competitiveness, learning basic skills, developing entrepreneurial spirit, and creating structures that make educators accountable for what they do (Apple, 2007). Given pressures to reduce government debts and faced with an aging population, federal and provincial governments in Canada have to make difficult decisions about where to put scarce resources. As provincial funding for schools, colleges, and universities has declined in the past decades, fundraising has become a major role of school and university administrators. Furthermore, as an increasing amount of private money is required to finance education, the potential to fundamentally change what public education means arises. This is of greater concern in post-secondary education, as critics of this shifting funding model are worried that private interests are becoming more powerful in deciding what type of research and scholarship can take place at Canadian universities (Polster and Newson, 2010; Sears, 2003).

Another goal of neoliberalism is to reduce the role of government and to seek free-market solutions to social issues. In its most extreme form, neoliberal education would replace Canada's current system of public, comprehensive education with a purely private system in which parents would receive school vouchers or credits, which they could spend on the school of their choice. This, it is argued, would make schools more accountable and responsive to the demands of parents, students, and communities, as the schools would need to compete for these educational dollars.

Finally, neoliberal reforms also emphasise accountability. Largely, this is to be achieved through standardized testing and publication of test results. Elements of this neoliberal vision of education are found in the *No Child Left Behind* policy that was instituted during the Bush administration across the United States. Schools (and students) must undergo annual standardized testing programs. If schools fail to perform at or above a certain threshold repeatedly, parents are given the opportunity to move their children to other, better-performing schools, leaving underperforming schools at risk of closure and further decline. Although this policy was meant to create incentives for schools to do well and to give families more educational choice, research has shown that it has disproportionately harmed the most disadvantaged children and families (Lauen, 2007). To move a child out of an underperforming school requires resources, such as means of transportation, and more importantly, knowledge about schools and how to make educational choices. The latter is tied to middle-class forms of habitus and capital. This creates a situation in which the most disadvantaged families have no option but keeping their children at "problem" schools, which under the *No Child Left Behind* policy are sent on a downward spiral, leaving indeed many children behind. Moreover, standardized tests cannot measure whether schools fulfill important community functions beyond preparing children for doing well on these tests. Schools in disadvantaged communities may especially do much to help those they serve, something that may never manifest in standardized test results.

More broadly, critics of neoliberal educational reform argue that market-based solutions rest on a complete misunderstanding of the role of education and would lead to undemocratic and unfair outcomes, effectively creating a two-tier education system in which affluent Canadians will gain access to very good schools and solidify their privileged status, while low-income Canadians living in poor neighbourhoods will see the quality of their schools decline. If evidence from the United States' *No Child Left Behind* program is any indication, these concerns are well justified.

Conclusion

In many aspects, the concerns inherent in the neoliberal reform movement bring us full circle to early functionalist goals for education. Although neoliberals are not concerned with Durkheimian notions of moral education or social cohesion, they do believe that the ultimate social good derives from economic participation through a free, unfettered market. Thus, schools need to be set up not only to reflect this ideal (for example, through a shift from public to private education) but also in what they teach and how they teach it. Refocusing pedagogical strategies on basic competencies is meant to increase the ability of young people to participate in the economy, which in turn is to make one's nation globally competitive through a highly educated and skilled workforce. Standardized testing, another hallmark of neoliberal educational reform, is said to increase accountability in the school system but could also be argued to socialize children into accepting the competitive nature of a market economy. The explicit nature of the goals may be different, but they are strongly reminiscent of Parsons' (1959) notion that education is foremost about socializing young people into accepting the dominant norms and values of a given social order. Conflict sociologists challenge this assumption and look for ways in which this often taken-for-granted or hegemonic relationship between schools and social norms can be disrupted. Although research and scholarship from a conflict perspective can be taken to task for stopping at the level of critique and not offering constructive solutions to the problems they have identified, it is nonetheless implied in this research that equipping students with the ability to identify oppression and their role in it (whether as oppressor or oppressed) should be a key goal of any schooling. These debates will continue as we struggle to understand education as fostering social justice, reproducing social inequalities, or preparing students for success in a post-industrial knowledge economy.

Questions for Critical Thought

1. Assess this statement from a functionalist and a conflict perspective: "Canada is a modern country in which people are rewarded for working hard."
2. Do Africentric or First Nation schools violate Canada's commitment to multiculturalism?
3. Should schools be responsible for teaching children about alternative gender and sexual identities?
4. Are standardized tests a good measure of whether a school is a good school?

Glossary

Anti-racism A perspective that goes beyond multiculturalism by investigating and trying to erase the power relations at the root of ethnic and racial inequalities.

Conflict perspectives Unlike the consensus implicit in functionalism, conflict perspectives look at power relations that create inequality and stratification.

Functionalism A sociological perspective that looks at the ways in which social institutions and processes work together to serve the needs of a social structure.

Gender norms Feminist sociologists argue that gender norms do not emerge biologically but culturally. Strong cultural expectations about how to be a man or a woman shape how we behave as men and women.

Multiculturalism The existence, acceptance, and promotion of multiple cultural traditions; it is a key aspect of Canada's stance toward diversity.

Neoliberalism An economic principle that believes in the benefits of small government, fiscal austerity, privatization, and free trade.

Note

1. Information for individual schools in Ontario is available through the Educational Quality and Accountability (EQAO) website: www.eqao.com/results/?Lang=E

References

Abada, T., Hou, F., and Ram, B. "Ethnic differences in educational attainment among the children of Canadian immigrants." *Canadian Journal of Sociology* 34(1) (2009): 1–28.

Anisef, P., Axelrod, P., Baichman-Anisef, E., James, C., and Turrittin, A. *Opportunity and Uncertainty: Life Course Experiences of the Class of '73.* Toronto: University of Toronto Press, 2000.

Apple, M. "Whose markets, whose knowledge?" In *Sociology of Education: A Critical Reader*, Alan R. Sadovnik (ed.), (177–93). New York and London: Routledge, 2007.

Aries, E., and Seider, M. "The interactive relationship between class identity and the college experience: The case of lower income students." *Qualitative Sociology* 28(4) (2005): 419–43.

Baxter, A., and Britton, C. "Risk, identity and change: Becoming a mature student." *International Studies in Sociology of Education* 11(1) (2001): 87–101.

Bernstein, B. "Social class, language and socialisation." In *Power and Ideology in Education*, J. Karabel and A.H. Halsey (eds.), (473–86). New York: Oxford University Press, 1977.

Bougie, E., and Senécal, S. "Registered Indian children's school success and intergenerational effects of residential schooling in Canada." *The International Indigenous Policy Journal* 1(1) (2010). Retrieved from: http://ir.lib.uwo.ca/iipj/vol1/iss1/5

Bourdieu, P. *Outline of a Theory of Practice*. New York: Cambridge University Press, 1977.

Bourdieu, P. *The Logic of Practice*. Cambridge: Polity, 1990.

Bourdieu, P., and Passeron, J.C. *Reproduction in Education, Society and Culture*. Second edition. London: Sage, 1990.

Bowles, S., and Gintis, H. *Schooling in Capitalist America*. New York: Basic Books, 1976.

Brown, P. "Education, opportunity and the prospects for social mobility." *British Journal of Sociology of Education* 34(5–6) (2013): 678–700.

Brown, P., Lauder, H., and Ashton, D. *The Global Auction: The Broken Promises of Education, Jobs and Incomes*. Oxford and New York: Oxford University Press, 2011.

Buchman, C., DiPrete, T.A., and McDaniel, A. "Gender Inequalities in Education." *Annual Review of Sociology* 34 (2008): 319–37.

Butler, J. *Gender Trouble: Feminism and the Subversion of Identity*. New York: Routledge, 1990.

Calarco, J.M. "'I Need Help!' Social class and children's help-seeking in elementary school." *American Sociological Review* 76(6) (2011): 862–82.

Canadian Council on Learning. *Post-secondary Education in Canada: Meeting Our Needs?* Ottawa: Canadian Council on Learning, 2009.

Canadian Education Statistics Council. *Education Indicators in Canada: Report of the Pan-Canadian Education Indicators Program December 2010*. Statistics Canada cat. no. 81-582-X. Ottawa: Statistics Canada, 2010. www.statcan.gc.ca/pub/81-582-x/81-582-x2010004-eng.htm

Coleman, J., Campbell, E.Q., Hobson, E.J., Portland, J., Mood, A.M., Weinfeld, F.D., and York, R.L. *Equality of Educational Opportunity*. Washington: Government Printing Office, 1966.

Collins, R. *The Credential Society: An Historical Sociology of Education and Stratification*. San Diego: Academic Press, 1979.

Davies, S., and Guppy, N. *The Schooled Society*. Third edition. Don Mills: Oxford University Press, 2014.

Dei, G. "The role of Afrocentricity in the inclusive curriculum in Canadian schools." *Canadian Journal of Education* 21(2) (1996): 170–86.

Dei, G. "Knowledge and politics of social change: The implication of anti-racism." *British Journal of Sociology of Education* 20(3) (1999): 395–409.

Durkheim, E. *Moral Education: A Study in the Theory and Application of the Sociology of Education*. (Trans. E.K. Wilson and H. Schnurer). New York: Free Press, 1961.

Erwin, L., and MacLennan, D. "Introduction: Historical backgrounds and critical perspectives." In *Sociology Education in Canada: Critical Perspectives on Theory, Research and Practice*, Lorna Erwin and David MacLennan (eds.), (1–25). Toronto: Copp Clark Longman, 1994.

Finnie, R., Lascelles, E., and Sweetman, A. *Who Goes? The Direct and Indirect Effects of Family Background on Access to Post-secondary Education*. Ottawa: Statistics Canada, 2005.

Goldthorpe, J. "Class analysis and the reorientation of class theory: The case of persisting differentials in educational attainment." *British Journal of Sociology of Education* 47(3) (1996): 481–505.

Gordon, C.E., and White, J.P. "Indigenous educational attainment in Canada." *The International Indigenous Policy Journal* 5(3) (2014). Retrieved from: http://ir.lib.uwo.ca/iipj/vol5/iss3/6

Hall, E.M., and Dennis, L. *Living and Learning: The Report of the Provincial Committee* on *Aims and Objectives of Education in the Schools of Ontario*. Toronto: Ontario Department of Education, 1968.

Jackson, S., and Gee, S. "'Look Janet,' 'No you look John': Constructions of gender in early school reader illustrations across 50 years." *Gender and Education* 17(2) (2005): 115–28.

Jones, S., and Myhill, D. "'Troublesome boys' and 'compliant girls': gender identity and perceptions of achievement and underachievement." *British Journal of Sociology of Education* 25(5) (2004): 547–61.

Krahn, H. "Choose your parents carefully: Social class, post-secondary education, and occupational outcomes." In *Social Inequality in Canada: Dimensions of Disadvantage*, E. Grabb, J. Reitz, and M. Hwang (eds.). Sixth edition. Toronto: Oxford University Press, Forthcoming.

Lareau, A. *Unequal Childhoods: Class, Race and Family Life*. Berkeley: University of California Press, 2003.

Lauen, D. "False promises: The school choice provisions in no child left behind." In *Sociology of Education: A Critical Reader*, A.R. Sadovnik (ed.), (461–86). New York and London: Routledge, 2007.

Lehmann, W. *Choosing to Labour? School-Work Transitions and Social Class*. Montreal and Kingston: McGill-Queen's University Press, 2007.

Lehmann, W. "Becoming middle class: How working-class university students draw and transgress moral class boundaries." *Sociology* 43(4) (2009): 631–47.

Lehmann, W. "Extra-credential experiences and social closure: Working-class students at university." *British Educational Research Journal* 38(2) (2011): 203–18.

Lehmann, W. "Working-class students, habitus, and the development of student roles: A Canadian case study." *British Journal of Sociology of Education* 33(4) (2012): 527–46.

Lehmann, W. "Habitus transformation and hidden injuries: Successful working-class university students." *Sociology of Education* 87(1) (2014): 1–15.

Li, C., Gervais, G., and Duval, A. *The Dynamics of Overqualification: Canada's Underemployed University*. Ottawa: Statistics Canada, 2006.

McCormack, M., and Anderson, E. "'It's just not acceptable any more': The erosion of homophobia and the softening of masculinity at an English Sixth Form." *Sociology* 44(5) (2010): 843–59.

McDowell, L. *Redundant Masculinities?: Employment Change and White Working Class Youth*. Malden: Blackwell, 2003.

Ogbu, J. "Understanding cultural diversity and learning." *Educational Researcher* 21(8) (1992): 5–14.

Organisation for Economic Co-operation and Development (OECD). *Education at a Glance 2014: OECD Indicators*. Paris: OECD, 2014.

Panel on Fair Access to the Professions. *Phase 1 Report: An Analysis of the Trends and Issues Relating to Fair Access to the Professions*. London: The Panel on Fair Access to the Professions, 2009.

Parsons, T. "The school class as a social system: Some of its functions in American Society." *Harvard Educational Review* 29 (1959): 297–318.

Polster, C., and Newson, J. *Academic Callings: The University We Have Had, Now Have, and Could Have*. Toronto: Canadian Scholars' Press, 2010.

Porter, J. *The Vertical Mosaic: An Analysis of Social Class and Power in Canada*. Toronto: University of Toronto Press, 1965.

Reay, D., Crozier, G., and Clayton, J. "Fitting in or standing out: Working-class students in UK higher education." *British Educational Research Journal* 36(1) (2010): 107–24.

Ringrose, J. "The future is female: The post-feminist panic over failing boys." In *Canadian Perspectives on the Sociology of Education*, Cynthia Levine-Rasky (ed.), (213–32). Don Mills: Oxford University Press, 2009.

Rist, R.C. "On understanding to processes of schooling: The contributions of Labeling Theory." In *Power and Ideology in Education*, J. Karabel and A.H. Halsey (eds.), (292–305). New York: Oxford University Press, 1977.

Royal Commission on Bilingualism and Biculturalism. *Report of the Royal Commission on Bilingualism and Biculturalism*. Ottawa: Queen's Printer, 1968.

Sears, A. *Retooling the Mind Factory: Education in a Lean State*. Aurora: Garamond Press, 2003.

Smith, G. "The ideology of 'fag': The school experience of gay students." *The Sociological Quarterly* 39(2) (1998): 309–35. (Edited for publication by Dorothy E. Smith.)

Usher, A. *A Little Knowledge Is a Dangerous Thing: How Perceptions of Costs and Benefits Affect Access to Education*. Washington, Toronto, and Melbourne: Educational Policy Institute, 2005.

Wanner, R. "Social mobility in Canada: Concepts, patterns and trends." In *Social Inequality in Canada: Patterns, Problems, and Policies*, E. Grabb and N. Guppy (eds.), (116–32). Fifth edition. Toronto: Pearson Prentice Hall, 2004.

Willis, P. *Learning to Labour: How Working Class Kids Get Working Class Jobs*. Farnborough: Saxon House, 1977.

2

Where Do Educational Achievement Gaps Come From?

Scott Davies, Darren Cyr, Jessica Rizk, and Magdalena Janus

Introduction: The Problem of SES Achievement Gaps

Reducing student **achievement gaps** is a prime priority for education policy today. Children from socio-economically advantaged backgrounds repeatedly outperform their less advantaged peers on virtually all schooling indicators, from standardized test scores to grades, high school graduation rates, and post-secondary attendance. School boards, departments, and ministries across Canada are aiming to reduce these gaps. Their aims come in a striking context. Over the past few decades, Canadians from all walks of life have attained more formal education. Post-secondary attendance has grown immensely. This expansion has reflected profound change in Canadian labour markets. Over the past century, jobs have shifted from agricultural and industrial sectors to post-industrial or "knowledge" sectors. School credentials have become an essential ticket for individual prosperity.

In some respects, policy-makers are simply catching up with what sociologists have demonstrated for a half century: that socio-economic status (SES) is a prime determinant of children's school achievement and attainment. Whether conceived as a series of related family attributes like family income, poverty level, parent education, employment status, and/or occupational prestige, SES is a robust predictor of children's educational outcomes (Sirin, 2005). In fact, the impact of SES may have become increasingly powerful over the past 30 years (see Duncan and Murnane [2011]). At the upper end of student achievement, record numbers of youth are attending advanced tiers in higher education, including professional (for example, law, MBA) and graduate degree programs. But at the lower end, attainments are rising more slowly. In the United States, disadvantaged youth still have sizable high school dropout rates (Heckman, 2008). In Canada, those rates fell between 1990 and 2005 (Bowlby, 2005), but have not declined since[1]. Further, Willms (2009) reports that literacy levels among Canadian youth do not appear to be rising, particularly at the lower reaches of reading ability. Aggregate levels of school attainments are continuing to rise, but they may be polarizing as well.

The Original Reproduction Theory of Achievement Gaps

The 1960s created a great deal of optimism in education. Prior to that decade, elementary and high schools still resembled those of the early twentieth century. "Chalk and talk" teaching methods and strict discipline prevailed. High schools sent most of their students to job markets and prepared only small numbers of students for further study. There were fewer students in attendance in Canadian institutions of higher education. Whereas in 2012, 22 per cent and 62 per cent of Canadians over age 15 had a university degree or some post-secondary attainment, respectively, the corresponding figures in 1951 were 2 per cent and 6 per cent[2]. The 1960s brought several transformations to education in Canada. Elementary and secondary schools introduced a host of reforms. Curricula were revised; seemingly "outdated" courses such as ancient languages were replaced by "relevant" courses in current social studies. Students could choose from more elective courses. Pedagogies became more progressive, de-emphasising memory and drill-based learning in favour of group discussion, personal expression, and critical thinking. Discipline codes were loosened; old forms of corporal punishment were outlawed, giving students more latitude in their conduct at school. Teacher qualifications were raised so that all would graduate from university and become steeped in the newest pedagogies. All in all, these changes promised to make schools more welcoming and humane.

One immediate impact was to raise high school graduation rates and channel record numbers of youth to a transformed higher education system. Community colleges were created with the hope of meeting emerging labour market needs for advanced technical training. Dozens of new universities sprang up in previously underserved locales, and many older ones were enlarged to handle larger influxes of students. In addition to addressing new economic climates, policy-makers hoped these changes would also enhance equity. They reasoned that an expanded number of slots, coupled with affordable tuition, would eventually erase SES, gender, and racial inequalities in access to Canadian higher education. But by the mid-1970s, one decade after this expansion, SES disparities still persisted, despite rising educational attainments among all strata. Disadvantaged youth were attaining more formal schooling than ever, but so too were advantaged youth. "So much reform, so little change," the saying went.

This failure of a broad assortment of reforms generated a re-think in sociology. A new pessimism occurred from witnessing recurring outcomes despite great institutional change. Whereas previous generations of sociologists had amply documented disparities in school outcomes, the new generation saw them in a new light, not as soon-to-disappear relics of a bygone era, but as products of active design. They imagined unequal school outcomes to be built into the very structure and functioning of modern schooling. Their pessimism was expressed in what became known as Reproduction Theory.

This theory had two main variants. One version, associated with the work of Herbert Bowles and Samuel Gintis (1976), emphasises the role of school "structures" in maintaining inequality. Its basic tenet was that capitalist economies need stratified labour forces. Upper-end job markets need highly educated graduates to become managers, supervisors, and professionals. Lower-end jobs need less educated workers to staff factories, warehouses, and retail outlets. Schools were organized to meet those needs. In what Bowles and Gintis dubbed the **correspondence principle**, levels of schooling subtly mirror different types of workplaces. Distinct streams were seen to have a hidden curriculum that socialized students for their eventual job. For instance, vocational streams stress rule following and rote activity in order to prepare students for manual and factory work, while academic streams give students more autonomy and discretion in order to ready them for occupations requiring more independence and less direct supervision. Bowles and Gintis further contended that working-class youth tended to be directed into the lowest streams because their schools were generally poorly resourced, because they were often funnelled into lower ability groups by stereotyping teachers, because they were often discouraged by institutional gatekeepers (like guidance counsellors) who mistook class and/or ethnicity for indicators of students' ability, and because they could not afford post-secondary tuition fees. Thus, this variant of Reproduction Theory proposed that school streams, funding, tiered curricula, tuition fees, and guidance systems each perpetuated SES gaps.

A second variant of Reproduction Theory, associated with the work of French sociologist Pierre Bourdieu (Bourdieu and Passerson, 1977) had a more cultural emphasis. Bourdieu contended that success in school required a familiarity with the dominant culture. In France during the 1970s, the culture of the upper classes and professionals dominated. Their highbrow culture comprised formal works of high status literature, music, and art, as well as more informal styles of interacting, conversing, and expressing personal taste. Bourdieu contended that wealthy and highly educated parents exposed their children to great works of art and literature, taking them to galleries and museums and inculcating its most subtle manifestations through daily conversations and interactions. From that premise, he delivered his famous punchline: schools claimed to be fair, objective, and meritorious but actually rewarded this dominant culture. Schools misrecognized having knowledge of great works of literature and art, having an expansive vocabulary, speaking in a professional style with flair, having polished manners, and being an agile debater as signs of intelligence and ability. But Bourdieu saw them not as markers of aptitude but as merely arbitrary, as cultural accoutrements of advantaged social classes. Bourdieu dubbed these class-rooted capacities cultural capital, his signature concept. With credentials being increasingly used in modern society to allocate youth to top positions in professions, corporations, and government, Bourdieu saw cultural capital as the pivotal mechanism that reproduced class inequality through schooling.

These two variants of Reproduction Theory—structural and cultural—continue to be hugely popular in the sociology of education. Both recognize that inequalities beyond schools set the stage for educational inequalities but trace achievement gaps to school structures, practices, and cultures, and assert that schools are the prime causal force that generates disparities.

We offer a different position. While SES disparities in educational outcomes have persisted since the 1970s, school structures, practices, and cultures are no longer viewed as their primary causes. Yes, biases in curricula, teaching and school organization directly generated disparities when Reproduction Theory was originated. But many aspects of schooling and society have since changed. Reforms have continually altered school structures, practices, and cultures at all levels. Further, higher education has expanded immensely, along with an elaborate second-chance system by which non-traditional students can re-enter high schools and/or post-secondary institutions. The sum impact of these changes, we believe, is that SES achievement gaps in Canada are now perpetuated by other forces that have emerged over the past few decades: (1) evolving forms of upper-middle-class parenting that are widening disparities in children's out-of-school learning; (2) emerging "secondary mechanisms" that enhance the competitiveness of students from upper-middle-class origins; and (3) deepened neighbourhood effects on schooling that stem from entrenched patterns of income and wealth inequality in society. We end by discussing educational reforms that might attenuate these generators of achievement gaps.

New Times: The Crosscutting Effects of Continual School Reform and Rising Societal Inequality

Canadian schools today are different from what they were 40 years ago. Higher education was once "foreign territory" to youth from humble origins. But now the overwhelming majority—over 80 per cent—of Canadian parents, including those from the lowest income categories, expect their children to go to college or university (Davies, 2005). Most young Canadians now attend post-secondary institutions (Zeman, 2007) and most possess more school credentials than their parents, regardless of social origin (Corak, Lipps, and Zhao, 2003; Finnie, Lascelles, and Sweetman, 2005). These changes have been facilitated by evolving school structures. Many secondary schools have been de-streamed. While some informal streaming still occurs, Canada's secondary schools are increasingly structured to channel most students into higher education. Further, students who lacked success during their regular high school years can now be considered mature students and enter an increasingly elaborate "second-chance" system. They can earn high school credits, graduate, enter transitional year programs, and access post-secondary studies via alternate means. High school diplomas are more accessible than ever, as are post-secondary admissions. Rather than being sorted mostly into vocational streams, more working-class youth are heading to colleges and universities. Schools are encouraging, rather than discouraging, this movement.

As a result, secondary schools do far less gatekeeping than they did 40 years ago, when sociologists could credibly characterize guidance counsellors as influential actors who cooled out the mark and discouraged working-class students from considering university (for example, Clark [1960]; Cicourel and Kitsuse [1977]). But for the past two decades, high schools have been mandated to retain (almost) all of their students, graduate the vast majority, and embrace a "college for all" spirit (Rosenbaum, 2001). Many have dropped "zero tolerance" forms of student discipline in favour of "progressive discipline" that aims to re-integrate rather than suspend and expel rule breakers (Milne and Aurini, 2015). While some believe this new discipline has harmed educators' moral authority and created "marshmallow schools" that tolerate misconduct to the detriment of others, perhaps even to rule-breakers themselves (Paulle, 2013), it is consistent with the mandate of retaining greater numbers of students.

In terms of culture, teachers are now trained in ways unimagined in the 1970s. Teachers colleges have since emphasised equity and awareness of teacher biases. Perhaps as a result, studies rarely detect forms of teacher bias by student SES, gender, or race (for example, Farkas et al., [1990]; Kingston [2001]; Paulle [2013]). Today's curriculum also differs from that described by Bourdieu. The overwhelmingly technical content of science and math is difficult to link to a socio-economic origin, as are social studies and humanities curricula, which are written by professional specialists and vetted by bureaucrats, often with multicultural sensitivities. Few guardians of traditional, elite culture prize public school curricula. Further, interaction styles in classrooms are more populist and casual than those of a half century ago, as teacher and student conduct has undergone what Randall Collins (2004, 371) has dubbed a "Goffmanian revolution": teachers with stiff, formalizing demeanours who demand deference from their students have given way to those with more relaxed, engaging, and informal manners.

Thus, high schools have changed over the past 40 years, and far more working-class youth go through to higher education. But the wider political economy in Canada has also changed. Unemployment has since been higher; wealth and income inequality has worsened with the rising of upper- and upper-middle-class earnings over the past 30 years, coupled with the stagnation of other classes' incomes (Fortin et al., 2012). Further, inequalities across urban neighbourhoods have deepened in many Canadian cities (Hulchanski, 2010).

These overlapping trends—worsening disparities among families and neighbour-hoods versus continuing public school reform and expansion—have prompted some con-temporary sociologists to re-think elements of Reproduction Theory. Noting that broader socio-economic conditions provide the "ecology" in which schools operate, they question whether school structures, cultures, and practices still necessarily reinforce societal in-equalities at every turn. They reason that these structures, cultures, and practices may be actually weakening connections between schools and their immediate locales to some de-gree, having more positive impacts but also having been undermined by societal trends.

This newer reasoning focuses on the fact that families and neighbourhoods shape skills, stresses, orientations, and expectations children bring to school. School-level achievement clearly reflects local neighbourhood conditions: public schools in poor areas tend to under-achieve on virtually all performance indicators relative to schools in wealthy areas (Duncan and Murnane, 2011). Children from the poorest neighbourhoods and families have the most "complicated" lives, dealing with parental unemployment, family instability, local vio-lence, meagre household resources, and multiple residential moves.

This reasoning also focuses on the organization of public schooling. As government in-stitutions, public schools are far more uniform than their surrounding communities. Cen-tralized funding and governance effectively standardize children's experiences while they attend public schools. Those schools receive provincial funds through a universal formula that directs the same monies to schools in rich and poor areas alike, and also funnels extra funds to schools deemed in need because of large proportions of poor, recent immigrant or special needs students. This creates a sharp contrast between schools and household and neighbourhood environments, which as noted above, have become increasingly disparate. Further, governments set common standards for curricula, discipline, teacher qualifications, physical plant, class sizes, testing, and so on. Through this funding and governance, public education bureaucracies partly dis-embed schools from their neighbourhood ecologies.

Indeed, this process has reminded sociologists of an old ideal: schools may be great equal-izers after all. In their earliest days, public schools were lauded for their potential to level playing fields and generate upward mobility. The Reproduction theorists of the 1970s, as noted above, emphasised the very opposite view. But new research is suggesting something more nuanced. For instance, **summer learning** studies find that socio-economic gaps in learning growth are markedly smaller during the school term than they are during the summer when children are not in school (Alexander, Entwisle, and Olson, 2007; Downey, von Hippel, and Broh, 2004). Schools appear to provide learning opportunities that are more equal than those in families and neighbourhoods. Similarly, public schools offer working-class and poor students better access to sports and other extracurricular activities than do their neighbourhoods (Bennett et al., 2012). Likewise, the physical conditions of public schools are more equal than those across households. In disadvantaged neighbourhoods, for instance, schools have resources to fix vandalism and graffiti, as well as provide safe spaces. Privately owned buildings typically lack those resources. Reflecting this contrast, Cyr and Davies (2014) found only weak correlations between the amount of disorder on school grounds in Hamilton and nearby neighbourhood poverty. Indeed, schools in dangerous neighbourhoods seemed to serve as oases that tempo-rarily shielded youth from harsher conditions beyond (see also Cyr [2014]; Paulle [2013]).

For these reasons, we believe some core tenets of Reproduction Theory need to be revised. Many outcomes remain the same—low SES youth have markedly lesser school achievements than high SES youth—but the mechanisms that generate them have changed. What are these mechanisms?

New Sources of SES Achievement Gaps

Before outlining these mechanisms, we make a key distinction. A "primary mechanism" is a social force that affects children's capacity to learn school material. A "secondary mechanism" influences their aspirations and expectations for schooling. We use this distinction to help untangle a variety of processes that generate achievement gaps. We draw on Canadian research to illustrate these processes and examine American research where there is a lack of Canadian data.

New Primary Mechanisms: Out-of-School Learning

Parenting has changed over the past 40 years. In previous generations, mothers and fathers, even those in the middle class, rarely purchased toys or games for their children based on their promised educational benefits. Few parents prioritized reading to their children in search of an educational payoff, but instead prized reading for reading's sake. Aspiring parents may have forced their children to do homework, but few regarded themselves as home-based educators who were responsible for developing their children's cognitive skills. But much has changed, especially in the middle class. A new culture has emerged, especially among mothers, who charge themselves with responsibility not only for their children's health, safety, security, nutrition and morality, but also for their children's cognitive stimulation and growth (Quirke, 2006). In this new culture, even small infants are seen to need cognitive nurturing. Mothers are told to play Mozart for babies still in the womb. This culture has taken hold most strongly among the most educated parents (Aurini, 2011). Despite being employed for longer hours, mothers and fathers are spending more time on children's educational activities (Sayer, Bianchi, and Robinson, 2004). As a result, there are growing SES gaps in the monies parents spend on enriching goods and services for their children, such as books, computers, and private tutoring (Duncan and Murnane, 2011).

This culture has been imprinted in what is known as "school readiness." A growing stockpile of research on preschool children consistently reveals SES gaps in early cognitive measures taken before children enter formal public schools. For instance, American studies show marked SES gaps in achievement, particularly in reading, as early as age two (Farkas and Hibel, 2008). Canadian data show that five year old children from poor families have much lower school readiness than those from well-off families (Janus and Duku, 2007). Importantly, these early disparities predict achievement in later grades. In a British Columbia study, students with low readiness in kindergarten had below average cognitive skill levels four years later (Lloyd and Hertzman, 2009). Similarly, Ontario children with low readiness in kindergarten had more academic problems as far as Grade 9 (Yau et al., in preparation). Between 60 per cent and 70 per cent of kindergarten students in Toronto, who were not vulnerable on any dimension of school readiness met provincial standards in reading three and six years later, while the corresponding rates among vulnerable children were 29 per cent and 35 per cent. In the United States, Foster and Miller (2007) estimated that children with low reading readiness fell two years behind those with high reading readiness by the end of Grade 1. A well-known study from Baltimore (Alexander et al., 2007) tracked this process further by following children from Grade 1 into high school and found that eventual drop outs had academic problems as early as Grade 1. These longitudinal studies show how SES gaps emerge before children enter formal public schooling and often widen as they progress through schools.

The key question is: Why? A core challenge for researchers is to untangle the effects of schools versus families. Reproduction Theory suggests that schools actively generate disparities, but much research points to the potent impacts of families. The literature reviewed above shows clear effects of SES on preschool children's cognitive skills and how highly educated parents continue to pass on their vocabulary, reasoning, and literacy skills to their children. Their greater disposable incomes allow them to provide learning resources like books, crayons, and toys, and pay for lessons for swimming, dance, soccer, music, and so forth. Higher SES parents can also assist more effectively with homework (McNeal, 1999) and tend to have higher expectations for their children's education (Hill et al., 2004). Parenting clearly permeates children's learning opportunities, and SES influences parent's material and human resources and practices.

Among school-age children, summer is the extended period of non-school time. As discussed above, summer learning studies suggest that schools actually reduce the tendency for family-generated gaps to widen, since they equalize students' exposure to learning resources and opportunities. For instance, in Baltimore, Alexander et al. (2007) traced more than half of the SES gap in cognitive skills by Grade 9 to summertime gaps that had accumulated over several years. In an Ontario study, children from the top SES quartile continued to acquire literacy during the summer, even matching school year rates of learning, while those from the bottom quartile lost some of their previously acquired literacy (Davies and Aurini, 2013). This evidence suggests that non-school time is an important primary mechanism of SES gaps because children are exposed to greatly varying learning opportunities and resources outside of school.

New Secondary Mechanisms: Evolving Parenting Strategies for Educational Competition

Whereas "student achievement" is typically indicated by test scores and grades, "student attainment" refers to progressing through institutional channels like successive credential tiers, enrolling in lucrative fields of study, and attending schools of varying prestige. Benefitting economically from schooling requires more than acquiring fundamental skills and mastering the curriculum. One must comply with institutional dictates and acquire the right credentials. A key finding in sociology is that SES affects student attainment beyond their achievement. That is, even taking into account skill levels and grades, youth from higher SES origins are likelier to graduate from high school, enter higher education, and attend higher ranked universities (Radford, 2013; Davies, Maldonado, and Zarifa, 2014). What triggers a SES gap in student attainment, beyond those gaps in student achievement? In this section, we argue that SES differences in parenting have become important generators of SES attainment gaps. Whereas Bourdieu originally portrayed schools as rewarding a time-honoured elite culture, today's gaps stem from relatively novel practices that are altering what counts as cultural capital. Shifting family-school connections have given advantaged parents new tools that offer their children a competitive edge.

Norms of family involvement in schooling have changed. Today's schools expect parents to be "active, involved, assertive, informed, and educated" (Lareau and Weininger, 2003, 589). Until two decades ago, few teachers or parents expected parents to assume strong educational roles at home (Ong-Dean, 2009; Irwin and Elley, 2011). Lareau (2002, 2003, 2011) argues that class differences in parenting practices, rather than differences in participation in highbrow culture, are prime generators of inequality. She traces these evolving cultures to rising educational disparities among parents, particularly mothers, and growing anxieties over downward mobility in an increasingly uncertain economy.

Lareau (2003, 3, 2011, 3), describes working-class and poor parents as enacting a logic of "natural growth." This logic prioritizes meeting children's basic needs for love, shelter, and sustenance, but otherwise taking a hands-off attitude in educational matters, instead prizing children's autonomy and independence. This logic assumes a division of labour in which professional teachers are responsible for children's education, and parents play supporting roles rather than closely monitoring their children's schooling or feelings and feeling entitled to intervene when needed. Lareau compares that logic to middle-class parents' "concerted cultivation." This form of parenting takes several guises. First, these parents prefer to use elaborate language and reasoning when disciplining their children, which builds those children's sense of entitlement when dealing with teachers. Building on this idea, Calarco (2011) found that middle-class children in an elementary school made the most requests for help and were most successful at eliciting assistance from teachers, thereby boosting their learning opportunities. Second, concerted cultivation also involves parents directing all sorts of structured activities for their children—music, dance, arts, and sports lessons—that loosely simulate schooling in that children follow the formal dictates of adults. Third, it strengthens home-school connections. These parents embrace school-like activities in their homes, structuring their children's play and searching for "teachable moments" in the hopes of nurturing cognitive skills (Devine, 2004; Henry, 1996; Irwin and Elley, 2011). At school, these parents volunteer more regularly in their children's classrooms, PTA meetings, and school councils. Some concerted cultivators seek advantages by bypassing public schooling altogether, hiring tutors and/or enrolling their children in private schools. Concerted cultivation also involves intervening on behalf of one's child, whether by choosing the best teacher, the best special program, or the best school (Demerath, 2009; Ong-Dean, 2009).

Viewing these elements of concerted cultivation as a whole, Lareau emphasises how it boosts parents' capacity to "work" educational institutions for their children's benefit and adapt their lifestyles to "align" home life with schools' institutional rewards. If schools assign a lot of homework, the concerted cultivator sets aside family time for monitoring, assisting with, and completing it. If some teachers or programs are better than others, the concerted cultivator inquires and intervenes to secure the best options. If transitions from high school to post-secondary institutions require a great deal of knowledge about course and grade requirements, deadlines, and institutional choices, the cultivator is "on it." Lareau does not regard concerted cultivation to be intrinsically better than the accomplishment of natural growth, but observes that one facilitates educational competitiveness more than the other.

What implications do these changing family practices have for Reproduction Theory? As noted above, Bourdieu (1973) originally conceived "cultural capital" as a scarce resource that upper-class families impose on schools' evaluation criteria, and that class-biased teachers use to reward students most familiar with high status culture, thereby alienating most working-class youth. But how realistic is this imagery in contemporary Canada? Today, it is increasingly difficult to link public school curricula to a social class. Researchers rarely detect class bias among teachers, who are generally unimpressed by highbrow cultural participation, and instead reward prosaic things like reading ability and work habits (Kingston, 2001; Sullivan, 2001). Bourdieu's followers may deem basic literacy and hard work to be "middle-class" attributes, "exclusionary practices," or "arbitrary cultural accoutrements," but perhaps they are just basic skills needed by all. And the continual expansion of post-secondary tiers is shifting the meaning of educational disadvantage. Today's gaps are no longer products of the virtual absence of working-class students in university but of the rising attainments of their middle-class peers. A new line of research is examining adjustments among newly arrived youth from working-class origins in universities. Those students appear to enjoy having their repertoire of cultural influences broaden, yet also recognize newly strained relationships with parents or former friends (for example, Lehmann [2014]). Finally, many of today's middle-class parents were not themselves raised in that class, and so their resources and sensibilities were acquired through a process of upward mobility. Many of this generation's "reproducers" were cultural arrivistes in the previous generation. Much concerted cultivation represents cultural production, not reproduction. So, we revise Bourdieu's imagery by downplaying the imposition of upper-middle-class culture in favour of recognizing these parents' active adaptation to evolving school demands and rewards, emphasising their innovative activation of resources (Lareau 2003, 2011; Looker, 1994).

New Neighbourhood Effects: Inequality, Stress, and Disorder

A third mechanism focuses on the impacts of schools and neighbourhoods. The core idea behind research on "neighbourhood effects" is that children's attainments can be influenced by surrounding circumstances in ways independent of their personal and family characteristics. For a quarter century, American sociologists have found that neighbourhood poverty, beyond its association with children's family background, is also associated with lower school achievement and attainment, verbal ability, test scores, graduation rates, and heightened problem behaviour (reviewed in Cyr [2014]). Canadian researchers have found similar though generally weaker neighbourhood effects (for example, Boyle et al. [2007]; Lloyd and Hertzman [2010])[3].

A variety of mechanisms create these neighbourhood effects. First, areas with greater poverty are proximate to crime, violence and threats of physical harm, health dangers, and precarious parental employment, and tend to strain family relationships. Each of these can expose children to great amounts of stress (Duncan and Magnuson, 2011). McLoyd (1990) argues that poverty impacts children by harming their family's relationships by triggering conflict, undermining social support, and exposing children to mental health stressors. Second, neighbourhoods in which many people have difficult lives tend to generate certain peer dynamics. Youth cultures can be diverted from school-sponsored activities in the cause of daily survival. Distrust of police and other authorities can foster "street" codes in which interactions among youth are inflected by norms of intimidation and hostility rather than co-operation. Street codes can force many students, even those otherwise positively oriented toward school, to embrace interaction styles that violate school norms in order to save face among peers (Anderson, 1999). In this way, neighbourhoods can shape "school climates." Schools with unhealthy climates have been shown to lower student motivation, heighten disengagement and frustration, and ultimately lessen achievement (Thapa et al., 2013). In response, schools sometimes implement dress codes, security systems, and strict rules of conduct in attempts to buffer street norms and re-orient children to classroom learning. But otherwise, peer groups can de-align many youth from pro-school norms and practices, such as prioritizing homework, identifying with the student role, or even enjoying school.

One example of how neighbourhood contexts can penetrate school processes comes from a recent Canadian study. "Physical disorder"—strewn garbage, graffiti, derelict lots, broken windows, vandalized property—is often construed as symbolizing a deep malaise and public incivility in urban public spaces. Vandalism, graffiti, and broken windows can spring up almost anywhere, but they can become relatively permanent features of poor communities that lack resources to prevent or remove them. Such disorder can provoke fear, attract criminals, and stigmatize blighted neighbourhoods if interpreted as a signal of weak social controls. Research shows that high levels of disorder are correlated with a variety of social problems, including concentrated poverty, crime, lack of social support, lower self-esteem, and worse physical and mental health (reviewed in Cyr [2014]).

Applying similar ideas to schooling, Cyr and Davies (2014) examined relationships between disorder and academic outcomes in a mid-size, de-industrializing Ontario city. They reasoned that physical disorder in areas surrounding schools might affect their educational outcomes via two possible mechanisms. Disorder might encourage student deviance. Large urban schools are daily destinations for thousands of students, many of whom must pass through public spaces strewn with graffiti, garbage, and vandalism. Some youth may interpret that disorder as indicating that rule-breaking can go undetected and unpunished, especially in secluded spots near schools, such as laneways, back areas of stores, abandoned buildings, and littered ravines. For some youth, these spots can be enticing refuges for smoking, drug use, drinking, fighting, and stealing, although others may avoid them out of fear. In either event, high levels of disorder around schools can distract students from academic work and disrupt core learning processes.

Or disorder can divert high-achieving and rule-abiding students toward more orderly schools. While most schools are vandalized and littered at some point in time, those that are regularly disordered can get spoiled reputations. Those reputations can affect the composition of schools' student populations. In most Canadian jurisdictions, families can send their children to public schools beyond their catchment boundaries if space is available. Disorder around a school may influence this choice if achievement-oriented and ambitious parents associate graffiti, litter, and vandalism with a school's academic quality being less. If they do make that association, ambitious families may self-select out of highly disordered schools and, instead, choose schools in more orderly settings.

To test these ideas, Cyr and Davies (2014) measured the amount of disorder in streets surrounding each school, as well as disorder on school buildings and grounds, for every elementary and secondary school in an Ontario city. They uncovered an intriguing pattern of findings. For starters, disorder and graffiti on streets surrounding schools was strongly correlated with neighbourhood poverty; poorer locales had more disorder. Further, neighbourhood disorder had significant net effects on school outcomes like student achievement, rates of suspension, and perceptions of safety. Those schools with higher levels of disorder in their surrounding streets had more students with below-standard test scores, higher suspension rates, and more students reporting they felt unsafe at school. Put simply, neighbourhood disorder was correlated with school outcomes.

The authors also found patterns that supported a different kind of argument, however. They found that disorder and graffiti on school grounds and buildings—unlike disorder on surrounding streets—was not significantly associated with neighbourhood poverty or with school outcomes. That is, levels of disorder for schools did not always mirror their surrounding neighbourhoods. Why? Cyr and Davies reckoned that institutional governance partly "detach" schools from their broader neighbourhoods. Public funding formulae can standardize school grounds and equalize their upkeep, while other nearby buildings lack a parallel mechanism. In public schools, children spend their weekdays in settings with fairly common conditions and not only in terms of their physical upkeep. Mandatory teacher qualifications, universal disciplinary rules, and standardized curricula equalize other social conditions. Across full ranges of neighbourhoods, from the richest to the poorest, these institutional processes create more common experiences while students are in schools than during their non-school lives.

Discussion: Can School Reforms Keep Pace with Societal Change?

Canadian education policy-makers want more youth to pursue post-secondary studies, and so they also wish to reduce achievement gaps. Yet schools are finding it harder to create level playing fields as societal inequality worsens. What educational policies are governments pursuing to counteract the effects of deepening inequality?

Policies for Equalizing Learning Opportunities

Research suggests that SES gaps are forged during children's early years and then widen during long stretches of non-school time, such as summers, because of family inequalities in learning opportunities and resources. This implies that schools need to compensate for those family-based inequalities. Several policies have been developed under this rationale: free preschool programs, full-day junior and senior kindergarten, learning supports for families with young children, and summer learning programs. Many hail early learning programs as a solid return on investment (for example, Pascal [2009]). Some American studies find lasting positive effects of early learning programs for low-income children, while others find that effects can "fade out" after several years (for example, Foster and Miller [2007]). In Canada, large-scale programs like full-day junior kindergarten are relatively new, so there are few definitive data as yet, although full-day kindergarten appears to help certain populations of children (Warburton, Warburton, and Hertzman, 2012). Similarly, summer learning programs appear to reduce 15 per cent to 30 per cent of pre-existing gaps in early literacy and numeracy (Borman and Boulay, 2004; Davies and Aurini, 2013; Kim and Quinn, 2013). These compensatory programs appear to be more effective than those that narrow learning opportunities for struggling youth, such as streaming, ability grouping, and grade retention. Evaluations of the latter programs find that their students tend to have lesser subsequent achievement than similar children who remain in mainstream environments (Condron, 2008), likely because of constricted ranges of learning opportunities.

Policies for Secondary Mechanisms: Hitting a Moving Target?

A variety of structure-oriented and cultural-oriented policies might counteract SES disparities in family "alignments" with school systems. In terms of structures, the expanded "second-chance system," mentioned above, provides more routes than ever by which former dropouts can re-enter and graduate from high schools and post-secondary programs.

Along with student loans, scholarship, and bursary initiatives, these programs can assist young adults whose families previously lacked information about post-secondary requirements, studying strategies, or the intricacies of navigating mass educational systems. In terms of cultures, more educators are aware of the need to encourage and nurture aspirations among disadvantaged youth, many of whom enter schools with restricted mental horizons about their possible futures. Yet our analysis of new parenting cultures suggests these policies may have limited impacts if today's gaps are mainly fuelled by the agency of upper-middle-class parents, since these policies cannot restrict that agency.

Policies for Disadvantaged Contexts: Supporting Neighbourhoods and Stress Reduction

To counteract children's exposure to stressful contexts, some policy-makers have championed neighbourhood-based supports for all families, such as the Ontario Early Years Centres (OEYCs) and Best Start programs, as well as similar initiatives in Manitoba and Australia. These initiatives aim to provide local communities with reliable resources and training for early childhood health and education. It is difficult to judge whether these initiatives are particularly effective for poorer children, since they are accessible to all. Within schools, student discipline reforms are attempting to be less punitive, since they disproportionately impact disadvantaged youth. Programs like progressive discipline and restorative justice, for instance, may be having some positive impacts (Milne and Aurini, 2015). In another vein of policy, some are championing programs aimed at promoting greater integration by family income across schools, with the hope of re-engineering peer dynamics. Finally, the effects of physical disorder around schools imply that if educators work with local communities to clean up and monitor areas adjacent to schools, they may have positive effects on student outcomes.

Conclusion: Renewing Our Understandings of Achievement Gaps

When Reproduction Theory was first popularized in the 1970s, biases in curricula, teaching, and school organization actively generated achievement gaps. But many aspects of schooling and society have since changed. Schools' professional norms and structures have evolved, becoming more accommodating of more students than before, and expanding opportunities for higher education. As a result, new forces are fuelling achievement gaps. Wealth and income inequality among families have risen, harming social conditions in many neighbourhoods, while middle-class parents are creating new alignments between their homes and schools. Thus today, achievement gaps are reproduced less through any imposition of a longstanding elite culture on public schools, and more through micro-level innovations by which advantaged parents adapt to school arrangements and effectively advocate for their children. Schools have largely worked around these trends. They can be faulted for assuming that children can get help at home with their homework, but can be praised for developing policies that partly compensate for disparities in home support. Educators face twin pressures: They are expected to provide a level playing field yet also welcome all of their constituents, including concerted cultivators. Despite great school reform, Canada has seen a subtle shifting of educational responsibility from schools to families, and that has likely strengthened SES effects on school outcomes.

Questions for Critical Thought

1. Do you see evidence of the "correspondence principle" in your university? Give examples.
2. Think about your upbringing as a child. Can you recognize any of the parenting "logics" described by Annette Lareau? For instance, were you "concertedly cultivated" by your parents? If so, do you think that upbringing helped you attend university? Explain.
3. Think again about your upbringing. What activities, both formal and informal, did you do during the typical summer? Did any sharpen your literacy and/or numeracy skills? Did you ever experience a "summer setback"?
4. Have high schools changed over the past 50 years? Ask a grandparent about his or her experiences with teachers, curricula, or testing, and compare them to your own.
5. When you see physical disorder around a school, does it shape your image of that school? Why or why not?

Glossary

Achievement gaps Disparities in learning school material that emerges over time between various groups such as social strata.

Correspondence principle The idea that school streams mirror different kinds of workplaces in order to socialize future workers into various positions in stratified workplaces.

Summer learning A strategic area of study that compares school-year patterns of learning to those in the summer months. These studies allow researchers to examine learning disparities that emerge outside of school, thus allowing them to distinguish family effects from school effects.

Notes

1. Heckman (2008) argues that "official" high school graduate rates in the United States may be masking a key trend wherein many recent graduates merely attain a "diluted" secondary education in the form of a General Educational Development (GED), many of which are obtained by prison inmates. He claims the skill profiles of GED holders resemble those of high school dropouts more than those of regular high school graduates. Ou (2008) finds that GED recipients have significantly worse income, life satisfaction, and symptoms of severe depression and substance use than high school graduates, though they fare better than high school dropouts. We are unaware of any Canadian studies that similarly compare skills or labour market fortunes of on-time high school graduates versus mature graduates.
2. See www4.hrsdc.gc.ca/.3ndic.1t.4r@-eng.jsp?iid=29
3. Canada's weaker neighbourhood effects likely reflect its lesser concentration and persistence of poverty (Ley and Smith, 2000).

References

Alexander, K.L., Entwisle, D.R., and Olson, L.S. "Lasting consequences of the summer learning gap." *American Sociological Review* 72(2) (2007): 167–80.

Anderson, E. *Code of the Street: Decency, Violence, and the Moral Life of the Inner City.* New York: W.W. Norton & Company, 1999.

Aurini, J. "How upper-middle-class Canadian parents' understand the transmission of advantages." *Education and Pedagogy* 23(60) (2011): 19–43.

Bennett, R., Lutz, A.C., and Jayaram, L. "Beyond the schoolyard: The role of parenting logics, financial resources, and social institutions in the social class gap in structured activity participation." *Sociology of Education* 85(2) (2012): 131–57.

Borman, G.D., and Boulay, M. (eds.). *Summer Learning: Research, Policies, and Programs.* Mahwah: Lawrence Erlbaum Associates, 2004.

Bourdieu, P. "Cultural reproduction and social reproduction." In *Knowledge, Education and Cultural Change: Papers in the Sociology of Education,* R. Brown (ed.), (71–84). London: Tavistock, 1973.

Bourdieu, P., and Passerson, J. *Reproduction in Education, Society and Culture.* London: Sage Publications, 1977 [1990].

Bowlby, G. "Provincial drop-out rates—trends and consequences." *Education Matters* cat. no. 81-004-XIE, 2(4). Ottawa: Statistics Canada, 2005.

Bowles, S., and Gintis, H. *Schooling in Capitalist America: Educational Reform and the Contradictions of Economic Life.* New York: Basic Books, 1976.

Boyle, M.H., Georgiades, K., Racine, Y., and Mustard, C. "Neighborhood and family influences on educational attainment: Results from the Ontario Child Health Study follow-up 2001." *Child Development* 78(1) (2007): 168–89.

Calarco, J.M. "I need help!" Social class and children's help-seeking in elementary school." *American Sociological Review* 76(6) (2011): 862–82.

Cicourel, A.V., and Kitsuse, J.I. "The school as a mechanism of social differentiation." In *Power and Ideology in Education,* J. Karabel and A.H. Halsey (eds.), (282–92). New York: Oxford Press, 1977.

Clark, B.R. "The 'cooling-out' function in higher education." *American Journal of Sociology* 65(6) (1960): 569–76.

Collins, R. *Interaction Ritual Chains.* New Jersey: Princeton University Press, 2004.

Condron, D.J. "An early start: Skill grouping and unequal reading gains in the elementary years." *The Sociological Quarterly* 49(2) (2008): 363–94.

Corak, M.R., Lipps, G., and Zhao, J.Z. *Family Income and Participation in Post-secondary Education.* Ottawa: Statistics Canada, 2003.

Cyr, D. "Physical graffiti and school ecologies: A new look at 'Disorder', neighbourhood effects and school outcomes." PhD thesis, McMaster University, 2014.

Cyr, D., and Davies, S. "Neighbourhood disorder and school outcomes in a de-industrializing city." Unpublished manuscript, McMaster University, 2014.

Davies, S. "A revolution of expectations? Three key trends in the SAEP data." In *Preparing for Post Secondary Education: New Roles for Governments and Families,* Robert Sweet and Paul Anisef (eds.), (149–65). Montreal: McGill-Queen's University Press, 2005.

Davies, S., and Aurini, J. "Summer learning inequality in Ontario." *Canadian Public Policy* 30(2) (2013): 287–307.

Davies, S., Maldonado, V., and Zarifa, D. "Effectively maintaining inequality in Toronto: Predicting university destinations of Toronto District School Board graduates." *Canadian Review of Sociology* 51(1) (2014): 22–53.

Demerath, P. *Producing Success: The Culture of Personal Advancement in an American High School.* Chicago: The University of Chicago Press, 2009.

Devine, F. *Class Practices: How Parents Help Their Children Get Good Jobs.* Cambridge: Cambridge University Press, 2004.

Downey, D., Von Hippel, P., and Broh, B. "Are schools the great equalizer? Cognitive inequality during the summer months and the school year." *American Sociological Review* 69 (2004): 613–35.

Duncan, G.J., and Magnuson, K. "The nature and impact of early achievement skills, attention skills, and behavior problems." In *Whither Opportunity: Rising Inequality, Schools, and Children's Life Chances,* Greg J. Duncan and Richard J. Murnane (eds.), (47–70). New York: The Russell Sage Foundation, 2011.

Duncan, G.J., and Murnane, R. "Introduction: The American dream, then and now." In *Whither Opportunity: Rising Inequality: Schools and Children's Life Chances,* Greg J. Duncan and Richard J. Murnane (eds.), (3–26). New York: Russell Sage Foundation, 2011.

Farkas, G., Grobe, R.P., Sheehan, D., and Shuan, Y. "Cultural resources and school success: Gender, ethnicity, and poverty groups within an urban school district." *American Sociological Review* 55(1) (1990): 127–42.

Farkas, G., and Hibel, J. "Being unready for school: Factors affecting risk and resilience." In *Disparities in School Readiness: How*

Families Contribute to Transitions into School, Alan Booth and Ann Crouter (eds.), (3–30). New York: Erlbaum, 2008.

Finnie, R., Lascelles, E., and Sweetman, A. "Who goes? The direct and indirect effects of family background on access to postsecondary education." Research paper. Ottawa: Statistics Canada, 2005.

Fortin, N., Green, D.A., Lemieux, T., Milligan, K., and Riddell, W.C. "Canadian inequality: Recent developments and policy options." *Canadian Public Policy* 38(2) (2012): 121–45.

Foster, W.A., and Miller, M. "Development of the literacy achievement gap: A longitudinal study of kindergarten through third grade." *Language, Speech, and Hearing Services in Schools* 38(3) (2007): 173–81.

Heckman, J. "Schools, skills and synapses." UCD Geary Institute Discussion Paper Series, 2008.

Henry, M. *Parent-School Collaboration: Feminist Organizational Structures and School Leadership*. Albany: State University of New York Press, 1996.

Hill, N.E., Castellino, D.R., Lansford, J.E., Nowlin, P., Dodge, K.A., Bates, J.E., and Pettit, G.S. "Parent academic involvement as related to school behavior, achievement, and aspirations: Demographic variations across adolescence." *Child Development* 75(5) (2004): 1491–509.

Hulchanski, J.D. *The Three Cities within Toronto: Income Polarization among Toronto's Neighbourhoods, 1970–2005*. Toronto: Cities Centre, University of Toronto, 2010.

Irwin, S., and Elley, S. "Concerted cultivation? Parenting values, education and class diversity." *Sociology* 45(3) (2011): 480–95.

Janus, M., and Duku, E. "The school entry gap: Socioeconomic, family, and health factors associated with children's school readiness to learn." *Early Education and Development* 18(3) (2007): 375–403.

Kim, J.S., and Quinn, D.M. "The effects of summer reading on low-income children's literacy achievement from kindergarten to Grade 8." *Review of Educational Research* 83(3) (2013): 386–431.

Kingston, P. "The unfulfilled promise of cultural Capital Theory." *Sociology of Education* (Extra issue) 74 (2001): 88–99.

Lareau, A. "Invisible inequality: Social class and childrearing in black families and white Families." *American Sociological Review* 67(5) (2002): 747–76.

Lareau, A. *Unequal Childhoods*. First edition. Berkeley: University of California Press, 2003 .

Lareau, A. *Unequal Childhoods*. Second edition. Berkeley: University of California Press, 2011.

Lareau, A., and Weininger, E. "Cultural capital in educational research: A critical assessment." *Theory and Society* 32(5/6) (2003): 567–606.

Lehmann, W. "Habitus transformation and hidden injuries: Successful working-class university students." *Sociology of Education* 87(1) (2014): 1–15.

Ley, D., and Smith, H. "Relations between deprivation and immigrant groups in large Canadian cities." *Urban Studies* 37(1) (2000): 37–62.

Lloyd, J.E.V., and Hertzman, C. "From kindergarten readiness to fourth-grade assessment: Longitudinal analysis with linked population data." *Social Science & Medicine* 68(1) (2009): 111–23.

Lloyd, J.E.V., and Hertzman, C. "How neighborhoods matter for rural and urban children's language and cognitive development at kindergarten and Grade 4." *Journal of Community Psychology* 38(3) (2010): 293–313.

Looker, D.E. "Active capital: The impact of parents on youths' educational performance and plans." In *Sociology of Education in Canada: Critical Perspectives on Theory, Research and Practice*, L. Erwin and D. MacLennan (eds.), (164–87). Toronto: Copp Clark Longman Ltd., 1994.

McLoyd, V.C. "The impact of economic hardship on black families and children: Psychological distress, parenting, and socioemotional development." *Child Development* 61 (1990): 311–46.

McNeal, R.B. "Parental involvement as social capital: Differential effectiveness on science achievement, truancy, and dropping out." *Social Forces* 78(1) (1999): 117–44.

Milne, E., and Aurini, J. "Schools, cultural mobility, and social reproduction: The case of progressive discipline." *Canadian Journal of Sociology* 40(1) (2015): 51–74.

Ong-Dean, C. *Distinguishing Disability: Parents, Privilege, and Special Education*. Chicago: The University of Chicago Press, 2009.

Pascal, C. *With Our Best Future in Mind: Implementing Early Learning in Ontario*. Toronto: Queen's Printer for Ontario, 2009.

Paulle, B. *Toxic Schools: High-Poverty Education in New York and Amsterdam*. Chicago: University of Chicago Press, 2013.

Quirke, L. "'Keeping young minds sharp': Children's cognitive stimulation and the rise of parenting magazines, 1959–2003." *Canadian Review of Sociology* 43(4) (2006): 387–406.

Radford, A.W. *Top Student, Top School? How Social Class Shapes Where Valedictorians Go to College.* Chicago: University of Chicago Press, 2013.

Rosenbaum, J. *Beyond College for All*. New York: Russell Sage, 2001.

Sayer, L., Bianchi, S., and Robinson, J.P. "Are parents investing less in children? Trends in mothers' and fathers' time with children." *American Journal of Sociology* 107 (2004): 1–43.

Sirin, S.R. "Socioeconomic status and academic achievement: A meta-analytic review of research." *Review of Educational Research* 75(3) (2005): 417–53.

Sullivan, A. "Cultural capital and educational attainment." *Sociology* 35(4) (2001): 893–912.

Thapa, A., Cohen, J., Guffey, S., and Higgin, D. "A review of school climate research." *Review of Educational Research* 83(3) 2013: 357–85.

Warburton, W.P., Warburton, R.N., and Hertzman, C. "Does full day kindergarten help kids?" *Canadian Public Policy* 38(4) 2012: 591–603.

Willms, J.D. "Successful transitions: Findings from the National Longitudinal Survey of Children and Youth." Context paper presented at the Successful Transitions Conference, Human Resources and Skills Development Canada. Ottawa, Ontario, 28–29 April 2009.

Yau, M., Janus, M., Duku, E., and Brown, R. "Kindergarten school readiness and later school achievement." Unpublished manuscript. Offord Centre for Child Studies, McMaster University. (In preparation.)

Zeman, K. "A first look at provincial differences in educational pathways from high school to college and university." Statistics Canada cat. no. 81-004-XIE. *Education Matters* 4(2) (2007): 1–15.

3

Intergenerational Transfers of Advantage

Parents' Education and Children's Educational and Employment Outcomes in Alberta[1]

Harvey Krahn and Gary R.S. Barron

Introduction

Sociologists have been studying patterns of status attainment in the United States (for example, Sewell, Haller, and Ohelndorf [1970]) and Canada (for example Boyd, Pineo, and Porter [1981]) for many decades, asking why some people obtain more education and, in turn, higher status occupations than others. This research tradition has revealed consistent patterns of **intergenerational transmission of advantage**, that is, a strong tendency for the children of more educated parents (with higher status occupations) to themselves acquire more education and, hence, better jobs (Potter and Roksa, 2013).

This chapter examines the links between parents' and children's social standing in Alberta in the late 1990s and early 2000s, a time when post-secondary educational opportunities in the province were expanding and the economy was very strong, offering many employment opportunities to young people. Data from a seven-year longitudinal survey of Alberta high school graduates are analysed to see if patterns of intergenerational transfer of advantage are altered in such a context.

Following the lead of previous researchers, we focus on university education but also ask whether a trades-related post-secondary education provides an alternative pathway to employment success in a provincial economy dominated by resource extraction industries (particularly the oil and natural gas industries). In discussing the data patterns, we draw on a vocabulary of concepts developed by the French sociologist Pierre Bourdieu to describe patterns of cultural reproduction of social inequalities or, in other words, the intergenerational transmission of advantage.

"Getting Ahead" in Canada

A century ago, only a tiny minority of young Canadians—typically men and those from the wealthiest families—went on to college or university after completing high school. Most young people did not finish high school, since this was required for few jobs. But by the 1980s, Canada's occupational structure had changed dramatically (Krahn, Hughes, and Lowe, 2015), and typical advice to teenagers from parents and teachers had become "get a good education if you want to get ahead in life." This was good advice indeed since, today, on average, those with a college or university education earn considerably more from their jobs (Boothby and Drewes, 2006; Frenette, 2014).

The rapid expansion of Canada's post-secondary educational system in the post–Second World War era (Davies and Guppy, 2006) meant that university and college education was now more accessible to young people from working-class and lower-middle-class families. Even so, one of the strongest predictors of a young person completing university continues to be whether one or both of her or his parents had acquired a university degree. For example, a recent national study of 25- to 39-year-old Canadians revealed that 56 per cent of those from families where at least one parent had finished university had themselves acquired a degree. In contrast, only 23 per cent of similarly aged Canadians from families where neither parent had a degree had personally completed university (Turcotte, 2011). Thus, we continue to see the intergenerational transfer of educational advantages in Canada. In turn, young people with university degrees are more likely to get better jobs (Krahn et al., 2015).

University-educated, and typically more affluent, parents pass along advantages to their children in various ways (Davies and Guppy, 2006; Mueller, 2008). They can more easily pay for their children to attend college or university but also, much earlier, for tutoring that can improve a child's chances of getting accepted into a better-resourced elementary or secondary school (Lee and Burkam, 2002). In addition, children of university-educated parents are more likely to have completed academic (non-vocational) high school programs that are required for university entrance (Taylor and Krahn, 2009), no doubt because their parents, with greater knowledge of how the education system works (Lareau, 2003), insisted that they do so. University-educated parents also instill higher educational and occupational aspirations in their children (Krahn, 2009) and serve as useful role models and information sources.

Vocational post-secondary education (technical school training or apprenticeships), however, has generally been under-valued in Canada (Lyons, Randhawa, and Paulson, 1991). Shuetze (2003, 71) calls it the "poor cousin" of academic (that is, university) education, noting that (middle-class) parents and high school teachers typically encourage young people to choose university (or a community college) over vocational training. At the same time, because they do not have the advantages of their middle-class peers, working-class youth are more frequently streamed into high school vocational programs (Taylor and Krahn, 2009) that close doors into university and open doors into post-secondary technical training. If they do want to continue their education, working-class youth might also choose vocational post-secondary training because it costs less and is less foreign to them (Lehmann, 2014).

Because of the more limited appeal of vocational education to most Canadian youth, and because Canadian employers have been reluctant to invest in training for their employees (McKenna, 2013), Canada has relied heavily on immigration for skilled trades workers (Lyons et al., 1991). In contrast, countries like Germany have an extensive vocational educational system (particularly apprenticeships) tightly integrated with industry needs for employees (Heinz, 2003; Lehmann, 2007a), leading to higher occupational status for the skilled trades.

Workers with skilled trades certification (for example, carpenters, electricians, pipefitters), a subset of those with any type of vocational post-secondary training, account for less than 10 per cent of total employment in Canada today (Pyper, 2008). In Alberta, the trades comprise a higher proportion of total employment (15 per cent). Most workers in the skilled trades are men. While some workers with post-secondary vocational training can earn high salaries in some settings, national Census data from 1981 to 2001 show that the earnings premium for trades certification (compared to only a high school education) was not as large as was the earnings advantage received by workers with a college diploma (Boothby and Drewes, 2006). For example, in 2000, for 25- to 34-year-old male workers, those with trades training earned 15 per cent more than those with only high school education while those with a college diploma earned 19 per cent more. For 25- to 34-year-old women, the earnings premiums for trades and community college training were 5 per cent and 20 per cent, respectively. The earnings premium in 2000 for young workers with a university degree (compared to only high school education) was much higher, 52 per cent for men and 61 per cent for women.

Along with parents' education, a number of other factors shape post-secondary educational attainment in Canada and, through it, labour market outcomes. Until a few decades ago, women were less likely than men to complete university. Today women are more likely to attend and complete university (Turcotte, 2011). Nevertheless, young women continue to be over-represented in traditional "female" university programs such as education, nursing, and the humanities, which, on average, lead to lower paying jobs compared to the jobs (for example, in science or engineering) typically obtained by university-educated men (Davies and Guppy, 2006; Krahn et al., 2015). Women are also less likely than men to obtain technical post-secondary qualifications that also lead to higher-paying employment in some settings.

Previous research has highlighted problems faced by rural youth seeking a university or college education (Looker and Dwyer, 1998; Andres and Looker, 2001; Mueller, 2008). Unlike their urban counterparts who might have several post-secondary options in their community, rural youth typically must leave home to continue their education, making the transition more difficult and costly. This problem is not as severe in provinces where community colleges have been established in smaller urban centres (Frenette, 2003).

Aboriginal youth face the most barriers to acquiring a good education (Davies and Guppy, 1998). They are more likely to have grown up in poor families and also more likely to be living in smaller rural communities or on Indian reserves, far from any post-secondary institutions. As a result, in 2011, only 10 per cent of working age (25 to 64) Aboriginal Canadians had acquired a university degree, compared to 26 per cent of the rest of the population (Aboriginal Affairs and Northern Development, 2013). Consequently, Aboriginal youth would have many fewer family and community members who might be educational role models and information sources.

Immigrant youth, who also frequently face discrimination, language barriers, and problems of low income, tend to have higher than average post-secondary educational goals (Krahn and Taylor, 2005). They are also more likely than native-born Canadians to attend and complete university (Abada, Hou, and Ram, 2009). In part, this is because immigrant parents, often very well-educated but still underemployed (Krahn et al., 2000), strongly encourage their children to obtain a post-secondary education (Taylor and Krahn, 2013).

Cultural Reproduction and Inherited Advantage: Bourdieu's Key Concepts

Pierre Bourdieu wrote extensively about how social hierarchies are reproduced. He paid close attention to people's everyday social lives, and the cultural practices these involve, including those in schools and universities (Bourdieu, 1980, 1984, 1988). He developed some useful theoretical concepts to help people think about their own personal situation so that they might have "some means of doing what they do, and living what they live, a little bit better" (Bourdieu, 2007, 113). He thought of his concepts as tools for strategically thinking about one's position in the world and how to navigate it effectively. Sociologists have found Bourdieu's concepts particularly useful for interpreting processes of **cultural reproduction** and the transmission of advantage across generations.

Bourdieu imagined that life was much like a game played on a field (like rugby), with players positioned according to how they had individually accumulated different forms of capital (Grenfell, 2008). He envisioned an over-arching **field of power**, a social space upon which individuals accumulate and exchange economic (money), social (useful relationships with other people), and symbolic capital (of which there are many types including cultural, intellectual, and scientific) in order to move to a more desirable position. Of course, people can play at many games and each game has its own field where certain **forms of capital** are more or less valuable.

One option is to go to university and play that game and the various smaller games it offers, like the sociology game or engineering game. Getting through university requires that one have particular economic and symbolic capital in order to do well. Overall, people invest in university because they realize that it will create symbolic capital (a degree) that can then be used to acquire a more advantageous position on the field of power such as a higher status and better paying job.

A key question is how do people learn to play these games and use their different forms of capital effectively? As Bourdieu explained, a child is born into a particular time, place, and position on the field of power—those of its parents. As the child grows up, she or he becomes accustomed to certain types of clothing, food, and recreation, along with many other specific cultural (lifestyle) practices. For example, wealthier parents with higher levels of education may read to their children more often, use a wider selection of words in conversations, and expose their children to a variety of experiences such as international travel and the fine arts (Sullivan, 2001). When it is time for the child to go to school, sit still in a desk, and respond to teachers' questions, the ability to do so may come more naturally. The child will have a predisposition to academic schooling and feel comfortable with the context and challenges it presents.

This predisposition is what Bourdieu called **habitus** (Bourdieu, 1980; Maton, 2008). Habitus is an embodied sense of what one should do and how one should do it, and, therefore, directs how people engage with the world. A habitus that is well-suited for a particular field involves a well-developed understanding of the game that is being played and how different forms of capital can be used to accomplish goals. Returning to the example of the child from the more advantaged family, one can see some elements of habitus. The child is comfortable sitting still (embodied experience), is versatile at listening and speaking with teachers (using cultural capital such as words and knowledge of the fine arts and the larger world effectively), and takes the schooling game seriously. Moreover, habitus is shaped by practice. Over time, the child becomes more adept at playing the schooling game. Growing up in a particular position on the field and developing a particular habitus does not mean that one's choices are always pre-determined. While habitus describes a degree of structural constraint for an individual person, Bourdieu meant to demonstrate that it is also generative and can shift over time. Children are not exact copies of their parents. They are exposed to different experiences and different fields, and grow up in a different time and context (a different field of power) and, perhaps, even in a different place. While a young person's interests and choices are shaped through interactions with their parents and in their community, an individual might nevertheless take an interest and choose to get involved in games (for example, attending university) their parents had never imagined, even though they might not be as adept at these games as other more advantaged peers (Lehmann, 2007b, 2014).

Bourdieu's theory and concepts help us to better understand how patterns of intergenerational transfer of advantage are maintained, but it is also important to note that he was writing about France, a country with a very different cultural and educational history than Canada, at least four decades ago. As Davies and Rizk (2014) observe in a review of how Bourdieu's concept of cultural capital has been studied over the years, among other significant changes in the North American educational field, we have seen a substantial expansion of the post-secondary education system. There is now room for more people to play the higher education game. What effect has this had on post-secondary educational opportunities, and subsequent career outcomes, for young people from less advantaged backgrounds?

Along with changing over time, the post-secondary educational field also differs across space. In Alberta and British Columbia, for example, post-secondary systems allow young people to move relatively easily from the college system into the university system, and vice versa (Andres and Krahn, 1999). Furthermore, even though university education has typically been valued more than a technical post-secondary education (Davies and Guppy, 2006), there are likely locales in which unique industrial structures offer employment opportunities that might favour a technical over a university post-secondary education.

This chapter focuses on Alberta at the turn of this century, and asks whether long-standing patterns of intergenerational transfer of advantage are still observed in a province where improving access to higher education has been a government priority, and where unemployment rates have typically been low and the demand for young workers with technical training has been high for the past several decades. In addition, we highlight differences in educational attainment and employment outcomes in early adulthood on the basis of gender, urban-rural background, immigrant status, visible minority status, and Aboriginal status.

Getting Educated and Finding Work in Alberta

Over the past 60 years, Alberta's economy has shifted from a heavy reliance on agriculture (and to a lesser extent, forestry) to an equally heavy reliance on the oil and gas industries. In the past several decades, massive development of oil sands deposits around Fort McMurray (in the north-central part of the province) and large gas field developments in various regions, has led to rapid population growth in mid-sized cities in regions where the oil and gas industries dominate, but also in the province's two major cities, Calgary and Edmonton. Unemployment rates in the province have generally been low, and average incomes, particularly in the oil and gas industries, have been relatively high. As a result, the province has experienced extensive in-migration, from other provinces and from other countries. Fort McMurray, which has grown even faster than other urban centres (Dorow and O'Shaughnessy, 2013), is often described as Canada's second largest Newfoundland city because of the thousands of former Newfoundland residents now living and working there! But alongside wealth and opportunity, there are also groups that have not benefitted nearly as much. As in other provinces, recent immigrants (Krahn et al., 2000) and members of First Nations (Luffman and Sussman, 2007) experience much higher levels of unemployment and underemployment.

Alberta was one of the first provinces to improve access to post-secondary education by opening community colleges in smaller urban centres (for example, Lethbridge Junior College, Canada's first community college, was opened in 1957) and by eliminating barriers to the transfer of academic credits between colleges, technical schools, and universities

(Andres and Krahn, 1999). In the early 1970s, Athabasca University began to experiment with distance learning programs that allowed students across the province to enroll in university courses. In the last several decades, Alberta has also provided financial incentives to post-secondary institutions to add new programs and to attract students from previously under-represented geographical areas and population sub-groups. In addition, it has given degree-granting status to a number of public (for example, Mount Royal University in Calgary) and private (for example, Concordia University College in Edmonton) colleges[2]. The emphasis on improving access has been driven not so much by a desire to reduce social inequality (although that might be a by-product) but to promote economic growth (Taylor, 2001; Alberta Innovation and Advanced Education, 2014). Consequently, a strong emphasis on skills training and vocational education characterizes the province's secondary and post-secondary systems (Taylor, 2001; Titley, 2005).

When our study was completed (1996–2003), Alberta had 4 universities (University of Alberta, University of Calgary, University of Lethbridge, Athabasca University), 14 publicly funded colleges in urban centres of various sizes (including 3 in communities with fewer than 7000 residents), 2 large technical institutes (1 in Edmonton and 1 in Calgary), and 9 private university colleges (8 with religious affiliations). In this chapter we ask whether traditional patterns of intergenerational transfer of advantage through the post-secondary system are still found in a province where access to post-secondary education has been substantially improved and employment opportunities have been more abundant. We also ask whether, in a setting where demand for workers with trades-related education has been high, vocational (trades-related) education offers an alternative (to university) pathway into well-paying jobs. We then return to Bourdieu's theoretical framework to discuss our findings.

Research Methods

In late spring of 1996, 2691 Grade 12 students (18 years old, on average) in 58 Alberta high schools completed questionnaires asking about their educational and work experiences and aspirations (Krahn and Hudson, 2006). The sample of schools was representative of the population with two exceptions; a small minority of Alberta youth (about 5 per cent) graduating from private high schools and schools on First Nations were not sampled. Seventy-three per cent of the study participants provided contact information so that they could be re-interviewed in the future.

Seven years later, in 2003, 1218 Time 1 respondents (now 25 years old, on average) completed a follow-up survey (96 per cent by telephone, 4 per cent by mail)[3], resulting in a response rate of 45 per cent (62 per cent of those who provided contact information at Time 1). Older respondents (19 or older in 1996) as well as immigrant, visible minority, and disabled youth were less likely to respond in 2003. Time 2 response rates did not differ by gender, region of the province, community size, family background, or respondents' school and work experiences. The 2003 sample was weighted to make it representative of the 1996 Alberta high school graduating class in terms of school size, community size, and school district (Krahn and Hudson, 2006).

The 2003 sample ($n = 1218$) contained slightly more females than males. One in 10 (9 per cent) Time 2 respondents were immigrants (born outside of Canada), 14 per cent self-identified as a member of a visible minority group, and 4 per cent stated that they were of Aboriginal origin. One-third (34 per cent) were from families where at least one parent had a university degree. By age 25, 4 out of 10 study participants were married (24 per cent) or co-habiting (14 per cent), and 16 per cent had become parents. Thirty per cent of Time 2 participants were currently enrolled in a post-secondary program; some were continuing in advanced programs, while others had returned to college or university after some years away.

Findings

Post-secondary Educational Attainment by Age 25

A large majority (60 per cent) of Time 2 respondents had acquired a post-secondary educational credential (university degree, college or technical school diploma, apprenticeship) by 2003 (Table 3.1). This high level of post-secondary attainment suggests that the Alberta government's efforts to improve access to post-secondary education have been relatively successful. In fact, 88 per cent of Time 2 respondents had started some kind of post-secondary program; about two-thirds had completed the program (Krahn and Hudson, 2006).

Almost one-third (32 per cent) of Time 2 respondents had acquired a university degree, 15 per cent had obtained a community college diploma, the same proportion had received a technical school diploma, and 4 per cent had completed an apprenticeship (Table 3.1)[4]. Overall, women (65 per cent) were significantly more likely than men (55 per cent) to have acquired a post-secondary credential[5]. Women were more likely to have received a community college diploma or a university degree, while men were more likely to have completed an apprenticeship.

We now turn to a multivariate analysis of the factors, in addition to gender, that determined who acquired a technical post-secondary education (that is, they received a technical school diploma and/or completed an apprenticeship). Multivariate analyses take into account the degree to which some factors that might influence an outcome such as educational attainment may be correlated with others. For example, immigrant youth are more likely to live in large cities, while Aboriginal youth are less likely to do so. A multivariate analysis adjusts the findings so the unique effect of each factor is highlighted[6].

Along with gender differences, our multivariate analyses revealed that study participants whose parents (at least one) had completed university, and those who had themselves completed an academic (rather than vocational) high school program, were less likely to have acquired a technical post-secondary education. Those who were living in a major city (Edmonton or Calgary) when completing high school were more likely to have obtained a

Table 3.1 Post-secondary Attainment (1996–2003) by Gender*

	Female (%)	Male (%)	Total (%)
Obtained any post-secondary credential**	65	55	60
Completed an apprenticeship**	2	7	4
Received a technical school diploma	13	16	15
Received a community college diploma**	19	10	15
Obtained a Bachelor's degree**	37	27	32
(n)	645	573	1218

Notes: * Weighted estimates; sub-sample sizes vary slightly across dependent variables because of differing levels of non-response.
** Gender differences are statistically significant ($p < 0.05$).

technical post-secondary credential, perhaps a result of their easier access to the province's two large technical colleges.

Compared to completion of a technical post-secondary program, a larger number of factors were associated with the acquisition of a university degree by age 25. As already noted, women were more likely to have completed a university degree. So, too, were members of visible minority groups. In stark contrast, Aboriginal respondents were one-tenth as likely as non-Aboriginals to have completed university. Sample members living in Edmonton and Calgary in 1996 were no more likely to have completed university than were those from elsewhere in the province.

Study participants whose parents (at least one) had completed university were three times more likely to have done so themselves, compared to their peers whose parents were not university educated. The effect of having completed a high school academic program was even stronger. These study participants were six times more likely than vocational program graduates to have acquired a university degree by age 25.

Employment Outcomes by Age 25

At age 25, 85 per cent of the sample members were holding one or more jobs, 6 per cent were unemployed, and 9 per cent were not working or looking for a job (that is, they were out of the labour force). In our analysis of the monthly income (before taxes) that employed respondents received from their main jobs, we exclude any current students since many students work in low-paying part-time student jobs that would not be valid indicators of the income they could expect to receive after graduating. This reduces our sample to 855 employed non-students. Their average monthly income was $2953. Female sample members were earning significantly less ($2412), on average, than were male study participants ($3478).

Our multivariate statistical model (Figure 3.1) looks complicated but actually is quite easy to understand. The path diagram brings together all of the important (statistically

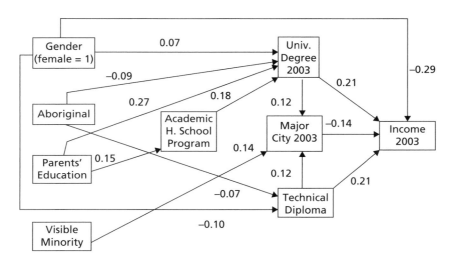

Figure 3.1 Ascribed and Achieved Determinants of 2003 Income

significant) factors that influenced the earnings of the 855 employed (non-student) study participants[7]. The arrows' (paths) indicate the causal direction of the statistical relationship (for example, parents' education has an effect on children's education, not vice versa). The size of the path coefficients (called Beta, or β) tells us about the strength of the effect (for example, a β of 0.30 is twice as strong as a β of 0.15). The sign of the path coefficient shows whether the statistical relationship is positive (for example, higher parents' education → higher children's education) or negative (for example, live in a larger city → lower income).

Figure 3.1 clearly illustrates the strong impact, both directly and indirectly, of parents' education on their child's income at 25 years of age. Children of university-educated parents are more likely to complete an academic high school program ($\beta = 0.15$), which, in turn, means they are more likely to obtain a university degree ($\beta = 0.18$). Along with this indirect effect, we also see a strong direct effect ($\beta = 0.27$) of parental university education on their child's acquisition of a university degree. And, as previous research has shown, university degree holders earn more money, on average ($\beta = 0.21$), than people with only a high school education.

Previous research also leads us to expect that women are more likely to have acquired a university degree ($\beta = 0.07$). Even so, at age 25, women earn substantially less than men ($\beta = -0.29$), because of the types of jobs they typically hold and a greater likelihood of working part-time. Somewhat surprisingly, given previous research, visible minority youth are no more or less likely to have completed university, controlling for the other variables in this model. Even so, visible minority status has a negative effect on income, indirectly as a result of being more likely to live in a major city at age 25 ($\beta = -0.14$). Aboriginal youth face a double disadvantage. Aboriginal status has negative effects both on acquiring a university degree ($\beta = -0.09$) and on getting a technical diploma ($\beta = -0.07$), both of which, in turn, are strong predictors of higher income at age 25.

Figure 3.1 also highlights two unusual findings that previous research would not have led us to expect. First, a technical post-secondary credential and a university degree have similar impacts on income at age 25 ($\beta = 0.21$). In real dollar terms (not shown in Figure 3.1), however, controlling for all the other variables in the model, having a technical diploma by age 25 translates into an additional $1035 per month (before taxes), compared to an additional $869 per month for having completed university. Second, while incomes are generally higher in larger urban centres (Beckstead et al., 2010), we find that living in a major city (Edmonton or Calgary) at age 25 is associated with a lower income ($\beta = -0.14$) compared to living elsewhere in the province.

Discussion

We observed an unusually high level of post-secondary educational attainment within this cohort of Alberta high school graduates. By age 25, 6 out of 10 had obtained some type of post-secondary credential, suggesting that the Alberta government's efforts to increase access to higher education have had some success. University education was most popular (32 per cent had received a degree), followed by a technical (trades-related) education (19 per cent). Interestingly, and unlike previous research, in the resource-driven Alberta economy, young people with technical training were enjoying a higher (dollar) return to their education by age 25 than those who had completed university. Related to this, study participants living in Edmonton or Calgary, the province's largest urban centres, were earning less than those who worked elsewhere. Young women's educational attainment (more university and less technical training compared to men) and earnings (lower than men's), however, reflected patterns observed elsewhere.

Given the high level of access to post-secondary education, do we see evidence of a decline in the intergenerational transfer of advantage? For university education, the answer is no. Children of university-educated parents were still more likely to complete high school academic programs and, consequently, more likely to acquire a university degree. We also observed a direct effect of parental education on children's university education, likely reflecting the greater ability of university-educated parents to pay for their children's education. A university degree, in turn, translated into significantly higher earnings at age 25. In this particular provincial setting, however, the acquisition of a technical post-secondary credential offered an alternative pathway to higher earnings, at least by age 25. Children of university-educated parents, however, were no more or less likely to acquire technical training[8]. What stands out most, perhaps, is the double disadvantage faced by Aboriginal high school graduates who were less likely to go to university and also less likely to acquire a technical post-secondary education. Aboriginal youth were being left behind in both the university and technical training races to higher earnings and career success.

Thinking about the data patterns as Bourdieu might, we can describe the province of Alberta during this particular time period as a unique field of power with alternative pathways to career success that may not be available elsewhere or in other eras. While university degrees still provide strong symbolic capital that can be converted into higher earnings, in Alberta a technical post-secondary education also helps develop unique skill sets that are particularly valuable in specific resource extraction (for example, oil and gas) and related (for example, construction) industries. Children of university-educated parents grow up with an academically oriented habitus that prepares them for competition in a field where having the capacity to succeed, first in an academic high school program and then, later, in university, leads to future employment success. However, a working-class habitus may not disadvantage young people as much in this provincial setting as it may elsewhere. In fact, growing up in a family where one or both parents are employed in the trades might lead children to develop a habitus more suited to success in the natural resource-based Alberta labour market.

That women receive lower income than men, on average, is not a new finding, but it is useful to examine it from Bourdieu's perspective (Fowler, 2003). A female habitus (social psychologists might call this a process of socialization), shaped in one's family of origin with traditions of caring and less dominant roles for women, may re-exert itself in the post-secondary education system and labour market when women make gendered career choices. In turn, women continue to be under-represented in higher paying skilled trades and upper-level management and professional positions, and over-represented in caring occupations (for example, childcare, eldercare) which pay considerably less. Also, within any workplace there is a tacit arena of gendered games being played that involve a combination of subjectively and structurally defined stakes and rules (Williams and Dempsey, 2014). Such micro-power games typically advantage men to the detriment of women's income and career progress. Furthermore, women are also under much greater pressure to balance home and (paid) work responsibilities (Milan, Keown, and Urquijo, 2011), leading them to place more emphasis on the former, with the result being more limited career success. All of these processes help explain why women continue to report lower average incomes than men, even though young women today are more likely to complete university. Women are also less likely to complete trades-related post-secondary educations (Boothby and Drewes, 2006), so while this pathway to income success exists in Alberta today, it is still infrequently followed by young women.

Another important finding is the disadvantaged situation of Aboriginal high school graduates who, regardless of their parents' education, are much less likely to acquire a university degree or technical diploma. People of Aboriginal status in Canada have a unique and unfortunate history, and there are many structural and cultural factors that help explain their less advantaged educational and employment situation. The history of colonization and the residential school system, the last of which closed only in 1996 (Woods, 2013), did substantial damage to Aboriginal cultures and tore many families apart. For a variety of related reasons, unemployment and poverty rates have been much higher for Aboriginal households (Luffman and Sussman, 2007). As a result, many young Aboriginal Albertans may have grown up in a family environment where parents were less able to provide them with the material and cultural advantages enjoyed by middle-class non-Aboriginal youth. In Bourdieu's language, Aboriginal youth completing high school may have a habitus that is not very well-suited for participation in post-secondary education. Their parents are also often less able to provide the economic capital required to pay for post-secondary education and the social capital (contacts and networks) that will lead to success in the post-secondary field of power. Moreover, and similar to the gender related micro-power games that disadvantage women, micro-power games related to race may also disadvantage Aboriginal people in schools and workplaces.

We conclude with a few observations about vocational post-secondary education. In general, compared to university degrees, technical diplomas and apprenticeships have had a lower "earnings premium" in Canada (Boothby and Drewes, 2006). In Alberta, at the end of the twentieth century and the beginning of the twenty-first century, this has not been the case, at least for younger workers. We wonder whether the same findings would be observed in other provinces (for example, Newfoundland and Labrador, Saskatchewan) that have experienced natural resource-driven economic booms? Also, with the global collapse of oil prices that began in late 2014 we may no longer see such patterns in Alberta. Furthermore, when our study participants are 50 or 60 years old, will the earnings of those with a technical post-secondary education still be higher than the income of those who completed university? Technical training may be very valuable in a specific place and time (for example, the oil sands of Alberta in the first decades of this century) while training in more general skills might be useful in a wider range of situations. As Heinz (2003) notes, university credentials, less focused in their scope than technical credentials, may be more portable. It is also possible that, over the long term, university credentials are more likely to lead to jobs in industries (for example, government, health, education) where pay is generally higher, promotions and fringe benefits are more extensive, pensions are more common, and, to some extent, job security is greater.

We make these comparisons, recognizing that they appear to have a university bias, which is not our intention. Compared to university education, technical diplomas and apprenticeships have historically had lower status in Canada. This is unfortunate, in our opinion, because the demand for skilled-trades workers will continue in Canada. Furthermore, we recognize that working in the trades can be highly satisfying for many young people (including from university-educated families) who don't necessarily enjoy more academic pursuits (Lehmann, 2007a). At the same time, we believe that there are aspects of a broad liberal arts university education (for example, an emphasis on critical thinking, citizenship, and openness to other ideas and cultures) that would benefit all young people. We need to seek ways to bridge the gap between vocational and academic education (Axelrod, Anisef, and Lin, 2003), in high schools and in post-secondary institutions, so that all young people, regardless of their backgrounds and disposition, can improved their career opportunities while also broadening their experiences.

Questions for Critical Thought

1. What are some of the ways in which your own decision to attend college or university were shaped by your family and community experiences?
2. Can some of Pierre Bourdieu's key theoretical concepts help you understand your own educational experiences?
3. What are some of the unique employment opportunities in your city or region? How well do local high schools and post-secondary institutions prepare youth for these opportunities?
4. Do you think vocational (technical) education has lower status than college or university education? Is this a problem, and if it is, what could be done about it?

Glossary

Intergenerational transmission of advantage A process whereby the economic advantages and cultural tools for success in a particular society are inherited by children; similar to **cultural reproduction**.

Field of power A social-cultural space upon which individuals interact and compete with one another for success and on which various cultural practices and symbolic resources serve as forms of capital.

Forms of capital Along with economic capital (for example, money), within a society (on a particular field of power), individuals and families have differing amounts of cultural capital (for example, ways of speaking or dressing), symbolic capital (for example, a university degree), and social capital (for example, exclusive social networks); different forms of capital (for example, time and money) can be invested to obtain other forms (for example, a university degree).

Habitus An embodied disposition, formed over time in relation to a field, which can structure individual human practices but also generate creative possibilities.

Acknowledgements

The data analysed in this study were collected by the Population Research Laboratory (PRL), Department of Sociology, University of Alberta, with funding from the Social Sciences and Humanities Research Council of Canada (SSHRC grant no. 410–96–0804) and the Government of Alberta.

Notes

1. A draft of this chapter was presented at the Annual Meetings of the Canadian Sociological Association in Ottawa in June 2015. Parts of the chapter were discussed by Krahn and Hudson (2006).
2. Titley (2005) observes that, while the Alberta government opened many new colleges and gave degree-granting status to some established colleges, it did not provide adequate operating grants to allow post-secondary institutions to deliver high-quality programs.
3. Data collection methods used at Time 1 (1996) and Time 2 (2003) were approved by a University of Alberta Research Ethics Board.
4. These four types of post-secondary credentials total to more than 20 per cent since a small number of study participants had acquired more than one credential by age 25.

5. Here, and in the following discussion, we comment on only those differences between groups that were statistically significant ($p < 0.05$). This means that, with a sample of this size, differences this large would occur by chance alone less than 5 per cent of the time.

6. In this particular analysis, we employed logistic regression techniques. Detailed tables are available from the authors.

7. Seventeen per cent ($n = 147$) of the 855 employed non-students in our Time 2 sample did not report their income, a typical finding in survey research. We employed Full Information Maximum Likelihood estimation (FIML) techniques (Allison, 2003) to estimate these missing data. Further information on the structural equation model is available from the authors.

8. If we had included in our model a variable measuring whether or not parents of study participants had acquired a technical post-secondary credential, we likely would have seen a significant effect on the likelihood of their child acquiring technical post-secondary training. Unfortunately, information provided by study participants at age 18 about their parents' technical education was not sufficiently reliable for us to use it in our analysis.

References

Abada, T., Hou, F., and Ram, B. "Ethnic differences in educational attainment among the children of Canadian immigrants." *Canadian Journal of Sociology* 34 (2009): 1–28.

Aboriginal Affairs and Northern Development Canada. *Fact Sheet: 2011 National Household Survey Aboriginal Demographics, Educational Attainment and Labour Market Outcomes.* Ottawa: Aboriginal Affairs and Northern Development Canada, 2013.

Alberta Innovation and Advanced Education. *Alberta Sets Vision for Future Economic Growth*, 2014. Retrieved 12 August 2014 from: http://eae.alberta.ca/

Allison, P.D. "Missing data techniques for structural equation modeling." *Journal of Abnormal Psychology* 112(4) (2003): 545–57.

Andres, L., and Krahn, H. "Youth pathways in articulated post-secondary systems: Enrolment and completion patterns of urban young women and men." *Canadian Journal of Higher Education* 29(1) (1999): 47–82.

Andres, L., and Looker, E.D. "Rurality and capital: Educational expectations and attainments of rural, urban/rural and metropolitan youth." *Canadian Journal of Higher Education* 31(2) (2001): 1–46.

Axelrod, P., Anisef, P., and Lin, Z. "Bridging the gap between liberal and applied education." In *Integrating School and Workplace Learning in Canada: Principles and Practices of Alternation Education and Training*, H.G. Schuetze and R. Sweet (eds.), (217–42). Montreal, Kingston: McGill-Queen's University Press, 2003.

Beckstead, D., Brown, M.W., Guo, Y., and Newbold, K.B. *Cities and Growth: Earnings Levels across Urban and Rural Areas: The Role of Human Capital.* The Canadian Economy in Transition Series, cat. no. 11-622-M, no. 20. Ottawa: Statistics Canada, 2010.

Boothby, D., and Drewes, T. "Post-secondary education in Canada: Returns to university, college and trades education." *Canadian Public Policy* 32(1) (2006): 1–21.

Bourdieu, P. *The Logic of Practice.* Stanford: Stanford University Press, 1980.

Bourdieu, P. *Distinction: A Social Critique of the Judgement of Taste.* (Trans. by R. Nice). Cambridge: Harvard University Press, 1984.

Bourdieu, P. *Homo Academicus.* Stanford: Stanford University Press, 1988.

Bourdieu, P. *Sketch for a Self-analysis.* (Trans. by R. Nice). Cambridge: Polity, 2007.

Boyd, M., Pineo, P.C., and Porter, J. "Status attainment in Canada: Findings from the Canadian Mobility Study." *Canadian Review of Sociology and Anthropology* 18(5) (1981): 657–73.

Davies, S., and Guppy, N. "Race and Canadian education." In *Racism and Social Inequality in Canada: Concepts, Controversies and Strategies of Resistance*, V. Satzewich (ed.), (131–56). Toronto: Thompson Educational Publishing, 1998.

Davies, S., and Guppy, N. *The Schooled Society: An Introduction to the Sociology of Education.* Don Mills: Oxford University Press, 2006.

Davies, S., and Rizk, J. "The third generation of cultural capital research." Paper presented at the Annual General Meeting of the Canadian Sociological Association, St. Catharines, Ontario, May 2014.

Dorow, S., and O'Shaughnessy, S. "Fort McMurray, Wood Buffalo, and the oil/tar sands: Revisiting the sociology of 'community'." *Canadian Journal of Sociology* 38(2) (2013): 121–40.

Frenette, M. "Access to college and university: Does distance matter?." Analytic Studies Branch research paper no. 201. Ottawa: Statistics Canada, 2003.

Frenette, M. "An investment of a lifetime? The long-term labour market premiums associated with a postsecondary education." Analytic Studies Branch research paper no. 359. Ottawa: Statistics Canada, 2014.

Fowler, B. "Reading Pierre Bourdieu's masculine domination: Notes towards an intersectional analysis of gender, culture and class." *Cultural Studies* 17(3/4) (2003): 468.

Grenfell, M. (ed.). *Pierre Bourdieu: Key Concepts.* Durham: Acumen, 2008.

Heinz, W. "The restructuring of work and the modernization of vocational training in Germany." In *Integrating School and Workplace Learning in Canada: Principles and Practices of Alternation Education and Training,* H.G. Schuetze and R. Sweet (eds.), (25–43). Montreal, Kingston: McGill-Queen's University Press, 2003.

Krahn, H. "Choose your parents carefully: Social class, post-secondary education, and occupational outcomes." In *Social Inequality in Canada: Patterns, Problems, and Policies,* E. Grabb and N. Guppy (eds.), (171–87). Fifth edition. Toronto: Pearson/Prentice Hall, 2009.

Krahn, H., Derwing, T., Mulder, M., and Wilkinson, L. "Educated and underemployed: Refugee integration into the Canadian labour market." *Journal of International Migration and Integration* 1 (Winter 2000): 59–84.

Krahn, H., and Hudson, J. "Pathways of Alberta youth through the post-secondary system into the labour market, 1996–2003." *Pathways to the Labour Market Series,* no. 2. Ottawa: Canadian Policy Research Networks, 2006.

Krahn, H.J., Hughes, K.D., and Lowe, G.S. *Work, Industry, and Canadian Society.* Seventh edition. Toronto: Nelson Education, 2015.

Krahn, H., and Taylor, A. "Resilient teenagers: Explaining the high educational aspirations of visible-minority youth in Canada." *Journal of International Migration and Integration* 6 (3/4) (2005): 405–34.

Laureau, A. *Unequal Childhoods: Class, Race, and Family Life.* Berkeley: University of California Press, 2003.

Lee, V.E., and Burkam, D.T. *Inequality at the Starting Gate: Social Background Differences in Achievement as Children begin School.* Washington: Economic Policy Institute, 2002.

Lehmann, W. *Choosing to Labour: School-Work Transitions and Social Class.* Montreal, Kingston: McGill-Queen's University Press, 2007a.

Lehmann, W. "'I just don't feel like I fit in': The role of habitus in university drop-out decisions." *Canadian Journal of Higher Education* 37(2) (2007b): 89–110.

Lehmann, W. "Habitus transformation and hidden injuries: Successful working-class university students." *Sociology of Education* 87(1) (2014): 1–15.

Looker, E.D., and Dwyer, P. "Education and negotiated reality: Complexities facing rural youth in the 1990s." *Journal of Youth Studies* 1(1) (1998): 5–22.

Luffman, J., and Sussman, D. "The Aboriginal labour force in western Canada." *Perspectives on Labour and Income* (January 2007): 13–27.

Lyons, J.E., Randhawa, B.S., and Paulson, N.A. "The development of vocational education in Canada." *Canadian Journal of Education* 16(2) (1991): 127–50.

Maton, K. "Habitus." In *Pierre Bourdieu: Key Concepts,* M. Grenfell (ed.), (49–65). Durham: Acumen, 2008.

McKenna, B. "When employers duck responsibility for training, Canada loses." *The Globe and Mail* online (19 May 2013). Retrieved 10 September 2014 from: www.theglobeandmail.com/report-on-business/when-employers-duck-responsibility-for-training-canada-loses/article12022931/

Milan, A., Keown, L., and Urquijo, C.R. "Families, living arrangements, and unpaid work." In *Women in Canada: A Gender-Based Statistical Report,* cat. no. 89-503-X. Ottawa: Statistics Canada, 2011.

Mueller, R.E. "Access and persistence of students in Canadian post-secondary education: What we know, what we don't know, and why it matters." In *Who Goes? Who Stays? What Matters?: Accessing and Persisting in Post-secondary Education in Canada*, R. Finnie, R.E. Mueller, A. Sweetman, and A. Usher (eds.), (33–62). Montreal, Kingston: McGill-Queens University Press, 2008.

Potter, D., and Roksa, J. "Accumulating advantages over time: Family experiences and social class inequality in academic achievement." *Social Science Research* 42(4) (2013): 1018–32.

Pyper, W. "Skilled trades employment." *Perspectives on Labour and Income* 9(10) (October), Statistics Canada cat. no. 75-001-X: 5–14. Ottawa: Statistics Canada, 2008.

Schuetze, H.G. "Alternation education and training in Canada." In *Integrating School and Workplace Learning in Canada: Principles and Practices of Alternation Education and Training*, H.G. Schuetze and R. Sweet (eds.), (66–92). Montreal, Kingston: McGill-Queen's University Press, 2003.

Sewell, W.H., Haller, A.O., and Ohlendorf, G.W. "The educational and early occupational status attainment process: Replication and revision." *American Sociological Review* 35(6) (1970): 1014–27.

Sullivan, A. "Cultural capital and educational attainment." *Sociology* 35 (2001): 893–912.

Taylor, A. *The Politics of Educational Reform in Alberta*. Toronto: University of Toronto Press, 2001.

Taylor, A., and Krahn, H. "Streaming in/for the new economy." In *Canadian Perspectives on the Sociology of Education*, C. Levine-Rasky (ed.), (103–24). Toronto: Oxford University Press, 2009.

Taylor, A., and Krahn, H. "Living through our children: Exploring the education and career 'choice' of racialized immigrant youth in Canada." *Journal of Youth Studies* 16(8) (2013): 1000–21.

Titley, B. "Campus Alberta Inc.: New directions for post-secondary education." In *The Return of the Trojan Horse: Alberta and the New World (Dis)Order*, T.W. Harrison (ed.), (254–268). Montreal: Black Rose Books, 2005.

Turcotte, M. "Intergeneration education mobility: University completion in relation to parents' education level." *Canadian Social Trends* (Winter 2011): 38–44.

Williams, J.C., and Dempsey, R. *What Works for Women at Work*. New York, London: New York University Press, 2014.

Woods, E. "A cultural approach to a Canadian tragedy: The Indian residential schools as a sacred enterprise." *International Journal of Politics, Culture & Society* 26(2) (2013): 173–87.

4

Identifying the Complexity of Barriers Faced by Marginalized Youth in Transition to Post-secondary Education in Ontario

Karen Robson, Robert S. Brown, and Paul Anisef

Introduction

In Canada, the topic of access to post-secondary education (PSE) has been taken up by a variety of researchers, both academic and applied. A number of established correlated factors associated with participation in PSE have also been identified, including Aboriginal status, family socio-economic status (SES), urban and rural status, immigrant status, race, ethnic group membership, family structure, parental educational attainment, and academic engagement (Finnie, Childs, and Wismer, 2011; McMullen, 2011). These characteristics have also been found to be contingent upon each other; for example, low income is negatively associated with PSE *but* has a lessened effect if a student has good high school grades (McMullen, 2011). The interaction of different characteristics has been explored to some degree by previous researchers. For example, Abada, Hou, and Rams (2009) and Finnie, Childs, and Wismer (2011) examine how children from different immigrant groups as well as those born in different generations (that is, first, second, or third) have PSE uptake rates that are dramatically different from each other as well as from the native-born population (the "immigrant paradox," Suárez-Orozco and Rhodes [2009]). They argue that some differences may be accounted for because of differing parental expectations and social and cultural capital possessed by the various groups under consideration. Focusing on Ontario, Lennon et al. (2011, 151) have come to similar conclusions, finding that students with foreign-born parents were more likely to go on to PSE and that previous academic success and parental background were also significant factors in this outcome. What remains to be uncovered, however, is how these characteristics impact upon PSE transitions in their combination. Individuals possess various **status traits** that shape their life courses based upon their mutual interaction (Collins, 1998). This framework recognizes that risk factors interplay with various SES and demographic factors, often increasing or compounding the at-risk situation. Being black, male, and from a single-parent family provides one illustration.

Life Course and Intersectionality:
A Review of Literature

The theoretical underpinnings of this study are rooted in both life course and intersectionality theoretical orientations. **Life course theory**, as it applies to PSE, comprises three elements. The first element is time—an essential element of life course research, it includes examination of stages of human development, as well as detailing the contexts within which human development occurs. Included within the element of time is the theme of stability and change, which acknowledges both the constraints and the opportunities for individuals to alter their values, beliefs, and self-evaluations as they move through their life course. The time element also suggests an educational sequence that comprises three stages: planning for PSE; participating in PSE; and making the transition from PSE to the workforce. Each is enacted across an extended age range from early childhood, through adolescence and into adulthood. The second element recognizes the tension between the constraints imposed by social structures such as gender, ethno-racial status, and social class with the expression of personal agency or the individual's capacity to make choices based on personal knowledge, skills, personality, and values, such as the pursuit of higher or further education. The third element identifies the interactions between the individual and the various social institutions encountered on "life's way." These include family, school, university or college, and the workplace. Throughout the life course, individuals are engaged in the task of moving through and between all these major institutions (Anisef et al., 2000; Berger and Motte, 2007; Sweet and Anisef, 2005).

Berger and Motte (2007) emphasise the utility of the life-course perspective in capturing the complexities of the journey to PSE and in better understanding the access, persistence, and completion barriers faced by many individuals and groups. Specifically, they emphasise two points: (1) factors that determine PSE access (and completion) lie in the individual's life circumstances and are already present in early childhood; and (2) social factors like socioeconomic status interact with individual characteristics and do so in different ways throughout the life course. When examining PSE transitions through a life course lens, it is important to view the individual as an agent who constructs a personal pathway within the larger context of social, cultural, and economic forces. Structure and agency work together in helping shape the life course including educational attainment and other forms of social mobility.

While the life course orientation underscores the importance of accounting for the individual and combined effects of social structure and personal agency, studies that have been conducted to date rarely examine the impact of multiple social factors (for example, ethno-racial status, gender, social class) and their intersections on life course outcomes (McCall, 2005). By way of illustration, prior studies have rarely considered how race and ethnicity as well as gender jointly differentiate the health status of older adults; instead they have examined race and ethnicity as well as gender as if they were separate dimensions of social stratification (Warner and Brown, 2010). By contrast, an intersectionality approach systematically examines the interactive influences of race and ethnicity as well as gender on health and health trajectories across the life course (Schulz and Mullings, 2006). That is, an intersectionality approach begins with the premise that forms of oppression (for example, racism, sexism) overlap, and thus posits that the consequences of race and ethnicity as well as gender cannot be understood sufficiently by studying these phenomena separately. Personal characteristics can combine to serve as cumulative advantages or disadvantages over the life course (for example, being black, male, and from a low-income household).

The concept of intersectionality emerged in the late 1960s and early 1970s in conjunction with the multiracial feminist movement and as part of a critique of radical feminism that had developed in the late 1960s. The critique, known as revisionist feminist theory, questioned the assumption that sex was the main factor that determined the fate of women (hooks, 1984). More specifically, women of colour disputed the idea that women composed a homogeneous category, arguing that the forms of oppression experienced by white middle-class women were distinct from the forms of oppression experienced by women of colour. As Crenshaw (1991, 1243), who later coined the phrase "intersectionality identities" points out, the intersectionality experience within black women is more powerful than the sum of their race and sex. Collins (1998, 2000, 2005) is also associated with a popularization of the term, as her work has highlighted the intersectionality of gender, race, and class, particularly as it relates to the experience of black women's paid employment in the United States.

Generally, scholars agree that intersectionality refers to the notion that social identities such as race, gender, and class interact to form qualitatively different meanings and experiences (Warner, 2008). Rather than conceptualizing social identities as functioning independently and being subsequently "added together to form experience" (Warner, 2008, 454), those that employ the intersectionality notion agree that identity cannot be reduced to a summary of the social groups to which a person belongs. In fact, social groups interact with each other and, as a consequence, create specific manifestations that cannot be explained by each alone (Warner, 2008, 1).

Objectives and Research Questions

In this chapter we raise the following question: "How do gender, race, family SES, and special education needs interact to either facilitate or hinder access to and participation in PSE among Ontario students?" While several studies exist which point to how students' various individual characteristics serve to lessen or increase their likelihood of attending PSE, our objective in this study is to examine these various status traits in combination with one another using a unique longitudinal data set consisting of students who were 17 years of age and enrolled in secondary schools in the Toronto District School Board (TDSB) in the autumn of 2006.

The data analysis reported in this chapter will (1) identify and clarify the current PSE trajectories of Ontario youth and the relationship of these trajectories to status traits; and (2) examine and identify differences between those secondary students who successfully access or confirm PSE and those who do not. This examination will be conducted with respect to status traits, in isolation and in combination. Our objective is to determine what combinations of status traits serve to either advantage or disadvantage secondary students in transitioning to PSE. The development of detailed knowledge around individual combinations of traits that facilitate or hinder PSE transition is an important first stage in creating effective policy around widening access to PSE.

Data and Methods

The data employed in this study are derived from a survey (often called the Student Census) administered from November 6 to 10 in 2006 in all TDSB secondary schools and all Grades 7 to 8 in elementary schools. A total of 289 Toronto schools were involved. After all the data were processed and verified, a student census database was created consisting of 34,219 students in Grades 7 to 8, and 71,222 students in Grades 9 to 12. In social science research, our confidence in the findings we discover often hinges on the proportion of people that respond to surveys. In recent years, response rates over 50 per cent are considered to be quite good. The use of Board enrolment figures as of 31 October 2006 revealed a high response rate of 92 per cent for Grades 7 to 8 and 81 per cent for Grades 9 to 12. The response rate for 17 year old students, in particular, was 74 per cent. Student surveys were administered in classrooms and gathered information on who the students were in addition to how they felt about their school and personal lives. To ensure student confidentiality, teachers were instructed to ask their students to leave their identification numbers, but to black out their names before placing their completed surveys in a return box at the front of the classroom. While the survey was confidential, it was not anonymous. Student identification numbers were linked to other centrally available data sources, such as the TDSB Student Information System, EQAO (standardized testing) and student report cards. Access to data was granted through the TDSB research department to which one of the authors belongs.

The specific subset of data employed for these analyses are based on 14,048 students aged 17 who were surveyed in the census conducted in Fall 2006. These students were age appropriate for Grade 12, the age in which most Ontario students start their transition to PSE. Added to these data were other pieces of additional information: data from the Fall 2006 Student Census completed by Grade 9 to 12 students in the TDSB on a range of socio-economic, demographic, and attitudinal variables (see Brown [2009]); data from the 2001 Canadian Federal Census on household income (matched by postal code to the census dissemination area of around 300 households)[1], and data on post-secondary applications and confirmations as supplied to the Toronto District School Board (TDSB) by the Ontario University Applications Centre (OUAC) and Ontario College Applications Centre (OCAS)[2]. Because it has been found that students will apply over multiple years (see Sweet et al. [2010]), OUAC and OCAS information from the 2007, 2008, and 2009 application cycles were also merged with the data set.

Dependent Variable—College and University Confirmations

When social scientists rely on empirical methods to collect information or data and then to subsequently analyse the data collected, they frequently rely on what is called variable language. Two main concepts related to the use of variable language are dependent and independent variables. When social scientists speak of dependent variables, they refer to attitudes or behaviours that they are seeking to understand and/or to predict. Variables, by their very nature, are not fixed. They vary. Thus, when we speak of college and university confirmations as dependent variables, we assume that some people will wind up enrolling in a PSE institution while others will transition to other pathways (for example, jobs). When understanding or explaining a dependent variable (in this case PSE confirmations), social scientists employ independent variables or factors that they believe or theorize to be related to the dependent variable in question. It should be understood that the selection of independent or predictor variables chronologically precede (come before) the dependent variable or the variable to be explained.

This limited cohort study allowed us to examine the PSE pathways of 17-year-old students over three years in the TDSB (to the end of 2009). We examined three possible pathways: (1) confirmed an offer of admission to an Ontario university; (2) confirmed an offer of admission to an Ontario college; or (3) neither of these two options[3]. Just over half of the sample (50.7 per cent) confirmed university acceptance, while 15.2 per cent confirmed college acceptance[4]. The term *confirmed acceptance* applies to the situation where a student has applied to a college or university, has been accepted, and has accepted the offer. It is more substantial than a simple acceptance at a university or college—it implies the additional intentionality of the student to actually attend the university or college.

Independent Variables—Gender, Race, and Class

Intersectionality theory has traditionally focused on gender, race, and class to understand how such combinations of traits are highly connected to one another and to constrained sets of choices that individuals are able to make. In our analyses, sex was dummy-coded so that "male" is equal to 1 (and "female" is equal to 0), (self-reported) race was divided into White, Black, East Asian, South Asian, Southeast Asian, Latin American, and Middle Eastern. Our data also contained information on those who self-identified as "Mixed" and those who did not fall into any of the major groups ("Other"). Because "Mixed" and "Other" are very heterogeneous categories, these cases (approximately 6 per cent of the original sample) have not been included in our analyses. In terms of operationalizing the social class of the student, we used median neighbourhood family income data from the 2001 Canadian Census. In the student census and administrative records, there is no record of parental income. The Census neighbourhood figures, while cruder than individual-level data, do provide a measure of family socio-economic status based on the general neighbourhood income characteristics. They also give us an indication of the wider characteristics of the neighbourhood for a more macro understanding of the students' environments. In other words, because income within neighbourhoods is relatively homogenous, we are estimating individual incomes because we have neighbourhood data for our sample members.

Other Independent Variables of Interest

We included several other independent variables in order to both account for existing research on the determinants of transition to post-secondary education (and thus not overstate the relationship between gender, race, and class and our outcomes of interest) and augment the status traits typically associated with intersectionality. As such, we also recognize *immigrant status*, *streaming*, and *special education needs* to be traits that will impact on the trajectories of students' learning paths. Race, immigrant generation status, and income are highly associated in Toronto (Yau, Rosolen, and Archer, 2013), as are immigrant generational status, ethno-racial group, and post-secondary attainment (Sweet et al., 2010). Therefore, we argue that we cannot really conceptualize "race" without accounting for how strongly this concept is tied to generation status and income in Toronto.

Immigrant generation of the student was derived from information on students' region of birth and where their parents were born. First-generation students were those who were born outside of Canada (as were their parents), second-generation students were born in Canada but had one parent born outside Canada, and third-generation students had both parents born in Canada (Anisef et al., 2010). In terms of *streaming* and *special education needs*, we understand both to be highly associated with educational attainment in general. Students whose course work is mostly in applied subjects have a very low rate of post-secondary attainment. Students in the applied stream (in Toronto) are also more likely to be from families with lower incomes (People for Education, 2014) and to be black and to be male. Another related factor is that students in the applied stream are more likely to be identified as having special education needs (Brown and Parekh, 2010; Toronto District School Board, 2012). These findings point to the highly correlated nature of race, income, perceived ability, and streaming.

Information on the *academic stream* of students in Grade 9 was available[5]. A variable measuring academic and applied streams in Grade 9 was included in the analysis and was coded so that "1" was equal to being in the applied stream and "0" was equal to the academic stream. In terms of *special education needs*, we also had information from the administrative file that indicated whether a student fell under the EQAO definition of special education needs, which excludes students identified as Gifted: that is, those students with an active exceptionality or an active Individual Education Plan. Students who had these characteristics were dummy code "1" on the special education needs variable.

Control Variables

Social scientists will frequently hold certain variables constant in order to assess the real impact of a series of independent variables. This is particularly true when the research literature has established the important influence of these so-called control variables with regard to the dependent variable being analysed. This being the case, we controlled for two additional concepts: *parental education* and *grades* so as not to overstate the relationship between our key variables of interest and post-secondary confirmations. Recent Canadian research has demonstrated that parental education is a stronger predictor of post-secondary attainment than income (Davies, Maldonado, and Zarifa, 2014), and therefore this variable's inclusion in any statistical model predicting transition to PSE is crucial. In terms of *parental education*, the students were asked about the highest educational attainment of their parents. The data were recoded into a single variable to capture the highest level of education of either parent with possible response categories being "High School," "College," "University," and "Don't Know." The variable was dummy-coded so that "1" was equal to university or college (that is any PSE).

High school grades are of course a strong determinant of school success and post-secondary transition and were based on Grade 11 marks (expressed in percentages) and derived from the administrative database.

Analytic Strategy

Social scientists usually employ different sorts of statistics to first describe the variables employed in their studies and then to understand or predict the dependent variable of critical importance in their studies. The techniques employed in predicting dependent variables are complex and need not be discussed here in any great detail. What students should understand, though, is that these techniques permit the social scientist to sort out the impact of personal characteristics (that is, age, race, gender) and the impact of more meso and macro factors that exist beyond the individual level. By way of illustration, high school students planning for PSE are influenced by values and expectations related to their gender as well as their socio-economic origins and ethnicity. At the same time, they attend schools (meso-level factors) that vary in many ways including the nature of the neighbourhood (macro-level factor) in which the school is situated.

The techniques we employed in our analysis also allow us to explore the application of **intersectionality theory** in which it is argued that gender, race, and income impact on the life chances of individuals. The theory also suggests that the distinctive combinations of these factors or variables will have unique effects, depending upon sub-group membership. In this study, we employ a statistical application that allows us to evaluate the impact of different intersectional ties of students and examine how these different combinations of fixed characteristics can impact upon their life chances (McCall, 2005). Through the application of statistics used in this study we can assess, for example, if the effect of being black on post-secondary confirmation is different for males and females. It will also tell us if median family income differentially impacts on PSE confirmations according to ethno-racial group. Previous literature cited above has suggested that blacks and males, as well as those who are from lower socio-economic backgrounds, are more highly represented among students identified with special needs. We aimed to examine how the combinations of these specific status traits impacted upon their PSE pathways.

Results

Table 4.1 presents the descriptive statistics of variables used in this study. After all missing variable information was taken into account, we were left with a usable sample of 11,835. In our sample, over half of the students confirmed university, while 16 per cent confirmed college and 30 per cent confirmed neither. Our sample was very racially diverse and is thus reflective of Toronto's population of students, with just over a third white and around 20 per cent East Asian and South Asian. Southeast Asians, Middle Easterners and Latin Americans compose smaller groups between 2 per cent and 5 per cent. Males compose half of the sample and the average median family income was just over $58,000 per year, although the range on this variable was substantial. We can also see that the average grade for students was around 70 per cent and that two-thirds of parents had post-secondary education of some sort. In terms of generational status, the biggest group were first-generation students at 44 per cent, followed by second-generation students at 36 per cent. Third-generation students accounted for just under 20 per cent of the entire sample. Around 20 per cent of students were in the applied stream while 10 per cent of students had been identified with special education needs.

Our next step in analysing post-secondary confirmations was to employ an advanced form of statistics to assess the odds of students with certain background characteristics confirming either university or college. We found that being

Table 4.1 Descriptive Statistics ($n = 11,835$)

Variable	Average
Post-secondary Pathways	
Confirmed university	54%
Confirmed college	16%
Neither	30%
Race	
Black	10%
East Asian	23%
Latin American	2%
Middle Eastern	5%
South Asian	21%
Southeast Asian	3%
White	37%
Male	50%
Median family income	$58,430
Grade 11/12 marks	69.68%
Parents have PSE	66%
Immigrant Generation	
First generation	44%
Second generation	36%
Third generation	19%
Applied stream	19%
Special education needs	10%

male (compared to female) reduced the likelihood of university and college confirmation. In terms of race, the findings varied greatly by group. Compared to whites, East Asians, South Asian, and Southeast Asians were more likely to confirm university and college. Blacks were less likely than whites to confirm university but more likely to confirm college. Latin Americans were less likely to confirm university than whites, but no different from whites in terms of college confirmations. In terms of income, there was a positive effect for university and a negative one for college. These findings show that gender, race, and income certainly do matter for PSE confirmations.

We then sought to more closely explore sub-group differences based on gender, race, and income. These sub-group differences are best understood when presented graphically (see Figures 4.1–4.3).

Figure 4.1 Illustrates the sub-group of gender and black. This relationship shows that black males are at an additional disadvantage in terms of their likelihood of confirming university. Their predicted probabilities of confirming university are at around 0.14, compared to 0.45 for their white male counterparts.

Figure 4.2 illustrates the significant intersections between selected racial groups and income. As can be seen in all of the graphs, the relationship between gender and income is expressed as lines that have different trajectories in terms of likelihood of confirming PSE. In all cases, females were above males, but as income increased the lines converged. In other words, the impact of income on PSE confirmation was different for males and females and narrowed at higher median family income levels. The different race and income intersections were illustrated by the very distinctively differentiated trajectories that the lines in each graph portrayed. In fact, if income had the same effect on university confirmations for all races, the lines in each of these graphs would look similar. Instead, their shapes were very different.

In the case of East Asians and South Asians, even at low median income levels, the likelihood of confirming PSE was fairly high (and much higher for females), and this increased steadily with income as well, although the trajectory changed for females at mid-to-high income levels. In the case of college confirmations, income steadily decreased the likelihood of confirming college for East Asians, and this also narrowed for males and females at the higher income levels. In contrast, the lines for white males and females and university confirmations were somewhat parallel, although they did converge at higher income levels.

When we included the additional measures of *grades*, *parental post-secondary education*, *immigrant generation*, and whether the student was in the *applied stream*, we found that grades were positively associated with university and college confirmation, and that

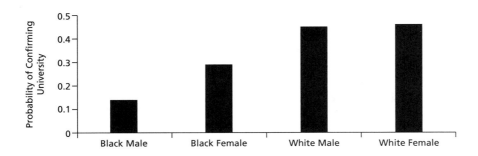

Figure 4.1 Intersection of Gender with Being Black

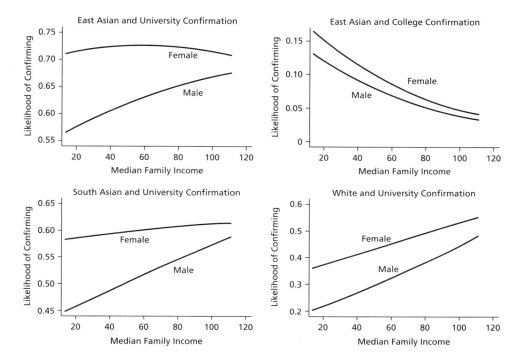

Figure 4.2 Intersections of Race with Income on Predicting University and College Confirmation

parental PSE was positively associated with university but not college confirmation. Relative to third-generation Canadians, students who were first generation were most likely to confirm both college and university. As expected, being in the applied stream strongly diminished the likelihood of confirming university, but not college. Having special education needs reduced the likelihood of university and college confirmations, with the negative effect on the odds of university confirmations being stronger than the odds on college confirmations.

In further explorations of intersectionality, we found that the combination of special education needs with income was statistically significant. We graphically illustrate the relationships in Figure 4.3.

As illustrated, the relationship between income and confirming both university and college was certainly dependent on whether a student had been identified as having special education needs. In the case of university confirmations, an increase in income steadily increased the likelihood of confirming, although the gap between those with special needs and those without was sizable. In the case of college confirmations, the relationship with income was completely reversed for those with special needs compared to those without. For those with special needs, their likelihood of confirming college steadily increased with income. However, for those without special education needs, as their income rose their likelihood of confirming college was virtually nil. In the case of university confirmations, an increase in income steadily increased the likelihood of confirming, although the gap between those with special needs and those without was sizable. In the case of college confirmations, the relationship with income was completely reversed for those with special needs compared to those without.

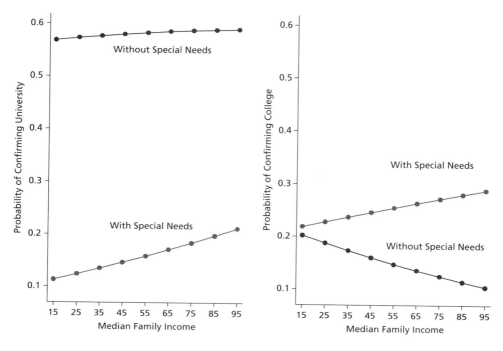

Figure 4.3 Intersection of Special Education Needs with Median Family Income

Discussion and Conclusions

Our findings revealed that issues of race, class, gender, and special education needs matter very much to the post-secondary transitions made by Toronto high school students. We found that income, race, and gender were intimately linked in explaining the PSE confirmations of students. For example, black males were significantly less likely to attend university compared to other groups. Students with special education needs had limited post-secondary horizons, and only those with sufficient economic resources stand a chance of attending college. These findings raise the question as to what sorts of interventions are possible to alter these existing situations that limit the life chances of young people.

To review, our research is motivated by an intersectionality approach, which is based on the premise that individuals' combinations of characteristics (for example, race, ethno-racial group, disability, social class) put them at the intersection of various social groupings. These combinations of characteristics must be considered when making recommendations for advancements in social mobility, including the transition to post-secondary education. This perspective, we argue, provides us with a fresh look at public policy and a new lens for examining marginalized student populations in terms of their access to PSE, their persistence in PSE, and their successful transition to the labour market.

We are not the first researchers to suggest that an intersectionality framework has direct policy implications. In fact, the Institute for Intersectionality Research and Policy at Simon Fraser University has developed guidelines for implementing the key tenets of intersectionality into policy recommendations (Hankivsky, 2012). They argue that it is of central importance to understand that an intersectionality perspective requires that individuals be conceptualized as occupying many characteristics, none of which can be prioritized. Additionally, the social categories that individuals occupy are socially constructed and as such, they are not fixed. These socially constructed identities are shaped by larger processes of power and influence and are dependent on time and place. The recognition of these factors as they exist thus necessitates efforts to promote social justice and equity (Hankivsky, 2012; Hankivsky and Cormier, 2011).

Our analyses pinpointed certain intersectionality groupings—race, gender, class, and special education needs. An intersectionality approach may suggest, in fact, that a single technique of disseminating information to students about PSE may not fit all marginalized student populations. We need to dig deeper and gear information to specific sub-groups using targeted strategies. If we are to tackle lack of awareness of information and programs, we must focus on information that is of relevance to these groups.

Cultural Capital and Trust

There are at least two important aspects to the notion of information dissemination. The first is that the type of information regarding PSE applications and processes is definitely demarcated by familial experience with PSE—a notion that is relevant to Bourdieu's concepts of cultural and social capital (Bourdieu, 1986). The second is that students need *trusted sources* from which to receive relevant information.

Middle-class families where at least one parent has attended PSE have a wealth of knowledge that they use to guide their children. Rosenbaum and Naffziger (2011, 2) argue that secondary students not only need encouragement to attend PSE but also require "cultural capital translators." There is a plethora of assumed knowledge that is required to successfully transition to PSE: entrance requirements; funding possibilities; the simple process of acquiring the right forms; deadlines; and so forth. What may seem like "common sense" to students whose parents have PSE is a foreign world to first-generation students. In fact, common sense is knowledge—cultural knowledge—that comes with lived experience. As argued by Bourdieu (1986), this type of tacitly understood knowledge allows the people who have it to be at an advantage, particularly with regard to social mobility. If they are lacking particular knowledge, it is very likely they have access to a network (parents, friends) from which they can safely obtain that information. In other words, they have the social capital necessary to obtain needed information. While students with parents who have PSE may have been groomed from an early age to have the correct information about how, when, and where to apply, it is certainly not a taken-for-granted reality for students without this kind of family experience (or social and cultural capital). Also, it is simply not enough to direct these students to the right information because students who are not familiar with these types of processes will invariably become discouraged or intimidated, or make incorrect assumptions. In fact, Rosenbaum and Naffziger (2011) emphasise that it is precisely this step—*the inability to deal with this type of information*—that may surprise middle-class policy-makers. It is not simply about the complexity of the forms themselves, but also the risk of incurring student debt and the fear of being pulled into a foreign world with which they have no experience. Rosenbaum and Naffziger (2011) also point out that students from lower SES backgrounds may have acquired a cultural value of avoiding debt, making the prospect of student loans seem daunting and unacceptable. Such students must not be forced to rely on their own assumptions, which may be misinformed and short-sighted. They must be shown how to apply for funding, the implications of this funding, and the different career paths that will, as a consequence, be open to them. Being led to a four-year liberal arts degree that accrues a heavy student debt is very possibly not the best match for students who want the guarantee of a job. Being informed about the programs that are most likely to help them realize their goals is far more helpful.

As stated above, a second component of disseminating information to groups revealed by our intersectionality analysis is very likely related to trust. Trust requires that information received by intersectionality groups be viewed as valid. There are several issues that should be highlighted regarding trust. Rosenbaum (2011) argues that simply increasing the aspirations of youth who are typically under-represented in PSE programs will enhance neither their transition to PSE nor their ability to complete PSE. Rather, information about the realities of PSE must be provided, which includes the wide range of different types of degree and certificate programs that exist (that is, a four-year Bachelor's degree is not the only option) and that the successful completion of PSE is itself demanding and will require diligence and strong effort at the secondary school level. Rather than encouraging a university for all approach, apprenticeship and college paths occupy a place in this discourse as second- or third-rung choices. These alternative paths are quite attainable, require less investment in terms of tuition, consist of shorter-term programs of study, and are often financially and personally rewarding.

As mentioned earlier, Rosenbaum argues that simply raising the aspirations of disadvantaged youth is not enough and may actually be a disservice as this type of strategy fails to equip students with the right kinds of social capital and information they need to succeed. Specifically, first-generation students must be provided with information about how to succeed in post-secondary education and to overcome the hurdles they must clear in order to even gain a place at such an institution. They need to be told earlier in their educational process what kinds of courses and grades they need to be able to gain entrance to PSE institutions. For example, People for Education (2014) recently found that while applied courses are theoretically eligible to be considered for university entrance, the hard reality is that students who take applied courses very rarely attend university. There is currently a major disconnect between what students are told about the possibilities of following an applied route and what the actual outcomes have been for such students.

Most importantly for the immediate future, concrete suggestions should be given to counselling staff in secondary schools and student success personnel in order to maximize the chances that every student will be aware of the possibilities that exist. This means that all students should be given the appropriate guidance to wade through the institutional and bureaucratic complexities associated with implementing post–high school educational and career choices and be able to speak to similarly situated young adults who have managed to negotiate these hurdles in the recent past. But who is the person doing the showing and mentoring? Again, this relates to the issue of information coming from trusted sources. Rosenbaum and Naffziger (2011, 2) and Stephan (2013, 1) call these individuals "college coaches." Specifically, these individuals help students navigate this unfamiliar world that assumes a certain degree of cultural capital. While a natural assumption is that school counsellors can serve in this role, the reality is that many students are underserved by school counsellors given the very high student-counsellor ratio. Moreover, many of these students will require extended attention and repeat sessions. This is something that pressured school counsellors cannot provide to all students on a one-to-one basis. Stephan (2013) also argues that the standard counselling model that was initially developed to serve middle-class students with PSE preparation often remains unquestioned. This model may not work well in providing guidance to more disadvantaged students.

Our findings have revealed evidence of distinctly different PSE outcomes based on the intersectionality of race, sex, class, and special needs education. Clearly, a one-size-fits-all policy approach will be of limited use, as it denies the existence of a starting place of disadvantage for a large proportion of students. Policy-makers must look at the intersections of students' lives and target initiatives to them. This is not a suggestion that every student requires a custom-made policy initiative, but that ministerial and institutional policy-makers should recognize that there are many factors that act to constrain the choices made by youth. Our analysis of intersectionality groupings and an understanding of the process of communicating useful information to such groups revealed that there are at least two major issues to be considered: (1) the social networks of students and taken-for-granted assumptions that surround the provision of information, and (2) that such information must come from trusted sources.

Questions for Critical Thought

1. Using an intersectionality approach, identify your particular intersections (for example, race, gender, social class). Describe how your particular intersectionality influenced your post-secondary trajectory.
2. The findings from this chapter suggest that post-secondary access differs significantly by race, sex, and special education needs. If you were a policy-maker, what would you suggest to make post-secondary access more equitable? List three suggestions.
3. List three ways that an intersectionality approach could be used to inform public policy on post-secondary education.
4. Using the website of your university or college, find out what policies and/or programs your institution has for attracting students from non-traditional or marginalized groups. What groups are targeted? How do the policies or programs you have identified assist these groups in the successful transition to post-secondary education?

Glossary

Intersectionality theory The theoretical approach that individuals' lives and opportunities are inextricably linked to the multiple identities that they occupy in relation to their ethno-racial group, gender, and social class. Many using this approach also include additional characteristics such as sexual orientation and (dis)ability in their understanding of the intersections of identity.

Life course theory A theoretical approach that is used to understand sociological phenomena by focusing on the structure and context of people's lives over time.

Status traits The characteristics that are assigned to individuals and have social significance in a society, such as ethno-racial group, age, gender, and social class.

Notes

1. The 2001 Canadian Federal Census was the most recent Canadian Census data that were available when the data set was constructed in 2007. The 2006 Canadian Census had not yet been publically released.
2. All students applying to post-secondary in Ontario do so through one of the two institutions. It should be noted that while academic researchers can, upon approval by the TDSB, gain access

to student census data, only TDSB staff can analyse information containing PSE confirmation information.

3. This latter category includes those who applied to post-secondary but were not accepted by an Ontario college, those that graduated from high school but did not apply to post-secondary over the three years, and those who dropped out or were still in school at the end of the three years. For the purposes of our analyses, such individuals were similar insofar as they all shared the characteristic of not being accepted to university or college.

4. Approximately 9 per cent had applied to PSE and had not been accepted, while nearly 10 per cent graduate but do not apply to PSE. Just over 15 per cent had dropped out or were still in school.

5. Academic stream was determined through the majority of courses taken according to the Grade 9 to Grade 10 Program of Study. Most students took a majority of Grade 9 to Grade 10 courses in the Academic program of study (excluding courses that are Open, that is, without a defined program of study).

References

Abada, T., Hou, F., and Rams, B. "Ethnic differences in educational attainment among the children of Canadian immigrants." *Canadian Journal of Sociology* 34 (2009): 1–28.

Anisef, P., Axelrod, P., Baichman-Anisef, E., James, C., and Turrittin, A. *Opportunity and Uncertainty: Life Course Experiences of the Class of '73*. Toronto: University of Toronto Press, 2000.

Anisef, P., Brown, R.S., Phythian, K., Sweet, R., and Walters, D. "Early school leaving among immigrants in Toronto secondary schools." *Canadian Review of Sociology* 47 (2010): 103–28.

Berger, J., and Motte, A. "Mind the access gap: Breaking down the barriers to postsecondary education." *Policy Options* 28(10) (November, 2007): 42–46.

Bourdieu, P. "The forms of capital." In *Handbook of Theory and Research for the Sociology of Education*, J. Richardson (ed.), (241–58). New York: Greenwood, 1986.

Brown, R.S. *An Examination of TDSB Postsecondary Patterns: 17 Year Old Students, 2007*. Toronto: Toronto District School Board, 2009.

Brown, R., and Parekh, G. *Special Education: Structural Overview and Student Demographics*, research report no. 10/11–13). Toronto: Toronto District School Board, 2010.

Collins, P.H. *Fighting Words: Black Women and the Search for Justice*. Minneapolis: University of Minnesota Press, 1998.

Collins, P.H. *Black Feminist Thought*. London: Routledge, 2000.

Collins, P.H. *Black Sexual Politics: African-Americans, Gender, and New Racism*. New York: Routledge, 2005.

Crenshaw, K.W. "Mapping the margins: Intersectionality, identity politics, and violence against women of color." *Stanford Law Review* 43(6) (1991): 1241–99.

Davies, S., Maldonado, V., and Zarifa, D. "Effectively maintaining inequality in Toronto: Predicting student destinations in Ontario universities." *Canadian Review of Sociology* 51 (2014): 22–53.

Brown, R., Parekh, G., Presley, A., and Toronto District School Board. *The TDSB Grade 9 Cohort 2006–2011: Special Education Fact Sheet No. 4*, 2012.

Duquette, C. *Students at Risk*. Second edition. Markham: Pembroke Publishers, 2013.

Finnie, R., Childs, S., and Wismer, A. *Underrepresented Groups in Postsecondary Education in Ontario: Evidence from the Youth in Transition Survey*. Toronto: Higher Education Quality Council of Ontario, 2011.

Gauthier, M. "Youth Studies in Canada: Introduction." In *Spotlight on Canadian Youth Research*, M. Gauthier and D. Pacom (eds.), (11–20). Quebec City: Les Presses de l'Université Laval, 2001.

Hankivsky, O. (ed.). *An Intersectionality-based Policy Analysis Framework*. Vancouver: Institute for Intersectionality Research and Policy, Simon Fraser University, 2012. Retrieved 23 April 2014 from: www.sfu.ca/iirp/documents/IBPA/IBPA_Framework_Complete%20Collection_Hankivsky_2012.pdf

Hankivsky, O., and Cormier, R. "Intersectionality and public policy: Some lessons from existing models." *Political Research Quarterly* 64(1) (2011): 217–29.

hooks, bell. *Feminist Theory: From Margin to Center*. Second edition. Cambridge: South End Press, 1984.

Lennon, M.C., Zhao, H., Wang, S., and Gluszynski, T. *Educational Pathways of Youth in Ontario: Factors Impacting Educational Pathways*. Toronto: Higher Educational Quality Council of Ontario, 2011. Retrieved 5 August 2015: www.heqco.ca/SiteCollection Documents/YITS%20ENG.pdf

McCall, L. "The complexity of intersectionality." *Signs* 30(3) (2005): 1771–800.

McMullen, K. *Postsecondary Education Participation among Underrepresented and Minority Groups*. 81-004-x, 8(4). Ottawa: Statistics Canada, 2011.

Organisation for Economic Co-operation and Development (OECD). *Education at a Glance 2013: OECD Indicators*, Paris: OECD Publishing, 2013. Retrieved from: http://dx.doi.org/ 10.1787/eag-2013-en

People for Education. *Choosing Courses for High School*, 2014. Retrieved 28 February 2014 from: www.peopleforeducation.ca/wp-content/ uploads/2014/02/choosing-courses-for-high-school-2014.pdf

Rosenbaum, J.E. "The complexities of college for all beyond fairy-tale dreams." *Sociology of Education* 84(2) (2011): 113–17.

Rosenbaum, J., and Naffziger, M. "Information is not enough: Cultural capital, cultural capital translators, and college access for disadvantaged students." IPR working paper 11-04, 2011.

Schulz, A.J., and Mullings, L. (eds.). *Gender, Race, Class and Health: Intersectional Approaches*. San Francisco: Jossey-Bass, 2006.

Stephan, J.L. "Social capital and the college enrollment process: How can a school program make a difference?." *Teachers College Record* 115 (2013): 1–39.

Suárez-Orozco, C., Rhodes, J., and Milburn, M. "Unraveling the immigrant paradox academic engagement and disengagement among recently arrived immigrant youth." *Youth & Society* 41(2) (2009): 151–85.

Sweet, R., and Anisef, P. (eds.). *Preparing for Postsecondary Education: New Roles for Families and Governments*. Montreal: McGill-Queen's University Press, 2005.

Sweet, R., Anisef, P., Brown, R., Walters, D., and Phythian, K. *Post-high School Pathways of Immigrant Youth*. Toronto: Higher Education Quality Council of Ontario, 2010.

Warner. L.R. "A best practices guide to intersectional approaches in psychological research." *Sex Roles* 59 (5–6) (2008): 454–63.

Warner, D.F., and Brown, T.H. "Understanding how race/ethnicity and gender define age trajectories of disability: an intersection approach." The Center for Family and Demographic Research, working paper series 2009–2010. Toledo: Bowling Green University, 2010.

Yau, L.R., and Bryce, A. *Toronto District School Board Facts. 2011–12 Student & Parent Census*, 2013. Retrieved 21 May 2014 from: www.tdsb.on.ca/Portals/0/AboutUs/Research/ 2011-12CensusFactSheet1-Demographics-17June2013.pdf

5

Education–Job Mismatch and Underemployment among Post-secondary Graduates with Disabilities

Brad Seward, David Walters, and David Zarifa

Introduction

In the last few decades, the face of higher education has changed dramatically. Enrolments have reached unprecedented numbers, as governments and international organizations have called for higher education to expand and maintain a healthy economy. Students from a variety of socio-demographic backgrounds are being encouraged to attend, and consequently their educational expectations have heightened dramatically. Human capital theories explain higher education as a means for individuals to increase their productivity, marketability, and skill acquisition in preparation for the workforce. In its aggregate form, "knowledge economy" rationales are positioning universities and their graduates as increasingly pertinent to societal prosperity. However, these theories assume that all individuals who choose to invest in education and training and hold the skills and abilities valued will be rewarded equally. Indeed, research has long shown that those who obtain a degree experience higher paying and more stable jobs and shorter bouts of unemployment. However, youth from disadvantaged backgrounds remain less likely to succeed in school, to complete their programs, and to transition successfully into the labour market (Krahn, 2009; Lehmann, 2007; Anisef et al., 2000; Andres et al., 1999; Looker, 1997).

This chapter provides an empirical example of the difficulties new graduates face in their school-to-work transitions. Our focus is on the early employment experiences of disabled post-secondary graduates. Despite trends indicating a growing proportion of post-secondary students who self-identify as having a disability (CUSC, 2009), their unique experiences and difficulties transitioning from school-to-work remain largely unexplored, particularly in the Canadian context. To provide a comprehensive picture of the disconnect between education and work, we examine two related concepts—underemployment and self-perceived education–job mismatch. Further, our study examines nationally representative survey data from the 2005 cohort of post-secondary graduates in Statistics Canada's National Graduate Survey.

Our study sheds light on the following research questions. First, what are the educational characteristics of post-secondary graduates with disabilities? That is, are persons with disabilities more likely to graduate from certain fields of study and levels of education in comparison to students without disabilities? Second, do disabled graduates report higher levels of self-perceived mismatch and underemployment in their early workforce experiences in comparison to non-disabled post-secondary graduates? That is, are disabled graduates more likely to experience difficulties securing work to match their education level? Finally, are there any differences in terms of mismatch and underemployment levels reported by new graduates?

Human Capital Theory, Structural Inequality, and Credentialism

With a shrinking primary sector and the reliance on a **knowledge-based economy** becoming more prominent in Canada, human capital theorists have called for the expansion of post-secondary education provision. **Human capital theory** posits that people invest personal resources (time, effort, and money) into higher education as a utility function to secure greater labour market returns. Made popular by economist Gary Becker (1975), human capital theory conceives the pursuit of higher education as a rational cost-benefit analysis undertaken by individuals hopeful to enter the labour market. The theory suggests that prospective workers intentionally and rationally incur the costs of training through higher education as a means to secure future employment. This self-investment is recognized by employers—who identify the worker as being more skilled and productive—and they are therefore prepared to pay higher wages (Fevre et al., 1999).

The issue, however, is that the returns on investment that are predicted by human capital are not necessarily guaranteed. While a great deal of evidence suggests that individuals with higher levels of human capital earn more over the course of their careers, those individuals typically have higher annual incomes, and greater probabilities of securing full-time, permanent work, as the labour market is not simply an open arena where individuals with similar credentials compete with similar resources for available jobs (Lowe, 2004, 150). Not everyone has the same means or constraints. Structural factors, such as social class, gender, region, as well as race and ethnicity, change the nature of the relationship between education and work.

At the same time, the expansion of higher education has led to increasingly intense competition among labour market hopefuls, resulting in the inflation of credentials. This process, referred to as **credentialism**, is the belief that formal education is rewarded less for its knowledge base, abilities, and skills and more for the symbolic value of having completed a given credential tier (Collins, 1979; see Brown [2001] for a review). As a result, many scholars believe that the connections between earned credentials and the skills required for the job are weakening (Mclean and Rollwagen, 2010; Walters, 2004; Bills, 2003). Hiring decisions may be increasingly supply driven, based less on matching up skilled candidates with skill shortages and more about taking candidates with higher levels of formal education simply because a surplus of such individuals exists. The end result leaves graduates employed in positions that require abilities below their formal level of education—a mismatch that we will discuss further below.

Some research suggests that credentialism is the result of dominant class structures attempting to maintain the status quo (Sykes et al., 2009). According to Maximally Maintained Inequality (MMI) theory, as historically disadvantaged groups attain the educational credentials previously held by dominant groups, the credential requirements for prestigious jobs that are necessary for status maintenance and mobility are inflated (Raftery and Hout, 1993). For example, as greater proportions of the population pursue undergraduate degrees, the relationship between social origins and graduate and professional school admission may strengthen (Zarifa, 2012a). That is, as access opens up at lower credential tiers, privileged groups may seek out higher levels of education to maintain their advantaged position. Additionally, researchers are finding support for theories of Effectively Maintained Inequality (EMI), where privileged groups seek out prestigious segments (for example, lucrative fields, selective institutions) within credential tiers (Davies, Maldonado, and Zarifa, 2014; Zarifa, 2012b; Lucas, 2001). In these ways, despite increased educational access to the post-secondary system, the social class advantages of the elite may be maintained through finer distinctions.

Linking Education and Work for Youth with Disabilities

Much existing work on disabled youth's school-to-work transitions has focused on employment status to determine success rates of labour market outcomes. In the majority of studies, regardless of disability type, disabled youth were significantly less likely to be gainfully employed than their able-bodied counterparts (Zarifa, Walters, and Seward, forthcoming; Janus, 2009; Madaus et al., 2001; Blackorby and Wagner, 1996). Conventional measures of employment provide an insufficient view of the problem. They often overlook the quality of employment disabled post-secondary graduates are able to secure (Livingstone, 2010). Indeed, looking at disabled workers within the entire working population, these individuals are significantly more likely to be employed in precarious and non-standard working arrangements (Shuey and Jovic, 2013; McMahon, 2012; Schur et al., 2009). Moreover, post-secondary educational attainment may not necessarily buffer the risk for disabled graduates as these trends have been seen to persist for university graduates, leading to mismatched labour market outcomes (Officer, 2009; Fichten et al., 2012).

Overall, empirical data looking at Canadian disabled graduates' education match is limited. Part of the problem is that disabled graduates have traditionally represented such a small population that a great deal of research has involved post-secondary access for disabled youth (Cheatham et al., 2013; Trainor, 2008; Wilkens and Hehir, 2008) rather than the outcomes of post-secondary education. Recent research suggests, however, that this trend may be changing in Canada, as the population reporting a disability begins to rise. In Ontario, for example, disability rates increased from 21 per cent to 27 per cent of the population between 1999 and 2008 (McCloy and DeClou, 2013). Similar upward trends can be seen when examining post-secondary enrolments. Between 2003–4 and 2010–11, the number of students with disabilities registering with university and college disability offices increased about 66 per cent (McCloy and DeClou, 2013). In fact, many universities across Canada are now reporting that nearly 10 per cent of their graduating cohorts have a disability (CUSC, 2009). As the population of disabled graduates expands, it has become increasingly necessary to examine the extent to which these graduates are finding work that links up with their level of education.

We briefly discuss two ways of assessing the degree to which education and work match up—underemployment and perceived mismatch—before turning to our empirical analyses using the National Graduates Survey.

Underemployment

Underemployment typically refers to the situation that occurs when an individual's career expectations are not realized upon transitioning into the labour market. This tends to occur most often when an individual's skill or potential is underutilized or when the expected pecuniary returns on investment (that is, the salary expected based on the price paid for education) are unmet (Athey and Hautaluoma, 1994). The most common example for new graduates occurs when an individual secures a job with requirements that are below his or her level of formal education. Past research in Canada has estimated that approximately 20 per cent of the entire employed workforce is underemployed (Robst, 2007). This proportion could be on the rise as younger, more highly educated workers continue to enter the workforce. Moreover, this trend may be exacerbated as the number of jobs that do not require higher education decline. One of the major problems with underemployment is that it effectively alienates post-secondary graduates from the knowledge they have obtained; it is this wasted ability of the eligible workforce that poses problems for the tightly linked education-work relationship suggested by human capital theory (Livingstone, 1999). Where education should be providing individuals with the tools necessary to secure lucrative employment (consistent with human capital assumptions), the competition inherent in slack labour markets forces these individuals to accept exploitative employment arrangements for which they are often overqualified (Athey and Hautaluoma, 1994).

With respect to disability, Fichten and colleagues (2012) note that disabled post-secondary graduates were significantly less likely to find employment in a field closely related to their educational field of study. This is consistent with other research documenting the difficulty disabled graduates have securing relevant employment (Hale et al., 1998; Officer, 2009; Livingstone, 2010; Holmes and Silvestri, 2011).

Part of the problem is the fact that employers often have negative perceptions of applicants with disabilities. Perceptions that disabled workers are not able to meet the pace and organizational demands of the job or that they are more expensive to employ than able-bodied workers have often resulted in these individuals struggling to find standard work arrangements for which they are qualified (Shuey and Jovic, 2013; Robert and Harlan, 2006). Although legal protections and recent policy changes have attempted to increase accommodation for disabled workers in lucrative employment arrangements (for example, Lynk [2008]), institutional barriers remain for these individuals.

Self-Perceived Mismatch

Self-perceived mismatch is related to (but distinct from) underemployment in a number of ways. As a subjective measure of mismatch, this process captures several employment-related factors unconsidered in underemployment. Handel (2003), for instance, rejects the notion that the workforce is increasingly facing a skills-based mismatch. While there may be little evidence for a decline in human capital returns, employer's expectations of employment are often disconnected with that of their employees. Workers can feel unsatisfied with many aspects of the job not traditionally considered in objective measures of underemployment. The level of control over decision making (Handel, 2003), access to benefits (Schatzel et al., 2012), and agency over the work process (Livingstone, 2010) all contribute to self-perceived (mis)match in employment. In this way, while underemployment focuses on skill match and pecuniary returns exclusively, self-perceived mismatch incorporates other potential areas of job satisfaction that contribute to finding valuable employment for the level of education attained.

Of course, self-perceived mismatch may not always be a negative association. There is evidence that some disabled graduates find employment for which they are under-qualified

(Officer, 2009; Trupin and Yelin, 2003). In these cases, however, the proportion of under-qualified graduates is small and usually overshadowed by those who are underemployed.

One major aspect that may contribute to self-perceived mismatch among disabled workers is the access to employment benefits and the level of disability accommodation. Despite legal obligation in Canada with respect to the employment of disabled workers, employers' perceptions of differences in abilities often result in unequal access to accommodation requirements, benefits, and job security (Schur, 2002). It is estimated that even at high levels of education, nearly one-third of disabled workers may have unmet accommodation needs (Hale et al., 1998). The unique position of disabled graduates transitioning into the labour market calls for the use of a number of measures of mismatch; utilizing both objective and subjective measures can potentially include additional returns to schooling not considered by employment status or income levels.

Methods

The National Graduate Survey (NGS)

Our task in this chapter is to expand our knowledge of difficulties disadvantaged groups face in their education-work transitions by charting the experiences of youth with disabilities. To explore these differences empirically, we utilize data obtained from Statistics Canada's 2005 National Graduate Survey (NGS). The NGS serves as a valuable resource for determining the labour market outcomes of post-secondary graduates. Previous cycles have been used extensively in the research literature. However, few studies have used the survey to examine the transitions of disabled graduates or have examined the early workforce experiences of 2005 cohort of post-secondary graduates.

The 2005 NGS contains information on 31,025 post-secondary graduates of various programs across all Canadian provinces and territories, 1,604 of whom self-identified as having a disability. The survey population consists of all graduates who had completed the requirements of their post-secondary degrees, diplomas, or certificates during the 2005 calendar year. Computer Assisted Telephone Interviews (CATI) were conducted regarding the educational history and employment profiles of respondents in 2007, two years after completing their degrees.

It is important to identify several limitations to the National Graduate Survey data. First, the cancellation of the 2010 follow-up survey has restricted the 2005 to 2007 wave of graduates to only allow for the study of short-term labour market outcomes. Second, because of the aggregate coding of disability in the data, this study can only assess the experiences of individuals living with a self-identified disability as one homogenous group. Thus, it is not possible to disentangle the impact of physical and learning disabilities on employment outcomes, nor is it possible to assess the severity of disability. Finally, the data only allow for analysis among post-secondary graduates. As such, we cannot compare the labour market outcomes of those with and without post-secondary credentials.

Variables

The key explanatory variables used in this study are disability, field of study, and level of education. Disability status was coded as a dichotomous "Yes" or "No" response to the survey question asking respondents to indicate whether they had a lasting disability or handicap that had persisted for at least six months. Level of education refers to the program that graduates completed in 2005. The levels were broken down into trades and vocational certification, college diploma, and below Bachelor's-degree level university programs, university undergraduate degree programs, and advanced university degree programs, which include graduates of Master's, PhD and professional programs (for example, law, medicine, and dentistry). Finally, NGS respondents were asked to report their field of study. Their responses were originally converted into a field of study code applicable for all graduates, using the Classification of Instructional Programs (CIP) system to match university, college, and trade-vocational institutions' field of study categories. Consistent with previous studies on fields of study and employment outcomes using the NGS, we grouped fields into the following six categories:

1. Liberal arts (for example, fine arts, humanities, and social sciences)
2. Commerce, management, and business administration
3. Physical, agricultural, and biological sciences
4. Engineering, computer sciences, and math
5. Health and related fields
6. Other[1]

The regression models also included the primary socio-demographic variables age, marital status, number of dependent children, visible minority and immigrant statuses, and parental education, and whether the respondent received funding from various sources[2]. These variables have been shown to influence labour market outcomes based on research conducted using the 2000 NGS and have been, therefore, included as control variables in the models (Zarifa, 2012a; Zarifa and Walters, 2008; Walters and Zarifa 2008). With the exception of age, all of the explanatory variables used in the analysis were treated as categorical[3].

Two key response variables measure the extent to which graduates' work matches their educational qualifications and skills. The first key response variable taps into the self-perceived (mis)match between education and employment by utilizing the following survey question: Considering your experience, education, and training, do you feel that you are overqualified for the (main) job you held last week? The variable was recoded as the dichotomous response: (1) "Yes"; and (2) "No." Underemployment was measured using the survey question analysing the respondent's completed level of education required to get his or her current job, compared with the highest level of education of the graduate by 2005. This variable was recoded as (1) The respondent held more education than was required for his or her job at the time of hiring; or (2) The respondent held the same or less education than was required for his or her job. In both cases, we are comparing the extent to which the degree or program completed by the graduate in 2005 matches up with the education required for the job held by the graduate two years later in 2007.

Analyses

The statistical analyses contain descriptive statistics and binary logistic regressions. Descriptive analyses are used to uncover statistically significant differences between disabled and non-disabled graduates across a number of key variables. Regression analyses are then used to examine the extent to which group differences hold when controlling for a number of factors. In other words, regression analyses allow us to observe whether relationships between explanatory and response variables remain consistent when other important factors are taken into consideration. Key variables are entered into three separate models to observe the impact of disability on the two key response variables. The first set of models compares the perceived mismatch and underemployment variables separately against only the disability variable. Model 2 looks to see if the relationships witnessed in Model 1 persist when controlling for socio-demographic variables and introduces the independent variables level of education and field of study. Model 3 looks at the relationship between disability and qualification match when taking income into consideration[4].

Results

Descriptives

Do disabled graduates hold different credentials than their non-disabled counterparts? When considering the level of education graduates obtained, a few differences do emerge. Individuals without disabilities were more likely to graduate from higher levels of education. The bar graph in Figure 5.1 indicates that about 31 per cent of disabled individuals obtained undergraduate degrees compared to 39 per cent of non-disabled persons. Disabled

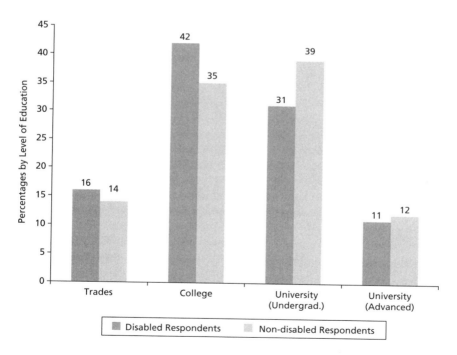

Figure 5.1 Level of Education by Disability Status, National Graduates Survey, 2005 Cohort

Note: Differences by disability status are statistically significant ($p < 0.001$; chi-square test). $n = 23{,}744$.

and non-disabled graduates held advanced degrees at similar rates (11 per cent and 12 per cent, respectively). At the same time, disabled respondents were more represented in the trades (16 per cent compared to 14 per cent) and college programs (42 per cent versus 35 per cent).

Figure 5.2 reveals a few noteworthy differences across fields of study. Disabled graduates were more likely to pursue liberal arts fields than their non-disabled counterparts. Moreover, disabled graduates were less likely to graduate from engineering, business, and health-related fields relative to non-disabled graduates—fields that have been identified in the literature as yielding more lucrative labour market outcomes upon graduation (for example, Zarifa and Walters [2008]; Walters [2004]; Finnie [2001]; Finnie and Frenette [2003])[5].

Are disabled graduates more likely to report higher levels of education–job mismatch? Indeed, Table 5.1 suggests that they are significantly more likely than their non-disabled counterparts. In fact, about 42 per cent of disabled graduates perceived a mismatch between their education and employment, compared to approximately 31 per cent of non-disabled respondents ($p < 0.001$)[6].

Do graduates with disabilities report higher levels of underemployment than graduates without disabilities? The results presented in Table 5.1 indicate that disabled graduates

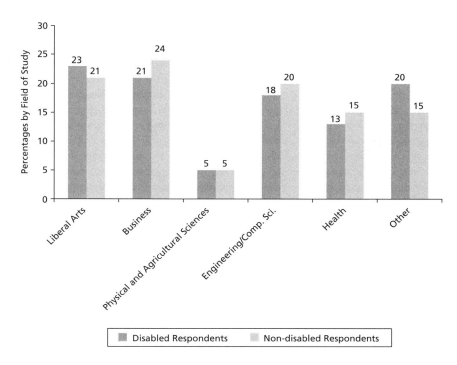

Figure 5.2 Field of Study by Disability Status, National Graduates Survey, 2005 Cohort

Note: Differences by disability status are statistically significant ($p < 0.001$; chi-square test). $n = 23,744$.

Table 5.1 Descriptive Statistics for Recent Graduates with and without Disabilities (2005 National Graduates Survey)

Variable	Respondents with Disability Percentage/Mean	Respondents without Disability Percentage/Mean
Perceived Education/Employment Mismatch*		
Yes	42	31
No	58	69
Underemployed for Current Job*		
Yes	58	49
No	42	51
Sex		
Male	42	42
Female	58	58
Marital Status		
Not married	41	41
Married	59	59
Dependent Children		
No	28	22
Yes	72	78
Age*	33	30
Visible Minority Status*		
Visible minority	10	19
Non-minority	90	81
Immigrant Status*		
Immigrant	5	14
Non-immigrant	95	86
Parental Education*		
Parents did not attend post-secondary	44	41
At least one parent with post-secondary	56	59
Bursaries/Grants*		
Yes	24	20
No	76	80
Government Loans		
Yes	41	44
No	59	56
Scholarships		
Yes	32	31
No	68	69

Table 5.1 continued

Variable	Respondents with Disability Percentage/Mean	Respondents without Disability Percentage/Mean
Other Loans		
Yes	30	27
No	70	73
Region*		
Ontario	36	35
Atlantic provinces	7	6
Quebec	24	33
Western provinces	33	26
Field of Study*		
Liberal arts	22	21
Business	21	23
Physical and agricultural sciences	5	5
Engineering/comp. sci.	19	20
Health	12	16
Other	21	15
Level of Schooling*		
University (undergrad.)	32	39
Trades	15	14
College	42	35
University (advanced)	11	12
Income*	38,487	42,212
n	1,026	22,718

Note: * $p < 0.001$. The asterisks denote the results from chi-square tests used to compare sample proportions and t-tests for differences in sample means. Percentages are shown for all variables except for age and income. Age is measured in years and income in dollars.

were significantly more likely to experience underemployment in their early workforce outcomes. While both groups report disturbing levels of underemployment, the inequalities are greater for disabled individuals. Specifically, 59 per cent of disabled respondents were underemployed for their current job, compared to 49 per cent of non-disabled graduates[7].

Regressions

Perceived Qualification Match

Our first series of regression analyses (see Table 5.2) indicate whether or not an individual perceived his or her education as being related to his or her employment across a number of key variables and controls[8]. Our particular interest is to see whether or not disability status is significantly related to one's perception of qualification match, and if this relationship

Table 5.2 Binary Logistic Regressions Predicting Perceived Qualification Match for the 2005 Cohort of Canadian Post-secondary Graduates

	Model 1		Model 2		Model 3	
	Coeff.	p	Coeff.	p	Coeff.	p
Constant	0.816	***	0.292	**	−12.577	***
Disability						
Yes	−0.48	***	−0.566	***	−0.411	***
No	-	-	-	-	-	-
Sex						
Male			−0.125	*	−0.337	***
Female			-	-	-	-
Age			0.012	-	−0.08	*
Age²			0.012	-	0.107	***
Marital Status						
Not married			0.219	***	0.135	*
Married			-	-	-	-
Dependent Children						
Yes			−0.081	-	−0.064	-
No			-	-	-	-
Visible Minority Status						
Visible minority			−0.355	***	−0.309	***
Non-minority			-	-	-	-
Immigrant Status						
Immigrant			−0.477	***	−0.406	***
Non-immigrant			-	-	-	-
Parental Education						
Parents did not attend post-secondary			−0.044	-	−0.056	-
At least one parent with post-secondary			-	-	-	-
Region				*		**
Ontario			-	-	-	-
Atlantic provinces			0.035	-	0.258	***
Quebec			0.15	*	0.238	**
Western provinces			0.153	*	0.109	-
Bursaries/Grants						
Yes			−0.005	-	0.001	-
No			-	-	-	-

Table 5.2 continued

	Model 1		Model 2		Model 3	
	Coeff.	p	Coeff.	p	Coeff.	p
Government Loans						
Yes			0.034	-	0.037	-
No			-	-	-	-
Scholarships						
Yes			0.115	-	0.068	-
No			-	-	-	-
Other Loans						
Yes			−0.107	-	−0.148	*
No			-	-	-	-
Field of Study				***		***
Liberal arts			-	-	-	-
Business			0.365	***	0.084	-
Physical and applied sciences			0.326	***	0.179	*
Engineering/comp. sci.			0.818	***	0.451	***
Health			1.05	***	0.799	***
Other			0.88	***	0.749	***
Level of Schooling				***		***
University (undergrad.)			-	-	-	-
Trades			−0.082	-	0.387	***
College			0.004	-	0.29	***
University (advanced)			0.407	***	0.137	-
Income					1.24	***

Wald chi²(1) = 16.24	Wald chi²(24) = 396.48	Wald chi²(25) = 748.99
$p >$ chi² = 0.0001	$p >$ chi² = 0	$p >$ chi² = 0
Pseudo R² = 0.0015	Pseudo R² = 0.0432	Pseudo R² = 0.091
n = 23,744	n = 23,744	n = 23,744

Notes: *$p < 0.05$. **$p < 0.01$. ***$p < 0.001$. Asterisks aligned with variable names indicate the results of multiple parameter likelihood ratio chi-square tests. Additional models included interactions between disability status and field of study, level of education, and income, but none of these additional terms significantly improved the overall model fit. Standard errors are available upon request.

holds when taking into consideration other possible influences at the same time. Indeed, the regression analyses show that even while controlling for socio-demographic, educational, and income characteristics, graduates with disabilities are found to be much less likely to report that their education matches their employment characteristics than their non-disabled counterparts. This finding is statistically significant ($p < 0.001$), indicating that we can be 99.9 per cent confident that the relationship between disability status and perceived qualification match is not due to chance.

In addition to disability status, men, visible minorities, and immigrants were also significantly less likely to report a close education-to-employment match ($p < 0.001$). The results also show that educational characteristics play a role, as both field of study and level of education were found to have a significant association with qualification match. After accounting for controls, graduates in the health and fitness, engineering, mathematics, and computer science fields were most likely to view their qualifications as closely related to their employment ($p < 0.001$), while graduates from physical and applied sciences, business, and liberal arts programs were, respectively, the least likely to view their qualifications matching their employment characteristics ($p < 0.001$). In terms of education level, college graduates were more satisfied with their work/educational qualification match than university graduates ($p < 0.001$). Graduates with trades and vocational certification also became significantly more likely than Bachelor's graduates to view a close connection between their educational qualification and the job they held ($p < 0.001$). These findings are consistent with existing studies that suggest college graduates may feel they are better fitted for the labour market demands of employers than their university counterparts (Athey and Hautaluoma, 1994; Livingstone, Wolff, and King, 2007)[9].

Underemployment

The second series of regressions (see Table 5.3) indicate whether or not an individual was underemployed for the employment held at the time of interview. As in the previous regressions, our goal is to see whether or not disability status has a significant impact on an individual's chances of being underemployed, and the extent to which disability may be a factor, when including other possible influences in the mix. Interestingly, the results reveal that disabled graduates were significantly more likely to be underemployed than their non-disabled counterparts, even when accounting for socio-demographic and educational characteristics. Yet this relationship no longer holds once income was also taken into consideration. These findings suggest that the disparity in disabled graduates' underemployment is dependent upon their income level.

As expected, educational characteristics also have a significant impact on one's chances of being underemployed. When looking at level of education, the results showed that graduates with trades and vocational certification were the most likely to be overeducated for the job they held ($p < 0.001$). College graduates, and those with advanced training (Master's, doctorate, or professional degrees), were also less likely to have their qualifications closely relate to their employment than those with a Bachelor's degree (the reference category) at $p < 0.001$. As stated earlier, a significance level of $p < 0.001$ indicates that we can be 99.9 per cent confident that the relationships witnessed are not due to chance.

Moreover, field of study was also found to have a significant association with underemployment. Those in the "Other" fields had the least risk of underemployment ($p < 0.001$), followed by graduates listed in the health and fitness fields and graduates from engineering, mathematics, and computer science, respectively ($p < 0.001$). Graduates from liberal arts fields were the most likely to be underemployed ($p < 0.001$).

Table 5.3 Binary Logistic Regressions Predicting Job Qualification for the 2005 Cohort of Canadian Post-secondary Graduates

	Model 1		Model 2		Model 3	
	Coeff.	p	Coeff.	p	Coeff.	p
Constant	0.057	*	−0.033	-	−9.721	***
Disability						
Yes	−0.394	***	−0.298	*	−0.162	-
No			-	-	-	-
Sex						
Male			−0.299	***	−0.471	***
Female			-	-	-	-
Age			−0.137	***	−0.218	***
Age²			0.104	***	0.185	***
Marital Status						
Not married			0.091	-	0.027	-
Married			-	-	-	-
Dependent Children						
Yes			−0.162	*	−0.152	*
No			-	-	-	-
Visible Minority Status						
Visible minority			−0.063	-	−0.015	-
Non-minority			-	-	-	-
Immigrant Status						
Immigrant			−0.131	-	−0.061	-
Non-immigrant			-	-	-	-
Parental Education						
Parents did not attend post-secondary			0.012	-	0.003	-
At least one parent with post-secondary			-	-	-	-
Region				***		***
Ontario			-	-	-	-
Atlantic provinces			−0.053	-	0.097	-
Quebec			0.035	-	0.093	-
Western provinces			−0.2	***	−0.257	***

continued

Table 5.3 continued

	Model 1		Model 2		Model 3	
	Coeff.	p	Coeff.	p	Coeff.	p
Bursaries/Grants						
Yes			0.081	-	0.09	-
No			-	-	-	-
Government Loans						
Yes			0.015	-	0.018	-
No			-	-	-	-
Scholarships						
Yes			0.206	***	0.174	**
No			-	-	-	-
Other Loans						
Yes			0.088	-	0.068	-
No			-	-	-	-
Field of Study				***		***
Liberal arts	-	-	-	-	-	-
Business			0.534	***	0.328	***
Physical and applied sciences			0.351	***	0.246	**
Engineering/comp. sci.			0.848	***	0.583	***
Health			0.848	***	0.648	***
Other			0.882	***	0.784	***
Level of Schooling				***		***
University (undergrad.)	-	-	-	-	-	-
Trades			−1.019	***	−0.699	***
College			−0.671	***	−0.488	***
University (advanced)			−0.554	***	−0.785	***
Income					0.932	***

Wald chi²(1) = 11.62   Wald chi²(24) = 600.03   Wald chi²(25) = 800.96

$p > $ chi² = 0.0007 $p > $ chi² = 0 $p > $ chi² = 0

Pseudo R^2 = 0.0010   Pseudo R^2 = 0.0492   Pseudo R^2 = 0.0757

n = 23,744 n = 23,744 n = 23,744

Notes: * $p < 0.05$. ** $p < 0.01$. ***$p < 0.001$. Asterisks aligned with variable names indicate the results of multiple parameter likelihood ratio chi-square tests. Additional models included interactions between disability status and field of study, level of education, and income, but none of these additional terms significantly improved the overall model fit. Standard errors are available upon request.

Summary and Implications

This study makes several contributions to our current understanding on the impact of disability on school-to-work transitions in Canada. Much of the existing research has not drawn on nationally representative data to characterize the experiences of young workers. The NGS provides a nice picture of the inequalities faced by graduates with disabilities who graduated in 2005.

Overall, the link between school and work is much looser than human capital theory suggests. Consistent with previous studies (Frank and Walters, 2012; Walters, 2004; Bills, 2004; Livingstone, 1999; Athey and Hautaluoma, 1994), a substantial portion of new post-secondary graduates enter jobs that do not often utilize their skills' potential. Both objective measures of underemployment and subjective measures of mismatch tell a similar story—finding work at one's level of expertise continues to be a problem for many new graduates.

The situation was especially problematic for youth with disabilities. Disability was shown to have a significant effect on graduates' perspectives of qualification match to the employment they have secured. Disability was also observed to have an impact on underemployment, although the relationship weakened when income was taken into consideration.

In addition to graduates with disabilities, visible minorities and respondents who held immigrant status were all significantly more likely to perceive education-to-work mismatch. These findings complement previous work that revealed visible minorities (Maume, 1999; Louie, 2004; Ogbu and Simons, 1998; Ong, 2005) and immigrants (Li, 2001) are more likely to face blocked mobility opportunities in securing lucrative employment. Interestingly, however, women were less likely to perceive education-work mismatch and experience underemployment than men.

Our results suggest that field of study and level of education choices of graduates also play a role in influencing both perceived and actual qualification match, even after controlling for income. Certain degrees and fields are more likely to mesh with labour market demands than others. The outcomes experienced by recent graduates echoes that of previous cohorts of the NGS (Finnie, 2001; Walters, 2004). Interestingly, college, trades, and advanced university graduates in our analyses were found to have weaker qualification matches to their employment than university undergraduates, despite being more likely to perceive a close match between education and work than Bachelor's graduates.

The fields of study results are also consistent with previous cohorts. That is, liberal arts degrees still remain the least likely to provide satisfactory results in terms of qualification match. Unfortunately, disabled graduates, compared to their non-disabled counterparts, were significantly more likely to graduate from liberal arts programs. At the same time, however, disabled individuals were also more likely to graduate from the trades and college, so their likelihood of perceived or actual mismatch may have been partially offset by virtue of their institution choices.

It is important to note that because the aggregate measure of disability within the National Graduate Surveys, we are unable to distinguish among disability types. Recent research has shown that workforce outcomes vary both by disability type (learning and physical disabilities) as well as disability severity (Sanford et al., 2011; Garlaneau and Radulescu, 2009; Janus, 2009; Robert and Harlan, 2006; Trainor, 2008; Blackorby and Wagner, 1996). Should such data become available in Canada, our understanding of the school-work match would benefit from analyses that capture the heterogeneity of individuals with disabilities.

According to credentialist theory, we might expect that employers will select candidates on the basis of their credentials, yet the disconnect between formally credentialed youth with disabilities and job qualifications shows evidence that additional structural barriers exist in the workforce. Despite controlling for the effects of educational characteristics and socio-demographic differences, disability continued to have a significant impact on employment match. While the current data will not allow us to disentangle the issue, our results do align with previous work that suggests the relative inequalities in the mismatch of education and work indicate that new graduates with disabilities continue to face barriers in the workforce.

Questions for Critical Thought

1. Consider human capital theory and credentialism: in what ways do these two perspectives view the link between education and work differently?
2. Discuss the similarities and differences between underemployment and self-perceived mismatch. Is it possible to have one without having the other? Explain.
3. How does credentialism relate to underemployment and self-perceived mismatch; in what ways are they conceptually linked?
4. You have been appointed as a policy-maker responsible for addressing the difficulties new graduates face transitioning into the labour market; what suggestions would you propose to encourage equality for (1) disabled graduates; and (2) all post-secondary graduates?

Glossary

Credentialism The practice of hiring individuals with higher levels of formal education because of a surplus of such individuals rather than satisfying the demands of a job. A consequence of this is that formal education becomes rewarded less for its knowledge base and abilities, and more for its symbolic representation of completing a credential tier.

Human capital theory The perspective that people intentionally and rationally invest their time, effort, and money into higher education as a means to acquire greater labour market returns. This self-investment is recognized by employers (identifying the worker as being more skilled and productive), who in turn are willing to pay higher wages.

Knowledge-based economy A system of consumption and production that is characterized by the production of intellectual goods and services, emphasises technological advancement, and rewards workers for their knowledge and skills.

Self-perceived education–job mismatch A subjective measure of education–job match that shows how much an individual believes the skills required to perform on the job differ from those acquired in his or her formal education.

Underemployment The situation where an individual's employment fails to utilize the level of training or skill that he or she has obtained through formal education or when there are unmet expectations for monetary returns on investment in formal education.

Notes

1. This category included areas that could not be adequately captured in the above fields such as education, recreational and counselling services, interdisciplinary studies, unknown, or unclassified fields not specified and undeclared.

2. Parental education, coded as whether or not an individual had at least one parent with a post-secondary education, serves as a proxy for socio-economic status.

3. Indicator coding (0/1) was used for categorical variables.

4. Additional models (not shown) include interactions between disability and field of study, level of education, and income to see if the gaps between disabled and non-disabled graduates vary across educational characteristics. None of these additional terms significantly improved the model fit, and thus are not presented.

5. Subsequent analysis of Table 1 reveals that disabled graduates were approximately four years older on average ($p < 0.001$), were less likely to have dependent children than non-disabled graduates ($p < 0.05$), were less likely to have a parent who had attended post-secondary education ($p < 0.001$), were more likely to be a visible minority ($p < 0.001$) and less likely to hold immigrant status ($p < 0.001$), and had equal instances of scholarships and bursaries than their non-disabled counterparts ($p < 0.001$). Disabled graduates' earned roughly 91 per cent of the annual income earned by non-disabled graduates ($38,487 and $42,212, respectively).

6. Additional analyses (not shown) revealed that about 31 per cent of all graduates in the NGS perceived a mismatch between their education and employment.

7. Additional analyses (not shown) indicate that about 51 per cent of all graduates in the NGS were underemployed.

8. The following set of results applies to all post-secondary graduates in Canada who provided responses for each of the variables included in our analyses. A filter was applied to the data to rule out any missing cases via list-wise deletion, ensuring that all models used in these analyses had the same sample size ($n = 23,744$).

9. It is important to note that a number of controls were no longer significant after income was added to the model, including age, the presence of dependent children, the access to student grants and scholarships as well as other loans, and immigrant status.

References

Andres, L., Anisef, P., Krahn, H., Looker, D., and Thiessen, V. "The persistence of social structure: Cohort, class and gender effects on the occupational aspirations and expectations of Canadian youth." *Journal of Youth Studies* 2(3) (1999): 261–82.

Anisef, P., Axelrod, P., Baichman-Anisef, E., James, C., and Turrittin, A. *Opportunity and Uncertainty: Life Course Experiences of the Class of '73.* Toronto: University of Toronto Press, 2000.

Athey, T., and Hautaluoma, J. "Effects of applicant over education, job status, and job gender stereotype on employment decisions." *The Journal of Social Psychology* 134(40) (1994): 439–52.

Becker, G.S. *Human Capital: A Theoretical and Empirical Analysis.* Chicago: University of Chicago Press, 1975.

Bills, D. "Credentials, signals, and screens: Explaining the relationship between schooling and job assignment." *Review of Educational Research* 73(Winter) (2003): 441–9.

Bills, D. *The Sociology of Education and Work.* Malden, MA: Wiley, 2004.

Blackorby, J., and Wagner, M. "Longitudinal postschool outcomes of youth with disabilities: Findings from the National Longitudinal Transition Study." *Exceptional Children* 62 (1996): 399–413.

Brown, D. "The social sources of educational credentialism: Status cultures, labor markets, and organizations." *Sociology of Education* 74(Special issue) (2001): 19–34.

Cheatham, G.A., Smith, S.J., Elliott, W., and Friedline, T. "Family assets, postsecondary education, and students with disabilities: Building on progress and overcoming challenges." *Children and Youth Services Review* 35(7) (2013): 1078–86.

Collins, R. *The Credential Society.* New York: Academic Press, 1979.

Canadian University Survey Consortium (CUSU). *Graduating Students Survey.* 2009. Retrieved 17 December 2013 from: www .cusc-ccreu.ca/publications/rpt_CUSC_ Master_V3_2009-1.pdf

Davies, S., Maldonado, V., and Zarifa, D. "Effectively maintaining inequality in Toronto?

Predicting student choice of Ontario universities." *Canadian Review of* Sociology 51(1) (2014): 22–53.

Fevre, R., Rees, G., and Gorard, S. "Some sociological alternatives to Human Capital Theory and their implications for research on post-compulsory education and training." *Journal of Education and Work* 12(2) (1999): 117–40.

Fichten, C.S., Jorgensen, S., Havel, A., Berile, M., Ferraro, V., Landry, M.-E., Fiset, A.D., Juhel, J.-C., Chwojka, C., Nguyen, M.N., Amsel, R., and Asuncion, J. "What happens after graduation? Outcomes, employment, and recommendations of recent junior/community college graduates with and without disabilities." *Disability & Rehabilitation* 34(11) (2012): 917–24.

Finnie, R. "Fields of plenty, fields of lean: The early labour market outcomes of Canadian university graduates by discipline." *Canadian Journal of Higher Education* 31(1) (2001): 141–76.

Finnie, R., and M. Frenette. "Earning differences by major field of study: Evidence from three cohorts of recent Canadian graduates." *Economics of Education Review* 22(2) (2003): 179–92.

Frank, K., and Walters, D. "Exploring the alignment between postsecondary education programs and labour market outcomes." *Canadian Journal of Higher Education* 42(3) (2012): 93–115.

Garlaneau, D., and Radulescu, M. *Employment among the Disabled.* Cat. no. 75-001-X. Ottawa: Statistics Canada.

Hale, T.W., Hayghe, H.V., and McNeil, J.M. "Persons with disabilities: labor market activity, 1994." *Monthly Labor Review* 121(9) (1998): 3–12.

Handel, M.J. "Skills mismatch in the labor market." *Annual Review of Sociology* 29(1) (2003): 135–65.

Holmes, A., and Silvestri, R. *Employment Experience of Ontario Postsecondary Graduates with Learning Disabilities.* Toronto: Higher Education Quality Council of Canada, 2011.

Janus, A.L. "Disability and the transition to adulthood." *Social Forces* 88(1) (2009): 99–120.

Krahn, H. "Choose your parents carefully: Social class, post-secondary education, and occupational outcomes." In *Social Inequality in Canada: Patterns, Problems, and Policies*, E. Grabb and N. Guppy (eds.), (171–89). Toronto: Pearson Prentice Hall, 2009.

Lehmann, W. "'I just didn't feel like I fit in': The role of habitus in university

drop-out decisions." *Canadian Journal of Higher Education* 37(2) (2007): 89–110.

Li, P. "The market worth of immigrants' educational credentials." *Canadian Public Policy* 27, 1 (2001): 23–38.

Livingstone, D.W. *The Education–Jobs Gap: Underemployment or Economic Democracy.* Toronto: Garamond Press, 1999.

Livingstone, D.W, "Job requirements and workers' learning: Formal gaps, informal closure, systemic limits." *Journal of Education and Work* 23 (3) (2010): 207–31.

Looker, E.D. "In search of credentials: Factors affecting young adults' participation in postsecondary education." *The Canadian Journal of Higher Education* 27(2) (1997): 1–36.

Louie, V.S. *Compelled to Excel: Immigration, Education, and Opportunity among Chinese Americans.* Palo Alto: Stanford University Press, 2004.

Lowe, G. "Labour markets, inequality, and the future of work." In *Social Inequality in Canada: Patterns, Problems and Policies*, J. Curtis, E. Grabb and N. Guppy (eds.), (148–64). Fourth edition. Toronto: Pearson Education, 2004.

Lucas, S.R. "Effectively maintained inequality: education transitions, track mobility, and social background effects." *American Journal of Sociology* 106(6) (2001): 1642–90.

Lynk, M.S. "Disability and work: The transformation of the legal status of employees with disabilities in Canada." In *Law Society of Upper Canada Special Lectures, 2007: Employment Law*, R. Echlin and C. Paliare (eds.), (189–257). Toronto: Irwin Law, 2008.

Madaus, J., Foley, T., McGuire, J., and Ruban, L. "A follow-up Investigation of university graduates with learning disabilities." *Career Development for Exceptional Individuals* 24(2) (2001): 133–46.

Maume Jr, D. "Glass ceilings and glass escalators: Occupational segregation and race and sex differences in managerial promotions." *Work and Occupations* 26 (1999): 482–509.

McCloy U., and DeClou, L. *Disability in Ontario: Postsecondary Education Participation Rates, Student Experience and Labour Market Outcomes.* Toronto: Higher Education Quality Council of Ontario, 2013.

McLean, S., and Rollwagen, H. "Educational expansion or credential inflation? The evolution of part-time study by adults at McGill University, Canada." *International Journal of Lifelong Education* 29(6) (2010): 739–755. DOI 10.1080/02601370.2010.523944

McMahon, B.T. "An overview of workplace discrimination and disability." *Journal of Vocational Rehabilitation* 36 (2012): 135–9.

Officer, S. "Struggling to remain employed: Learning strategies of workers with disabilities and the education-job match." In *Education and Jobs: Exploring the Gaps*, D.W. Livingstone (ed.), (257–79). Toronto: University of Toronto Press, 2009.

Ogbu, J.U., and Simons, H.D. "Voluntary and involuntary minorities: A cultural-ecological theory of school performance with some implications for education." *Anthropology and Education Quarterly* 29(2) (1998): 155–88.

Ong, M. "Body projects of young women of color in physics: Intersections of gender, race, and science." *Social Problems* 52(4) (2005): 593–617.

Raftery, A., and Hout, M. "Maximally maintained inequality: Expansion, reform, and opportunity in Irish education, 1921–75." *Sociology of Education* 66 (1993): 41–62.

Robert, P.M., and Harlan, S.L. "Mechanisms of disability discrimination in large bureaucratic organizations: Ascriptive inequalities in the workplace." *Sociological Quarterly* 47(4) (2006): 599–630.

Robst, J. "Education, college major, and job match: Gender differences in reasons for mismatch." *Education Economics* 15(2) (2007): 159–75.

Sanford, C., Newman, L., Wagner, M., Cameto, R., Knokey, A.M., and Shaver, D. *The Post-high School Outcomes of Young Adults with Disabilities up to 6 Years after High School. Key Findings from the National Longitudinal Transition Study-2 (NLTS2)* (NCSER 2011-3004). Menlo Park: SRI International, 2011.

Schatzel, K., Strandholm, K., and Callahan, T. "An educational option for those facing lay-off: A human capital perspective." *Human Resource Development International* 15(3) (2012): 303–19.

Schur, L. "Dead-end jobs or a path to economic well-being? The consequences of non-standard work among people with disabilities." *Behavioral Sciences and the Law* 20 (2002): 601–20.

Schur, L., Kruse, D., Blasi, J., and Blanck, P. "Is disability disabling in all workplaces? Workplace disparities and corporate culture." *Industrial Relations* 48(3) (2009): 381–410. DOI 10.1111/j.1468-232X.2009.00565.x

Shuey, K., and Jovic, E. "Disability accommodation in nonstandard and precarious employment arrangements." *Work and Occupations* 40(2) (2013): 174–205. Retrieved from: http://resolver.scholarsportal.info/resolve/07308884/v40i0002/174_dainapea. DOI 10.1177/0730888413481030.

Sykes, G., Schneider, B.L., Plank, D.N., and Ford, T.G. *Handbook of Education Policy Research.* New York: Routledge, 2009.

Trainor, A. "Using cultural and social capital to improve postsecondary outcomes and expand transition models for youth with disabilities." *The Journal of Special Education* 42(3) (2008): 148–62.

Trupin, L., and Yelin, E.H. "Disability and the characteristics of employment: An analysis of the California Work and Health Survey." *Monthly Labor Review* May (2003): 20–31.

Walters, D. "The relationship between postsecondary education and skill: Comparing credentialism with human capital theory." *The Canadian Journal of Higher Education* 34(2) (2004): 97–124.

Walters, D., and Zarifa, D. "Earnings and employment outcomes for male and female postsecondary graduates of co-op and non-co-op programmes." *Journal of Vocational Education & Training* 60(4) (2008): 377–99.

Wilkens, C.P., and Hehir, T.P. "Deaf education and bridging social capital: A theoretical approach." *American Annals of the Deaf* 153(3) (2008): 275–84.

Zarifa, D. "Persistent inequality or liberation from social origins? Determining who attends graduate school in Canada's expanded postsecondary system." *Canadian Review of Sociology* 49(2) (2012a): 109–37.

Zarifa, D. "Choosing fields in an expansionary era: Comparing Canada and the United States." *Research in Social Stratification and Mobility*" 30(3) (2012b): 328–51.

Zarifa, D., and Walters, D. "Revisiting Canada's brain drain: Evidence from the 2000 cohort of Canadian university graduates." *Canadian Public Policy* 34(3) (2008): 305–20.

Zarifa, D., Walters, D., and Seward, B. "The earnings and employment outcomes of the 2005 cohort of Canadian postsecondary graduates with disabilities." *Canadian Review of Sociology.* (Forthcoming).

Part II

Dimensions of Inequality
Class, Gender, Race, Ethnicity, and Sexuality

Introduction

Although issues of inequality were already fundamental to chapters in Part I, the chapters in Part II more directly look at the experiences of specific groups that struggle at school for various reasons. These chapters also reflect changes in the discipline more broadly. Early research about educational inequality was exclusively concerned with issues of social class. Comparing schools working- and middle-class neighbourhoods, Anyon (1980) showed that children are taught differently depending on their class background. Children in the working-class schools were exposed to pedagogical strategies that are rote, mechanical and inflexible, thus learning to become obedient workers. In contrast, the teaching styles used with children in middle-class schools allowed for flexibility, creativity, and students' input, which Anyon interpreted as the types of skills needed to enter the managerial class. Oakes (2005) showed that the same differences can be observed between pedagogical strategies in vocational and academic streams in public schools. Moreover, her research identified that working-class and African-American children were far more likely to be placed in vocational streams, which not only affected their learning environment, but also suggested unfair stream placement processes.

Countering this structuralist claim, Willis (1977), in his famous ethnography of the "Hammertown" Lads, put forward his resistance thesis, claiming that rather than being the victims of structural conditions over which they have no control, working-class youth actively resist the middle-class norms and culture of schools. Bourdieu's (1977, 1990) cultural reproduction approach seeks to find a compromise between structural and agency explanations, suggesting that a middle-class habitus (that is, the attitudes and behaviours that emerge from a middle-class upbringing and social background) is rewarded, whereas working-class knowledge is not. This in turn sets up students for success or struggle at school. As Davies and his co-authors have already argued in Chapter 2, middle-class parents, indeed, more successfully engage on behalf of their children and thus increase their chances of success at school. Middle-class parents can do this, because their own educational experiences are better aligned with that of teachers and school administrators. Parents with lower levels of education tend to approach schools in a more guarded, deferential, or hostile way, as they themselves may have had difficult schooling experiences in the past.

The research of Janice Aurini, Emily Milne, and Cathlene Hillier in Chapter 6 investigates these claims. Drawing on over 100 interviews with parents, they argue that while all parents consider themselves vigilant and concerned about their children's well-being and learning at school, middle-class parents do this to better effect than working-class parents, partly because they are more comfortable and persuasive in their interactions with school staff. As more educational responsibility is offloaded on to parents, the authors argue that we need to be aware that some parental voices are heard more clearly than others.

Especially in North America, concerns about class inequalities were eventually eclipsed by questions about observable and often stark differences in the educational attainment of ethnic minorities. Complicating debates about ethnic achievement in education is the fact that members of some minority groups substantially outperform those of the white majority, while others have historically struggled in schools. In Canada, two ethnic minority groups with attainment far below average are African-Canadians and members of First Nations. In contrast, in Chapter 7 Alison Taylor, Shadi Mehrabi, and Thashika Pillay ask why the educational aspirations of 15-year-old racialized immigrant youth are noticeably higher than those of Canadian-born white youth. The authors point to a far greater complexity in the educational experiences of these young students, as their academic success is accompanied by particular challenges related to their bi-cultural identity and uncommonly high parental aspirations and pressures, which often lead to strongly instrumental approaches to education.

The schooling of Indigenous Canadians is complex and forms one of the saddest chapters in Canadian history. Separated from their families, their home communities, and their Indigenous cultures, many First Nations children were subjected to physical and emotional abuse in the Residential School system. The trauma of Residential School continues to haunt Aboriginal Canadians not only in their struggles with the effects of abuse, but also in their ability to trust formal schooling with the safekeeping of their children and the transmission of valuable knowledge. In Chapter 8, Catherine Gordon and Jerry White chart the history of colonial education policy in Canada. Using data from four Censuses and the 2011 National Household Survey, they show how this colonial educational approach has left a legacy of Indigenous alienation and low attainment. Given the importance of formal educational credentials, Indigenous Canadians find themselves excluded from participation in a modern knowledge economy. Gordon and White conclude their chapter with a discussion of the *First National Control of First Nations Education Act* and a number of further recommendations for reform, that include the indigenization of curriculum and schools, more investment into First Nations schools, control by Indigenous Canadians, and the use of mentors and role models for the next generations of young First Nations students.

Jayne Baker, in Chapter 9, engages with the complex nature of understanding gender differences in education. Public discourse suggests that this is a reversal of fortune story. Whereas policy-makers were concerned with the educational prospects of girls and young women not so long ago, our attention has shifted to what many have called a boy crisis. Women now outperform boys in standardized tests in primary and secondary schools, they have lower rates of school non-completion, and they outnumber men in most university programs. Yet whether boys are in crisis and why that may be is hotly contested. Feminists have asked why the success of girls needs to be reconstructed as a problem for boys, rather than as an achievement to celebrate. Furthermore, it has been pointed out that women have yet to fully convert their educational advantage on the labour market, as they continue to earn lower incomes and are less likely found in positions of authority. Interestingly, whether the issue is girls' achievement problems in the past or that of boys today, an often-suggested solution is to institute single-gender schooling. In the past, single gender schooling was to free girls from more aggressive boys who dominate the learning environment. Today, all-boy schools are designed to re-engage boys who have become alienated by schools that are said to have become too feminized. Drawing on ethnographic observations in an elite all-boys and an elite all-girls school, Baker suggests that rather than fulfilling the potential to disrupt, such schools more likely reinforce traditional gender norms. Furthermore, her findings also lead us to be cautious about research that highlights the educational benefits of single-gender schools, as most of it conflates issues of gender and class.

Part II concludes with a chapter extending the discussion of gender at school, especially about the changing nature of being a boy. Michael Kehler argues, in Chapter 10, that changing images of what constitute an ideal form of masculinity are putting stress on boys' sense of self-worth. He shows that schools are key sites in which young people adapt to, reinforce and challenge heteronormative masculinities, perhaps nowhere more so than in the gym locker room. The physical appearance and prowess of boys has long been associated with their status in the school hierarchy (see, for example, Evans and Eder [1993]). Despite much greater acceptance of alternative sexualities, the pressure to be muscled and "buff" may have increased, which Kehler argues, oppresses and silences boys whose bodies do not conform to these ideals.

As with other dimensions of inequality discussed in Part II, even if the schooling conditions of traditionally disadvantaged social groups has improved (for example, that of women or many ethnic minorities), other social processes continue to have powerful, socially reproductive effects.

References

Anyon, J. "Social class and the hidden curriculum of work." *Journal of Education* 162(1) (1980): 67–92.

Bourdieu, P. *Outline of a Theory of Practice*. New York: Cambridge University Press, 1977.

Bourdieu, P. *The Logic of Practice*. Cambridge: Polity, 1990.

Evans, C., and Eder, D. "No exit: Processes of social isolation in middle school." *Journal of Contemporary Ethnography* 22(2) (1993): 139–70.

Oakes, J. *Keeping Track: How Schools Structure Inequality*. Second edition. New Haven & London: Yale University Press, 2005.

Willis, P. *Learning to Labour: How Working Class Kids Get Working Class Jobs*. Farnborough: Saxon House, 1977.

6

The Two Sides of "Vigilance"

Parent Engagement and Its Relationship to School Connections, Responsibility, and Agency

Janice Aurini, Emily Milne, and Cathlene Hillier

Introduction

In principle everyone is "for" parent engagement (Duch, 2005; Epstein, 2005; Sheldon and Epstein, 2005). The term **parent engagement** is used to describe parents' involvement in their children's schooling, including communicating with the school, volunteering, attending school functions, and supporting learning at home. These activities are seen to facilitate children's successful movement through the education system. Despite the widespread support for parent engagement, quantitative research has failed to consistently find a strong relationship between parent engagement and children's academic achievement (El Nokali, Bachman, and Votruba-Drzal, 2010; Fan and Chen, 2001; McNeal, 2012). These findings (or non-findings), however, have not diminished enthusiasm for parent engagement initiatives, nor the general belief that school success depends on high levels of parent engagement (Deslandes and Bertrand, 2005).

Drawing on interviews with 122 parents, we examine how parents understand what it means to be an "engaged parent" and the concrete actions they associate with those definitions. While all parents see themselves as "vigilant," the lower socio-economic status (SES) families in our sample are unable to translate those values into effective advocacy, the identification of learning difficulties, and the acquisition of resources for their children. The results of this study demonstrate the diversity of actions associated with what it means to be an engaged parent and help explain why many parent engagement initiatives have little impact on students' behavioural and academic outcomes.

Literature Review

Since the 1960s (for example, Coleman et al. [1966]), a large body of research has found that parent-SES predicts educational outcomes more than "school-effects" (for example, school funding, location, class size) (Alon, 2009; Davies and Aurini, 2013; Frenette, Mueller, and Sweetman, 2010; Gamoran, 2001; Sirin, 2005). Children from disadvantaged backgrounds tend to have lower grades and are less likely to finish high school or enter post-secondary education. Achievement gaps are present even before students begin school. Students from lower-SES families are less likely to be "school ready"; they have a less expansive vocabulary and knowledge of numbers and have shorter attention spans (Coleman et al., 1966; Conley and Albright, 2004; Janus and Duku, 2007; Statistics Canada, 2005, 2008; Willms, 2009). Lower-SES families are also less likely to understand how schools work, where to get resources, or how to navigate institutional processes such as how to get a child into a special program (Lareau, 2011).

While not specifically targeting lower-SES families, the emphasis on parent engagement emerges from this empirical reality. Parent engagement policies encourage parents to monitor their children's school progress, participate in school activities, and have ongoing communication with educators. Efforts to strengthen parent engagement are also believed to recalibrate parenting practices and give lower-SES parents the tools to align with academic expectations. The following quote from a recent policy document captures how parent engagement is framed in most provinces in Canada (Ontario Ministry of Education, 2010, 14):

> Parental involvement is a broad term and includes such things as good parenting, helping with homework, serving on school councils and board committees, communicating and meeting with teachers and volunteering in the classroom or on school trips. All forms of parental involvement are beneficial. In every form, parental involvement in education shows children that their parents care about what they are doing and learning, and that they value a good education.

The question must be asked is "all" and "every form" of parent engagement beneficial? A few studies have found moderate to strong associations between parent engagement and schooling outcomes including grades and disciplinary problems (Barnard, 2004). Most research, however, has been mixed at best (Fan and Chen, 2001). A recent meta-analysis of parent involvement and homework help found a positive relationship for elementary and high school students, but not for middle-school students. This analysis also found a positive association for verbal achievement outcomes, but a negative association for mathematic achievement (Patall, Cooper, and Robinson, 2008). A handful of studies have been more damning, finding a negative relationship (Senler and Sungur, 2009) or no relationship between parent involvement and academic achievement or student well-being (Reay, 2005). As McNeal (2012, 80) observes, "[T]he degree of inconsistency surrounding parent involvement effects on student outcomes is perhaps the most troubling aspect of the research done to date."

Researchers have sometimes turned to the "reactive hypothesis" to explain these less than impressive results (Epstein, 1988). The reactive hypothesis is premised on the assumption that parents become more involved when their child is experiencing acute behaviour or academic difficulty. In other words, some parents adopt a "reactive" rather than "proactive" approach to their children's schooling. McNeal (2012), however, found no empirical support for this hypothesis. Instead, his research found that behaviour or academic challenges often lead to less rather than more parent involvement. As McNeal (2012, 80) asks: "Can it be that some forms of involvement are good and others bad?" (for examples, see Lareau and Munoz [2012] and Lareau and Shumar [1996]).

Our analysis extends this question and considers whether some forms are more or less optimal in terms of benefitting children's literacy or numeracy, accessing resources or resolving behavioural or other difficulties. In this chapter we examine how parents define parent engagement, the actions they associate with that definition, and how those understandings inform the resulting parent engagement strategy that is adopted.

Methods

This project started with two basic questions: How do parents define parent engagement? How do these understandings inform the nature of the parental engagement strategies adopted? To answer these questions, we interviewed parents at Smith Academy School (SAS) and Central Alexander School (CAS). These schools are located in Ontario, approximately one hour apart, in economically depressed neighbourhoods. Both schools are in urban locations that are peppered with a mixture of family homes, apartment buildings, businesses, and industry.

Almost 33 per cent of SAS and 50 per cent of CAS students live in low-income households, compared to the provincial average of 16.5 per cent. Only 18 per cent of SAS and 8 per cent of CAS parents have some university education, compared to almost 37 per cent of the province's adult population. Almost 25 per cent of SAS and 31 per cent of CAS students receive special education services compared to just over 14 per cent of the province's student population. The median family income of SAS and CAS families is just over $40,000, much lower than the provincial average of $69,000 (Statistics Canada, 2006)[1]. CAS and SAS consistently fare poorly on provincially mandated standardized tests.

In total we conducted 118 interviews with 122 participants. Parent interviewees also included a handful of grandparents, aunts, and a step-mother who currently fill the role of primary caregiver. Interviews were conducted on-site, lasted 45 minutes to 3 hours, and were digitally recorded with the permission of the interviewee. Most interviews were conducted by only one member of the research team to accommodate scheduling and to develop a more intimate exchange with the participant.

What became obvious from our analysis is the difference within our sample. While CAS and SAS are situated within relatively economically depressed neighbourhoods, a proportion of families in our sample included college diploma and university degree holders. Some of these interviewees experienced downward mobility as a result of a marriage break-up, divorce, or illness. In rarer cases, some respondents' current financial circumstance will likely improve once they complete their education at the local university or secure employment that is commensurate with their education (see Table 6.1 below). Not shown here, we also asked participants their total family income. Of the 95 families who responded to this question, 28 per cent had family incomes less than $30,000 and 32 per cent had family incomes that range from $30,000 to $69,999. Approximately 20 per cent of the participants in our sample earn more than $70,000 per year. We use these parents with higher levels of education and income as a point of comparison to highlight vastly different orientations toward schooling processes.

Table 6.1 Description of Education: 2012 and 2013

	No Response	Less than High School	High School Diploma	College / Some College Education	University / Some University Education
SAS (n = 72)	16.7% (12)	4.2% (3)	16.7% (12)	33.3% (24)	29.2% (21)
CAS (n = 50)	20.0% (10)	14.0% (7)	14.0% (7)	40.0% (20)	12.0% (6)
Total (n = 122)	18.0% (22)	8.2% (10)	15.6% (19)	36.1% (44)	22.1% (27)

Note: Percentages have been rounded to the nearest tenth. Participants only, not including spouses or partners.

Findings

While many parents describe themselves as "highly engaged," these shared value systems do not necessarily generate an optimal parent engagement strategy or outcome for their children in terms of advocating effectively, accessing resources, or identifying potential behaviour or academic problems. Our data finds that parent engagement varies along three key dimensions: (1) Connections and Comfort Level; (2) Roles and Responsibility; and (3) Agency.

Connections and Comfort Level

The importance of home-school connections has been at the forefront of education policy-making and research. In theory positive home-school relationships afford schools the opportunity to communicate expectations, share pedagogical strategies, and, in some cases, work closely with parents. Researchers have noted that lower-SES parents have greater difficulty connecting with schools; in particular such families feel less comfortable talking to teachers and staff (for example, principals, social workers) compared to higher-SES parents (see for example, Lareau [1987]).

Interestingly, many of our interviewees believe they have a strong relationship with their child's teacher. Several described feeling "very comfortable" engaging with the professionals at the school and readily provided an example of past communications with school staff. Yet problems remain. Parents vary greatly in terms of their "**linguistic capital**"—the relative ability to communicate effectively (Bourdieu, 1992; Reay, 1999).

In our sample, feelings of connection and comfort do not necessarily translate into meaningful and productive relationships with teachers or staff members. Parents' journey through the education system, personal biographies, or status differences between themselves and staff loom large. While lower-SES families felt "comfortable" talking to teachers at the school BBQ or school outing, they do not feel empowered to challenge the authority of school staff or to push for additional educational services even when they are acutely aware that their child is struggling. The higher-SES parents in our sample felt no such deference. Such parents readily question the materials, programs, and services offered and do not take "No" for an answer. These findings question whether attempts to improve connections with parents, however sincere and well-meaning they are, improve parents' ability to effectively manoeuvre complex institutional processes.

Lower Levels of Comfort

> I found my daughter's kindergarten teacher difficult to talk to. . . . It was really hard to open up to her because she seemed stand offish.
>
> Elaine, SAS parent

In the abstract, almost all of our interviewees described feeling connected to the school and comfortable with staff. Yet in practice, the lower-SES interviewees had difficulty engaging with teachers or the materials that were sent home. Many of these parents mentioned that they did not enjoy school. Several of these parents had not finished secondary school or had returned to school as an adult to earn a GED. Such parents described watching helplessly from the sidelines as their children experienced the same challenges.

Elaine (SAS parent), a stay-at-home mother of three young children (ages five, three, and five months), describes her own difficulties helping her daughter. Elaine has a high school diploma and her husband has a college certificate in IT. At the suggestion of a friend, Elaine's oldest daughter sees a speech therapist. However, she continues to worry about her daughter's speech delays and weak literacy skills. She attended the first parent-teacher interview night at the beginning of the year, but felt her concerns were not taken seriously:

> I needed some help and some guidance and I wasn't given that from the teacher. All I got from her kindergarten teacher was "Oh, it's all good, she's in kindergarten. We don't really get on it until they are in grade one so just feel it out, by grade one then we'll know." But then my argument was I don't want to wait until grade one to see if my daughter is behind. I want my daughter to always be, you know, up with the other kids because it affects her self-esteem when she sees all these other kids are reading and she's struggling.

Describing the teacher as "stand offish," Elaine no longer attends parent-teacher interviews. Her own experience as a struggling reader makes her feel uncomfortable approaching the teacher with confidence. She describes feeling ill-equipped to work with her daughter effectively at home, and home reading sessions often end in tears. Elaine, like many of the lower-SES parents we spoke to, wants to help her daughter succeed at school. Yet low levels of comfort, "not liking the teacher" and her own schooling experiences, limit Elaine's ability to help her child overcome learning, behavioural, or emotional challenges at school and at home.

Higher Levels of Comfort

> Parents need to put themselves out there to put themselves in a path of advice. You've got to get to the school, you've got to introduce yourself.
>
> Shannon, SAS parent

Unlike parents like Elaine, higher-SES parents not only felt more comfortable engaging with school officials but more importantly felt entitled to make demands on the school. Shannon, a mother of four children (ages 10, 9, 4, and 2), is a good example of how such parents engage comfortably and confidently with educators. Shannon is a Canada Post letter carrier and is currently working toward a Bachelor's degree; however, she was clear to point out that "[her] job is [her] kids." Her husband has completed some university and works as a private investigator. Based on the family income, they would be considered middle class (Statistics Canada, 2007).

Jonathan, her four-year-old son, has been diagnosed with Autistic Spectrum Disorder. At one and a half, she noticed her son was struggling with speech development. She was proactive in expressing her concerns to her pediatrician, who then connected her to speech services within her community. While on wait lists, Shannon made sure that her son was supported through other service providers and at home. When Jonathan was two years old, she began attending the Parent and Family Literacy Centre (PFLC) every day. Here, Shannon and her children receive guidance on socialization and learning strategies. The centre is located inside her children's school, and when Jonathan enters junior kindergarten in the following September, he will already be familiar with the school, the routine, the teachers, and the staff.

I have a history with the principal because I've been at that PFLC, so she's familiar with me. We already have a good relationship. Going into the school year, I'm very confident. In September, I will still be at the PFLC program with my youngest. It's kind of like I'm on call. If they've got an issue they can't handle, then they know where to find me, I'm there.

Shannon has spent a considerable amount of time within the school building and has become familiar with the teachers, the principal, and the school staff. She considers herself to be "part of the school," describing that she has "a feel for the school and how it's being run and how people are."

Roles and Responsibility

Fundamentally parent engagement initiatives encourage parents to be more directly involved in their children's schooling. Creating the daily agenda, sending home materials, and encouraging parents to help with homework are seen to help parents "institutionally align" with schools (see Lareau [2011]). Yet not all parents see themselves as "parent educators," nor do they believe it is their responsibility. Lower-SES parents "perceive a separation between home and school" (see Lareau and Shumar [1996, 30]), with the parent taking responsibility for food and shelter and the school taking responsibility for all matters related to their children's cognitive development and problems that arise when their child is on school grounds. Among our interviewees this perception is rooted in the parents' philosophy of parenting and also the deference they afford teachers' relatively high level of education and training. By way of contrast, our higher-SES interviewees see schools as a critical resource; but they believe that parents are ultimately responsible for their children's emotional, social, and cognitive development.

Lower Levels of Responsibility

> I'm more the type of parent where if it's not broken, you don't fix it.
>
> Matthew, CAS parent

While feelings of trust and connectedness with professionals—including teachers, doctors, and social workers—are tenuous at best, lower-SES parents are highly dependent on them. Part of this dependency is rooted in their philosophy of parenting. These parents articulate a distinct division of labour between families and schools, with the former taking responsibility for more basic care (for example, shelter), and the latter taking more responsibility for education (Lareau, 2011).

Matthew, a father at CAS, has a learning disability that prevents him from working. When his former common-law partner left his daughter alone for long periods of time at home, Social Services stepped in and the daughter was placed in a foster home. He worked with Social Services, taking parenting and cooking classes that enabled him to develop the necessary parenting skills to gain custody of his daughter. Matthew had dropped out of high school. He hopes his daughter will complete high school and work for the government after graduation. Matthew describes himself as "vigilant" when asked about his involvement in his daughter's education. He sets up learning games for her on the computer and buys math and literacy workbooks from the dollar store for her to work on at home. Matthew's knowledge of what his daughter is doing at school, however, is limited. Although he attends the parent-teacher interview each year, his engagement with teachers consists of greetings at drop-off and pick-up at his daughter's school. Matthew's daughter has some difficulty with math and he relies on the teacher to let him know what she needs to work on at home:

> I really don't have anything that I approach the teachers with because I figure if there's no complaints coming from my daughter, there's no complaints coming from the school, then there's no problems . . . a lot of the times the teachers will write down if she's having trouble with something and it gives me an idea on what I need to work with.

Matthew is clearly a loving and dedicated father who wants his daughter to succeed. Yet parents like Matthew defer to the nature and definition of parent engagement articulated by their children's school.

Higher Levels of Responsibility

> I constantly work with the teachers and we try to work together towards achieving goals for each child. . . . They let me know what they are doing [in class] or what we could practice [at home], if there are books we could read or stuff we could practice ahead of time.
>
> Loren, SAS parent

Higher-SES parents associate a wider range of actions with what it means to be an "engaged" parent. More than a mere "partner," these parents see themselves as directing their children's academic trajectories. Like most of our interviewees, these parents dutifully check their child's agenda, attend school events, ensure that homework is complete, and describe ongoing communication with their child's teacher. But beyond these actions, the higher-SES parents in our sample are also extremely proactive and hands-on. Loren, a mother of four children (ages nine, eight, six, and three months) believes parents are the primary educator. Loren and her husband each obtained a Master's degree in business and see it as their responsibility to ensure their children enjoy similar success:

> [Parents] play the principle role. At the end of the day it's your child. There's nobody who is going to take responsibility, it is yours. I only have this one chance to do it right. [Teachers] are preparing them for maybe work and I'm preparing them for life. The school is more concerned about learning skills. Literacy, numerical skills and stuff like that. The parent is building up a whole human being that encompasses so much more aspects than the school.

Beyond participating at school events and parent-teacher meetings, Loren's role also involves actively seeking out teachers and educational materials in order to support her children's learning at home. At the time of our interview, Loren had acquired the next year's curriculum for each of her children. She describes working on the curriculum at home and using it as a way to prepare and motivate her children. She actively monitors her children's learning and uses her interactions with teachers as an opportunity to design home learning activities that match each of her children's unique learning styles.

Agency

> the reliance on consensual language such as "partnership," "involvement" and "dialogue," which features strongly in the home-school literature, edits out tension and conflict, as well as the inequalities underlying them. (Reay [1999, 160] paraphrasing Vincent [1996])

Agency, the capacity of an individual or a group to make a choice and to act, is a fundamental assumption that is embedded in much of the parent engagement policy literature. Importantly, this belief assumes that families, with the right guidance, knowledge, and encouragement, have the ability to align with schooling processes in a manner that improves their children's academic trajectories. Yet efforts to include parents do little to improve parents' ability to challenge school authorities. Some parents also fear that questioning teachers or the principal could lead to the further intrusion of social service agencies. The higher-SES parents in our sample have no such reservations and readily push for changes and challenge teachers' authority.

Lower Levels of Agency

> If there is a problem, we have to be notified in order to help rectify the problem, if you're not then what do you do? . . . That is the general role of a teacher. You make sure they are learning. That is your responsibility. That is your job. That is what you get paid for.
>
> Christine, CAS parent

Christine exemplifies how the dependency on teachers creates feelings not only of helplessness but also disillusionment when a problem or issue has not been taken care of by the school or other professionals. Christine is a stay-at-home mother of three young children and her oldest child attends CAS. Christine struggles financially and emotionally, and various social service agencies have been involved intermittently since her first born was a baby. A high school drop-out, Christine hopes her children will finish high school.

Christine believes she has a good relationship with the staff and sees herself as highly engaged. She describes writing notes in the school agenda (a communication binder that is sent home daily), telephoning the school when her daughter is teased, and talking to the principal when her daughter came home with bruises from a "Twilight" game the children had been playing at recess. "Engaged" however does not mean "interfering," but rather communicating with the school when a problem arises.

The only time I see the need to communicate with the teacher is if there is a problem or something that I think she would need help with. The way I see it is leave it alone, if there is no need to interfere with it, then don't do it, because the second you do that, then they're going to introduce something else, then it's just going to get confusing.

As she explained, "When I see it at home I automatically assume they see it here." This assumption turned ugly in the spring leading up to our interview. Christine was "blindsided" when her daughter's teacher told her that she is "significantly" behind in her reading and writing. When asked about other forms of communication that should have signalled a problem much earlier on, Christine told us that if the problem was acute, the school should have initiated communication with her. Interestingly, this experience has not changed Christine's approach to parent engagement and when asked about how she plans to address her daughter's literacy problems next school year, she told us that she is waiting to hear back from the school.

Parents like Christine want to help their children succeed in school. They are not "reactive" in the classic sense of the term (Epstein, 1988), nor are they "proactive" (McNeal, 2012). Instead, they rely heavily on the school or other professionals to diagnose problems; when directly confronted with a problem, they readily accept assistance offered by the school but they rarely initiate contact. In these cases, the philosophical division between home and school limits communication with the school and ultimately affects their children's academic progress.

Higher Levels of Agency

I think parents should do everything they can to have a positive relationship with the teacher, know the teacher, and support being in regular contact with the teacher: what can I do at home to kind of help this?

Audrey, SAS parent

Not all of our interviews shared Christine's sense of powerlessness. The higher-SES parents in our sample do not hesitate to contact the school. These parents not only feel capable helping their child but also feel that it is their right. For such parents, schools and teachers are a part of an arsenal of resources at their disposal, along with online sources and books, professionals, community or parent groups, and friends.

Audrey (SAS parent) described a situation that had occurred when her son was in Grade 2. Placed in a split Grade 2/Grade 3 class, his teacher "Ms M" sent home work that was clearly at a Grade 3 level, rather than creating different homework for the Grade 2 students. Audrey and her husband, both teachers, scheduled a meeting and were shocked when Ms M told them to buy Grade 2 level books from a bookstore for their son to work on in class. Dissatisfied with this response, they talked to the principal and had their son moved to a Grade 2 class.

Parents like Audrey respect teachers and seek their advice. However, by their very definition of parenting, they are responsible for identifying various problems and potential solutions. As described by Audrey: "In order to get the answers that you want for your kids, you have to push through any obstacle. You just have to keep on pushing and *No* is not an answer, it's not in my vocabulary, especially for my kids." These parents "can't just sit back and wait for it to work itself out," and they have the confidence to trust their gut instinct. Although the outcome does not always address all of these parents' concerns, it nonetheless optimizes the potential outcome.

Conclusion

Parent engagement policies are a popular institutional response to family practices that may limit school success. The benefits of parent engagement strategies, however, hinge on the type of engagement including parents' connection and comfort level, how parents view their role in their children's schooling, and the degree to which parents feel empowered to advocate for their children's educational needs. While all of our parents saw themselves as "engaged," the lower-SES parents in our sample were not as successful at solving their children's social or academic difficulties. These parents often expressed a lot of frustration at their inability to access resources and problem-solve with teachers.

In our study, examples of "engagement" provided by lower-SES parents like Elaine included showing up to school on time, attending information sessions, volunteering, writing in the agenda, and helping with homework. While important, these actions speak more to parents' ability to align with a series of discrete administrative tasks; they do not necessarily translate into effective advocacy, problem identification, or the ability to access resources. At the other end of the spectrum, higher-SES parents like Shannon differ not necessarily in the intentionality of their actions, but rather in their ability to navigate the school system, advocate for resources, and, ultimately, facilitate their children's social and academic outcomes. Research on time use has also made this point by recognizing not only the type or quantity of time use but also the quality of time use and the intensity of parent involvement. As Leibowitz (1977, 244) notes, "[H]ow time is spent with children may be as important as how much time is spent."

Parent engagement policies are designed with the very best intentions, and we observed how such initiatives have a positive impact on how parents and their children felt about the schools where we conducted data collection. However, we should not be surprised that parent engagement policies do little to stem socio-economic effects. As Furstenberg (2011, 476) observes, "It is unrealistic to build a policy to reduce educational inequalities by mobilizing parents to adopt and mimic the techniques of most motivated and capable families." Higher-SES families by virtue of their high levels of education, occupational, or financial resources are simply better equipped to negotiate their children's successful movement through the education system.

Questions for Critical Thought

1. Define parent engagement and its theorized relationship to academic achievement.
2. What is the "reactive hypothesis"? Does this theory adequately explain higher levels of parent engagement? Why or why not?
3. Parent engagement is theorized to improve academic outcomes. Has research substantiated this theory?
4. Why have school boards in Canada and abroad adopted formal parent engagement policies?

5. How do lower-SES and higher-SES families see the "division of labour" between school and home when it comes to their child's education?

Glossary

Agency The capacity of an individual or a group to make a choice and to act.

Linguistic capital The mastery of language and the relative ability to effectively communicate with other people.

Parent engagement Describes parents' involvement in their children's lives inside and outside of schooling. The actions associated with parent engagement range widely and include everything from communicating with the school, volunteering for and attending school functions, and supporting learning at home. These activities are seen to facilitate children's successful movement through the education system. Parent engagement is also seen to improve children's emotional and social well-being and reduce behavioural problems.

Acknowledgements

This research was generously supported by an Insight Grant, funded by the Social Science and Humanities Research Council. We also thank the parents and school staff who generously gave us their time.

Notes

1. Data also come from school board websites hosted by the Ministry. To protect the confidentiality of participating schools and families, the links are not provided.

References

Alon, S. "The evolution of class inequality in higher education: Competition, exclusion, and adaptation." *American Sociological Review* 74 (2009): 731–55.

Barnard, W.M. "Parent involvement in elementary school and educational attainment." *Children and Youth Services Review* 26 (2004): 39–62.

Bourdieu, P. *Language and Symbolic Power*. Cambridge: Massachusetts Policy Press, 1992.

Coleman, J.S., Campbell, E.Q., Hobson, C.J., McPartland, J., Mood, A.M., Weinfeld, F.D., and York, R.L. *Equality of Educational Opportunity*. Washington: US Department of Health, Education & Welfare. Office of Education (OE-38001 and supp.), 1966.

Conley, D., and Albright, K. *After the Bell–Family Background, Public Policy, and Educational Success*. New York: Routledge, 2004.

Davies, S., and Aurini J. "Summer learning inequality in Ontario." *Canadian Public Policy* 30(2) (2013): 287–307.

Davies, S., Aurini, J., Jean-Pierre, J., and Milne, E. "Les effets des programmes d'été de littératie : Les théories d'opportunités d'apprentissage et les élèves « non-traditionnels » dans les écoles ontariennes francophones." *Canadian Journal of Sociology*. (Forthcoming).

Deslandes, R., and Bertrand, R. "Motivation of parent involvement in secondary-level schooling." *The Journal of Educational Research* 98 (2005): 164–75.

Duch, H. "Redefining parent involvement in Head Start: A two-generation approach." *Early Child Development and Care* 175 (2005): 23–35.

El Nokali, N.E., Bachman, H.J., and Votruba-Drzal, E. "Parent involvement and children's academic and social development in elementary school." *Child Development* 81 (2010): 988–1005.

Epstein, J.L. "How do we improve programs for parent involvement?" *Educational Horizons* 66 (1988): 58–9.

Epstein, J.L. "Links in a professional development chain: Preservice and inservice education for effective programs of school, family, and community partnerships." *The New Educator* 1 (2005): 125–41.

Fan, X., and Chen, M. "Parental involvement and students' academic achievement: A meta-analysis." *Educational Psychology Review* 13 (2001): 1–22.

Frenette, M., Mueller, R.E., and Sweetman, A. "Introduction: Deepening our understanding of young Canadians' participation in post-secondary education." In *Pursuing Higher Education in Canada: Economic, Social and Policy Dimensions*, Ross Finnie, Marc Frenette, Richard E. Mueller and Arthur Sweetman (eds.), (1–12). Montreal, Kingston: McGill-Queen's University Press, 2010.

Furstenberg, F.F. "The challenges of finding causal links between family educational practices and schooling outcomes." In *Whither Opportunity*, G.J. Duncan and R.J. Murnane (eds.), (465–82). New York: Russell Sage Foundation, 2011.

Gamoran, A. "American schooling and educational inequality: A forecast for the 21st century." *Sociology of Education* (Extra issue) (2001): 135–53.

Janus, M., and Duku, E. "The school entry gap: Socioeconomic, family, and health factors associated with children's school readiness to learn." *Early Education and Development* 18 (2007): 375–403.

Lareau, A. "Social class differences in family-school relationships: The importance of cultural capital." *Sociology of Education* 60(2) (1987): 73–85.

Lareau, A. *Unequal Childhoods. Class, Race, and Family Life: With an Update a Decade Later.* Second edition. Berkeley: University of California Press, 2011.

Lareau, A., and Munoz, V. "You're not going to call the shots: Structural conflict between the principal and the PTO at a suburban public elementary school." *Sociology of Education* 83 (2012): 201–18.

Lareau, A., and Shumar, W. "The problem of individualism in family-school policies." *Sociology of Education* 69 (1996): 24–39.

Leibowitz, A. "Parental inputs and children's achievements." *Journal of Human Resources* 12 (1977): 242–51.

McNeal, R.B. "Checking in or checking out: Investigating the parent involvement reactive hypothesis." *The Journal of Educational Research* 105 (2012): 79–89.

Ontario Ministry of Education. *Parents in partnership: A parent engagement policy for Ontario, 2010.* Retrieved 1 May 2012 from: www.edu.gov.on.ca/eng/parents/involvement/PE_Policy2010.pdf

Patall, E.A., Cooper, C., and Robinson, J.C. "Parent involvement in homework: A research synthesis." *Review of Educational Research* 78 (2008): 1039–101.

Reay, D. "Linguistic capital and home: School relationships: Mothers' interactions with their children's primary school teachers." *Acta Sociologica* 42(2) (1999): 159–68.

Reay, D. "Doing the dirty work of social class? Mothers' work in support of their children's schooling." *The Sociological Review* 53 (2005): 104–16.

Senler, B., and Sungur, S. "Parental influences on students' self-concept, task value beliefs, and achievement in science." *The Spanish Journal of Psychology* 12 (2009): 106–17.

Sheldon, S.B., and Epstein, J.L. "Involvement counts: Family and community partnerships and math achievement." *The Journal of Educational Research* 98 (2005): 196–206.

Sirin, S.R. "Socioeconomic status and academic achievement: A meta-analytic review of research." *Review of Educational Research* 75(3) (2005): 417–53.

Statistics Canada. "Student achievement in mathematics—The roles of attitudes, perceptions and family backgrounds." *Education Matters* (2005). Retrieved on 31 March 2013 from: www5.statcan.gc.ca/bsolc/olc-cel/olc-cel?lang=eng&catno=81-004-X20050017836

Statistics Canada. Census Tract Profile, 2006 Census (2006). Retrieved on 17 April 2013 from:

www12.statcan.ca/census-recensement/2006/dp-pd/prof/92-597/index.cfm?Lang=E

Statistics Canada. Study: Income Inequality and Redistribution (2007). Retrieved on 17 April 2013 from: www.statcan.gc.ca/daily-quotidien/070511/dq070511b-eng.htm

Statistics Canada. "Are 5-year-old children ready to learn at school? Family income and home environment contexts." (2008). Retrieved on 17 April 2013 from: www.statcan.gc.ca/pub/81-004-x/2007001/9630-eng.htm

Willms, J.D. "The critical transition from 'Learning-to-read' to 'Reading-to-learn.'" Paper presented at the Successful Transitions Conference sponsored by Human Resources and Skills Development Canada. Ottawa, 2009.

7

"You Have to Get That Degree"

Influences on the Educational and Career Aspirations of Racialized Immigrant Youth

Alison Taylor, Shadi Mehrabi, and Thashika Pillay

Introduction

Data from the Youth in Transition (2000) survey of 15-year-old Canadians suggest that the educational aspirations of racialized immigrant youth are noticeably higher than those of Canadian-born white youth. Even after controlling for parents' education and family income, an aspirational gap persists (Krahn and Taylor, 2005). Since a higher proportion of foreign-born youth are enrolled in university education, it also appears that, for many, these aspirations are being attained (Boyd, 2002; Dinovitzer, Hagan, and Parker, 2003). At the same time, there are large group differences in university attainment among children of immigrants with Asian Canadians, for example, showing higher levels of attainment than black or Filipino Canadians (Abada and Tenkorang, 2009).

This paper addresses the question of why **racialized** immigrant youth are aiming so high, with particular attention to family interactions and parent-child relationships. We share the view that families are an important focus for analysis since, like schools, they are often key sites for social reproduction. In particular, Bourdieu's concepts of social, cultural, and economic capital have been helpful in understanding the processes that lead to differential outcomes for youth from working-class and middle-class families (for example, Reay [1998]). However, minority ethnic groups' trajectories and experiences often contradict analyses based only on social class (Archer and Francis, 2007; Modood, 2004). An explanation for their drive for **social mobility** despite disadvantage is, therefore, required. Drawing on interviews with racialized immigrant youth and parents, this paper considers the extent to which Bourdieu's concepts of social and cultural capital and other conceptions inspired by his work—for example, "ethnic capital," and "aspirational capital"—are useful in explaining the experiences of racialized immigrant youth and parents.

Bourdieu's Concepts and Racialized Immigrant Youth

The strategies of a "player" and everything that defines his [sic] "game" are a function not only of the volume and structure of his capital at the moment under consideration and of the game chances . . . they guarantee him, but also of the evolution over time of the volume and structure of his capital, that is, of his social trajectory and of the dispositions (habitus) constituted in the prolonged relation to a definite distribution of objective chances. (Bourdieu and Wacquant, 1992, 99)

The concepts of **cultural capital** and **social capital** can be useful in explaining different participants' feel for the game and the disadvantageous outcomes experienced by those who lack such capital. For example, the unequal educational achievement of children from different class backgrounds has been explained using the concept of cultural capital, which includes knowledge, skills, taste, lifestyle, and qualifications (Bourdieu, 1985). Cultural capital has been shown to be transmitted through the family; for example, as more educated parents are better able to promote cultural capital for their children through schooling using their material resources, time, educational knowledge, qualifications, and social confidence (Reay, 1998, 2000; Lareau, 1987). While the concept of cultural capital has been seen as applicable in some non-Western countries (Byun, Schofer, and Kim, 2012), Modood (2004) suggests that it is limited in its ability to explain how subordinate groups achieve upward mobility.

Modood (2004) argues that the concept of social capital is more useful in this regard, particularly the idea of ethnicity as a way of linking people across classes to those in positions of power or influence. Bourdieu (1985, 248) describes social capital as "the aggregate of the actual or potential resources which are linked to possession of a durable network of more or less institutionalized relationships of mutual acquaintance or recognition." Social capital is composed of the social relationships that allow one to access resources and the amount and quality of those resources (Portes, 1998). Through social capital, individuals can gain access to economic resources, increase their cultural capital, or affiliate with institutions that confer credentials.

However, there is also uncertainty associated with individuals' ability to use social capital; different forms of such capital can be contradictory, and, therefore, it can have negative as well as positive consequences. For example, Portes (1998) suggests that social capital can exclude outsiders, make excessive claims on group members, and restrict individual freedoms. Similarly, Putnam (2000) distinguishes between *bonding* and *bridging* capital where bonding capital is inward looking and supports exclusive identities and group homogeneity, while bridging capital is outward looking and encompasses people across diverse social divisions. It is possible to imagine tensions between these forms of social capital and to expect that bounded solidarity and trust are likely to have different effects for different groups (see also Portes [1998]).

Writers have made other claims about social capital and immigrant groups. For example, Portes (1998) cites research suggesting that immigrant families compensate for the absence of outside networks beyond the family with an emphasis on social capital in the form of familial support, including preservation of the cultural orientations of their home country. Similarly, Dinovitzer, Hagan, and Parker (2003) argue that *familial social capital* in immigrant families can provide necessary supports and networks for youth who may lack other sources of social capital. However, as Sweet, Anisef, and Walters (2010) note, non-material forms of family capital are not likely to fully resolve a shortfall in the family's economic resources without careful planning.

Modood (2004) uses the term *ethnic capital* to explain the aspirations of minority ethnic parents for their children and the educational success of some youth from disadvantaged ethnic minority groups. This ethnic capital is seen as transmitted from adults in families to children through norms (for example, pursuit of higher education as a means of social mobility) and norms enforcement (including use of parental authority and the provision of resources to realize ambitions). The term *emotional capital* has also been used to describe a set of emotional competencies that is essential for an individual's effective use of social and human capitals (Gendron, 2004). Like social capital, emotional capital can be seen as advantageous or disadvantageous for racialized groups (Froyum, 2010). Reay (2000) describes emotional capital as a variant of social capital that can be understood as the stock of emotional resources built up over time within families upon which children can draw.

Finally, Basit (2012) introduces the concept of *aspirational capital* to address what she sees as shortcomings in other conceptions. Aspirational capital is presented as an extension of cultural and social capital in families where it already exists and as a substitute for cultural and social capital in minority ethnic families where it does not exist:

> An important component of aspirational capital is the desire for upward social mobility, which was not only manifest in the comments of working-class families, but also in the remarks of those from educated middle-class backgrounds, indicating their desire for the young people to continue in the family tradition of successful careers and not be downwardly mobile. (Basit, 2012, 135)

The ideas above provide a starting point for thinking about why racialized immigrant youth may have higher educational aspirations and attainment than white, Canadian-born, youth despite the challenges facing immigrant families described in the section that follows.

Recent Immigrant Cohorts in Canada

Education and Labour Market Outcomes

Immigration has produced an increase in the racial diversity of the Canadian population (Reitz, 2007a). The proportion of immigrants from "non-traditional" sources other than Europe and the United States grew from about 5 per cent before 1960 to nearly 80 per cent in the 1990s (Reitz, 2007a, 23). Consequently, by 2006, 75 per cent of the more than 1.1 million immigrants who had arrived in Canada in the previous five years were non-Caucasian in race or non-white in colour (Statistics Canada, 2008). Most immigrants are also very well educated given the growing emphasis in immigration policy on attracting skilled workers (Phythian, Walters, and Anisef, 2009). The *Longitudinal Survey of Immigrants to Canada* showed that 69 per cent of newcomers aged 25 to 44 years who arrived in Canada between October 2000 and September 2001 had a university education compared to 22 per cent of the Canadian-born population in the same age group (Statistics Canada, 2003).

However, there are differences in educational attainment for different racial minority groups. For example, Thiessen's (2009) analysis of data from the longitudinal Youth in Transition Survey (cycles in 2000 and 2002) found, after controlling for structural and cultural differences, that Canadian-born East Asian youth were more likely to pursue a university education than European-born Canadian youth, while First Nations and African Canadians were less likely to pursue a university education. Drawing on data from the 2002 Statistics Canada Ethnic Diversity Survey, Abada, Hou, and Ram (2008) examined group differences in university completion among the children of immigrants, ages 25 to 34. They found that children of immigrant parents in most source region groups achieved higher university completion rates than children of Canadian-born parents. In particular, children of Chinese and Indian immigrants had higher university completion rates than children of Canadian-born parents, even when controlling for demographic and human capital factors. However, children of Filipino immigrants had a lower university completion rate than children of Canadian-born parents.

Policy-makers and others have assumed that immigrants selected on the basis of education, skills, and labour market demands will be more successful in the labour market than family class immigrants[1] and refugees. However, Census data suggest that throughout the 1990s, unemployment rates for recent immigrants with university degrees were at least three times higher than that of the native-born population (Statistics Canada, 2003). Furthermore, recent studies have documented a decline in immigrants' earnings relative to native-born Canadians and an increase in poverty among immigrants (Picot, 2004; Reitz, 2007a). While the 1960s cohort of adult male immigrants had earnings on par with those of their Canadian-born counterparts, the 1980s cohort earned 24 per cent less (Bonikowska and Hou, 2011). Thus, despite higher levels of education, immigrants appear to have more difficulty gaining access to work in knowledge occupations compared to those born in Canada, and experience an earnings disadvantage in occupations outside the knowledge sector (Reitz, 2007b).

One explanation for these outcomes is that immigrants' foreign credentials are undervalued in the Canadian labour market (Bauder, 2003; Fuller and Vosko, 2008), and their credentials are less transferable (Reitz, 2007b). Reitz (2007b) suggests that poor labour market outcomes may also occur because of employers' greater use of networks in recruitment and emphasis on interpersonal interactions in decision-making may disadvantage immigrants who are less integrated into local networks (Raza, Beaujot, and Gebremariam, 2013). Other explanations for a decline in relative earnings include possible labour market discrimination, a decline in returns to immigrants' foreign labour market experience and increasing education levels of the native-born workforce (Reitz, 2007a; 2007b). Studies of labour market discrimination based on race and ethnicity have documented systemic barriers to employment and exclusionary relations in the workplace (see also Vallas [2003]). In Canada, National Household Survey data suggest that the unemployment rate was 9.9 per cent for visible minority workers compared to 7.3 per cent for white workers in 2011; this rate was especially high for Arabs (14.2 per cent), blacks (12.9 per cent), and South Asians (10.2 per cent) (Jackson, 2014).

Racialized Immigrant Youth and Bicultural Identity

Despite the declining fortunes of immigrants over time, racialized immigrant youth in Canada tend to have higher aspirations than others. Research based on the 2000 Youth in Transition Survey found that 79 per cent of racialized immigrant youth (age 15) hoped to acquire a university education (one or more degrees), compared to 57 per cent of Canadian-born white youth, and immigrant parents' aspirations for their children were even higher (Krahn and Taylor, 2005). Further, longitudinal analysis demonstrates that the aspirations of racialized immigrant youth were very stable over time and that almost 75 per cent compared to 58 per cent of other youth were enrolled in post-secondary education by age 19 (Taylor et al., 2009).

Despite being remarkably resilient and capable of adapting (Soroka, Johnston, and Banting, 2007), racialized youth nevertheless face discrimination within the school system and society (for example, Kilbride [2000]; Anisef and Kilbride [2004]; Codjoe [2005]) because of an absence of teachers of colour, lower expectations, "colour-coded" streaming, and Eurocentric curricula. In addition, Lauer et al.'s (2012, 3) review of the Canadian literature and empirical analysis suggests that: "Like their parents, young immigrants are finding it difficult to secure jobs and are taking a longer period of time to reach income parity with their Canadian-born counterparts."

In sum, the literature suggests that visible minority immigrant youth have high educational goals and that recent immigrant cohorts have faced significant challenges in the Canadian labour market in terms of employment and earnings. The literature also suggests the danger in treating visible minorities as a homogeneous group. Through qualitative interviews with immigrant youth of colour and their parents, our study explores the question of why, given the barriers they often face, these youth have such high educational and career aspirations.

Method

Our qualitative research study examined the education and career trajectories of "visible minority" youth from immigrant families. Interviews with five female and five male youth between the ages of 18 and 23 were conducted in a Canadian city situated in a Western province. These youth were pursuing various education and career goals. Interviews with their parents—five fathers, three mothers, and both parents in two cases—were also conducted. Six of 10 youth were born outside of Canada and immigrated to Canada in childhood (the 1.5 generation) (Bonikowska and Hou, 2011). All youth had completed at least high school education in Canada and all were living at home with their parents at the time of the interviews.

Youth and parent interviews were conducted separately and were fully transcribed. The youth interviews focused on the process of immigrating to Canada, experiences in school, education and work plans, social networks and activities. Interviews with parents centred on their reasons for immigrating to Canada, their own education, immigration and labour market experiences, and aspirations for their children. Interview participants were also asked to complete a pre-interview questionnaire.

Eight of the 10 youth who participated in the study had at least one parent with a university degree (see Table 7.1). The extremely high levels of education among the families in the study are reflected in the high educational aspirations of the youth interviewed. Still, a previous study of 15-year-old Canadian youth found that even after controlling for parents' education and family income, there was a significant "visible minority immigrant" effect on their educational aspirations (Krahn and Taylor, 2005). In this cohort there were high levels of consistency between the accounts provided by youth and parents, indicating strong bonds between youth and parents and the development of shared family narratives (Taylor and Krahn, 2013).

Findings

Most families in our study, like many others who immigrate to Canada, found that their educational and work credentials were not recognized in the labour market, resulting in downward social mobility. For the majority of youth interviewed, monetary, emotional, and social support from parents, as well as support from shared ethnic and cultural community groups, became resources in families' quest for success and social mobility in Canada. Parents interviewed often provided economic support to help with their children's higher education at the expense of their own needs. Obligations to one's parents, in turn, provided motivation to children to do well academically (see also Abada and Tenkorang [2009]).

Table 7.1 Participant Profiles

Interview Number and Pseudonym (if applicable)	Gender	Parents' Country of Birth	Parents' Education (highest)	Youths' Education
1. Thomas	Male	China	High school (father)	Upgrading HS to enter university
2. Jon	Male	Vietnam	Less than high school	Enrolled in BSc
3. David	Male	Taiwan	Graduate degree (father)	Enrolled in BEd
4. Adnan	Male	Sudan	Undergraduate degree (both)	
5. Arad	Male	Iran	Graduate degrees (both)	Attending university
6. Cindy	Female	China	Undergraduate degree (father)	Attending university
7. Afshan	Female	Afghanistan	Undergraduate degree (father)	Upgrading HS to attend university
8. Alma	Female	Somalia	Graduate degree (father)	Enrolled in BSc
9. Julie	Female	Philippines	Undergraduate degrees (both)	Enrolled in BSc
10. Lili	Female	Iran	Graduate degree (father)	Enrolled in Bachelor's program in psychology

Basit (2012) suggests that an important component of *aspirational capital* is a desire for upward social mobility. Ethnic minority families' ambition to achieve social mobility was evident in everyday talk within families about the children's aspirations and future plans (see also Archer and Francis [2007]). In the subsections that follow, we argue that high educational and career aspirations are evident despite, and perhaps because of, the hardships faced by their families such as devaluation of their cultural capital (including linguistic capital and religious beliefs) as well as their human capital through non-recognition of their foreign credentials. Despite barriers, immigrant families found ways to help their children succeed within the Canadian educational system. Findings show that different forms of social capital help families compensate to a degree for a lack of other forms of cultural and social capital. At the same time, the findings are mixed since some youth also experienced parental involvement as a pressure that was not balanced with adequate support because the parents lacked understanding of the field.

Devaluing of Cultural Capital

To varying degrees, our interview participants perceived a devaluation of their language and culture, religion, and foreign credentials. One of the most common barriers experienced by immigrant parents and some youth was inadequate English language proficiency. While the multicultural vision of Canada involves creating a space in which different cultures keep their own values and languages, immigrants found that non-English language proficiency was seldom valued.

Further, lack of confidence in their English language skills (on the part of employers as well as immigrants) led several parents to take low-wage jobs despite their qualifications and skills. For example, Afshan says that her father has a four-year post-secondary degree from Afghanistan but had to work as a cleaner:

> When [my parents] came, English was a language barrier but they had other friends from Afghanistan who helped him find a night-time job cleaning, and that job didn't bother too much about speaking English.

For parents without post-secondary education, lack of English proficiency was even more of a barrier. For example, after arriving from Hong Kong, Thomas' father faced challenges in finding and keeping work. At the time of our interview, he was working over 10 hours a day at a grocery store and restaurant. Thomas' mother had worked as a seamstress but was unemployed at the time of our interview. While Thomas was born in Canada and did not experience the same struggles with English language proficiency, during high school, he thought that he would likely "end up just like my parents even if I did get a good education." He saw his cultural background as a deficit at that time:

> Yeah, it's funny because I never really felt like I fit in. I hope, I mean I don't think this is racist but I'm a person of different ethnicity and I don't really fit into the dominant Caucasian race group. So even though Canada's a multicultural society, I don't really feel like I fit in. But it's funny because if I go to Hong Kong where everybody's Chinese, I wouldn't really fit in either because I was born here.

Jon, a Vietnamese-Canadian male youth also acknowledged the pressures of a bicultural identity:

> My sister has had the most influence on me. She understands what it's like to be part of two cultures. My family is from Vietnam so they haven't really let go of that part of the culture, but I was born and raised here. . . . Being in two cultures is very dissatisfying. . . . My sister found a way to survive here and cope with it.

A few youth also felt that they did not receive the level of support needed at school. For example:

> [School counsellors] always limited your options kind of almost giving you the feeling that you weren't able to do it. . . . I said I want to go to the medical field but all along they gave me the impression I wasn't able to do it and stuck me into an area and said work in there, but they never gave me more feedback as to how I can get there and what I could do to get there (Afshan, Afghan female youth).

A male student also commented that he felt "less important than the other kids" in school (Adnan, Sudanese youth). These youth were uncertain about whether or not they had experienced discrimination, but it was noteworthy that youth from African and Middle Eastern countries were more likely to perceive lower school expectations than Asian youth (from Taiwan, China, and Vietnam).

Another area of diminished cultural capital was related to religious practices. According to the latest Canadian Census of population by religion (Statistics Canada, 2001), the majority of religious Canadians are Christians (77 per cent) and about 6 per cent of the population have identified themselves as Muslims (2 per cent), Jews (1.1 per cent), Hindu (1 per cent), Sikh (1 per cent), Buddhist (1 per cent), and other religions (0.3 per cent). Despite the value that Canadians are said to place on multiculturalism, our data show that some immigrant youth and their families felt that their religion was devalued.

For example, Alma was born in Somalia within a Muslim family, and practising her religion was an important part of her life. Her father sent Alma and her siblings to an Islamic school to ensure that they did not feel excluded:

> One of the things that I always have in mind is that my kids, and this is when they are young, they shouldn't get identity crisis. So in the public schools I feel most of the children they fear identity crisis. Teachers, where you are not white Christian, they ask where you come from, and that is what I hate for the public school because they teach the kids at young age that you don't belong to this country. OK? So all my kids go to the Islamic school because in that case they will never have identity crisis. They see in the class white Caucasian, Pakistan, India, Lebanon, Egypt, all this. So they don't have an identity crisis. So that's why I decide that . . . they grow up in their culture and their religion (Alma's father).

But when asked about the biggest obstacle that would stand in his daughter's way to reach her goals, Alma's father added:

> My daughters wear a hijab, a scarf. So in some industries maybe it is an obstacle. So they cannot work in fashion or design or as models or in commercials. So it is uncomfortable for them and it is a barrier.

In a similar way, an Iranian father talked with concern about his children's way of life after moving to Canada. He said that he and his wife hoped for their children to keep Iranian values, with roots in religious ideas, and to be faithful:

> I think looking at me and her mom and the faith that she has helps her. My main concern always was to have a daughter and my dad said, "Don't take your daughter to Canada and it will take her from you," and that's a normal situation. Unfortunately people coming from countries like Iran, especially when they are kids when they come here, and grew up in different culture like here, they change to different directions. But thanks God for her it was OK, and now my concern is for my son (Lili's father).

While a scarf, turban, yarmulke, and other religious symbols are considered part of their identity, religious minorities are often forced to assimilate (with the promise of success) or maintain their culture.

Devaluing of Human Capital

Our data further confirm that most parents faced challenges with the non-recognition of their foreign credentials. While most of these parents possessed university credentials from their home countries, few were able to find a job fitting their qualifications and skills. For example, Alma's father was born in Somalia and graduated from university there. After his graduation, he was hired as an Assistant Lecturer at a university in Somalia and then was sent for further education to Italy where he achieved a doctoral degree. He returned to Somalia and taught at a university until the civil war broke out. He and his family moved to Canada in the mid-1990s hoping to have a better life. However, economic pressures required him to seek work outside his field:

> Before I come to Canada I was hoping to . . . I can get a job that can at least, maybe not totally related to what I did but at least a job that is at least equivalent or I can say a white collar job. You know? But that was not the case and when I look around the first two or three years I worked at part-time community work and upgrading my English and then I entered taxi driving because that was the only way to survive, to feed my kids, to pay the bills.

In a few cases, the non-recognition of foreign credentials led families to move from one place to another in the hopes of finding a good job. This mobility, however, was not always a positive change in the lives of their children. For example, Arad was the only child of a physician and a dentist from Iran. His parents were among the top students in their country but neither could work in their fields when they came to Canada. To become employable, his mother immediately entered a Canadian dentistry school, but his father had to pass several exams to continue his studies. At the same time, he worked to support the family. After Arad's mother graduated, the family needed to move for her to find a job. This change was difficult for Arad to cope with, as his father recalls:

> [We moved] in the last three years of his education. It was very hard for him. The first five to six months that we came here, he was sitting at home and was depressed and not social, having difficulty with communicating with his classmates at the school. I tried to talk to his high school but it wasn't successful and I didn't get [an] appropriate response.

The devaluation of immigrant families' cultural capital raises questions about why youth have such high aspirations and attainment. We agree that the concept of cultural capital is limited in explaining this (Modood, 2004). As Abada, Hou, and Ram (2009) conclude, based on their analysis of the Canadian Ethnic Diversity Study, anticipated disadvantages can be an important motivator for immigrant youth to succeed academically. But our qualitative data further reveal that it may also lead immigrant families and youths to be more instrumental in their choices of academic programs and careers. For example:

> I was taught from a very early age to seek higher education and find financial security for myself as well as for the family (Jon, Vietnamese-Canadian male youth).

Jon's mother adds, "I would like [my children] to have a professional job here. It's good for everybody." Similarly, Lili's father recounts:

> I wanted [my daughter] to go to medicine and dentistry and she tried and she said, "This is not the area that I want to go."
> Q: Why did you think those areas would be good?
> Because of the job demand I would say. Because in engineering two years ago when everything was down and after five years of working with one of the biggest companies here they laid me off, even though I was a lead engineer, so I told her that you have to be related to health and those stuff because the health system is something that as long as we have human beings we need it.

The disappointments of parents therefore translate into high professional aspirations for children, which are double-edged—it appeared to act as a motivator for most of the youth interviewed but also led some to enter disciplines they may not have chosen on their own and, in a few cases, to pursue university education before they felt ready.

Value of Social Capital

In examining why immigrant youth aim high despite the devaluation of their cultural capital, it is also important to consider the compensatory role of social capital, defined by Bourdieu as the "possession of a durable network of relationships of mutual acquaintance and recognition" (Bellamy, 1994, 123). The literature indicates those immigrant youth who are part of a cultural network or community can benefit from role models and support coming from that community (Portes, 2000; Dinovitzer, Hagan, and Parker, 2003). Therefore, although immigrant families may lack social capital related to outside networks and career networks because of the lack of knowledge of those systems, they develop other forms of social capital described by the writers above as familial capital, ethnic capital, and emotional capital. The following section explores these concepts in relation to our interview data.

Our interviews confirm the role of family support as a resource of social capital in immigrant youths' attainment and success (Portes, 1998). Youth pointed to the role of *familial capital* in their academic and career life. Such supports were in the forms of financial assistance, help with school work, and/or providing for youths' material needs:

> My family supports me, basically. They give me a home and they give me a lot of support in helping me get to places, because currently I do not own a car. . . . So there's a lot of support there (Jon, Vietnamese-Canadian male youth).

While helping their children develop a strong work ethic and helping to finance their post-secondary education were common in the families interviewed, in a few cases we witnessed an extreme level of support, for example, being prepared to move for their children:

> [If my daughter] wants to continue to PhD . . . and it's very hard. . . . The number of people that can be accepted in [University Name], for example, first of all I don't think they have PhD program in all of psychology majors so we have to move

probably . . . and the reason that we're here is for her future. Because the stuff that happened to me, I didn't want those stuff happen to her (Lili's father).

At the same time, parents acknowledged their inability to support their children because of their lack of knowledge of the education system. However, this lack of knowledge did not hinder these families from drawing on other forms of support:

I try to support [my son]. I still have to let him know that I support him. . . . I still care about his education. Absolutely right now I cannot help him anymore, not like at junior high. From Grade 10, I cannot help him about homework any more, it's already difficult for me because of English. Right now all I can do is help him, support him what he want to do (Jon's father).

But again, social capital can be double-edged in that the supports families provide may also place additional pressure on youth, such as indicated by the following example:

[My parents] are helping me. But it's not without any strings. It's not like, I'm giving you money, just go do whatever you want. They want to see what you're doing, how you're doing, what's your goal. They want to make sure (David, Taiwanese-Canadian male youth).

While most participants pointed to familial capital, some also acknowledged support from their ethnic communities. *Ethnic capital*, in the form of strong family-community and/or parent-child relationships, was therefore an important resource for immigrant families who lacked other forms of social capital. Several families found refuge in communities that speak their own language and share similar values and goals. As this mother comments:

[I]n the beginning, we lived with my cousin's family and then we bought a house in the same neighborhood because . . . the Chinese community has a really strong emphasis on like this is a good school, this is a good neighbourhood, so we sort of followed that and we bought a house.

Probably because of parents' high educational attainment, education is highly valued as the most important means of social mobility. For example, when asked about their child's high aspirations, a Filipino parent suggested that aiming high is a norm in their family:

In the Philippines, parents would always tell the kids "the biggest thing is education, nothing can take that away from you." So that's always been the case with most Filipino parents (Julie's mother).

Lili also admitted that her Iranian parents' attitudes, which had an interesting gendered aspect, influenced her:

[M]y dad has always told me that he doesn't want me to get a job which makes me dependent to my husband, and he wants me to stand by my own.

Our data show that pursuing higher education is an expectation, whether children are interested or not. Lili's father wanted her to be a physician, so she enrolled in a program leading to medicine. However, she found that she preferred another field:

> I talked to [father] about it but he just stopped that because of Iranian mind set and Asian continent mindset and he was like: "You have to work harder," but it doesn't matter if I'm interested or not, and he said, "You will be interested eventually so just work harder."

Lili saw the fact that she was able to convince her father to let her switch to psychology and pursue a PhD rather than a medical degree as an important achievement. This example again points to parental pressure, perceived by some immigrant youth as motivating and by others as restrictive.

In the parent-child relationship, *emotional capital* is described as valued support, love, care, and concern that bond members of a family together (Reay, 2000). While this kind of capital is present in non-immigrant families also, immigration and settlement challenges appeared to lead to closer bonds within families. Almost without exception, the parents interviewed pointed to their children's future as the main reason they immigrated to Canada. Further, it was evident that their children's success has become an important focus; in fact, some parents appeared to be living through their children (Taylor and Krahn, 2013). Though in a few cases, these intense concerns about their children's future prompted resentment, in most cases, youth realized it came from a place of caring:

> Sometime I get home from work, I'm very tired. But when [son was] still a young kid and junior high, I will sit behind him. I said, "Why don't you study this, then maybe can help you a little bit." I will ask him a question about that homework and he will answer me. So make thing more interest. I help him a little bit, also to show him that I support him all the way. Sometime he see I can hardly open my eyes and he say, "Dad, you go to bed, I can see you very tired." That will maybe make him, okay my dad is very care about my education, I have to study hard (Jon's father).

Seeking Social Mobility (or Re-gaining Lost Status)

Archer and Francis (2007) and Basit (2012) contend that immigrant students' high aspirations result from their families' desire for them to achieve social mobility and to better themselves. Aspirations for youth were not a "personal, individual choice, but formed part of a family project of social mobility and escape" from current life conditions and from parents' failure to meet their own career aspirations (Archer and Francis, 2007, 120). Our data support this argument. For example, when asked about whether his parents' work experiences in Canada affected him, a male Vietnamese-Canadian youth, Jon, replied:

> It did, but not so much in the fact that I was exposed to [father's] kind of [unskilled] work and then realized that it was not something I wanted to do, but more in the fact that he would talk to me about his work and explain to me that he wanted me to be educated so that I would not have to [do low paid work]. I was

taught from a very early age to seek higher education and find financial security for myself as well as for the family.

Parents tended to communicate to their children that their lives would be easier than their parents' if they became educated. Thus, immigrant parents' valuation of education can be seen as "part of the process of reversing the initial downward mobility in the lives of their children" (Modood, 2004, 93).

Youth generally accept this discourse partly because they have been told about the sacrifices their parents have made on their behalf. For example:

> Q: What do you want for your children? What do you hope for them?
>
> I want so many things for them. One thing is what I want is one thing they can achieve. One thing I want is that all of them at least achieve a university degree, that's what I want. And I tell them days and night that I sacrifice my career for them. I could go for example, start university and finish my degree, a Masters you know, but I said I chose to put time in you and forgo my career and now I'm taking this job of taxi driving which is a job that everybody can do and I'm not happy of it and sometimes lose my prestige. So I said what I'm doing this I'm doing for you. So they have to understand that (Alma's father).

Youth reinforce the importance of parental sacrifice and hardship in their own life choices.

> Q: You said that you're happy with your grades, so what was the motivation around that?
>
> It's more around our parents, always encouraging us to do well, and supporting us. Like what [sister] said before, if we want to wash dishes our mom will be like no, you go do your homework. She'll tell us to always focus on school and she'll handle everything. Don't worry about the financial or anything (Cindy, Chinese-Canadian).

This theme of parents' sacrifices was also addressed when youth discussed the inability of parents to fit into life in Canada. As Thomas expressed, his mother's isolation because of language challenges motivated him to ensure that he became well integrated into Canadian society.

In sum, close familial relationships, respect for the sacrifices and downward mobility of parents, and the "valuing of education" by mostly well-educated parents appeared to come together to create high aspirations in the immigrant families in this study. But although our youth participants generally responded in a positive way to the strong aspirational push of parents, some also felt pressured by their parents. Youth were also affected adversely by the devaluing of parents' cultural and human capital and their lack of familiarity with the Canadian education system. Our research findings are, therefore, mixed.

Conclusion

Our study explored racialized immigrant youths' high educational and career aspirations in the face of challenges that include devalued cultural capital in families, and forms of social capital that are simultaneously enabling and restricting. We have, therefore, considered how Bourdieu's concepts fit the experiences of these families. The various forms of social capital described by different writers as familial capital, ethnic capital, emotional capital, and aspirational capital have been used to capture different aspects of these experiences. Some of these concepts may be better described in terms of the distinctive habitus (structures of mind characterized by a set of acquired sensibilities and dispositions) formed within immigrant families. Close parent-child and community bonds appear to form because of immigrant families' difficult settlement experiences, the desires of parents for their children's mobility (often because of their own disappointing labour market experiences), and, relatedly, the contradictory class location of families whereby well-educated parents are often forced to participate in lower skilled work. Our decision to interview both youth and their parents confirmed the importance of parents' experiences for youth motivation.

The response of youth to parental expectations was, with a few exceptions, compliant. They followed parents' wishes regarding their pursuit of university education, often in professional fields. However, as noted, these choices were not without consequences. While outwardly successful, a few youth felt restricted or burdened by parents' professional aspirations for them. And although they appeared to have a high level of bi-cultural competence, a number felt that their parents' (and others') belief that their lives will be easier was not necessarily accurate. Their experiences with the devaluation of their family's cultural capital lent credence to this view. In sum, despite the apparent good news story of immigrant youth educational aspirations and attainment, their own visions of the future were more ambivalent.

Questions for Critical Thought

1. How do you explain the higher aspirations of racialized youth from immigrant families, compared to other Canadian youth?
2. What are some of the reasons for the poor labour market outcomes of recent immigrant cohorts?
3. What are the effects of racial discrimination experienced by youth of colour?
4. Do you agree that different authors' adaptation of Bourdieu's concepts of social and cultural capital (for example, ethnic capital, aspirational capital) are helpful in understanding the situations of immigrant youth? Why or why not?

Glossary

Cultural capital The collection of symbolic elements such as skills, tastes, posture, clothing, mannerisms, material belongings, and credentials that one acquires through being part of a particular social class. Sharing similar forms of cultural capital with others creates a sense of collective identity and group position.

Racialization The act or process of imbuing a person with a consciousness of race distinctions or of giving a racial character to something or making it serve racist ends.

Social capital The actual or potential resources linked to possession of a durable network of relationships of mutual acquaintance or recognition. For example, the wealthy and powerful may use their "old boys' network" or other social capital to maintain advantages for themselves, their social class, and their children.

Social mobility The movement of individuals, families, households, or other categories of people within or between layers or tiers in an open system of social stratification.

Acknowledgement

We appreciate the help of research assistants Raja Amer and Tejwant Chana, and co-investigator Harvey Krahn in the study on which this chapter is based.

Notes

1. Family class immigrants are individuals, often parents, who are sponsored by other family members already resident in Canada.

References

Abada, T., Hou, F., and Ram, B. "Group differences in educational attainment among the children of immigrants." Statistics Canada, cat. no. 11F0019M—no. 308, 2008.

Abada, T., Hou, F., and Ram, B. "Ethnic differences in educational attainment among the children of Canadian immigrants." *Canadian Journal of Sociology* 34(1) (2009): 1–28.

Abada, T., and Tenkorang, E.Y. "Pursuit of university education among the children of immigrants in Canada: The roles of parental human capital and social capital." *Journal of Youth Studies* 12(2) (2009): 185–207.

Anisef, P., and Kilbride, K. "Introduction." In *Managing Two Worlds: The Experiences and Concerns of Immigrant Youth in Ontario*, P. Anisef and K. Kilbride (eds.), (1–36). Toronto: Canadian Scholars' Press, 2004.

Archer, L., and Francis, B. *Understanding Minority Ethnic Achievement: The Role of Race, Class, Gender and "Success."* London: Routledge, 2007.

Basit, T. "'My parents have stressed that since I was a kid': Young minority ethnic British citizens and the phenomenon of aspirational capital." *Education Citizenship and Social Justice* 7(2) (2012): 129–43.

Bauder, H. "'Brain abuse,' or the devaluation of immigrant labour in Canada." *Antipode* 35(4) (2003): 699–717.

Bellamy, L.A. "Capital, habitus, field and practice: An introduction to the work of Pierre Bourdieu." In *Sociology of Education in Canada*, L. Erwin and D. MacLennan (eds.), (120–36). Toronto: Copp Clark Longman, 1994.

Bonikowska, A., and Hou, F. "Reversal of fortunes or continued success? Cohort differences in education and earnings of childhood immigrants." Statistics Canada, Analytical Studies Branch Research Paper Series, cat. no. 11F0019M, no. 330 (January 2011).

Bourdieu, P. "The forms of capital." In *Handbook of Theory and Research for the Sociology of Education*, J. Richardson (ed.), (241–258). New York: Greenwood, 1985.

Bourdieu, P., and Wacquant, L. *An Invitation to Reflexive Sociology*. Chicago: University of Chicago Press, 1992.

Boyd, M. "Educational attainments of immigrant offspring: Success or segmented assimilation?" *International Migration Review* 36(4) (2002): 1037–60.

Byun, S., Schofer, E., and Kim, K. "Revisiting the role of cultural capital in East Asian educational systems: The case of South Korea." *Sociology of Education* 85(3) (2012): 219–39.

Codjoe, H. "Fighting a 'public enemy' of black academic achievement—the persistence of racism and the schooling experiences of black students in Canada." In *Inequality in Canada*, V. Zawilski and C. Levine-Rasky (eds.), (150–177). Toronto: Oxford University Press, 2005.

Dinovitzer, R., Hagan, J., and Parker, P. "Choice and circumstance: Social capital and planful competence in the attainments of immigrant youth." *Canadian Journal of Sociology* 28(4) (2003): 463–88.

Froyum, C.M. "The reproduction of inequalities through emotional capital: The case of socializing low-income black girls." *Qualitative Sociology* 33(1) (2010): 37–54.

Fuller, S., and Vosko, L. "Temporary employment and social inequality in Canada: Exploring intersections of gender, race and immigration status." *Social Indicators Research* 88 (2008): 31–50.

Gendron, B. "Why emotional capital matters in education and in labour: Toward an optimal exploitation of human capital and knowledge management." *Les Cahiers de la Maison des Sciences Economiques* 113(1) (2004): 31–42. Paris: Université Panthéon-Sorbonne.

Jackson, A. "Canadian-born visible minority youth face an unfair job future" (3 June 2014). Retrieved from: The Broadbent [Institute] blog: www.broadbentinstitute.ca/en/blog/canadian-born-visible-minority-youth-face-unfair-job-future#sthash.i7ihPXvH.vWGionPs.dpuf

Kilbride, K. "A review of the literature on the human, social and cultural capital of immigrant children and their families with implications for teacher education." CERIS working paper no. 13, 2000. Retrieved June 2004 from: http://ceris.metropolis.net/

Krahn, H., and Taylor, A. "Resilient teenagers: Explaining the high educational aspirations of visible-minority youth in Canada." *Journal of International Migration and Integration* 6(3/4) (2005): 405–34.

Lareau, A. "Social class differences in family-school relationships: The importance of cultural capital." *Sociology of Education* 60(2) (1987): 73–85.

Lauer, S., Wilkinson, L., Chung Yan, M., Sin, R., and Ka Tat Tsang, A. "Immigrant youth and employment: Lessons learned from the analysis of LSIC and 82 lived stories." *Journal of International Migration and Integration* 13 (2012): 1–19.

Modood, T. "Capitals, ethnic identity, and educational qualifications." *Cultural Trends* 13(2) (2004): 87–105.

Phythian, K., Walters, D., and Anisef, P. "Entry class and the early employment experience of immigrants in Canada." *Canadian Studies in Population* 36(3–4) (2009): 363–82.

Picot, G. "The deteriorating economic welfare of immigrants and possible causes." Statistics Canada, Analytical Studies Branch Research Paper Series, cat. no. 11F0019MIE, no. 222. Ottawa: Statistics Canada, 2004.

Portes, A. "Social capital: Its origins and applications in modern sociology." *Annual Review of Sociology* 24 (1998): 1–24.

Portes, A. "Social capital: Its origins and applications in modern sociology." In *Knowledge and Social Capital*, E.L. Lesser (ed.), (43–67). Boston: Butterworth-Heinemann, 2000.

Putnam, R. *Bowling Alone*. New York: Simon & Schuster, 2000.

Raza, M., Beaujot, R, and Woldemicael, G. "Social capital and economic integration of visible minority immigrants in Canada." *Journal of International Migration and Integration* 14(2) (2013): 263–85.

Reay, D. "Cultural reproduction: Mothers' involvement in their children's primary schooling." In *Bourdieu and Education*, M. Grenfell and D. James (eds.), (55–71). London: Falmer Press, 1998.

Reay, D. "A useful extension of Bourdieu's cultural framework?: Emotional capital as a way of understanding mothers' involvement in their children's education." *The Sociological Review* 48(4) (2000): 568–85.

Reitz, J. "Immigrant employment success in Canada, Part I: Individual and contextual causes." *Journal of International Migration and Integration* 8(1) (2007a): 11–36.

Reitz, J. "Immigrant employment success in Canada, Part II: Understanding the decline." *Journal of International Migration and Integration* 8(1) (2007b): 37–62.

Soroka, S., Johnston, R., and Banting, K. "Ties that bind? Social cohesion and diversity in Canada." In *Belonging? Diversity, Recognition and Shared Citizenship in Canada*, K. Banting, T. Courchene, and F. Seidle (eds.), (1–40). Montreal: McGill-Queens Press, 2007.

Statistics Canada. "Population by religion, by province and territory (2001 Census)." 2001. Retrieved August 2012: www.statcan.gc.ca/tables-tableaux/sum-som/l01/cst01/demo30a-eng.htm

Statistics Canada. "Characteristics of Canada's newest immigrants." (September 2003). Retrieved July 2012: http://statcan.ca/english

Statistics Canada. "Ethnic origins and visible minorities, 2006 Census" (2008). Retrieved September 2012: www.statcan.gc.ca/pub/89-611-x/4067689-eng.htm

Sweet, R., Anisef, P., and Walters, D. "Immigrant parents' investments in their children's PSE." *Canadian Journal of Higher Education* 40(3) (2010): 59–80.

Taylor, A., and Krahn, H. "Living through our children: Exploring the education and career 'choices' of racialized immigrant youth in Canada." *Journal of Youth Studies* 16(8) (2013): 1000–21.

Taylor, A., Krahn, H., Chana, T., and Hudson, J. "Exploring the post-secondary aspirations of immigrant youth." Presentation at the 11th National Metropolis Conference. Calgary, Alberta, 2009.

Thiessen, V. "The pursuit of post-secondary education: A comparison of First Nations, African, Asian, and European Canadian youth." Canadian Labour Market and Skills Researcher Network, working paper no. 19. Ottawa: Canadian Labour Market and Skills Researcher Network, 2009.

Vallas, S. "Rediscovering the color line within work organizations: The 'knitting of racial groups' revisited." *Work and Occupations* 30(4) (2003): 379–400.

8

An Overview of Indigenous Educational Attainment in Canada

Catherine Gordon and Jerry White

Introduction

Indigenous peoples have typically had lower educational attainment levels compared to the non-Indigenous population in Canada (Spence and White, 2009). Research indicates that low levels of education in specific populations are correlated with factors such as socio-economic status (Eagle, 1989), ethnicity (Gang and Zimmermann, 2000), geography (Garner and Raudenbush, 1991), and parental educational attainment (Krein and Beller, 1988). Several studies have indicated that low educational attainment levels among Indigenous peoples in Canada are also tied to colonialism (Miller, 1996). With an increasing number of Indigenous students at post-secondary institutions, some people feel more optimistic about the direction of attainment levels. Higher educational attainment will likely enhance individual labour market opportunities and possibly benefit Indigenous communities if educated individuals return home. In this article, recent attainment is examined in-depth. The objectives of the study[1] are the following:

a. To examine the most up-to-date data available for Indigenous educational attainment in order to determine whether there has been adequate progress since the 1996 Census in Canada. This assessment involves an examination of intra-Indigenous trends in educational attainment and a comparison between Indigenous and non-Indigenous populations in Canada across high school and post-secondary education (PSE).
b. To develop some preliminary policy assessments based on the data analysis. Cursory comments are made on the current reform proposed by the federal government of Canada announced in February of 2014.

For international and Canadian readers alike, it is important to present a brief history of Indigenous educational policy and practice in Canada first.

A Brief History of Colonial Education Policy in Canada: First Contact to 1996

Researchers and Indigenous peoples point to the history of **colonialism** and the approaches taken to education as necessary context in order to understand the present educational attainment of Indigenous peoples in Canada (see, for example, Miller [1996]). According to Peters (2013), the outcome and legacy of this history were:

> [P]overty, marginalization, and much despair. Deprived of an economic base, family relationships disrupted, and Indigenous ways of knowing denigrated, colonialism has taken an exacting toll on First Nations communities. First Nations have relatively high incarceration rates, infant mortality rates, and high school drop-out rates, higher rates of smoking, alcohol, and drug abuse, and have a disproportionate burden of ill-health. (First Nations Information Governance Centre [FNIGC], 2012; National Collaborating Centre for Aboriginal Health [NCCAH], 2012; Perrault, 2009, 43)

In order to explain and understand the impact of the past on present events, we begin at the earliest period when these processes began, at the beginning of the seventeenth century. France originally colonized Canada. The first schooling systems, dating to the early seventeenth century, had the goal of "Francization" of Indigenous peoples to convert them to Christianity (Jaenen, 1986). As White and Peters (2009) pointed out, the *Récollets* (Franciscan friars) trained small groups of boys, whom they hoped would lead the transformation in belief systems within communities.

In 1632, the Jesuits were given control of educating the Indigenous population. They decided first to set up community-based schooling (Magnuson, 1992) but later abandoned this approach for boarding schools (Jaenon, 1986). These efforts were very unsuccessful because of the "tenacity of the Indigenous cultures" (Magnuson, 1992, 61). By the beginning of the eighteenth century, the schools were largely abandoned (Miller, 1996). In addition to Indigenous resistance to converting to Christianity and French culture, part of the reason for school closure lay in the on-going politics and military situation in North America. The French began to realize that assimilation did not serve their colonial interests because both fur traders and soldiers found the Indigenous peoples valuable as partners in the fur trade and strong military allies (White and Peters, 2009).

The mindset that Indigenous peoples could be allies without being made into "Europeans" was also important in British thinking in North America in early periods. Prior to the War of 1812, the British were not very concerned with assimilating Indigenous peoples per se. They were more interested in the utility of Indigenous peoples as military partners against both the French and the Americans. However, the policy shifted after the War of 1812 when declining hostilities led to a British focus on rapid settlement of what is now Canada. A shift in thinking occurred whereby Indigenous peoples were no longer considered allies but impediments: "In the words of a former secretary of state for the colonies, 'reclaiming the Indians from a state of barbarism and introducing amongst them the industrious and peaceful habits of civilized life' became the order of the day" (cited in Wilson [1986, 66]).

This policy shift ushered in a dark time in Canadian history when the industrial boarding school system was launched. The system was designed to enhance the integration of Indigenous peoples into British North American society. In the same period, efforts were made to settle Indigenous populations on reserve land closer to white settlements. The objectives were to get Indigenous peoples, who were nomadic, to give up their nomadic way of life and to make Indigenous peoples who already had fixed communities adopt Western lifestyles. The reserves, however, proved to be a failure after many of the first experiments in this type of settlement were unable to retain a sizable Indigenous population (Miller, 1996).

From the 1840s to Canadian Confederation in 1867 the emphasis was on building "manual labour schools" that promoted Christianity, espoused general assimilation, and taught Indigenous peoples practical skills that fit the British view of development (Miller, 1996). By the 1860s, reports concluded that these, as well, were very unsuccessful (Miller, 1996).

From Confederation onward, the Constitution of Canada ceded control of Indigenous Affairs to the federal government. In the 50 years from 1871 to 1921, the Crown entered into treaties with many Indigenous peoples, known as Canada's First Nations. These **treaties** were designed by the state to facilitate settlement, resource development, and agricultural development in Ontario, as well as the Prairie provinces in Western Canada (Manitoba, Saskatchewan, and Alberta) and the territories of the northern regions. The arrangements and the treaties that came beforehand[2] laid a framework for Crown relations with Indigenous peoples. In these treaties, the Crown promised education; however, it is not clear that what the Crown meant by this was understood in the same way by the many Indigenous peoples who signed the agreement (White, Maxim, and Beavon, 2003). The first education efforts were day schools, but soon the Canadian government began to look south to the United States for a model of forced **residential schooling**.

The Davin Report of 1879 recommended that residential institutions be established in Western Canada (Haig-Brown, 1988). The acceptance of this proposal marked a massive growth in the residential schools that were run by various churches. White and Peters (2009, 17) noted: "the Indian Act was amended in 1894 to make school attendance at a day, boarding, or industrial school compulsory for ten months of the year for all Indigenous children over age six." Through residential schools, the state aimed to "take the Indian out of the child." The consequence included a long-term negative impact on educational attainment that is still witnessed today.

By 1910, reports made it clear that the schools were taking a significant toll on students' health. In many areas, 25 per cent of the student population were suffering from tuberculosis, and even the deputy superintendent of Indian Affairs indicated that less than half the students lived long enough to benefit from their education (White and Peters, 2009). Miller (1996) argued that, at this point in time, the Canadian government shifted its policy from education aimed at assimilating the Indigenous peoples to one of preparing them to live on their own reserves, in other words, segregation.

An examination of the policy and actions from 1910 up to the Second World War illustrates several key problems. First, the curriculum was always much less advanced than that of provincial schools[3]. Students received less than one half day in the classroom and the rest was spent in manual labour. Teachers often had minimal training and the churches used clergy as principals in the schools (Chalmers, 1972). These circumstances led to a situation whereby "few students progressed past the primary grades regardless of how many years were spent in school" (White and Peters, 2009, 18). This was far worse than the conditions for the settler population (Barman, Hébert, and McCaskill, 1986, 18). Second, White and Peters (2009, 19) noted:

> for many First Nations students residential schools were places of emotional, physical, and sexual abuse. Children were taken, often forcefully, from their homes, had their hair cut, were clothed in European style of dress, and were placed in unsanitary living conditions. Students were taught to be ashamed of their culture and to see themselves and their people as inferior and immoral, often facing punishment if they spoke their native language (Miller, 1996). Physical abuse was also commonplace in residential schools.

This history is being investigated by the Truth and Reconciliation Commission of Canada[4]. These conditions were not isolated events. Chrisjohn and Belleau (1991) estimated that in some schools 48 per cent to 70 per cent of residential school students were sexually abused (see also Milloy [1999]). Many researchers have documented similar conditions (see Haig-Brown [1988]; Knockwood [1992]; Miller [1996]).

The 1940s and 1950s marked another re-evaluation of government education policy. The whole education system was severely under-resourced given the Depression of the 1930s and during the Second World War. Many Indigenous veterans returning from Europe were not prepared to accept the poor treatment given to their peoples (Miller, 2000). A major government committee study concluded that residential schools were not succeeding and should be shut down and that the students should be integrated into the provincial systems (Bear Nicholas, 2001). In less than 10 years, 25 per cent of Aboriginal students were attending provincial institutions (Barman et al., 1986). However, the shift from residential schools was academically unsuccessful. In 1967, the federal government reported that drop-out rates from high school for Indigenous students were approaching 94 per cent. The drop-out rate for non-Indigenous students was less than 15 per cent (Indian and Northern Affairs Canada, 1967).

Despite the "decision" to move away from residential schools, the system was far from shut down even by the mid-1960s. However, public attitudes were shifting. There were liberation movements in the developing world, civil rights movements in the United States, and major government investigations that all contributed to a change in terms of public acceptance for discrimination (Miller, 1996). Two reports published in 1967, Caldwell's *Indian Residential Schools* and Hawthorn's *A Survey of the Contemporary Indians of Canada* were critical of the residential school system. According to Milloy (1999), the state opted to endorse the reports. Most schools shut their doors in the following decade.

Between 1967 and the 1990s, there was a period of public debate. Indigenous national organizations, like the National Indian Brotherhood, issued sharp rebukes to government proposals and called for **Indian control of Indian education**. This position was "inspired partly by events such as the 1970 Blue Quills Residential School sit-in, in which the community successfully resisted the school's closure, demanding it remain open under community control" (White and Peters, 2009, 23). The Canadian government had already steered away from residential schooling. With no clear policy direction to fall back on, the government accepted the Indian Brotherhood position of Indian control. However, this acceptance did not mean a major shift in how things were done. As White and Peters (2009, 19) reported:

> After accepting Indian Control of Indian Education as the national policy statement on Aboriginal education, the government began to devolve some administrative control of schools to First Nations communities. In most cases, the devolution of responsibility to First Nations communities resulted in very little actual control over the content and delivery of education.

In different provinces change was developing, albeit slowly. In 1988, the Assembly of First Nations (AFN) released the report *Tradition and Education: Towards a Vision of the Future,* which reiterated the concepts of Indigenous control, arguing that the government should devolve control to the Indigenous communities (AFN, 1988). The AFN argued that in practice the communities (First Nations) should acquire controls similar to those of the provinces as set out by the Canadian Constitution. This was a call for Aboriginal peoples' inherent right to self-government to be the basis for control over education (Abele, Dittubrner, and Graham, 2000). As White and Peters (2009, 24) reported: "It was argued that a Constitutional amendment was needed to formally recognize and affirm this inherent right, or, at the very least, federal legislation that would ensure future dealings between First Nations and the federal government were on a government-to-government basis." There was a demand for proper funding "to create a new administrative structure, establish national and regional educational institutions, formulate long-term education plans, [and] research First Nations learning styles and to develop new curriculum" (White and Peters, 2009, 24).

Since 1988, the landscape of change has become complex. New treaties have brought change in some provinces (for example, the Nishga'a treaty in British Columbia). More progressive provincial regimes have developed or are developing new curricula. At the same time, major finances for Indigenous educational systems have languished (AFN, 2010).

The Royal Commission on Aboriginal Peoples (RCAP, 1996) was a momentous undertaking in the mid-1990s. The RCAP had extensive involvement of Indigenous peoples themselves in research and leadership positions. The RCAP recommended that federal, provincial, and territorial levels of government recognize education as a core component of self-government and necessary to build Indigenous peoples' capacity to run their own affairs. Many of the groundbreaking policy suggestions from the RCAP have not yet been implemented.

The positive changes have led some people to hold hope that educational attainment would improve. That optimism is examined in this article. Our data analysis begins where this "history" leaves off, that is after RCAP in 1996. In the beginning of this introduction, it was stated that there are many things that are correlated with educational attainment. The history described above has taken a terrible toll on Indigenous peoples and has created conditions where educational attainment has been stifled. That said, it has not destroyed Indigenous peoples in Canada nor has it destroyed their drive for improving the educational process in the country. Indigenous languages, cultures, and knowledge(s) have not been obliterated although damage has been done. The call for control of Indigenous education by Indigenous peoples has actually grown (AFN, 1988, 2010; Castellano, 2000; National Indian Brotherhood, 1972; RCAP, 1996).

In this chapter, the data on attainment between 1996 and the present are examined. In the concluding sections, the current policy debate on Indigenous education will be discussed.

Methods

Data used in this chapter come from the 1996, 2001, and 2006 Censuses and the 2011 **National Household Survey (NHS)** of Canada. Publicly available data sets were downloaded that included variables relating to non-Aboriginal and Aboriginal populations, Registered Indian or Treaty Status Indian, on or off reserve status, and Aboriginal identity (First Nations, Inuit, Métis), as well as educational attainment, geographic location, and age group.

Highest educational attainment is defined as a person's "most advanced certificate, diploma, or degree" comprising (1) less than high school; (2) high school; and (3) post-secondary education (PSE). PSE is further broken down into the following categories: apprenticeship or trades, college or other non-university (herein referred to as college); university below the Bachelor's degree level; and university at or above the Bachelor's degree level (see Statistics Canada [2011b]). In each data set, there were additional categories that complicate the presumed general hierarchy (high school graduation, trades, college, and university). In order to avoid overestimating high school or PSE attainment, we combined certain categories. In the

1996 Census data set, categories of "some apprenticeship," "some college," and "some university" were collapsed into the high school educational attainment category because no diploma, certificate, or degree was obtained at the PSE level. Similarly, the "some high school" category was grouped with the "less than high school" category. The 2001 to 2006 Censuses and 2011 NHS had an option to examine whether a high school diploma was attained in addition to the highest education achieved. Those who had PSE yet no high school diploma are considered to have less than high school education[5]. In the labour market, potential employees typically have to show their resumés or fill in documentation about their educational achievements; employers will presumably consider those without high school completion to have a relatively lower educational attainment compared to high school graduates.

Limitations of NHS

The Indigenous population in Canada is a very diverse group and aggregate figures can obscure very different attributes. We have attempted to capture some of this diversity by reporting for the on and off reserve populations and by identity group: Métis, First Nations (Status and non-Status), and Inuit. Given the voluntary nature of the NHS, there are inherently more potential groups and geographical areas that may be under-enumerated. Therefore, the finer the analysis we do using the NHS data, the more likely there will be "under-enumeration impacts" on the findings. The most reliable situation is to have a stable methodology over time that has similar response patterns (like the mandatory long form Census).

Statistics Canada (2011a) reported that approximately 75.3 per cent of the Census sub-divisions in Canada were included in the releases. This is lower than the previous Census in 2006. The non-response bias is likely to affect Indigenous estimates generally and in rural centres particularly. Saskatchewan was the most under-reported province and has a high proportion of Indigenous peoples.

In the 2011 NHS, there were a total of 36 Indian reserves and Indian settlements that were incompletely enumerated. According to Statistics Canada (2011b), estimates associated with the on/off reserve variable are more affected than other variables because of the incomplete enumeration of these Indian reserves and settlements.

Results

The sheer number of post-secondary Indigenous graduates has increased tremendously over the past 15 years. From 1996 to 2011, there was a total increase of 183,170 Indigenous peoples between the ages of 25 to 64 years who attained PSE[6]. The change for each type of PSE by Census year during this time period is documented in Table 8.1. Between 2006 and 2011, there were 21,120 new college graduates and 23,085 new university graduates (at or above Bachelor's degree level [Bachelor]). For the most part, steady increases have been made at these educational levels over time. Conversely, apprenticeship or trades numbers are in decline. The drop in the 2006 to 2011 period reverses gains made in the 2001 to 2006 period. Possibly, this decline could indicate that Indigenous post-secondary students are choosing other paths at colleges and universities instead of participating in apprenticeship or trades. It is also possible that fewer apprenticeship opportunities were available for interested students following the 2008 recession.

The increased PSE attainment among the Indigenous population is a success. A real roadblock to a greater number of PSE graduates is low educational attainment. Table 8.2 shows

Table 8.1 Indigenous Population PSE Attainment, 25 to 64 years, 1996 to 2011, Absolute Numbers

	1996	2001	2006	2011	Change 1996–2011
Apprenticeship or trades	16,000	69,260	80,060	67,045	51,045
College or other non-university	66,935	66,795	103,905	125,025	58,090
University below Bachelor level	n/a	8,125	20,050	23,605	15,480*
University at Bachelor or above	15,660	26,340	43,010	66,095	50,435
Total post-secondary education	98,595	170,520	247,025	281,765	183,170
Total Indigenous population	346,485	443,600	555,420	671,380	324,895

Sources: Statistics Canada (1996, 2001a, 2006b, 2011a)
* The increase for this PSE type is for the 2001–2011 time period because data are not available for 1996.

the rising numbers over time of Indigenous peoples with no high school diploma or equivalent; the number increased by 80,165 in the 1996 to 2011 period. The number of high school graduates with no PSE completion also rose; however, this group is considerably smaller than its less educated counterpart. The Indigenous population in Canada is relatively young (Statistics Canada, 2011a), which means the numbers of those who are not high school or post-secondary graduates will likely rise if trends remain unchanged. A concern, then, is high school completion. Mendelson (2006, 31) reported: "the failure to complete high school explains 88% of the variation in PSE"[7]. Increasing the number of high school graduates increases the number of PSE graduates (Mendelson, 2006). Accordingly, high school completion is an important key to moving forward with regard to improving Indigenous PSE attainment.

In Canada's labour market, PSE attainment is critical for gainful employment. Unemployment rates[8] drop with each increasing level of higher education. Among the Indigenous population, the unemployment rate was a high 23.3 per cent for those who did not

Table 8.2 Indigenous Population High School with No PSE and High School Non-completion, 25 to 64 years, 1996 to 2011 Absolute Numbers, 2016 to 2021 Estimated Numbers

	1996	2001	2006	2011	Change 1996–2011	Projected 2016*	Projected 2021*
Less than high school	156,605	171,710	189,395	236,770	80,165	253,165	278,983
High school	91,275	101,355	118,960	152,840	61,565	166,683	186,913

Sources: Statistics Canada (1996, 2001a, 2006b, 2011a)
Note: In order to make the projections for 2016 and 2021, we assume that fertility and mortality rates for the Indigenous population remain at current levels and there are no major shifts in general economic or social conditions.
* Less than high school trend line: slope $a = 25,818$; x intercept $= 124,075$; $r^2 = 0.9182$.
High school only trend line: slope $a = 20,230$; x intercept $= 65,533$; $r^2 = 0.9336$.

complete high school; it fell to 11.4 per cent for those with high school only, and then to 9.3 per cent for those with PSE (Statistics Canada, 2011b). We estimate that 278,983 Indigenous peoples (25–64 years of age) will not have a high school education in 2021. Given the economic outcomes associated with higher education, this number is very high. We agree with Mendelson (2006) but also note that there are important considerations in terms of improving high school graduation rates. As noted earlier in this article, some are resources, curriculum, social capital, and normative issues, some relate to the policy and practice bred by colonialism, and still others relate to the lack of economic opportunity seen by Indigenous youth that dissuade them from seeking credentials.

The Indigenous population is a heterogeneous group. It is not surprising, then, that some groups fare better than others. Differences within the Indigenous population of Canada are discussed next.

Geographic Location

As noted earlier, the federal government in Canada has jurisdiction over Indigenous education. Yet attainment is disproportionate across provinces and territories. Seven provinces (Nova Scotia, Newfoundland and Labrador, Ontario, Quebec, New Brunswick, Prince Edward Island, and British Columbia) have a higher proportion of PSE than "less than high school" level of education. For example, among the Indigenous population in Nova Scotia, 53 per cent possess a PSE and 26 per cent have not completed high school. The pattern for the remaining provinces and territories is a higher proportion of "less than high school" education than PSE. This makes a useful benchmark for judging where the problems are most acute and where we might find positive approaches that are working.

The most alarming difference is Nunavut where 73 per cent of the Indigenous population has less than a high school education and 15 per cent has a PSE. A notable demographic trend in Canada is that the Northwest Territories and the Prairie provinces typically have the highest proportions of Indigenous peoples in their populations whereas, in terms of absolute numbers, Ontario has the largest Indigenous population (Statistics Canada, 2006a). However, the Indigenous populations of the territories and Prairies have lower educational attainment. In fact, they have the lowest provincial rates of high school completion with higher proportions of non-high school completion than PSE attainment. British Columbia stands out as a more successful Western province; two-thirds of its Indigenous population have at least a high school education. This province has 130 First Nations community schools, is engaged in defining new treaties, and has successfully integrated public and Indigenous run schools (First Nations Schools Association, 2014). At the other end of Canada, we see better educational attainment. Another more successful area of the country is Nova Scotia where the self-governing educational authorities of Mi'kmaw communities of the province reported high school completion rates of 88 per cent in the 2012 to 2013 school year (Mi'kmawKina'matnewey, 2014). This number is well above the national average for Indigenous students and is comparable to the average for the general population of Canada.

In Canada, recent job creation has been higher in Alberta and Saskatchewan (Burleton et al., 2013). However, these provinces rank relatively poorly with regard to Indigenous educational attainment. If PSE attainment is presumed to make individuals labour market ready, there is a geographical mismatch between a lesser trained Indigenous population and a very hot job market. Possibly, economic development projects are not localized in Indigenous communities.

Identity Group, Status, on or off Reserve

Differences within the Indigenous population of Canada also emerge by the identity group to which one belongs and whether one lives "on reserve" (in a First Nations designated community). Highest educational attainment over time for First Nations (North American Indian), Inuit, Métis, Status Indian and non-Status Indian, and peoples living on or off reserve[9] is shown in Table 8.3. One may expect that over the past 15 years, the percentages

Table 8.3 Highest Educational Attainment by Indigenous Group, 25 to 64 Years, 1996 to 2011, Percentages

	1996	2001	2006	2011
On Reserve				
Less than high school	54	48	50	55
High school	22	19	15	18
Post-secondary education	24	32	35	27
Off Reserve				
Less than high school	42	35	29	30
High school	28	24	23	24
Post-secondary education	30	41	47	46
Status				
Less than high school	47	42	40	43
High school	26	22	19	21
Post-secondary education	27	36	41	36
Non-Status				
Less than high school	42	35	28	29
High school	27	23	24	24
Post-secondary education	31	42	48	47
First Nations				
Less than high school	46	41	38	40
High school	26	23	20	22
Post-secondary education	27	37	42	38
Inuit				
Less than high school	53	48	51	59
High school	20	20	13	16
Post-secondary education	27	32	36	25
Métis				
Less than high school	41	34	26	26
High school	27	24	24	24
Post-secondary education	31	43	50	49

Sources: Statistics Canada (1996, 2001a, 2001b, 2006b, 2006c, 2011a)

of high school non-completions would decline and post-secondary attainment would in-crease. This is not the case for all identity and geographic groups. This trend was observed for Métis, off reserve, non-Status, and First Nations peoples[10]. These particular Indigenous groups have continuously had higher PSE attainment compared to Indigenous peoples living on reserve, Status Indians, or Inuit peoples. In 1996, all seven of these groups had roughly the same proportion of PSE attainment (range 24 per cent to 31 per cent). Fif-teen years later, Métis and off reserve peoples more than doubled their respective post-secondary proportions. For example, Métis PSE attainment numbers changed from 30,435 to 117,015—a growth of 285 per cent. Contributing to this growth is the great rise in high school completions. As stated earlier, an increase in high school completions will increase the number of PSE graduates.

This point in time appears to be a turning point for First Nations peoples. Although this population follows the higher education trend previously noted, in 2011, the proportions of those without a high school education and those with a PSE were about the same (40 per cent and 38 per cent, respectively). Likely in the next Census period, the First Nations popula-tion will have more PSE graduates than individuals without a high school education.

Attainment of higher levels of education over time is not evident among Inuit or those living on reserve. For on reserve Indigenous, educational attainment levels remained stable. Consistently, a greater proportion of this group has not completed high school than attained a PSE. Inuit educational attainment appears to be worsening; high school non-completions have risen about 11 percentage points over the past 10 years[11]. Among Status peoples, non–high school completion is higher compared to post-secondary completion.

Indigenous and Non-Indigenous Populations

We see no reason why Indigenous peoples in Canada could not achieve the same levels of education as non-Indigenous peoples if conditions were right. Figure 8.1 compares highest educational attainment between these populations over time. Similar trends are apparent for both populations: The proportion of those with less than high school education de-clined, which corresponds with a rise of those with a PSE; high school only attainment has been relatively stable at about 23 per cent from 2001 to 2011.

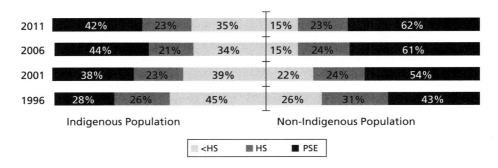

Figure 8.1 Indigenous and Non-Indigenous Highest Educational Attainment, 25 to 64 Years, 1996 to 2011, Percentages

Sources: Statistics Canada (1996, 2001a, 2006b, 2011a)

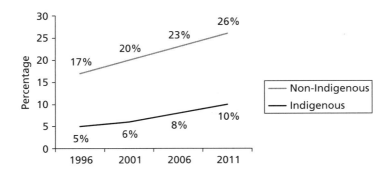

Figure 8.2 Indigenous and Non-Indigenous University Attainment, 25 to 64 years, 1996 to 2011

Sources: Statistics Canada (1996, 2001a, 2006b, 2011a)

Although both populations made gains in higher education, little change occurred to the gaps between them with regard to PSE attainment and high school incompletion. Between 1996 and 2011, Indigenous peoples had a higher percentage—about 19 percentage points—of those with less than high school education compared to non-Indigenous peoples. During the same time, the non-Indigenous population had a higher percentage of those with a PSE—ranging from 16 percentage points in 1996 to 20 percentage points in 2011—compared to the Indigenous population. The disparity between these populations is not narrowing. Indigenous PSE attainment was 65 per cent of the non-Indigenous PSE attainment in 1996, 70 per cent in 2001, 72 per cent in 2006, and 68 per cent in 2011. At best, the gap has remained at the same level. At worst, it is beginning to increase. Clearly, improving high school completion for Indigenous peoples is critical if we are to narrow the PSE gap between these groups.

In Figure 8.2 we compare university PSE attainment for our populations. We could produce figures illustrating all the PSE relationships[12]. We found that there is no gap in trades and apprenticeship attainment between Indigenous and non-Indigenous populations. For college the attainment remained fairly constant over time for both groups; there is a slight difference between them (a stable two percentage points). In Figure 8.2, there is a continuous and growing difference between the two trend lines for university attainment. The number of Indigenous degree holders is increasing both absolutely and proportionally, but the increase in non-Indigenous university completion is even greater. This gap is slowly widening; from 12 percentage points in 1996 to 16 percentage points in 2011. Considering the trends we see in these different types of PSE, we can say with certainty that university attainment carries the greatest weight in the PSE gap between the two populations.

Discussion

One objective guiding this article was to determine whether adequate progress has taken place with regard to Indigenous peoples' educational attainment in Canada. The answer to this question is of national and international importance. The short answer is that while improvements have been achieved, it should have been better. Below, this answer is elaborated upon. Afterward, we discuss policy attempts since 1996, including the 2014 proposed reforms, and make progressive policy recommendations.

Undoubtedly, strides have been made in Indigenous peoples' educational attainment in Canada. Among Indigenous peoples, the current working age group is more educated compared to this age group in earlier Censuses: Post-secondary attainment increased 186 percentage points between 1996 and 2011. The cumulative increase of PSE graduates reveals a source of labour that can make meaningful contributions to the Canadian economy and Indigenous communities. Another sign of moving forward is that this trend is observed for Métis, off reserve, non-Status, and First Nations peoples. Over the past 15 years, high school non-completion declined and PSE attainment rose for these groups. Also, Indigenous success is real in apprenticeships, trades, and colleges—Indigenous and non-Indigenous populations have about the same proportions of graduates for these PSE paths.

These gains connect to resources and economic development. Job creation is typically higher in urban areas than rural areas (Burleton et al., 2013). Perhaps Métis and off reserve peoples, who tend to live in cities, see the real value and payoff of high school completion and PSE through proximity to such economic activity. Time away from family and community are important factors among Indigenous peoples when determining whether to attend post-secondary institution (Restoule et al., 2013) and deciding among employment options (McKenzie et al., 2013). Urban centres are home to community colleges and many jobs that require PSE. Disruptions to familial relationships and responsibilities are minimal if urban Indigenous students attend local post-secondary institutions while living at home. Notably, apprenticeship, trades, and college programs require fewer resources, both financial and time, compared to university programs. In short, there may be real socio-cultural and economic explanations for the disparity we see between Status and on reserve Indigenous persons, and the Métis and non-Status populations, the latter having more improved educational attainment and a declining gap with the non-Indigenous population.

Our conclusion that there has not been adequate improvement in attainment rests on the continuing problems faced by on reserve, Status, and Inuit peoples with regards to high school completion. As well, there is the problem of a growing gap in university PSE attainment. This developing gap bodes poorly for engagement in the twenty-first century economy. The number of Indigenous post-secondary graduates increased, but PSE attainment among non-Indigenous peoples is increasing much more quickly. In summary, we would point out that the difference in attainment between populations is not narrowing. The disparity is driven by (1) continuing lower attainment of high school among Indigenous populations; (2) the increasing difference in university attainment; and (3) socio-cultural and economic disparities related to living on reserve, having Indian Status, and/or being Inuit.

Policy Attempts since 1996

We have briefly tracked Canadian policy from the seventeenth century to 1996 and looked at the data from 1996 Census to the 2011 NHS. In our discussion of the data, it was noted that while there have been improvements in the gross numbers of Indigenous persons who have completed high school and in the numbers attending and completing PSE, there are on-going serious problems. First, the high school non-completion rates are far too high. Second, there is an increasing gap between non-Indigenous Canadians and Indigenous people in Canada. Also noted above are intra-Indigenous differences whereby First Nations holding Status and Inuit are not doing as well as non-Status and Métis peoples.

The history of forced assimilation, residential schooling, abuse in some institutions, suppression of language and culture and the other violations that were pointed out earlier in this chapter, have surely contributed to the problems in educational attainment. That implies there are past policy failures and current policy shortcomings.

From 1996 to the present there have been quite a few partial and failed attempts to address policy deficits. While several initiatives were unveiled in the next few years[13], there was a continuing and growing critique of the state's approach. Many commentators are in agreement that the core problem has been that while there has been a formal acceptance of Aboriginal control of Aboriginal education, it has not been well translated into policy and action (Peters 2013, 40). It is widely accepted that control must be accompanied by the resources to exercise this power or it is vacuous (Gordon and White, 2014).

Fast forward to 2013, the same debate broke out into the public. The "Proposal for a Bill on First Nation Education" (see AANDC [2013]) came under intense criticism. The crux of the difference between First Nations and the Aboriginal Affairs and Northern Development Canada (AANDC) was the demand that any change reflect the First Nations people's proposals. Once again the same issues arose: "These include the central principle of First Nation control and the absolute need for a funding guarantee for First Nation children to learn in a safe, secure environment nurtured within their languages and cultures" (Atleo, 2013, 1).

The First Nations indicated that current proposals were not acceptable as they were not partnership driven and they did not respect treaty relationships (much less give control and resources to the First Nations (Atleo, 2013, 1). They called for substantial consultation, and the core demands included per capita funding equal to the provinces[14] and real control over the content and delivery of education[15]. The Department of Aboriginal Affairs and Northern Development (AANDC) argues that from its perspective, some consultation was done; the government notes that the First Nations saw the draft proposal and that it is still under discussion (Valcourt, 2013). Further, Aboriginal Affairs Minister Valcourt indicated that there would be funding with the new legislation; it simply had not been determined how much at this point (Valcourt, 2013). As well, the focus of the government seemed to be on accountability, standards, and quality of whatever might be allowed under the new Act. This raises the problem of real sovereignty for First Nations over their education.

The *First Nations Control of First Nations Education Act 2014*

In a surprise turn of events, February 2014 saw a joint announcement, from the Assembly of First Nations and the Canadian federal government, of a new approach and what appeared to be a new agreement. A supposedly new version of the *First Nations Control of First Nations Education Act* (FNCFNEA) was heralded as a real shift in policy. The Prime Minister, Stephen Harper, noted that "[The Act] will ensure First Nations control of First Nations education while establishing minimum education standards, consistent with provincial standards off-reserve" (PMO, 2014, 1) Finally Prime Minister Harper noted that the announcement has significant differences from the 2013 proposal including "adequate stable, predictable and sustainable funding" (PMO, 2014, 1).

The first response from the Assembly of First Nations (AFN, 2014) appeared to agree on several issues with the Canadian government. However, there was widespread opposition from different First Nations and regional leaders. The outcome was a reversal of the AFN position and the new draft bill was rejected. National Chief Atleo resigned citing the fact that the debate had shifted to his leadership and away from education. The Canadian government, for its part has removed the Bill from the legislative agenda, stating:

> As we have said all along, this legislation will not proceed without the support of AFN, and we have been clear that we will not invest new money in an education system that does not serve the best interests of First Nations children; funding will only follow real education reforms.

Policy for Moving Educational Attainment Forward

Aside from the debate over the 2013 proposals and the continuing disagreements over the recent 2014 redraft, there are several things that will need to change. For any policy to move forward to make real gains there will need to be several elements in place:

- Successful building of PSE attainment requires emphasis on high school completion strategies. This rests in improving the high school curriculum to reflect First Nations peoples in a historically proper light. It means in the short run, introducing more indigenization of the schools and ultimately will require schools built and operated in the territories of the First Nations by Indigenous-led school authorities.
- Decades of underfunding means large investments are necessary. This is not a form of welfare but rather an explicit recognition that over the colonial history there has been a deep problem created, and if we are going to make progress it requires investments. These investments should not be seen as a cost to the non-Indigenous population. It is truly an investment. It leads to improved health and social security for Indigenous peoples through improvement of the social determinants of health; it creates the possibility for hundreds of thousands of Indigenous peoples to engage in the economy. The collective wealth created by such engagement will far outweigh the investments. And lastly, it is simply unacceptable that a segment of the population living in Canada faces the gaps in education (health, labour force participation, and income) that exist today.
- Indigenous control of a properly funded system where voluntary agreements are developed with provincial education systems is a necessary component of any potential solution.
- Building on successes is critical. It was noted earlier that colleges are relatively successful in attracting and retaining Indigenous students. It was also noted that current self-governing educational authorities in select areas of the country have vastly improved high school graduation. These models need to be systematically examined and learned from in a practical sense.
- Creating a generation of mentors and role models will be an important step forward. Much of the research indicates that success leads to success. Parental educational attainment is highly correlated with children's success (see Krein and Beller [1988]). Improving attainment in each generation will build greater successes in the next.

Maintaining the status quo is in many ways the worst of all alternatives. Educational reform will require that a consensus be built. As Former National Chief Atleo pointed out:

> This work is simply too important to walk away and abandon our students to the next round of discussions, to tell them they will have to wait. . . . We owe it to

ourselves, our children and our nations to make our best efforts to achieve our lifelong goal of First Nations control of First Nations education. (Atelo, 2014)

Questions for Critical Thought

1. What role did assimilationist policies like "residential schools" play in creating a gap between Indigenous and non-Indigenous educational attainment?
2. Is the gap between Indigenous and non-Indigenous educational attainment narrowing, increasing, or staying the same?
3. Why do Gordon and White argue that improving high school completion rates is critical to improving post-secondary educational attainment?
4. Indigenous people's representative organizations argue that there should be "Aboriginal control of Aboriginal education." Do you understand their reasoning?
5. Improving the educational attainment of Indigenous peoples will benefit the people themselves and all Canadians at the same time. Do you agree? Why or why not?

Glossary

Colonialism The policy or practice of taking full or partial control, by force, over another territory, settling that territory with your citizens occupying it with settlers, and exploiting it socially, economically, and politically. British colonialism began in the late 1600s in Canada.

Indian control of Indian education The stated demand of Indigenous peoples to have sovereign control over the educational systems established for their peoples. This demand, put forward in the "Red Paper" by the National Indian Brotherhood in the 1970s, is seen as a cornerstone of policy to close the gap in educational attainment and protect Indigenous cultures.

Indigenous peoples The peoples descended from the original peoples who occupied North America when Europeans landed. In Canada this includes First Nations, Inuit, and Métis peoples.

National Household Survey (NHS) When the mandatory long form Census was cancelled in 2010 the federal government introduced a voluntary survey as part of the Census. This is called the National Household Survey.

Residential schools The history of Indigenous-settler relations in Canada is marked by many horrific attempts to assimilate the Indigenous populations. Residential schools refers to a school system set up by the Canadian government, run mostly by churches that stated objective of indoctrinating and assimilating the young people into Christianity and European ways of living. In an apology given on 11 June 2008 by Prime Minister Stephen Harper, he stated: "These objectives were based on the assumption Aboriginal cultures and spiritual beliefs were inferior and unequal. Indeed, some sought, as it was infamously said, 'to kill the Indian in the child.' Today, we recognize that this policy of assimilation was wrong, has caused great harm, and has no place in our country."

Treaties Between 1701 and present day, different groups of Indigenous peoples have entered into agreements with the Crown (first with the British and after with the federal government of Canada). These agreements are called treaties. These treaties speak to a variety of issues including the rights of peoples to use and enjoy lands occupied by Indigenous peoples and the responsibilities of government and Indigenous peoples. Treaties made prior to 1982 are recognized and protected by the Canadian Constitution. Modern treaties after 1982 are legally binding through other means.

Notes

1. For an in-depth analysis of educational attainment of Aboriginal peoples in Canada see the longer version of this report in *The International Indigenous Policy Journal*, Volume 5, Issue 3.
2. From the seventeenth century, protocols and treaties were signed in different areas. The most expansive period for treaty making was 1871 to 1921 when the so-called "numbered treaties" were consummated. These were the treaties that enshrined promises of state supported education.
3. In Canada the Constitution gives the provinces jurisdiction over education except for Registered Indians or First Nations and Inuit living on reserve.
4. For more information on the Commission please see: www.trc.ca/websites/trcinstitution/index.php?p=3
5. This is an example of how researchers have to be careful to investigate the specificities of Indigenous communities. Aboriginal Affairs Canada (AANDC) was in the habit of requiring Indigenous persons who were participating in certain transfer programs to enroll in upgrading seminars or short certificate programs. People taking these certificates would often report their engagement as PSE, thereby inflating the PSE numbers.
6. We utilized the 25- to 64-year-old population for two reasons: (1) the 15 and over age population inflates the number of people without high school completion; and (2) the 65 and over age groups are much more likely not to be employed compared to 25- to 64-year-olds.
7. The variables less than high school and PSE completion have a strong negative correlation ($r^2 = 0.8782$) (Mendelson, 2006).
8. The unemployment rate is the number of unemployed individuals ages 15 and over as a percentage of the labour force.
9. Canada has a rather unique system that is the result of colonialism. First Nations (in some documents called Indians) are Indigenous nations historically constituted prior to colonial first contact. They have, over the last four centuries, engaged in forced and voluntary agreements that have limited their traditional territories and created "reserves," which are defined through legislation and signed treaties. Status Indians are those who are registered and have status under the Indian Act and these peoples have reserved land. Some Status Indians live in their reserve communities and some do not (approximately 50 per cent; see White et al., 2003). Those who live on reserve are for all intents and purposes Status Indians. There is also a large population of non-Status Indians who have lost their recognition for various reasons and live in urban and smaller towns. These peoples very often identify in surveys as "First Nation-" so any data using "First Nation" includes both Status and non-Status First Nations persons. There are also mixed ancestry persons who identify as a separate Indigenous group known as Métis. These peoples live in more urban centres, and, finally, there are the Inuit who live in large part in Canada's North.
10. As noted, First Nations persons can be either Status or non-Status. Given that non-Status Indians have a higher level of educational attainment the mean levels of the First Nation category are inflated.
11. We caution readers that the 2011 NHS data were collected using a different methodology from previous Censuses; therefore it will be important to see the next collection periods for comparison (2016 and 2021).
12. For figures illustrating trades and college attainment trends see Gordon and White (2014) "Indigenous Educational Attainment" *The International Indigenous Policy Journal*, Volume 5, Issue 3.
13. The Education Partnerships Program (EPP) and the First Nation Student Success Program (FNSSP), for example.
14. It should be noted that "equal per capita funding" would in itself be inequitable given the decades of underfunding and the enormity of the problems to tackle (see Drummond in Galloway [2013]). See: www.theglobeandmail.com/news/politics/first-nations-schools-need-a-bigger-boost-economist-to-warn-chiefs/article15862012/#dashboard/follows/
15. In several areas (such as New Brunswick) Indigenous control has shown real improvements in the graduation rates from high school (see Valcourt [2013]).

References

Abele, F., Dittubrner, C., and Graham, K.A. "Towards a shared understanding in the policy discussion about Aboriginal education." In *Aboriginal Education: Fulfilling the Promise*, M.B. Costellano, L. Davis, and L. Lahache (eds.), (3–24). Vancouver: University of British Columbia Press, 2000.

Aboriginal Affairs and Northern Development Canada (AANDC). *Developing a First Nation Education Act: Discussion Guide*. Ottawa: Aboriginal Affairs and Northern Development Canada, 2013. Retrieved 21 July 2015 from: www.aadnc-aandc.gc.ca/eng/ 1355150229225/ 1355150442776b

Assembly of First Nations (AFN). *Tradition and Education: Towards a Vision of Our Future, a Declaration of First Nations Jurisdiction over Education*. Ottawa: Assembly of First Nations, 1988.

Assembly of First Nations (AFN). *First Nations Control of First Nations Education: It's Our Vision, It's Our Time*. Ottawa: Assembly of First Nations, 2010.

Assembly of First Nations (AFN). *A Clear Path Forward*. (2014). Retrieved 21 July 2015 from: www.afn.ca/uploads/files/education/a_clear_ path_forward_on_first_nations_education .pdf

Atleo, S. *Open Letter to Minister of Aboriginal Affairs and Northern Development*. Ottawa: Assembly of First Nations, 2013. Retrieved 21 July 2015 from: www.afn.ca/index.php/en/ national-chief/highlights-from-the-national-chief/open-letter-to-minister-of-aboriginal-affairs-and-northern-development

Atleo, S. "*First Nations Education Act* 'must act as a bridge'." CBC News (12 April 2014). Retrieved from: www.cbc.ca/news/aboriginal/ shawn-atleo-first-nations-education-act-must-act-as-a-bridge-1.2607454

Barman, J., Hébert, Y., and McCaskill, D. "The legacy of the past: An overview." In *Indian Education in Canada. Volume 1: The Legacy*, J. Barman, Y. Hébert, and D. McCaskill (eds.), (1–22). Vancouver: University of British Columbia Press, 1986.

Bear Nicholas, A. "Canada's colonial mission: The great white bird." In *Aboriginal Education in Canada: A Study in Decolonization*, K.P. Binda and S. Calliou (eds.), (9–33). Mississauga: Canadian Educators' Press, 2001.

Burleton, D, Gulati, S, McDonald, C, and Scarfone. S. *Jobs in Canada: Where, What and for Whom?* TD Economics. (Special report, 2013). Retrieved 21 July 2015 from: www.td.com/document/ PDF/economics/special/JobsInCanada.pdf

Caldwell, G. *Indian Residential Schools: A Research Study of the Child Care Programmes for Nine Residential Schools in Saskatchewan*. Prepared for the Department of Indian Affairs and Northern Development. Ottawa: Canadian Welfare Council, 1967.

Indian and Northern Affairs Canada. *A Survey of the Contemporary Indians of Canada Economic, Political, Educational Needs and Policies: Part 2*. Ottawa: Queen's Printer, 1967.

Castellano, M.B. "Updating Aboriginal traditions of knowledge." In *Indigenous Knowledges in Global Contexts*, G.F. Sefa Dei, B.L. Hall, and D.G. Rosenberg (eds.), (21–36). Toronto: University of Toronto Press, 2000.

CBC News. "Shawn Atleo resigns as AFN national chief." CBC News (2 May 2014). Retrieved from www.cbc.ca/news/politics/shawn-atleo-resigns-as-afn-national-chief-1.2630085

Chalmers, J.W. *Education behind the Buckskin Curtain*. Edmonton: University of Alberta Bookstore, 1972.

First Nations Information Governance Centre (FNIGC). *First Nations Regional Health Survey (RHS) 2008/10: National Report on Adults, Youth and Children Living in First Nations Communities*. Ottawa: First Nations Information Governance Centre, 2012.

First Nations Schools Association. *Home*. (2014). Retrieved 21 July 2015 from: www.fnsa.ca

Galloway, G. "First Nations schools need a bigger boost, economist to warn chiefs." *The Globe and Mail* 11 December 2013. Retrieved 21 July 2015 from: www.theglobeandmail.com/ news/politics/first-nations-schools-need-a-bigger-boost-economist-to-warn-chiefs/ article15862012/#dashboard/follows

Gang, I., and Zimmermann, K. "Is child like parent?" *The Journal of Human Resources* 35(3) (2000): 550–69.

Garner, C.L, and Raudenbush, S.W. "Neighborhood effects on educational attainment: A multilevel analysis." *Sociology of Education* 64(4) (1991): 251–62.

Gordon, C., and White, J.P. "Indigenous educational attainment in Canada." *The International Indigenous Policy Journal* 5(3) (2014). Retrieved 21 July 2015 from: http://ir.lib.uwo.ca/iipj/vol5/iss3/6

Haig-Brown, C. *Resistance and Renewal: Surviving the Indian Residential School.* Vancouver: Tillacum Library, 1988.

Office of the Prime Minister of Canada (PMO). *First Nations Control of First Nations Education Act.* Office of the Prime Minister of Canada, 2014. Retrieved 21 July 2015 from: www.pm.gc.ca/eng/news/2014/02/07/first-nations-control-first-nations-education-act

Indian and Northern Affairs Canada and Hawthorn, H.B, (ed.). *A Survey of the Contemporary Indians of Canada: A Report on Economic, Political and Educational Needs* (Volume 2). Ottawa: Indian Affairs Branch, 1967.

Jaenen, C.J. "Education for francization: The case of New France in the seventeenth century." In *Indian Education in Canada. Volume 1: The Legacy*, J. Barman, Y. Hébert, and D. McCaskill (eds.), (45–63). Vancouver: University of British Columbia Press, 1986.

Knockwood, I. *Out of the Depths: The Experiences of Mi'kmaw Children at the Indian Residential School at Shubenacadie, Nova Scotia.* Lockeport: Roseway, 1992.

Krein, S.F., and Beller, A.H. "Educational attainment of children from single-parent families: Differences by exposure, gender, and race." *Demography* 25(2) (1988): 221–34.

Magnuson, R. *Education in New France.* Montreal: McGill-Queen's University Press, 1992.

McKenzie, J., Jackson, A.P., Yazzie, R., Smith, S.A., Crotty, A.K., Baum, D., Denny, A., and Bah'lgai Eldridge, D. "Career dilemmas among Diné (Navajo) college graduates: An exploration of the Dinétah (Navajo Nation) brain drain." *The International Indigenous Policy Journal* 4(4) (2013). Retrieved 21 July 2015 from: http://ir.lib.uwo.ca/cgi/viewcontent.cgi?article=1154&context=iipj

Mendelson, M. *Aboriginal Peoples and Postsecondary Education.* Ottawa: Caledon Institute of Social Policy, 2006.

Mi'kmawKina'matnewey News. (2014). Retrieved from: http://kinu.ca/news

Miller, J.R. *Shingwauk's Vision: A History of Native Residential Schools.* Toronto: University of Toronto Press, 1996.

Miller, J.R. *Skyscrapers Hide the Heavens: A History of Indian-White Relations in Canada*, third edition. Toronto: University of Toronto Press, 2000.

Milloy, J.S. *A National Crime: The Canadian Government and the Residential School System, 1879 to 1986.* Winnipeg: The University of Manitoba Press, 1999.

National Collaborating Centre for Aboriginal Health (NCCAH). *The State of Knowledge of Aboriginal Health: A Review of Aboriginal Public Health in Canada.* Prince George: National Collaborating Centre for Aboriginal Health, 2012.

National Indian Brotherhood. *Indian Control of Indian Education.* Ottawa: National Indian Brotherhood, 1972.

Perrault, S. *The Incarceration of Aboriginal People in Adult Correctional Services.* Ottawa: Statistics Canada, 2009.

Peters, J. "Selected cases on the continuum of First Nations learning." PhD thesis, University of Western Ontario, 2013. Retrieved 21 July 2015 from: http://ir.lib.uwo.ca/cgi/viewcontent.cgi?article=3195&context=etd

Restoule, J., Mashford-Pringle, A., Chacaby, M., Smillie, C., Brunette, C., and Russel, G. "Supporting successful transitions to postsecondary education for Indigenous students: Lessons from an institutional ethnography in Ontario, Canada." *The International Indigenous Policy Journal* 4(4) (2013). Retrieved 21 July 2015 from: http://ir.lib.uwo.ca/cgi/viewcontent.cgi?article=1144&context=iipj

Royal Commission on Aboriginal Peoples (RCAP). *Report of the Royal Commission on Aboriginal Peoples.* Ottawa: Canada Communications Group, 1996.

Spence, N., and White, J.P. "First Nations educational success: Assessing determinants using a social context lens." In *Aboriginal Education: Current Crisis and Future Alternatives*, J.P. White, J. Peters, D. Beavon, and N. Spence (eds.), (225–47). Toronto: Thompson Educational Publishing, 2009.

Statistics Canada. *Census of Population, 1996* (Table 94-F0009XDB96001). Ottawa: Statistics Canada, 1996.

Statistics Canada. *2001 Census* (Catalogue No. 99-012-X2001042). Ottawa: Statistics Canada, 2001a.

Statistics Canada. *2001 Census* (Catalogue No. 97-F0011XCB2001058). Ottawa: Statistics Canada, 2001b.

Statistics Canada. *Chart 4: Provincial/Territorial Distribution of Aboriginal Identity Population, 2006*. Ottawa: Statistics Canada, 2006a. Retrieved from: www.statcan.gc.ca/pub/89-645-x/2010001/c-g/c-g004-eng.htm

Statistics Canada. *2006 Census* (Catalogue No. 97-560-XCB2006028). Ottawa: Statistics Canada, 2006b.

Statistics Canada. *2006 Census* (Catalogue No. 97-560-XCB2006038). Ottawa: Statistics Canada, 2006c.

Statistics Canada. *National Household Survey Users Guide* (Catalogue No. 99-001-x2011001). Ottawa: Statistics Canada, 2011a.

Statistics Canada. *2011 National Household Survey* (Catalogue No. 99-012-X2011044). Ottawa: Statistics Canada, 2011b.

Valcourt, B. *Open Letter to Assembly of First Nations*. Ottawa: Aboriginal Affairs and Northern Development, 2013. Retrieved 21 July 2015 from: www.aadnc-aandc.gc.ca/eng/1386958638702/1386958691700

White, J.P., and Peters, J. "A short history of Aboriginal education in Canada." In *Aboriginal Education: Current Crisis and Future Alternatives*, J.P. White, J. Peters, D. Beavon, and N. Spence (eds.), (13–33). Toronto: Thompson Educational Publishing, 2009.

White, J.P., Maxim, P., and Beavon, D. (eds). *Aboriginal Conditions: Research as a Foundation for Public Policy*. Vancouver: UBC Press, 2003.

Wilson, D.J. "'No blanket to be worn in school': The education of Indians in nineteenth-century Ontario." In *Indian Education in Canada. Volume 1: The Legacy*, J. Barman, Y. Hébert, and D. McCaskill (eds.), (64–87). Vancouver: University of British Columbia Press, 1986.

9

Single-Gender Education
Reinforcing and Challenging Gender Difference

Jayne Baker

Introduction

Although it seems self-evident, it is worth stating that single-gender schools are based on the notion of gender difference. Both boys' and girls' schools have mandates to meet the unique needs of their students. Where boys are concerned, this has been unproblematic; boys' schools have historically prepared boys for positions of leadership and labour market participation. For girls' schools, however, there have been significant changes in the role of women and larger societal goals around gender inequality largely via changes to women's role in the home and workplace. These schools have gone from "finishing" to "empowering" (DeBare, 2004). This chapter looks at one particular moment in the continuing history of single-gender schools through the vantage point of an **elite** all-boys' school and an elite all-girls' school, which I call Boy High and Girl High, respectively. I pay attention to the ways that these schools have been designed to address their students' supposed strengths and needs and the way understandings of gender are embedded in the everyday practices of the schools. For Girl High I also show the contradiction between girl power, stereotypes, and class privilege.

Gender and Class Reproduction

Many of the formative sociological theories at the core of the sociology of education typically pay insufficient attention to gender; they may assume a male student who will go on to participate in the paid labour market, or fail to use a gendered analysis in their discussions of the student experience of schooling, or may have female students on the periphery or absent altogether. Feminist sociologists in particular were quick to point out that early work in the sociology of education neglected to theorize on girls' experiences of class reproduction. Schools distribute messages about normative gender roles in keeping with broader class inequalities (Proweller, 1998), but this had remained invisible until feminist research documented girls' experiences as classed individuals (see especially Bettie, 2003; Gaskell, 1992; McRobbie, 2000).

Much like the broader sociology of education literature, the smaller literature on elite schools is also relatively silent on girls' experiences. The seminal Preparing for Power

(Cookson and Persell, 1985) surveys the American **private school** system but neglects girls' schools. Their analysis focuses most heavily on what Cookson and Persell call "The Select 16": a set of 16 elite boarding schools that stand out because of their long history of educating children of the most elite and significant families in the United States. Among the "The Select 16", none are all-girls schools; two were originally coeducational schools, one institution has always been all-boys, while the remaining 13 schools began as all-boys and converted to coeducation, typically in the 1970s. That this group composes "The Select 16" reflects the belief of the relative importance of boys' and girls' private schools; the majority of elite boarding schools have historically served the educational needs of boys. Gender is evidently present in Preparing for Power, but a gendered analysis is absent. For example, the authors discuss how private boarding schools provide leadership training and develop class consciousness: involvement with student government (which also leads to liaisons with school administration), competition, pressure, learning for its own sake, and the Socratic method of teaching and learning are all part of preparing for power. The authors state that these elements are less pronounced in girls' schools because the purpose of boys' and girls' education is distinct. Despite this acknowledgement, the authors do not analyse their observations with gender in mind.

More generally, very little sociological attention in North America has been paid to elite girls' schools as purveyors or conduits of the reproduction of social class advantage or to detailing some of the ways that elite girls' schools might contribute to the reproduction of gender inequality (exceptions include Proweller [1998], and Maxwell and Maxwell [1994], [1995]). This is despite significant changes in relation to the opportunities available to men and women. Girls can now anticipate a different kind of future than could the girls educated just a few decades ago. As women have gained ground in universities and workplaces, girls' schools have increasingly pitched themselves as central to developing girls' confidence, breaking down gender inequality, and engendering empowerment. This is especially the case among more privileged women in our society who have more opportunities available to them via their capital, including access to elite private schools. Most work on elite private schools focuses on coeducational environments. Comparative research on boys' and girls' private schools has not been particularly in-depth, focusing mainly on academic outcomes. Because of this relative silence on elite girls' schools and girls' experiences within elite schools—coeducational or single-gender—we know considerably less about girls' experiences of class reproduction in these contexts. We have far fewer examples of research that explores both class and gender reproduction in elite schools, especially elite girls' schools. As Connell et al. (1982) remark, it is not enough to consider how a private school serves largely privileged groups or that student X attends an all-girls school: "the fact that it [the private school] is both is important in understanding most facets of it" (180). With that as a starting point, this chapter will go on to provide a sketch of historical and contemporary private schooling, the debate about single-gender education, and the ways in which understandings of gender (especially gender difference) are evident in the classrooms of single-gender private schools.

Private Schooling in Canada—Then and Now

It wasn't until the mid-nineteenth century that the idea of universal, publicly funded education took hold. With this shift toward publicly funded education, private schooling came to mean a conscious rejection of the state-funded system by parents who wanted a religious-based education, specialized teaching, superior teaching, or a particular educational environment (Gossage, 1977). The Canadian private school system was modelled after the British system retaining, among other things, the association between education, religion, and class privilege. Most traditional Canadian private schools have Anglican roots, which "has traditionally been the religion of the well-to-do and influential" in Canada (Gossage, 1977, 4). By the early part of the twentieth century, the Church's influence declined, with more secular private school institutions opening. In Canada, private schools have a long history of educating political, social, and economic elites, much like is found in the United States and United Kingdom. Historically, a significant proportion of the Canadian elite have attended private schools (Clement, 1975; Porter, 1965).

Consistent with this history, contemporary Canadian private schools continue to provide an education to a relatively wealthy segment of the population. Although parents of all income, education, and occupational groups choose to send their children to private schools, parents choosing private schools tend, on average, to be better educated, earn higher incomes, and be employed in higher status occupations than those who opt to send their child(ren) to a publicly funded school (Van Pelt et al., 2007). For example, in a study comparing families in the province of Ontario, around half of all families with a child enrolled at a private school report a family income of $120,000 or more, while just under one-quarter of families with a child in the public system report the same level of family income (Van Pelt et al., 2007).

Private schools have historically been perceived to be designed to preserve elite norms and behaviours in their students (Maxwell, 1970), norms and behaviours that have looked very different for men and women. Accordingly, boys and girls were educated separately. Boys' schools believed their function to be the education of boys already born into privilege (Gossage, 1977). These schools focused not just on academic excellence but also character, notably on the ideals of integrity, fair play, service, and responsibility (Gossage, 1977). This was very often achieved through athletics. Sports were central to the school and athleticism was believed to be a dominant aspect of popularity and leadership (Weinzweig, 1970). Private school education for girls reflected their social and economic position. In these schools, girls were socialized to become the helpmates of the powerful, but not be powerful themselves. Education was academic, cultural, and social. Although the education of women became more commonplace in the late nineteenth century, popular opinion held that secondary education was certainly not essential for girls and that it was possibly even dangerous. Private schools could offer secondary education for girls, but it would not be funded through the public coffers (Gossage, 1977). Education for girls was terminal, not meant to be a path to post-secondary education. Many Canadian girls' schools retained aspects of "finishing schools" well into the twentieth century (Gossage, 1977). A look at the histories of some of these schools reveals classes offered in sewing, how to properly pour a cup of tea, and other duties expected of a wife of an upper-class gentleman. These courses fit the private girls' schools' goal of preparing "Christian gentlewomen" through social refinement.

Not surprisingly, single-gender private schools look quite different in many ways than the early private schools. One important shift in single-gender private schooling is actually a shift felt more generally across all school types and reflects a change in societal norms. That is, it is now taken-for-granted that girls' education is just as important as boys' education. A commitment to gender equality has moved to the foreground in all schools, including private schools. Likewise, the sense of appropriate norms and behaviours for girls and boys has also shifted. Research on a Toronto-area private boys' school in the mid-twentieth century found students' occupational choices that represented a narrow, male-dominated, professional part of the labour force: law, engineering, business and industry, and medicine (Weinzweig, 1970). Unequivocally, the students anticipated a university education and subsequent career, and the schools prepared them for this. Girls' schools, however, tended to focus less on university. In her 1965–6 study of an all-girls' school in Toronto, Maxwell (1970) uncovered a tension between the traditional education of the school and the possibility of a lifetime career. Marriage, children, and volunteering were presented by the school as incompatible with a career (Maxwell, 1970). Academic achievement was discussed in reference to marriage, not just because university attendance would bring more exposure to upwardly mobile men but also because academic achievement seemed to be an increasingly popular characteristic that men would want in a spouse (Maxwell, 1970). This changed by the mid-1980s, echoing second-wave feminism. Gone are the days of girls' schools offering classes in tea-pouring and sewing, and they are just as likely as boys' schools to instill the importance of academics and leadership. This is due, at least in part, to societal shifts in our understandings of gender inequality and patriarchy. These days, even a quick glance at a Canadian private school website—single-gender or coeducational—will reveal a commitment to academics and leadership for boys and girls. In fact, most are quite explicitly university-focused, many publicizing the national and international university destinations of their graduates.

The Zero Sum Game of Gender Equality

During the 1990s, a vast amount of research examined the experiences of boys and girls in elementary and secondary education. Many concluded that the educational system was not meeting girls' needs, the result of which was girls emerging from schools with less confidence and self-esteem (AAUW, 1992; Orenstein, 1994; Sadker and Sadker, 1994). Following this, research and public debate began posing the question "what about the boys?" in response to the perceived inattention to boys' issues within schools. Spurred on by higher rates of dropout and learning disabilities among boys (Kleinfeld, 2009), girls' higher grades (Buchman, DiPrete, and McDaniel, 2008), women outpacing men in university attendance, and the apparent **feminization of education** (Walkerdine, 1988), researchers, education leaders, and journalists questioned the focus on girls' experiences in education (recent examples of these ongoing discussions include Tyre [2006] and Abraham [2010]). Many argue that most of this literature is riddled with misguided assumptions and causal connections (see, for example, Mead [2006], Weaver-Hightower [2003])[1].

These debates about gender parity in education have raised questions about how to meet the needs of girls and boys. Given ongoing gender inequalities in education, single-gender classrooms and schools are frequently proposed as an answer to gender inequality in the classroom, a solution for both girls and boys. In keeping with this are the increasingly popular school board experiments with single-gender classes, particularly in specific subject matter (offering girls-only computer science and math courses, for example, or segregating boys and girls for English classes).

These new single-gender programs have proceeded without solid evidence backing gender segregated education. Research on the outcomes of single-gender education has at best produced mixed results. Where benefits are found, they are mostly rooted in the characteristics of the students attending and/or features of the schools, many of which are private, such as small class sizes (Lee, 1998). Lee and Bryk (1986) found positive outcomes for girls attending an all-girls Catholic private school versus a coeducation Catholic private school, including greater interest in math and science and higher educational aspirations (see also Lee and Marks [1992]). Other researchers have found no appreciable differences between students attending single-gender or coeducation institutions (Morse, 1998; LePore and Warren, 1997). A primary concern is the difficulty in measuring the impact of the school itself and not the kinds of characteristics that students bring with them to the school (such as academic engagement, studying habits, and so on, characteristics often rooted in social class).

While research on outcomes has produced mixed results, research on the practices within single-gender schools raises concerns that they may actually reinforce **gender stereotypes** and maintain sexist practices (Sax, 2009; Lee, Marks, and Byrd, 1994; Halpern et al., 2011). In a comparison of the classroom practices at boys', girls', and coeducation schools, Lee et al. (1994) found similar frequencies of sexism but also found that the type of sexism varied depending on the school type. Boys' schools were marked by confrontational teaching styles, explicit sexism (for example, a poster of a bikini-clad woman in a calculus class), and teachers encouraging sex stereotyping. Girls' schools were marked by expecting girls to need help, talking down to girls, and catering to stereotypical conceptions of females, including the expectation and even encouragement of dependence. Coeducation schools were marked by the kinds of practices found by Sadker and Sadker (1994) discussed earlier, such as boys receiving more classroom attention. Sexist practices may even exist in schools where gender equity is a deliberate curricular focus. For example, Spencer and colleagues (Spencer, Porsche, and Tolman, 2003) conducted research at a coeducational school intent on creating a gender equitable environment. Despite these intentions, the researchers found instances of inequality between boys and girls in the classroom. Students understood these differences to be a result of the fundamental differences between boys and girls, suggesting that deeply entrenched notions of difference may negate a school's attempts at gender equity. While Spencer's research was situated at a *coeducational* school intent on challenging gender inequality, it is relevant because many girls' schools are also intent on challenging gender inequality and nurturing the notion of "girl power." Indeed, female empowerment lies at the heart of what Girl High administrators and teachers believe Girl High does best, as I discuss in this chapter.

Data and Method

The data discussed in this chapter come from an ethnographic study of two elite, single-gender, academically selective private schools in Toronto, Canada. The schools offer elementary and secondary education, but this research focused mainly on students in Grades 11 and 12. The schools are single-gender; I refer to these schools as Boy High and Girl High, for simplicity. Both schools have many similarities that make them useful comparison cases, including similarly low teacher-student ratios, graduating class sizes, and classroom sizes, and similarly high tuition and fees (at over $20,000 per year per student, plus additional fees, expenses, and expected annual family donations). Boy High and Girl High are members of the national and provincial independent school associations, indicating that they are among the oldest and most elite of Canadian private schools (Davies and Quirke, 2007). Like most single-gender schools, Boy High and Girl High also affiliate themselves with national and international single-gender school organizations, such as the National Coalition of Girls' Schools.

The data consist of hundreds of hours of participant observation, interviews with administrators and students, and analysis of written and Web-based school documents like newsletters, school newspapers, and information packets for prospective families. Most fieldwork time was spent in classroom observation across a range of subject matter; this forms the bulk of the data. In addition to classroom observation, I attended assemblies and special events. This daily and ongoing participation in the everyday practices of the schools provided countless observations and casual conversations with students, teachers, staff, and administrators.

Because the private school community in Toronto is small, and because the schools themselves are also small, ensuring confidentiality is challenging. Unless something is relevant to the analysis—such as the subject matter a particular teacher is teaching—I have changed details of that nature. I have also altered the details of some circumstances, again in the interests of protecting the identities of my research participants. I am intentionally vague in some places about details that may jeopardize the confidentiality of the schools.

Girl Power, Boy Power

Administrators at both schools were strong in their conviction of the benefits of single-gender education, as were teachers, and were quick to itemize the benefits when asked. Many of these benefits echo the rhetoric in the popular press and promoted by various single-gender associations, like the National Coalition of Girls' Schools, revolving around gendered learning styles and the unique benefits of a single-gender environment. For example, administrators at both schools believed that the strength of the single-gender school is the comfort that comes with being in a class with same-gender peers, which enables students to take more risks. Students in single-gender classrooms will be less worried about saying the wrong thing or sounding dumb. In the words of Ms Harris, the Girl High principal: "It's wonderful to be focused and just relax in your classes and say what you want. That freedom is amazing. And the girls will tell you that." Indeed, students did tell me that, across both schools. The ability to be your self was a major strength identified by both sets of students. Students mentioned not feeling self-conscious, not worrying about appearance, and the freedom to behave however they wanted without worrying about impressing others.

Administrators and teachers at Boy High and Girl High identified other, unique benefits. At Boy High, the benefit is insulation from the features of a coeducational system that are believed to unfairly disadvantage boys, such as rules that limit physical movement in the classroom. Administrators and teachers are guided by their knowledge of the "boy crisis" in education and seemed well-versed in discussions of the under-performance of boys and the sense that boys will inevitably be seen as "less than" when boys' achievement is compared to that of girls. Like at Boy High, Girl High administrators and teachers also focused on the insulating qualities of an all-girls school and the ability for the school to be a "confidence factory" (Ms Harris). Administrators and teachers were very aware of women's under-representation in science, technology, engineering, and math (STEM) fields. They believed that girls' schools could correct societal pressures to play down their smarts in the interest of heterosexual romance.

This, however, led to an interesting tension at Girl High between addressing the "needs" of girls in stereotypical ways and the messages of girl power that are woven throughout the school. Girls are encouraged to believe they have unique and wonderful qualities that distinguish them from boys and deserve to be celebrated. At the same time, the approach to engaging girls is not a particularly feminist one; the administrators and teachers make use of many female stereotypes in their efforts to reach girls. The schools draw on gender stereotypes but, at Girl High, also tell the students to defy stereotypes in order to overcome obstacles like occupational glass ceilings. The remainder of this chapter compares Boy High and Girl High as a way to explore some of the differences in approaches and the belief in gendered learning styles, as well as the tension at Girl High between stated goals around leadership and empowerment and the realities of everyday practices at the school.

How Are Boys and Girls Educated?

Boy High: Competing with Your Brothers

A prominent belief among administrators and teachers at Boy High is that boys' learning hinges on having a relationship with their teachers. For example, Mr Fry, the Advanced Placement (AP)[2] economics teacher, talked about the importance of the boys feeling like they really know their teachers, and are known and understood by their teachers. What does this relational environment look like at Boy High? It becomes quickly apparent that it consists of what are stereotypical male behaviours: physicality, competitiveness, and sport. These stereotypically male traits frequently appear in debates around how coeducation is failing boys, particularly the notion that boys thrive in competition, need to move around the classroom rather than be confined to a desk, and have unique interests around which curriculum and instruction should be based. At Boy High it was not uncommon to see boys roaming the classroom, even in the midst of a teacher-driven lesson. Boy High students had the freedom to move about the classroom and the freedom to call out answers without raising their hands. Noise was readily tolerated. In fact, a steady din of noise was the norm in Boy High classrooms; where I commented on noise in the classroom, I made note of silences at Boy High, as they stood out as the exception.

Instead of fostering relationships among students, the classroom environment seemed to produce competition and one-upmanship. Some teachers merely tolerated the competition the students exhibited in the classroom. Others introduced competition as a way of motivating the students and facilitating their learning, as the following field notes from Mr Higgins' AP biology class at Boy High illustrate:

> They get put into three groups for a group challenge for multiple choice. Each group has to answer the first five questions right before they can move on to the next 6, and so on, until they finish the multiple choice questions. Students get really excited about this, are really racing to be the first team done. No prize for this. Definite tension and excitement. When this is done Mr Higgins notes there are only 12 minutes left, and he thinks that he'd be pushing it if they did more [test] prep, so instead they'll play biology Pictionary. The Pictionary competition (two teams, biology references) is evidently a favourite. The students are eventually mostly standing, cheering loudly, high-fiving, waiting in silent suspense for the next picture.

Competition within the Boy High classroom created a level of student excitement, tension, and interest.

These elements of physicality and competitiveness are consistent with the overarching dominance of sports at Boy High (and consistent with the history of Canadian single-gender boys' schools, as discussed earlier). Sports announcements were foremost at upper school assemblies; the results of recent competitions were shared, a "player of the game" was named and asked to come to the front for a handshake and sometimes a prize (like a jersey), and students would be urged to attend the next game. The celebrated athlete was often responsible for a game-changing play or a winning goal or had made a risky play as evidenced through the occasional bump, bruise, and broken bone. The bulletin boards lining the hallways were littered with tryout announcements, team rosters, and game results. Sports were a frequent topic of conversation between teachers and students, particularly since many of them worked together as coach and athlete on the same teams, and sports metaphors were woven throughout the school. In comparison, sports at Girl High were largely relegated to a less central area of the school, including their trophies, announcements, and sports-related facilities.

The emphasis on sports and competition is not necessarily at odds with the common belief at Boy High in the importance of relationships if we put it in the context of the sociological literature on masculinity and sport. As Messner (1990, 422) observes: "all boys are, to a greater or lesser extent, judged according to their ability, or lack of ability, in competitive sports." Boys' popularity in school settings is largely determined by their aptitude for sports (Adler, Kless, and Adler, 1992). Sports are also regarded as an acceptable venue for relationships to emerge or be focused around (Messner, 1990). This raises the possibility that sport is *intentionally* drawn on to create or support the relational environment at Boy High. However, it should be said that administrators and teachers never articulated athletics as the means through which relationships could develop at Boy High. They believed that an interest in sports came naturally to boys and provided a way for brotherhood to develop. But administrators and teachers tended to place their emphasis on the relationships that could develop in the *classroom* and not those related to sports. The predominant sentiment was that relationships develop out of the fraternity of a boys' school—a small and intimate environment where students and teachers have the opportunity to connect with one another.

Emphasising sports, physicality, and competition re-inscribes stereotypical notions of boys' natures and interests, notably at the exclusion of boys interested in the arts or not sports-inclined. The idea that relationships—to use the words of administrators: having teachers and students know and understand each other—are important to boys is counter to male stereotypes. In a sense then, emphasising relationships in the Boy High classroom would have been an opportunity to challenge gender stereotypes. Headmaster Mr Milton believes an all-boys environment presents many of these opportunities, discussed here via an anecdote about school dances:

> Not to be stereotypic on a dance, but when there is a dance, someone is going to do decorations. Well, I'm not sure what happened in your high school, but in this high—in my high school and in other high schools I know about, the guys don't get too much involved in that. Someone else can do that. They don't have to consider it. They *have* to consider it here. And by the way, it's an important job! So the paths to manhood are broader, they're more diverse. Homosexuality et cetera and macho-ism—all are tolerated in the [Boy High] environment because they're allowed to take . . . they are allowed to be what they are going to be.

In Mr Milton's eyes, an all-boys environment forced the boys to expand their idea of the boundaries of masculinity. But instead of witnessing a diverse range of masculinities, the everyday at Boy High resembles what we might expect based on the stereotypes of boys. At the end of the day, the link between boys and relationships is just an idea.

Girl High: Working Together on Things Girls Like

The most effective teaching methods for girls according to the senior school head, and the principal of Girl High, are those that harness the power of relationships. That might mean relating to teachers, relating to the community, or even just relating to the course material. Ms Middleton, senior school head, describes how girls learn math:

> We've got our own textbook for [Grades] 7 and 8 . . . it's really been hands-on applicable activities that get girls working in groups; that get girls working on real-life problems; a lot of math trails where you go out in the community and do math. All those kinds of things are really what get girls interested in math, and just doing the theoretical, abstract, reasoning piece by itself is not as interesting for them.

Ms Middleton believed that bringing the curriculum to the world outside of the school and having girls work together is the best way to match math learning with girls' strengths. She believed in the necessity of relating the subject matter to the girls' lives and to the "real world" in order for it to truly resonate with them. Notably, she describes as uninteresting the "theoretical, abstract, reasoning piece," all stereotypically masculine traits.

The idea that girls want to help, and that tapping into this would facilitate learning, came up repeatedly at Girl High. Helping was most typically conceived of as taking subject material and encouraging students to apply it to the world around them. Ms Harris, the principal, went as far as to say that the subject matter is almost peripheral to finding a good application of knowledge:

> Girls are overrepresented now in biology and medicine, and you know why? I think girls go to that because they like to help people, not because they care about learning biology, and I think that that's something we've learned about sciences in general. The kids will come to physics if they want to get the water to the village in Africa, and so we say to our teachers: design the projects, get the kids involved in the community and real problems that need to be solved and they'll learn the math and physics to do it.

Notably, Ms Harris attributes girls' representation in biology and medicine not to the earlier generations of women who carved a path, or to greater opportunities in accessing higher education, but to the idea of appealing to girls' (stereotypical) interests in helping others—by showing girls how to help others with problems, an interest in STEM is nurtured.

Girl High administrators also emphasised curricular tools that stress what is of interest to girls. Ms Middleton, the senior school head, offers an example:

> In Grade 8, the structures unit in science often has all these examples about bridges. Girls couldn't care less about bridges. So what's the application that will make sense to them? They *do* care about shoes, so why don't we use some of the same

things they like to do—shoes—high heels and all that kind of thing—what makes a shoe work? (emphasis hers).

These administrators were very aware of the long-standing trend of women's under-representation in STEM fields, and spoke to the ways they have found success in introducing and nurturing an interest in these subjects. In this example it is through high heels instead of bridges. In another example, a science teacher and "STEM strategic program leader" created a tradeshow of sorts meant to get girls interested in science through the use of cosmetics. (That they have a STEM leader signals the school's commitment to STEM.) At the tradeshow, girls rotated through different stations of lip balms, perfumes, and facial scrubs, learning the connection between chemistry and familiar make-up products. The examples of helping bring water to Africa, learning angles through high heels, and instituting a cosmetics tradeshow to nurture an interest in STEM fields reflect how Girl High administrators understand gender and, furthermore, underscores how they see stereotypical notions of girls and their interests.

While *both* Boy High and Girl High administrators and teachers believed in the importance of a caring relationship, the everyday practices at Girl High most closely support this vision. At Girl High, relations seemed to be built on sharing personal details. There were times that a teacher would break away from the lesson to talk about something related to his or her personal life, inviting the students to know about the teacher's non-school life with spouses and children. This level of intimate sharing was entirely absent from Boy High.

Within the classroom, Girl High fosters non-competitive relationships. An example involves pop quizzes that are taken up in class immediately following the quiz. Students quietly evaluated their own quizzes, which were then immediately and quietly put into student folders. Students very rarely compared scores. In addition, instead of competition, pitting students against each other, group work was the norm at Girl High. (Group work was very rare at Boy High. Only a few times did I see students working in pairs or groups on a non-competitive assignment or project.) At Boy High, pop quizzes looked more like a competition; they were likely to end in a public tally of who received what score, often with a prize going to the top earner.

The students at Girl High learned to work together, to support each other rather than see each other as competitors, and were not pushed beyond this comfort level. Given the administrators' belief that girls need to relate to each other, their teachers, the subject matter, and the world around them (through helping), these non-competitive relationships make sense. Indeed, *not* doing a public tally and rewarding the top scorer with a prize is probably typical of most school classrooms and is pedagogically most appropriate. The strong difference between these practices and the highly competitive approach at Boy High suggests that the gendered context—and the associated stereotypes—can have a strong influence on the educational environment.

Contradiction at Girl High

At Girl High, there is a tension between addressing the "needs" of girls in stereotypical ways and the messages of girl power woven throughout the school. Girl High students are routinely reminded about the strength of girls. In short, they learn about "girl power." This begins with the school motto: "Achieve Your Dream!"[3] The motto is meant to communicate to current and prospective students and families that girls can achieve anything imaginable.

It is plastered on school advertisements, internal documents, alumni communications, and staff memos, and sometimes makes its way into administrator speeches to the students. The message is that girls have the capacity to accomplish anything if they are immersed in an educational environment that believes in and nurtures their strengths. Laura, a quiet and studious Grade 12 student, said the motto accurately represents what the school does: instill confidence, provide opportunities, and prepare girls to take on new challenges. This view parallels that expressed by Principal Ms Harris, who also believed that the motto really captured what Girl High does—it expresses the kind of confidence gained by Girl High students between enrolment and graduation.

Empowerment was also evident in some of the classroom discussions between teachers and students right through to the more formal speeches made by teachers and administrators. Gender inequality was not discussed very much in most classes, the exceptions being those classes where group discussion was more typical or where a specific subject unit focused on women's issues, like English and social science classes. In Ms MacDonald's social science class, a variety of issues facing women around the world were discussed, especially during their unit on gender inequality. In discussing wage equity issues in North America, Ms MacDonald says this is changing: "it changed in my generation and it will change with you girls, *you* will make the change." In another exercise, Ms MacDonald asked the students to take as long as necessary to come up with a list of five female heads of state. This exercise encouraged a discussion of power, politics, and gender among the students. Ms MacDonald often discussed gender inequality in the context of change and how women can and should be at the helm of change in any part of the world. In these classes, the students learn to consider gender inequality, think about its relevance to their lives, grow comfortable talking about it, and imagine themselves as part of the solution.

In Principal Ms Harris' commencement address given to graduating Grade 12 students and their families, she too instilled notions of empowerment for girls, as captured in my field notes from graduation day:

> She says that they should remember that they live in a world where some girls still have no opportunity. The grads have opportunity and choices because of the old girls, their mothers, and grandmothers, who created choice for them by fighting against the expected. She says that you used to have to choose home. Then you used to have to choose a career. Now you can make ANY choice. You can be a philanthropist, an award-winning photographer, a journalist, the next astronaut, a scientist, a mom raising conscientious kids that will make change in the world. She says that it is not a question of having to make a path for themselves, but choosing which path to take or maybe even taking a way that isn't a path yet.

Ms Harris' speech echoes the fluid, choice-laden rhetoric common to third-wave feminism. She is encouraging the graduating class to realize their dreams, much like their school motto suggests. Ms Harris wants her graduating students to believe that they have any number of choices and should take advantage of them. They can choose whatever they want to do in life because of the women who came before them, the women who fought for future generations to have choice. Her message of overcoming gender inequality is devoid of the structural forces of inequality; gender inequality is individualized.

Ms Harris' speech also reveals the privilege enmeshed with gender at Girl High. They are not the girls who have no opportunity or are constrained financially. Instead, they can do whatever they choose to do or imagine possible. They are girls who can be philanthropists or journalists or scientists. Similarly, the girls in Ms MacDonald's social science class are taken through a gendered analysis of inequality, but most of that analysis is meant to understand the lives of women "out there" and especially in developing countries. Yes, through talking about wage gaps Ms MacDonald signals to the girls that they may yet experience inequality. But most of Ms MacDonald's course was centred on the students as vehicles for change in the lives of *other* women in other, less fortunate parts of the world.

The result of girl power on the one hand but class privilege on the other is Girl High students who feel empowered but seem to reject or be unaware of larger, structural dimensions of gender inequality. Their empowerment comes from years of receiving messages about the strength of girls and the attitude captured in their school's motto, which pointedly tells them that they can achieve whatever they dream. In their more privileged world, women do not experience inequality. Inequality is something that exists "out there" by other women in other contexts. It is something they talk about in class and read about in textbooks. They possess an awareness of inequality but no personal connection to it. They don't anticipate any obstacles to success, however defined. Instead, these girls anticipate the opportunity to develop and realize their goals.

And what do the students themselves make of girl power and the school's motto and message? Although a couple of girls were reflective and supportive of the motto, most of the students had negative reactions to the motto. For Krista, a graduating student occupying a leadership position, the intention of empowerment from administrators was falling on deaf ears; it did not resonate because it was an overused expression at the school. Another student, Rachel, felt the motto fell flat: "I think the motto is good in terms of how it shows that we're confident but it kind of makes us sound like feminists: 'Achieve Your Dream' . . . what about boys, can they achieve their dream? They make people think that we're capable of doing the impossible. I just don't think that's what [Girl High] should be advertising." Her use of the word "feminists" is clearly negative. Rachel strongly believed it was almost irresponsible to promote the idea that Girl High students are capable of doing the seemingly impossible.

The reasons why most Girl High students rejected the motto could be numerous. The girls expressed dislike of Ms Harris that may relate to their rejection of the school motto. Combining some dislike of Ms Harris with a message they hear ad nauseam, the motto may have seemed vacuous at best. Gender may not resonate with students as a key dimension of their experience, despite and because of their single-gender environment (Proweller, 1998). I would also add that gender pales as a key source of inequality in the life of a *privileged* Girl High student, because her experience of gender is filtered through their social class background. In their world, women have the choice to be whatever they want to be and can be a solution for the problems of other, less privileged women; gender inequality is simply one more thing for these future leaders to conquer.

In the end, girls are taught in ways that emphasise stereotypes and are simultaneously encouraged to try non-stereotypical paths, challenge gender inequality, and embrace girl power. The school encourages relationships between students and teachers and relies on group work and collaboration—not competition—to reach girls. They also encourage whatever means necessary to help girls learn, especially in STEM fields that traditionally do not attract women. This may come at the cost of reinforcing gender stereotypes, as is evident in teaching through high heels instead of bridges. These patterns are contradicted by messages of empowerment woven throughout the school, from the principal's speeches to classroom lessons to the school motto. In this environment, gender roles and expectations are simultaneously challenged and reinforced.

Conclusion

If the goal is to reach students and engage them with the material, single-gender private schools might be doing a good job. The students often seem genuinely excited about their learning. The beauty trade show at Girl High, for example, brought in girls who otherwise may not have been interested in science. One upper-year student said that it was her first time being involved in science outside of the classroom and that it was a good way to see science in the everyday. She said she now sees science as more than just "men in white lab coats." Given the lack of women in STEM fields and other gender-related issues in education, single-gender schools are likely seen as a viable and preferable way of reaching boys and girls.

Before committing to this alternative form of schooling, questions deserve to be raised about the practices and outcomes of single-gender schools, including as it relates to gender equity. Especially in light of earlier findings that single-gender schools are dominated by sexist practices, my own findings about reinforcing gender difference, and the increasing popularity of single-gender "experiments" in the public system, one should be attuned to the extent to which single-gender schools reproduce or challenge the gender order that they operate under. I find that single-gender education at Girl High reveals the difficulty and contradiction in basing education on gender difference while simultaneously attempting to challenge it. Single-gender schools might claim to address the so-called unique learning needs of boys and girls but, in doing so, gender is arguably reinforced. This happens first through supporting the notion of distinct and different gender categories and, second, by catering to this notion of difference in designing and enacting a vision for the school, including its curriculum.

In the past, there was no real contradiction between girls' schools' mandates and the broader social environment; at most all-girls schools across North America, girls were learning the skills and attributes that would help them excel in their lives once they were married. They would emerge from these schools ready to take on leadership roles in their community, charity, and events related to their husbands' work. Their lives were largely defined by the lives of their spouse and their education geared toward marriageability and maintaining a household once married. A career and family were incompatible. Canada (and other countries where girls' schools held this mandate) is a very different place now, however. We are living in an era where gender equality is valued. How does Girl High then justify their mandate of single-gender education? It is largely through engaging students with the subject matter through whatever means necessary and praising the unique strengths of girls through messages of girl power. As they see it, no other school is better equipped to give girls the confidence to "achieve their dream." At the same time, though, the methods for engaging students are very limited. The school may not be instructing tea-pouring as in days of old, but their methods are still rooted in narrow gender stereotypes. They have the resources to structure their curriculum however they want, but must also meet the needs of their market, a group of families who believe in the benefits of gender segregated education. This does not necessarily have to translate into a school culture rooted in narrow definitions of what makes a boy and what makes a girl, but that is the outcome at Boy High and Girl High.

It is also important to highlight how gender and social class intersect in this case. Single-gender private schools have largely been the domain of the privileged classes of Canadian society. Both the history of tea-pouring lessons to the present day focus on bettering the lives of other, less fortunate women and highlight how this population is relatively privileged. Much of what we know about single-gender schools is in fact mediated by social class[4]. It is worth pointing out that, of course, the same intersection of gender and social class exists at Boy High. However, gender remains largely invisible as an issue. From the earliest days of single-gender boys' schools like Boy High to the present day, academics, leadership, and character have been the focus. This has remained unchanged and is unproblematic in a social context that still generally privileges men and boys. There is no contradiction as it exists at Girl High. Moreover, discussions of gender relations and gender inequality were almost entirely absent at Boy High. A review of curriculum, classroom practices, and administrator and teacher beliefs about gender and social class suggests that gender is seemingly a non-issue. At Boy High, gender and social class are both sources of privilege, not complicated by the passing of time since the foundations of the school to the present day.

Questions for Critical Thought

1. Identify and discuss at least one example of how the students are regarded as gendered and classed individuals.
2. Imagine you have been asked by your local school district to identify a strength and weakness of single-gender schooling. Drawing on the data discussed in this chapter, what would you argue in support of single-gender schooling? Or would you argue in opposition to it?
3. Girl High and Boy High are schools that educate a wealthy segment of our population. Would you expect to find the same patterns at a single-gender school that serves a more mixed-SES population? Explain your answer.
4. Using this chapter as well as your Internet search results with the search terms "feminization of education," describe the predominant way that male learners are conceptualized. In your opinion, is this an accurate description? Explain.

Glossary

Elite Generally refers to a group of individuals that are economically, socially, and/or politically privileged in society. If one thinks of social stratification as a hierarchy, the elite occupy the uppermost position of that hierarchy.

Feminization of education A criticism sometimes levelled against contemporary schooling that argues schools are failing boys through such things as having a predominantly female teaching staff, having a curriculum geared toward the supposed interests of girls only, and discouraging physicality in the classroom in favour of orderly sitting, raising hands, and so forth.

Gender stereotypes Over-simplified beliefs about men and women, generally related to behaviour.

Private school An educational institution that does not receive any funding from the government. Funding comes from tuition and endowments. In Canada, private schools include well-established, elite schools, private religious schools, and smaller, newly established schools.

Notes

1. For more on how administrators at the research sites made use of this research, see Baker (2013).
2. Advanced Placement courses are offered at some public and private high schools throughout the world and are meant to be treated as a first-year university course credit in that subject. In Ontario, for example, students in a course like AP economics are learning the Ontario curriculum alongside the AP curriculum, and at the end of the term earn the credit toward their Ontario Secondary School Diploma (OSSD) and write the AP exam. Good performance on the AP exam results in a credit applied against post-secondary (university) education.
3. The motto has been re-worded to protect the confidentiality of Girl High.
4. This is taken up earlier in this chapter in the literature review discussing the inconclusive research on the benefits of single-gender schooling.

References

American Association of University Women (AAUW). *How Schools Shortchange Girls*. Washington: American Association of University Women, 1992.

Abraham, C. "Canada: Our time to lead/failing boys." *The Globe and Mail* 16 October 2010: A16.

Adler, P.A., Kless, S.J., and Adler, P. "Socialization to gender roles: Popularity among elementary school boys and girls." *Sociology of Education* 65 (1992): 169–87.

Baker, J. "Girl power, boy power, class power: Class and gender reproduction in elite single-gender private schools." PhD thesis, University of Toronto, 2013.

Bettie, J. *Women without Class: Girls, Race, and Identity*. Berkeley: University of California Press, 2003.

Buchman, C., DiPrete, T.A., and McDaniel, A. "Gender inequalities in education." *Annual Review of Sociology* 34 (2008): 319–37.

Clement, W. *The Canadian Corporate Elite: An Analysis of Economic Power*. Toronto: McClelland and Stewart Limited, 1975.

Connell, R.W., Ashenden, D.J., Kessler, S., and Dowsett, G.W. *Making the Difference: Schools, Families and Social Division*. Sydney: George Allen & Unwin, 1982.

Cookson Jr, P.W., and Persell, C.H. *Preparing for Power: America's Elite Boarding Schools*. New York: Basic Books, 1985.

Davies, S., and Quirke, L. "The impact of sector on school organizations: Institutional and market logics." *Sociology of Education* 80(1) (2007): 66–89.

DeBare, I. *Where Girls Come First: The Rise, Fall, and Surprising Revival of Girls' Schools*. New York: Penguin Group, 2004.

Gaskell, J. *Gender Matters from School to Work*. Buckingham: Open University Press, 1992.

Gossage, C. *A Question of Privilege: Canada's Independent Schools*. Toronto: Peter Martin Associations, 1977.

Halpern, D.F., Eliot L., Bigler, R.S., Fabes, R.A., Hamish, L.D., Hyde, J., Liben, L.S., and Martin, C.L. "The pseudoscience of single-sex schooling." *Science* 333 (2011): 1706–7.

Kleinfeld, J. "The state of American boyhood." *Gender Issues* 26 (2009): 113–20.

Lee, V. "Is single-sex secondary schooling a solution to the problem of gender inequity?" In *Separated by Sex: A Critical Look at Single-Sex Education for Girls*, Susan Morse (ed.), (41–52). Washington: American Association of University Women, 1998.

Lee, V., and Bryk, A.S. "Effects of single-sex secondary schools on student achievement and attitudes." *Journal of Educational Psychology* 78(5) (1986): 381–95.

Lee, V.E., and Marks, H.M. "Who goes where? Choice of single-sex and coeducational independent secondary schools." *Sociology of Education* 65(3) (1992): 226–53.

Lee, V.E., Marks, H.M., and Byrd, T. "Sexism in single-sex and coeducational independent secondary school classrooms." *Sociology of Education* 67(2) (1994): 92–120.

LePore, P.C., and Warren, J.R. "A comparison of single-sex and coeducational Catholic secondary schooling: Evidence from the National Educational Longitudinal Study of 1988." *American Educational Research Journal* 34(3) (1997): 485–511.

Maxwell, J.D., and Maxwell, M.P. "The reproduction of class in Canada's elite independent schools." *British Journal of Sociology of Education* 16(3) (1995): 309–26.

Maxwell, M.P. "Social structures, socialization and social class in a Canadian private school for girls." PhD thesis, Cornell University, 1970.

Maxwell, M.P., and Maxwell, J.D. "Three decades of private school females' ambitions: Implications for Canadian elites." *The Canadian Review of Sociology and Anthropology* 31(2) (1994): 139–67.

McRobbie, A. *Feminism and Youth Culture*. Second edition. London: Macmillan Press Ltd, 2000.

Mead, S. "The evidence suggests otherwise: The truth about boys and girls." *Education Sector, Research and Reports* 23(3) (2006): 1–21.

Messner, M.A. "Boyhood, organized sports, and the construction of masculinities." *Journal of Contemporary Ethnography* 18(4) (1990): 416–44.

Morse, S. *Separated by Sex: A Critical Look at Single-sex Education for Girls*. Washington: American Association of University Women, 1998.

Orenstein, P. *School Girls: Young Women, Self-esteem, and the Confidence Gap*. New York: Double Day, 1994.

Porter, J. *The Vertical Mosaic*. Toronto: University of Toronto Press, 1965.

Proweller, A. *Constructing Female Identities: Meaning Making in an Upper Middle Class Youth Culture*. Albany: SUNY Press, 1998.

Sadker, M., and Sadker, D. *Failing at Fairness: How America's Schools Cheat Girls*. New York: Simon & Schuster, 1994.

Sax, L.J. *Women Graduates of Single-Sex and Co-educational High Schools: Differences in Their Characteristics and the Transition to College*. Los Angeles: The Sudikoff Family Institute for Education and New Media; UCLA Graduate School of Education & Information Studies, 2009.

Spencer, R., Porche, M.V., and Tolman, D.L. "We've come a long way—maybe: New challenges for gender equity in education." *Teacher's College Record* 105(9) (2003): 1774–807.

Tyre, P. "The trouble with boys." *The Daily Beast*, 29 January 2006.

Van Pelt, D.A., Allison, P.A., and Allison, D.J. "Ontario's private schools: Who chooses them and why?" *Studies in Education Policy*. Vancouver: The Fraser Institute, 2007.

Walkerdine, V. *The Mastery of Reason*. London: Routledge, 1988.

Weaver-Hightower, M. "The 'boy turn' in research on gender and education." *Review of Educational Research* 73(4) 2003: 471–98.

Weinzweig, P.A. "Socialization and subculture in elite education: A study of a Canadian boys private school." PhD thesis, University of Toronto, 1970.

10

Behind Locker-Room Doors
Knowing Why Some Boys "Stay Away from Each Other"

Michel Kehler

Introduction

Amid ongoing concerns for youth, physical activity, and a ballooning "obesity epidemic," this chapter examines why some adolescent boys are reluctant to participate in secondary school health and physical education. Though it is often assumed that boys naturally like "gym" or health and physical education (PE) because they are boys, research has been slow to specifically examine the struggles and tensions for adolescent boys who regularly avoid, strategize, and purposefully withdraw from participating in high school health and physical education classes. It is commonly thought that parents encourage children to take academic courses instead of PE as requirements for post-secondary education. Health and physical education (HPE), like art education, become periphery courses for many students. There is, according to Messner and Musto (2014), a noticeable absence or dearth of research examining children and sport, in particular. While this chapter looks less at sport participation, it nonetheless contributes to the field by providing a closer look at adolescent male youth who struggle to participate in sport more generally and who strategically avoid participating in secondary school health and physical education classes in particular. The primary focus of this chapter is on developing and extending a deeper understanding of the intersection of **masculinities**, health education, and the sociology of the body.

Remarkably under-researched and often misunderstood is the relationship adolescent boys have to their bodies and the impact this has on how they come to know and understand health and physical education (see Hauge and Haavind [2011]; Martin and Govender [2011]; Wright, MacDonald, and Groom [2003]; Smolak [2004]; Wellard [2009]). Shilling (2010, 151) usefully highlights a shift toward a growing awareness and obsession with "the body as a visual symbol of distinction in the sphere of consumer culture, changing demands on the individual body—subject in the workplace and state sponsored promotions of performative conceptions of health." The intersection of bodily practices and a growing public hyper-visibility of the masculine body raises significant questions particularly at a time when issues of health, inactivity, and obesity are a part of the public mainstream discourse. Smolak (2004), for example, found a pattern in a review of the research indicating that there is "relatively few data on the nature of changes in body image itself, particularly if one wishes to examine either the components of body image or the differences in body image development by ethnicity, gender or culture" (21). As she has argued "body image [as] a strongly gendered phenomenon" (2004, 21), this has been wrongly misinterpreted to mean that boys and men do not have body image issues. It is increasingly evident that there is a glaring absence of attention on adolescent boys, bodies, body image, and the ways this may detract from positive healthy life practices, particularly participation in secondary school HPE among adolescent boys.

In the following sections I examine the experiences, influences, and ways some adolescent boys make sense of their own bodies in HPE classes. I draw on a subset of data from a three-year study conducted across three provinces in Canada (2008–2011). Broadly speaking this chapter looks more closely at socio-cultural factors intersecting health education, masculinities, and body image to better explain why some young men (14 to 15 years of age) are reluctant to participate in HPE. While I do not debate the obesity discourse as others have, I provide a more nuanced understanding of some possible underlying reasons some adolescent boys are increasingly marginalized and withdrawing from school HPE (for a useful discussion of the obesity debate see Evans, Davies, and Rich [2008] and Gard [2011])

This chapter begins with a broader look at the concerns for childhood inactivity. I argue that the locker-room space is a situational context in which adolescent boys negotiate body, space, and masculinities. It is in these school spaces, I argue, that there are deleterious and damaging conditions that go unchecked and uninterrupted. These conditions, locations, and interactions among youth and particularly male adolescents are implicated in a culture of fear, denial, and body image anxieties. As well, as Rich (2010, 818) argues in her examination of girls' bodies and surveillance mechanisms to address obesity and inactivity in schools, "the culture of schools cannot be ignored as coincidental, but rather as contributory in the development of these conditions when they should if anything, be involved in the prevention." Schools are significant and powerful contexts for the taken for granted lessons youth, both boys and girls, learn about bodies, health, and gendered identities.

Youth Inactivity, Quick Responses, and Research Trends

As I have previously argued, current health initiatives to increase physical activity among youth do not address sociocultural issues, such as homophobia, masculinities, femininities, and bullying, which are admittedly more difficult to assess and monitor in schools (see also Kehler [2010]; Atkinson and Kehler [2012]; Harwood and Wright [2012]; Markey [2010]; Rich [2010]). Instead, new initiatives are obsessed with an anti-obesity discourse that mobilizes action based on "health imperatives around 'eating well,' exercising regularly, and monitoring our bodies" (Harwood and Wright, 2012, 612). Attention has been focused on knowing how much or how often students participate in physical activity (see Dwyer et al. [2006]; Wright et al. [2003]). Rich (2010, 208) explains that in England and Wales "various mechanisms of surveillance are now being deployed in schools to monitor children's bodies." As such there continues to be a growing focus particularly in but not limited to education, where school practices and policies centre on managing, monitoring, and controlling youth health-related behaviour. At the same time there is a dearth of research given to the sociological or pedagogical perspectives that might explain what drives some students to withdraw from participating in school physical activity. Wright et al. (2003, 18) argue that the participation research, for example, does not account for "the social, and cultural contexts, local, national and global in which young people participate in physical activity . . . nor the circumstances of young people's lives which may allow or prevent their enacting their desires and wants in physical activity."

Research has been slow to question to what extent youth school experiences are influencing long-term health choices. Further research is needed to examine the impact mandatory school HPE courses has on healthy life choices. Mandatory physical activity and course requirements do not address nor respond to, for example, issues of safety in locker rooms, the manufactured image of male bodies, or connections between dominant heteronormative masculinity and sport culture (see Messner and Musto [2014]). Regardless of efforts to increase opportunities for physical activities in school, some students will not participate. In other countries including the United Kingdom, New Zealand, and Australia, governments are similarly investing in initiatives aimed at addressing youth inactivity and a perceived obesity crisis (see, for example, Rich [2010]).

Boys, Bodies, and Masculinities Explored

In public and visible ways male bodies, not unlike female bodies, become representative of a gendering process that values certain masculinities while marginalizing others. In their examination of sport and masculinity, MacKay, Messner, and Sabo (2000, 8) explain that "resistant inclinations and, sometimes rebellion against forms of hegemonic masculinity" prompts researchers to ask just what are men said to be resisting. Two directions for inquiry have dominated the sport and masculinity field including (1) examining highly institutionalized team sport such as football and hockey, as well as a more individualized, less centralized sport such as swimming or body building; and (2) exploring, within conventional and highly institutionalized athletic contexts, the degree to which there is room to negotiate gender identities. It is within the latter context, namely that of a high school physical education classroom, that I examine how adolescent young men, reluctant to participate in physical health and education class, are able to negotiate practices of masculinity within this space. By examining the gender movement available to young men, the following study draws attention to the limitations and restrictions young men routinely negotiate when reluctantly participating in health and physical education class. In short, this study provides a closer look at the ways some adolescent young men respond to and develop strategies to protect themselves and avoid harassment, for example, from other dominant, bodily privileged young men in high school locker rooms. This chapter also draws attention to the heteronormative behaviours of adolescent men that guide, restrict, and delimit interaction in high school locker rooms.

Many assume body image related issues are linked to femininity. However, as I argue, these assumptions may be related to cultural understandings of femininities and masculinities. Specifically, while girls' desire to be thin and the marketization and commodification of women is historically deep rooted, growing evidence suggests that the gaze upon male bodies, similar to that long reserved for women, is increasingly becoming an issue for young men (see Pope, Phillips, and Olivardia [2000]). Although Smolak (2004, 22) argues "messages to girls may be more consistent both in terms of number of sources and the clarity of the message," there is growing evidence that body image issues are increasingly prevalent across both boys and girls (see Diedrichs and Lee [2010]; Frost [2003]; Grogan and Richards [2002]; Hauge and Haavind, [2011]). The difference, I argue, is that the greatest divide for boys is one connected to denial and silencing that occurs in relation to North American stereotypes about what is masculine and what is not. As I have argued elsewhere:

> More so than any other private social space in which young boys interact, the gym classes and their associated locker rooms are zones of hyper-normative/dominant masculine affirmation. Heterosexual discourses involving the objectification of women, ideal-type male bodies, and coercively organized power differentials between boys are all on display therein. (Atkinson and Kehler, 2012, 172)

The association between the outward public display or expression of masculinity and body image has long been considered taboo or a girl issue among boys and young men. More recently, however, there is a growing acknowledgement and a deeper complex awareness of the relationship between masculinities and growing body image issues particularly among adolescent males and specifically with regard to body enhancing behaviours such a dieting and steroid use (see Eisenberg, Wall, and Neumark-Sztainer [2012]; Martin and Govender [2011]).

Masculinities research in particular and feminist theorizing more broadly has seen a shift and rejection of sex role and socialization models. While these dominant models remain well entrenched as part of the public mainstream discourse in relation to education, increased research has begun to challenge these views on various levels. Emerging research in education and gender and particularly the education of boys has begun to dislodge ideas of biological determinism long assumed to adequately explain why boys are active, aggressive, and dominant while girls are naturally passive, quiet, and demure. The binaristic thinking that positions all boys and all girls as naturally different is challenged by a more fluid and less essentialist or homogenous model for thinking of masculinity in school. With the work of Raewyn Connell (1995) masculinities are increasingly seen as agential, constructed, unfixed, and ever-changing as they intersect culturally as well as variably according to race, class, and gender.

Research in the last decade has unsettled normative understandings of masculinities, femininities, body image, physical health, and schooling (see Frost [2003]; Humberstone and Stan [2011]; Paechter [2011], [2003]; Wellard [2007]).

Building on past research and theorizing of gender identities, Smolak (2004, 23) draws attention to health education, body image, and masculinities. She found, for example, that there is a rise among boys concerned with body image issues. Specifically, Smolak (2004) found "adolescent boys report more negative comments about their bodies from their peers than girls do" and "boys are more likely to engage in teasing than girls." The increasing infatuation with body image among males and particularly adolescent males has, until recently, been largely unexplored. As Connell (1995, 45) explains, the significance of the body becomes emblematic of valued and undervalued masculinities from much theorizing in which "true masculinity is almost always thought to proceed from men's bodies—to be inherent in a male body or to express something about a male body." As I mention in the previous section, boys' decisions to engage or disengage with physical education within secondary schools are underscored by the socio-cultural understandings they have of their bodies and specifically how these understandings relate to the masculine identities. While it is important to promote physical activity among youth, schools in particular need to address and interrogate the social context in which students, boys and girls, constitute themselves in relation to others.

Billboard Bodies and Boys

The recent upsurge in advertising and marketing of male bodies is reason for concern. The male body is increasingly emblematic of a particularly valued form of masculinity captured in media advertising. In his study of 13- to 15-year-old boys, Norman (2011) describes a competing discourse for men who are both compelled to work on their bodies to look good while simultaneously rejecting and showing a disinterest in their bodies. The positioning and shifting of masculine subjectivities at a time of pronounced visibilities of the masculine body presents a powerful context for hearing the voices of young men who routinely move in and out of typically masculinized spaces. For Norman (2011, 443), his research highlights emerging discourse communities in which boys are found to "negotiate their masculine subjectivities by discarding unavailable discourses and investing more thoroughly in others." His research valuably suggests the intentional and purposeful ways boys and adolescent young men construct relationships not only with their own bodies but, significantly, with the bodies of others.

Research has shown that "images of extremely muscular models contribute to body dissatisfaction and muscle dysmorphia in young men" (Eisenberg, Wall, and Neumark-Sztainer, 2012, 1020). Schools are not neutral sites but are actively involved in a process that either perpetuates or challenges the reproduction of mainstream masculinities. It is evident that, depending on school cultures, some students, both boys and girls, are turning to muscle enhancing behaviours (see Eisenberg et al. [2012]). These behaviours are but one clear sign of a developing awareness among youth and a growing association between muscular bodies in the media and cultural images of masculinities and femininities (see DeVisser, Smith, and McDonnell [2009]; Ricciardelli, Clow, and White [2010]).

Pope et al. (2000) describe a trend and shift in male body obsession that traps young men in a "double bind" leaving boys and men bombarded by images of ripped, buff bodies manufactured in a burgeoning fashion industry intent on capitalizing on perfect male body images, while at the same time they are trapped by cultural norms that refuse, deny, and silence boys and men from talking or expressing their body insecurities.

The following section takes a closer look at a national study conducted in Canada to begin exploring why some adolescent boys struggle to participate in high school HPE. In this section I discuss the various ways boys make sense of their bodies in relation to other boys and how the HPE classroom context supports and denies particular forms of masculinities embodied in the masculine physique.

The Study

As I have argued above, locker rooms are troubled and troubling spaces for adolescent youth and adolescent boys in particular. Often overlooked or purposefully avoided because of the methodological challenges (see Fusco [2008]), researchers struggle to gain access both at the school level and at the university level. Ethics approval to engage in conversations that will permit and encourage adolescents to speak of body-related experiences is fraught with difficulties. In her research of 9- to 11-year-old girls, Paechter (2011, 310) describes the methodological challenges of overtly researching children's bodies, explaining that "she could approach questions of the body itself only obliquely" throughout her study. The tensions Paechter describes resonate with my own empirical research investigating how adolescent boys understand and know their bodies in the school context of HPE classes. The obstacles for allowing adolescent boys opportunities to speak to and from their bodies might explain the dearth of research into the socio-cultural meanings youth have of their bodies (see Smolak [2004]). In the area of body image, adolescent youth, and education, we are confronted with an ironic twist in which bodies remain somewhat invisible though highly visible and active in schools. Researchers are prohibited from and even limited by what is considered to be **ethnographic voyeurism**. We should not be surprised by the high level of gatekeeping, but we should be alarmed when this gate-keeping makes "an enquiry into bodies and bodily practices within school stand out as strange and out of place" (Paechter, 2011, 311). Having briefly noted here the significant difficulties of conducting this research, I will now offer an overview of the study and the context from which the data are taken for the discussion that follows in this chapter.

In the discussion section I draw on a subset of data taken from a larger three-year study conducted during the year 2008 through to 2011. The respondents included throughout this chapter are an accurate and consistent representation of the voices of the larger data set of 77 young men across three provinces in Canada, namely British Columbia, Ontario, and Nova Scotia. The participants included in this chapter participated in (1) a one hour semi-structured interview; (2) field observations conducted during scheduled secondary school HPE classrooms; and (3) Web blogging at a secure site in which participants described their experiences in HPE class. The names included are those selected by the participants and were chosen purposefully to maintain anonymity in the data reporting. Participants were invited on a voluntary basis to describe and explain why they were reluctant to participate in secondary school health and physical education classes. Students were recruited through public information talks in mandatory Grade 9 HPE classes. In addition, a snowball approach was used in which peers suggested classmates who also participated in the study. The interviews were conducted in places easily accessible and convenient for the students and included coffee shops, restaurants, and local libraries. These interviews were conducted during student arranged times both in school at lunch hour and after school depending on the availability of students. The willingness of the students to meet and participate is noteworthy particularly with the already mentioned logistical challenges many researchers face as well as the levels of discomfort and embarrassment that often accompanies this research for the participating interviewees (see Paechter [2011]).

Locker-Room Boundaries and Why Boys "Stay Away from Each Other"

This section examines the physical spaces in which adolescent young men learn about their bodies at school, namely HPE classes and school locker rooms. As HPE teachers begin to see the weight adolescent male body image and mainstream construction of masculinity and health has on boys' participation and withdrawal from HPE, it is increasingly important, too, that we begin to engage in disrupting and interrogating HPE spaces from which certain attitudes and beliefs among boys are allowed to manifest themselves. As I have argued along with Atkinson elsewhere (Atkinson and Kehler, 2012), school spaces make for interesting and troubling contexts in which boys sort out and navigate a meta-narrative of hegemonic masculinity:

> The ability for men to economically, politically, and culturally bully (*qua* masculine right) is no longer a universally accepted part of the social script, and discourses about gendered power expose those inequalities as deeply intolerable. (Atkinson and Kehler, 2012, 169)

It is, however, a different case in school locker rooms which continue to be "a zone wherein boys are sequestered from social control agents, and thus aggressively dominant boys are presented with an opportunity to bully/police the preferred sorts of masculinity mainly reified in physical education and sport settings" (Atkinson and Kehler, 2012, 169). There is a well understood tension between monitoring these spaces to provide safety *for* youth and the need to respect and protect the privacy *of* youth.

In many schools there remains a "do nothing" attitude regarding school locker rooms. In short, this allows for students, and in this case, boys to self-monitor the conduct and actions of their peers. There is a prevailing sense that locker-room culture, particularly with regard to boys, is a masculinized space that is the result of "boys being boys." Girl's locker rooms are similarly believed to be symbolic of girl culture and typical notions of femininity (see O'Donovan and Kirk [2007]). In short, school locker rooms and change rooms, like many sports arena locker rooms, are considered the boy's domain in which there is an allowance and acceptance of behaviours and attitudes among boys as natural and simply boys being boys.

Locker rooms and change rooms have gone relatively unquestioned and misunderstood as important social and cultural school spaces (see O'Donovan and Kirk [2007]; Pope et al. [2000]). Most troubling perhaps is the taken for granted and accepted attitude that underscores and indeed protects and maintains such school spaces. Essentialist arguments that *all* boys typically subscribe to a common set of beliefs and understandings of masculinity threaten to perpetuate and maintain a limiting and damaging version of heteronormativity in schools. I argue that it is these very school spaces, namely locker rooms and change rooms, that require greater scrutiny and deeper interrogation because "it is inevitable that the young people's interactions were shaped within the larger social, cultural, and political contexts" (O'Donovan and Kirk, 2007, 411). Space and the construction of specific school spaces, such as locker rooms, have an understood and accepted gendered resonance to them. Until recently, however, very little attention has been given to what O'Donovan and Kirk (2007, 400) argue are "the way in which interactions in the changing room impact on the engagement and experience of young people in physical education."

Pope et al. (2000) explain that locker rooms are uncomfortable places. They argue that for many younger men and boys they are:

Unwitting victims of one aspect of an insidious masculinity code: men aren't supposed to be bothered by preoccupations with their looks. Only women are supposed to get hung up about such things. To speak of anxieties about their bodies or physical appearance, for most men, is to violate the taboo. Many men would far prefer to disavow their worries—this internalizing their self-criticism—rather than risk the "loss of face" that would come with disclosure. (Pope et al., 2000, 25)

For many participants in this study the locker room was a threatening and unwelcoming space. In the following excerpts the students describe their experiences and explain how they understood locker rooms and change areas according to specific codes of masculinity. This research adds to what Hauge and Haavind (2011, 2) argue are a series of discourse communities among adolescent boys who "negotiate intersecting notions of how the body might appear masculine through engaging in various skills and activities," and moreover extends the argument within schools by providing a closer look at the deployment of bodily practices among boys and across competing forms of masculinities. In the following instance Connor reflects on the shower space and associations some boys made intersecting masculinity, homophobia, and bodily **surveillance**:

> There's a shower over in the corner that no one really ever uses because everyone thinks it's homo to use it and it's not . . . even though it's there to use but no one really uses it and there's a washroom that some people used to change so that other people don't watch them.

Connor elaborates, explaining the ways that boys actively and intentionally manage time and space in the school locker room:

> A lot of kids, they change really fast because they don't want other kids to make fun of them. They get in the locker room and they get out as fast as they can because they don't want to be in there long because if you're in there for a while, the chances are you're going to get picked on and then like I said, some of the kids, they go into the stalls to change so that no one can see them.

Connor draws attention to the delineation of spaces and cultural associations made between specific spaces within locker rooms. Physical spaces such as school showers are "homo to use." Students expressed a discomfort with the open space and the possible vulnerability intersecting masculinity, bodies, and shower spaces. I argue that spaces including showers and open areas in the change room are *normatively sanctioned spaces*. These spaces are characterized firstly by their openness as physical spaces. These spaces are prone to surveillance and peer scrutiny. In addition, these spaces are commonly understood as the most potentially threatening spaces in locker rooms. *Normatively sanctioned spaces* are arenas in which young men outwardly express heteronormative masculinity through physical means. Across the spectrum of the young men interviewed they spoke of physical intimidation, aggression, and the public display of traditionally masculine interactions such as posing, flexing, and physically encroaching on other boys' private spaces. In the following excerpt Jay describes the "edge of the room." He explains how lockers serve as dividers and boundaries among boys:

> They hang out in one edge of the room, the locker room but they hang out in this side or that side. Then we all like stay, we stay away from each other. The cool kids stay and then maybe have a few lockers to themselves, we have a few lockers to ourselves. We don't talk, honestly. The only way that they talk to us is, let's say, I'm on your team or you should do better or why did you throw that ball and then why didn't you pass it to me I was right open. You can never start a decent conversation with them and I honestly don't know how.

Harley similarly describes a form of silencing and physical alienation he experiences during HPE class:

> I don't know. We don't really speak to each other much. You know they don't really say too much to me. Maybe sometimes it's like . . . they started to pass the ball to me at the beginning of the year and then they kind of realized that I'm not very good and they just kind of ignored me.

The geography of the locker room is partitioned by divisive territories and appears to be boundaried according to an us versus them model. Jay and Harley describe clear tensions across the groups of boys that pit the "cool kids" against other kids who remain unnamed in the description. The nameless group, of which Jay is a member, is also a group without a voice. Harley describes a purposeful distancing some boys employ to physically marginalize other less skilled boys. His HPE class is best characterized by how he describes being increasingly silenced and gradually ignored. All the boys spoke of locker rooms in terms of **divisions** by sides and a physical distance where "we stay away from each other." In addition to physical divides between these boys, the boys spoke of a powerful sense of voicelessness in which "we don't talk" and we "can never start a decent conversation." The power among boys to silence others and alienate them, relegating them to sides of the locker room, is troubling and indeed reason for concern for teachers and coaches.

The physical and spatial divisions these boys create are also witnessed and expressed with regard to the resources and amount of investment boys dedicate to developing muscular bodies. Not dissimilar to other young men in this study Joseph describes a physical separation within the locker room, stating that "They're off in their little area they've kind of formed and we don't really, we don't bug each other." He identifies the other boys as:

> pretty buff and they're like, usually they, I don't know they seem really, like some of them are unsocial. I don't know why, you'd think you'd talk to a lot of people . . . usually they show up with like, you know full PE strip on, like gym shorts and you know and usually they're part of like school basketball team or something.

Noah describes the impact, privilege, and power that accompanies muscular bodies:

> They're muscular and thin. . . . He [the teacher] always calls on them and he gives them his keys and lets them like go pick up stuff and like stuff like that. You just feel that he likes them better than everybody else.

In addition to the privileges granted to the more dominant and body privileged boys, Noah also describes how those boys are able to control and define locker-room conversations:

> You see sort of different groups changing together and talking. . . . In the buff boys group it's usually they're talking about what sport we're playing today or what we're doing today, stuff like that.

Bob describes the symbolic significance muscularity has among adolescent boys:

> Maybe they look at other people and say oh I'm better than them. I have bigger muscles or something like that. I can run faster than them. The way they perform in certain activities makes them surpass other people. So it's kind of like comparing themselves to other people because if everybody's the same you can't really say you're better than them.

In the above conversation Bob describes the ways young men position themselves in relation to each other. Muscularity and speed, for example, are regular points of reference that these adolescent boys use to compare themselves.

Across this study the young men were consistent in how they drew the lines both physically and socially among their HPE classmates. The boys repeatedly made references that maintained and relied upon a polarization among their male counterparts based on a privileging of physical attributes as well as social status. Similar to Hauge and Haavind (2011, 12), the boys in this study adopted various discourses of the male body in which it could "be viewed as citing different masculine subjectivities that young boys may inscribe when constituting themselves as adolescents." Moreover, our research also indicates that "the process of constituting masculinity as an adolescent involves continuously negotiating ways of being and becoming as prescribed through such discourses" (2011, 12). According to these boys, the prevailing discourse heavily centred on male bodies that were "pretty buff" as well as "muscular and thin." Hauge and Haavind (2011, 10) refer to this as the "strong body" discourse which "acknowledges the body as strong and thus capable of attaining respect." These bodies also dominated specific spaces in the locker room. The power for the boys was both in the ability to project an aggressive outward bodily appearance but also in the management and control that accompanied particular dominant forms of masculine bodies. The awareness these boys shared and the ways it further manifested itself in how they come to understand their own bodies and physical activity in the context of HPE is again, an area requiring ongoing investigation.

Concluding Remarks: Voices from the Margins

The constructed-ness of masculinity and its representational forms in physical health education classes are visible in the daily interactions and exchanges of boys. There is a growing acknowledgement and awareness of the intersection between physical cultures and physical activity. Wright et al. (2003, 19) remind us that "young people draw on specific cultural resources to make sense of their participation; their engagement with physical activity and physical culture provides resources with which they make sense of their lives and their interactions with others." Mythic Artist explains that boys have fears and weaknesses and the effort to hide those weaknesses is evident in the expressions of masculinity conveyed through bodily performance:

I think they're showing off actually, they're probably showing off for some people like probably their friends or you know, girls that they have feelings for but maybe actually they're showing off for themselves because there's parts of them that aren't strong so they're showing off their physical strength kind of blocking out the other things.

During his interview Connor describes how other boys showed they were good in PE class:

I'd say it's fairly important. In the way they show it in class, it's more important than about how athletic they are around other people and how much better they are and how much they can do, how strong they are.

He further explains:

they can show off themselves and they can be tough around other people and it gives them an opportunity to be tough and be good at something because most of them, they don't excel in their academic classes. So gym is kind of their thing where they can be better than everyone else and they kind of take that to their heads a little bit more and the smaller kids.

Joey is aware of the power other boys have to include and exclude him in HPE class. His experiences in PE are captured by familiar and unsettling stories of bullying for the more privileged and physically dominant boys in his class:

> Usually when we're picking teams and stuff, I'm one of the last ones picked . . . and I try and participate as much as possible but it's hard to do when nobody passes you the ball in games and stuff. . . . I've been told one time in my gym class that we were doing a team game and the one guy came up to me and said that you're playing a very important role, the bench, and that didn't make me feel very good.

The young men in this study saw and were able to articulate the lines or boundaries that divided them. Spaces like boy's locker rooms make the invisible unspoken lines across boys more visually evident. The awareness and striking divisions that are predicated among boys on the basis of physical abilities, athletic prowess, and domination or outward physical strength and aggression is disturbing. These young men saw and knew the power of privileged masculine bodies. They routinely drew on a discourse of masculinity that allowed them to position themselves among other boys both physically and socially. The research interviews and the observations provided a way for these young men to make sense of their own bodies in relation to other, often at times, more powerfully bodied boys. Similar to the research of Hauge and Haavind (2011, 3), it is a poignant reminder for teachers and coaches to be aware that "the bodily practices boys perform should be seen as neither arbitrary nor accidental, but as intentional and directed." These young men have experienced the domination, the alienation, the oppressive acts of their peers who deploy their bodies to get privilege, to get recognized, and to get status among other boys. The discourse of the buff boys and the muscled bodies is juxtaposed with a discourse of silenced bodies and weak boys.

Gorely, Holroyd, and Kirk (2003, 444) argue for re-envisioning a gender-relevant physical education that embraces a socially critical pedagogy and extends previous work calling for a pedagogy of "care, concern and community." This study provides empirical regularities illustrating the ways boys make sense of school locker rooms and their relationship to these spaces in relation to masculinities, bodies, and physical health and education. Feelings of ridicule and inadequacies in health and physical education emerge for young men such as Mythic Artist when sport activities become a context for men to "show off for themselves because there's parts of them that aren't strong so they're showing off their physical strength kind of blocking out the other things." We are left with powerful stories and disturbing reminders of the taken for granted nature of school locker rooms. Frost (2003, 67) reminds us that for both boys and girls:

> the pressure to conform to them [the prescriptions of the body and appearance] and the outcomes of not meeting them sound sadly similar. Both young men and women speak of fears of, or the actual experience of, being excluded from the all-important group membership of youth, for being unable or unwilling to produce the necessary style, shape and size.

It is only fitting then that this chapter ends with the words from James who, not un-like many of the boys we interviewed and observed in this study, reminds us of what it is like to be on the margins or on the other side of the locker room. His comments not only reflect the embedded gendered assumptions intersecting masculinity and HPE, but also the real and apparent challenges before HPE teachers, coaches and administrators to change a culture and climate among boys that will allow for a greater diversity and broader reper-toire of masculinities so that *all* boys can participate in HPE classes without having to be a "superhero":

> I don't think that gym should expect us as males to be good . . . people like me, I get called a nerd because I'm up in my room playing on my computer all the time but people who go out and play football, they're not nerds, they're superheroes. I don't know, like they're not looked on like some person who nobody wants to be friends with.

Questions for Critical Thought

1. Consider other social spaces in schools and elsewhere that youth congregate. Keep in mind the concept of divisions. How do the spaces vary and on what basis? Consider shopping centres, common meeting areas. What are the rules of engagement? What kinds of surveillance can you identify?
2. Bodily privilege appears in many ways. Are you bodily privileged? Consider how you express your bodily privilege among peers and generate a list of reasons why and how boys and girls might do this. At what age do we notice bodily privilege? How might we interrogate or critique bodily privilege with adolescents?
3. Consider the increased visibility of the male body. What evidence do you have in your daily interactions that there is a shift in the degree to which boys and men are aware of their physical appearance?
4. The author suggests there needs to be a change in the culture and climate of school locker rooms. Debate how this might occur and or whether it is possible. What are the attributes of school culture that have made these stories resonate with many of us and moreover that reflect on the resilience of school culture?

Glossary

Divisions Locker rooms are explicitly and im-plicitly boundaried by physical and social divi-sions. The participants described intimidation practices that created separate spaces between different groups of boys. These were evident both physically by some boys being positioned on the fringes or boundaries of the locker room. The as-signment of boys to different places, particularly those marginalized in the locker room, was effec-tively done through verbal taunting and physically posing, taking up space to maintain separations among boys. Locker rooms like many social spaces can be mapped, reflecting power diff-erentials across the inhabitants in these spaces.

Ethnographic voyeurism This term is used to indicate the perception that ethnographers gaze upon participants in a voyeuristic manner. It is a term that is devoid of any evidentiary basis but rather heavily connected to stereotypes and assumptions. In this case the schools might, for example, assume boys do not have body image issues but girls typically would have these concerns. Additionally, schools might impose protective restrictions to researchers investigating issues associated with adolescent bodies suggesting that it is inappropriate to "look" at youths' bodies. The implicit and explicit fear outside of the research community is translated into gatekeeping that restricts and limits access to participants, usually youth, particularly in school settings and often under the age of consent.

Masculinities This term reflects a fluid way of being a man or boy and specifically relies on theories of gender as socially constructed. This term conceptually challenges long standing arguments that conflate sex with gender. Grounded in men's studies research, theorist Raewyn Connell (1995) problematizes a more restrictive understating of boyhood and manhood as biologically determined. As a term, masculinities reflects the possibilities of competing ways of being boys that are less restrictive and prescriptive than previously thought.

Surveillance As pertaining to school locker rooms, in particular, surveillance is a common practice among boys. The covert ways these young men, for example, would purposefully and strategically avoid the furtive glances of their peers reveals the level of surveillance. Boys expressed a discomfort in the locker room in which their peers took up space, imposing themselves through a physical as well as verbal dominance in these spaces. Boys monitor the actions of other boys to affirm they are suitably and appropriately masculine. Measures of harassment and bullying are often used to ensure boys conduct themselves as heteronormative boys.

References

Atkinson, M., and Kehler, M. "Boys, bullying and biopedagogies in physical education." *Thymos: Journal of Boyhood Studies* 6(1–2) (2012): 166–85.

Connell, R.W. *Masculinities*. Berkeley: University of California Press, 1995.

DeVisser, R.O., Smith, J.A., and McDonnell, E.J. "'That's not masculine': Masculine capital and health related behaviour." *Journal of Psychology* 14(7) (2009): 1047–58.

Diedrichs, P., and Lee, C. "GI Joe or Average Joe?: The impact of average size and muscular male fashion models on men's health and women's body image and advertisement effectiveness." *Body Image* 7(3) (2010): 218–26.

Dwyer, J.J., Allison, K.R., LeMoine, K.N., Adlaf, E.M., Goodman, J., Faulkner, G.E., and Lysy, D.C. "A provincial study of opportunities for school-based physical activity in secondary schools." *Journal of Adolescent Health* 39(1) (2006): 80–6.

Eisenberg, M.E., Wall, M., and Neumark-Sztainer, D. "Muscle-enhancing behaviors among adolescent girls and boys." *Pediatrics* 130(6) (2012): 1019–26.

Evans, J., Davies, B., and Rich, E. "The class and cultural functions of obesity discourse: Our later day child saving the moment." *International Studies in Sociology of Education* 18(2) (2008): 117–32.

Frost, L. "Doing bodies differently? Gender, youth, appearance and damage." *Journal of Youth Studies* 6(1) (2003): 53–70.

Fusco, C. "Naked truths?: Ethnographic dilemmas of doing research on the body in social spaces." In *The Methodological Dilemma: Creative, Critical and Collaborative Approaches to Qualitative Research*, K. Gallagher (ed.), (159–84). New York: Routledge, 2008.

Gard, M. *The End of the Obesity Epidemic*. Oxon: Routledge, 2011.

Gorely, T., Holroyd, R., and Kirk, D. "Muscularity, the habitus and the social construction of gender: Towards a gender-relevant physical education." *British Journal of Sociology of Education* 24(4) (2003): 429–48.

Grogan, S., and Richards, H. "Body image: Focus groups with boys and men." *Men and Masculinities* 4(3) (2002): 219–32.

Harwood, V., and Wright, J. "Policy, schools and the new health imperatives." *Discourse: Studies in the Cultural Politics of Education* 33(5) (2012): 611–15.

Hauge, M., and Haavind, H. "Boys' bodies and the constitution of adolescent masculinities." *Sport, Education and Society* 16(1) (2011): 1–16.

Humberstone, B., and Stan, I. "Health, (body) image, and primary schooling: 'Why do they have to be a certain weight?'" *Sport, Education and Society* 16(4) (2011): 431–49.

Kehler, M. "Negotiating masculinities in PE classrooms: Boys, body image and—want[ing] to be in good shape." In *Boys' Bodies: Speaking the Unspoken* M. Kehler and M. Atkinson (eds.), (143–65). New York: Peter Lang, 2010.

MacKay, J., Messner, M.A., and Sabo, D.F. (eds.). *Masculinities, Gender Relations, and Sport.* Thousand Oaks: Sage Publications, 2000.

Markey, C.N. "Invited commentary: Why body image is important to adolescent development." *Journal of Youth and Adolescence* 39(12) (2010): 1387–91.

Martin, J., and Govender, K. "'Making muscle junkies': Investigating traditional masculine ideology, body image discrepancy, and the pursuit of muscularity in adolescent males." *Men's Health* 10(3) (2011): 220–39.

Messner, M.A., and Musto, M. "For the sociology of sport: Where are the kids?." *Sociology of Sport Journal* 31(1) (2014): 102–22.

Norman, M. "Embodying the double-bind of masculinity: Young men and discourses of normalcy, health, heterosexuality, and individualism." *Men and Masculinities* 14(4) (2011): 430–49.

O'Donovan, T.M., and Kirk, D. "Managing classroom entry: An ecological analysis of ritual interaction and negotiation in the changing room." *Sport, Education and Society* 12(4) (2007): 399–413.

Paechter, C. "Power, bodies and identity: How different forms of physical education construct varying masculinities and femininities in secondary schools." *Sex Education* 3(1) (2003): 47–59.

Paechter, C. "Gender, visible bodies and schooling: Cultural pathologies of childhood." *Sport, Education and Society* 16(3) (2011): 309–22.

Pope, H., Phillips, K., and Olivardia, R. *The Adonis Complex: The Secret Crisis of Male Body Obsession.* New York: The Free Press, 2000.

Ricciardelli, R., Clow, K., and White, P. "Investigating hegemonic masculinity: Portrayals of masculinity in men's lifestyle magazines." *Sex Role* 63(1–2) (2010): 64–78.

Rich, E. "Obesity assemblages and surveillance in schools." *International Journal of Qualitative Studies in Education* 23(7) (2010): 803–21.

Shilling, C. "Exploring the society-body-school nexus: Theoretical and methodology issues in the study of body pedagogics." *Sport, Education and Society* 15(2) (2010): 151–67.

Smolak, L. "Body image in children and adolescents: Where do we go from here?." *Body Image* 1 (2004): 15–28.

Wellard, I. "Inflexible bodies and minds: Exploring the gendered limits in contemporary sport, physical education and dance." In *Rethinking Gender and Youth Sport*, I. Wellard (ed.), (84–98). London: Routledge, 2007.

Wellard, I. *Sport, Masculinities and the Body.* New York: Routledge, 2009.

Wright, J., MacDonald, D., and Groom, L. "Physical activity and young people: Beyond participation." *Sport, Education and Society* 8(1) (2003): 17–33.

Part III

Reform Pressures and Alternative Visions

Introduction

The chapters in Part III share a concern with the potential and pitfalls of education reform. Unlike any other social institution, those that loosely make up the education system are exposed to constant reform demands and pressures. I have already mentioned some of these demands in the introduction to this book; some are worth repeating here. Rather than promoting active labour market policies that create employment, governments tend to respond to high levels of unemployment by asking young people to stay in school longer, to study in programs that lead to better employability, or to upgrade their skills, as if these efforts magically were to create new employment opportunities. If levels of youth crime are perceived to be on the rise, schools are supposed to offer a fix by keeping young people who are at risk on track. As an immigrant nation, schools are to expand their offerings to integrate newcomers into Canadian society, but also to teach them the necessary skills (such as language skills) to succeed in Canada. We ask schools to solve the obesity crisis by offering more physical education and better food in their cafeteria. The list goes on.

Some reform pressures are more all-encompassing and challenge the status quo of how schooling is delivered. There is a long history of experimentation with alternative, anti-authoritarian, democratic school reform that eschews curriculum and structured learning in favour of students' self-discovery. Not only have these experiments remained relatively rare, they also exist outside the public realm and are therefore mostly accessed by families with relatively high levels of cultural capital. In fact, it has been argued that unstructured learning requires precisely the type of pro-learning mentality found in families with high levels of cultural capital (St Clair, 2001).

More pervasive has been the call to return schooling back to what supporters of such reform pressures call its basic functions of moral education and preparation for economic competitiveness. Michael Apple (2006) has linked these reform pressures in the United States to larger neoconservative and neoliberal movements. Two key obsessions of neoliberal school reformers are accountability and privatization. Accountability, to be achieved through regular standardized testing, has already become the norm for most students in Canada. In Ontario, for instance, the Education Quality and Accountability Office (EQAO) carries out annual province-wide tests on reading and math skills, although unlike in most of the United States, they are not formally linked to school funding or student records. Nonetheless, the public availability of school performance data, it has been argued, has led to destructive forms of inter-school competition and teaching-to-the-test mentalities, instead of improving learning and teaching (Moll, 2004). It also has been shown that those who already struggle at school suffer the most when tests become high stakes (Gillborn and Youdell, 2001).

Another hallmark of neoliberal reform is the belief that a privatized school system that offers parents and students choice over what kind of school suits their needs best will deliver better results than a one-fits-all public system. In the United States, Charter Schools are an attempt to introduce quasi-choice into the public system. In Canada, Alberta is the only province that has formally introduced Charter Schools, although Ontario offers similar levels of choice in its public high schools. For instance, parents can enroll their high school-aged children in French Immersion schools, performing arts-focused schools, academically focused schools, or the aforementioned Africentric School in Toronto. As public high schools have become increasingly diverse in what they offer, we still have seen a growing trend in private school enrolment, especially in Canada's larger cities. For instance, just under 9 per cent of children attend private schools in Ontario (Ontario Ministry of Education, 2014), although that number is higher in cities like Toronto. When we think of private schooling, we tend to imagine posh, elite private schools, such as All-Boys and All-Girls High studied by Baker in Chapter 9. As Linda Quirke and Janice Aurini point out in Chapter 11, however, there is tremendous diversity in the private school sector in Canada. Moreover, they found that many private schools (and private tutoring centres) are not led by qualified or certified teachers. Their research suggests that private schools and tutoring centres founded and managed by entrepreneurs rather than teachers prefer to hire non-certified teachers for relatively low salaries with few opportunities for professional development. Not only does this affect the quality of teaching, it also affects the professional status of those teaching.

Obviously, reform challenges do not only emerge from what Apple (2006) calls the neoliberal, neoconservative Right but also from what we may want to broadly call the Left. George Dei (1996) has published about the need for anti-racist education to provide a more politically aware and critical extension of multiculturalism in schools. In Chapter 12, he offers the concrete example of using Indigenous stories and proverbs to add anti-racist perspectives to curriculum. Concerned with the incongruity of educational curricula and teachers' pedagogies with students' Indigenous identity, Dei is hopeful that the use of Indigenous stories and proverbs creates interaction between the teacher and student where both are active participants in creative thinking and problem solving. Moreover, Dei argues that the use of proverbs and storytelling as a pedagogic strategy is fundamentally aligned with Indigenous peoples' ways of learning, knowing, collectivity, and interconnectedness.

Ryan Broll in Chapter 13 addresses the issue of student safety at school (and outside). A number of high-profile suicides in recent years have brought the issue of cyberbullying among young people to public attention. There is consensus that cyberbullying poses a significant thread to the well-being of young people, but policing it is difficult. Unlike traditional forms of bullying, such as schoolyard fights, cyberbullying can take place anywhere, anytime. It is thus not exclusively the responsibility of schools, but neither is it outside the school's purview, as being the victim of cyberbullying can have significant effects on one's ability to feel safe at school. Broll discusses the complex responsibility structure that has emerged in response to our concerns about the effects of cyberbullying, showing that each of the three main groups (school personnel, parents, and police) tend to see one of the other as more responsible.

Part III and the book close with a chapter by Delia Dumitrica and Amanda Williams who discuss the potential and problems of Massive Open Online Courses (MOOCs). MOOCs have been hailed by some as the great saviour of education, spreading knowledge around the globe and giving access to learning to people in remote parts of the world. Adding to the appeal of MOOCs is their association with elite, exclusive universities. Those hopeful of technical solutions to real-world problems see MOOCs as the answer to high tuition costs, skill shortages, and gaps in teaching expertise. Many working within academia fear commodification and corporatization of knowledge and see MOOCs as a threat to traditional face-to-face learning. Dumitrica and Williams, drawing on interviews with Canadian educators who have been involved in the development and delivery of MOOCs, highlight the complexity of this educational tool. They conclude that we cannot understand the role of MOOCs in education unless we link it to the social role educational institutions hope to fulfill. And herein lies much of the stories complexity: Being a good (global) citizen means that universities can use MOOCs to make what they offer accessible to ever-larger numbers of keen learners; dealing with budgetary restrictions in the age of austerity also makes MOOCs an attractive proposition to assume greater control of intellectual property and ultimately save on costs.

Despite the diversity of topics, the four chapters in Part III highlight the complexity of educational policy.

References

Apple, M. "Whose markets, whose knowledge?." In *Sociology of Education: A Critical Reader*, Alan R. Sadovnik (ed.), (177–94). New York: Routledge, 2006.

Dei, G. *Anti-Racism Education: Theory and Practice*. Halifax: Fernwood, 1996.

Gillborn, D., and Youdell, D. "The new IQism: intelligence, 'ability' and the rationing of education." In *Sociology of Education Today*, J. Demaine (ed.). Houndmills: Palgrave, 2001.

Moll, M. (ed). *Passing the Test: The False Promise of Standardized Testing*. Ottawa: Canadian Centre for Policy Alternatives, 2004.

Ontario Ministry of Education. *Quick Facts: Ontario Schools 2012–13*. Toronto: Queen's Printer for Ontario, 2014.

St. Clair, R. "No more classes? Framing pedagogy in a self-paced secondary school." *Alberta Journal of Educational Research* 47(3) (2001): 206–21.

11

"Teachers Can't Be Made, They're Born"
Teaching and Professionalism in Ontario's Private Education Sector

Linda Quirke and Janice Aurini

Introduction

The teaching profession is a "weak" profession, with lower levels of compensation, prestige, and authority than "full" professions, such as the legal or medical profession. Aspiring teachers may look to work in private tutoring or in a private school as a way to advance their career. Do workers in private education enjoy higher or lower status, compared to public school teaching? We examine the dynamics of professionalism in Ontario's private education sector according to Ingersoll and Merrill's (2011) seven criteria for professionalization. We analyse data from over 100 private education businesses, including 87 open-ended interviews with private school principals and private tutoring centre owners in Toronto and Hamilton, Ontario. Our findings suggest that entrepreneurs with no formal teaching experience are increasingly commonplace within Ontario private education. They actively foster a distinctly non-professional model of teaching in four ways: hiring uncertified staff; providing low wages; and providing few opportunities for either specialization or professional development. We conclude that private education workers' status is lower than the middling or semi-professional status associated with teachers in the public education sector.

Professionalism and Private Education in Ontario

The teaching profession has traditionally been understood to be a weak or a **semi-profession**, as it lacks the status enjoyed by "full" professions such as law and medicine (Etzioni, 1969). While many scholars have emphasised different elements of professions (see Adams [2010]), according to Brint (1994), professions are defined as:

> Those occupations exercising the capacity to create exclusive shelters in the labor market through the monopolization of advanced degrees and other credentials related to higher education that are required for the attainment of the social and economic opportunities of authorized practice. (Brint, 1994, 23)

Sciulli (2005, 935) emphasises the importance of structure when thinking about professions: "Professions always and everywhere provide expert services within . . . structured situations" to vulnerable clients. Sciulli (2005) argues that advanced formal education, collegiality, and an ethical sense of responsibility are important factors associated with professionalism.

While traditionally performed within large state-run bureaucracies (Etzioni, 1969), teaching work is increasingly performed outside of these customary settings. Canada's kindergarten to Grade 12 private education has witnessed unprecedented growth as more parents are enrolling their children in private school, and many seek out **private tutoring**. As such, a larger share of work traditionally performed by teachers is being carried out within the private education sector (Aurini, 2006, 2012; Aurini and Quirke, 2011; Davies and Quirke, 2005, 2006, 2007; Davies, Quirke, and Aurini, 2006; Quirke, 2009).

In this chapter, we ask the question: how do private education workers fare with respect to professional status, compared with teachers in state-run schools? Do private education workers enjoy higher **credentials**, pay and other markers of professionalism? Unlike schools, private tutoring businesses have not been traditional employers of teachers. Nevertheless, the widespread emergence of private tutoring across Canada is instructive and warrants further investigation. Drawing on interviews with private school principals and private tutoring centre owners in Toronto and Hamilton, Ontario, this paper examines the professional status of private education workers. What are the dynamics of teacher professionalism within a deregulated private sector? We argue that the private education field is characterized by a distinctly non-professional model of teaching. We find that private education organization leaders compromise teacher professionalism in four ways: (1) by hiring uncertified staff, (2) paying low wages, and failing to provide opportunities for either (3) specialization or (4) professional development.

Context: Teaching's Semi-professional Status

Teachers' weak professional status has been well documented (Dreeben, 2005; Ingersoll, 2003; Ingersoll and Merrill, 2011; Wilkinson, 2005; see also Rowan [1994]). Ingersoll and Merrill (2011) have looked specifically at the work of teachers, and have compiled seven key characteristics shared by full professionals, comparing how teachers fare according to these criteria (see Table 11.1).

Assessing teachers' status according to these criteria, one can determine that the teaching profession is not a full profession; it is weak with respect to several key characteristics. First, certification and formal credentials are a core trait of professions. Insofar as teachers are required to have professional certification and state-granted licences, teachers' professional status is maintained and preserved. Full professions must have a credential or licence to practise—usually both. Practising without the proper credentials is prohibited by law; someone who is not a member of the Royal College of Dental Surgeons of Ontario cannot practise dentistry in Ontario. However, anyone could open a private school or tutoring centre without any credential or experience in the field. Furthermore, while teachers in public schools are required to be certified and licensed by the state, they undergo only minimal training before starting work (for example, one year of teachers' college) compared to other professions. For instance, lawyers must undergo three years of law school after their undergraduate training. With respect to compensation, teachers earn far less than their counterparts in other professions.

One of the most essential characteristics of professions is specialization, which occurs when a task area becomes so complex that it becomes necessary to further sub-divide it

Table 11.1 Professional Characteristics: Full Professionals and Public Sector
Teachers as Semi-professionals

Criteria	Full Professionals (e.g. physicians)	Public Sector Teachers: Semi-professionals
Credentials	Licence, certification required	Licence, certification required
Compensation	High	Lower than most professions
Specialization	High (i.e. paediatrician would not perform brain surgery)	Low (much out-of-field teaching)
Professional development	Expected, ongoing	Moderate, not required
Induction	Extensive training for new practitioners	Few effective mentoring programs
Authority	High, self-governance	Moderate; high inside classroom, but no control over training, curriculum.
Prestige	High	Low compared to other professions

Source: Adapted from Ingersoll and Merrill (2011)

into more manageable chunks (for example, cardiology, urology, oncology). Professional training should, therefore, not be generic; full professionals specialize in a specific body of knowledge. For instance, a paediatrician would not be asked to perform brain surgery. Given the premise that professional knowledge is complex and requires skill and expertise, specialization is a hallmark of professionalism. Compared with other professions, specialization in teaching is low as teachers are routinely required to teach out of their "teachable" field of expertise (Ingersoll and Merrill, 2011; Ingersoll, 2003).

Teachers are not required to participate in thorough professional development throughout their careers. The requirement of practitioners to engage in ongoing in-service technical growth is associated with the notion that mastering and keeping a complex set of professional skills updated is an ongoing process (Ingersoll and Merrill, 2011). The norm of professional development is partially embraced by teachers. Most teachers participate in professional development (PD) workshops and programs when schools are closed on PD days during the school year. However, fewer than half of teachers go beyond this minimum to participate in professional development activities such as conferences, workshops or seminars sponsored by professional organizations (Ingersoll and Merrill, 2011).

Unlike other professions, teachers do not engage in extensive mentoring or induction programs. While doctors must spend years of training as a resident after completing medical school, teachers do not go through a similar stage of mentoring. After teachers complete teachers' college, they are considered fully fledged members of the profession. While teachers do enjoy a limited degree of authority within the classroom, the teaching profession is unable to establish a firmly based cognitive authority (see Larson [1977]; Freidson [1986]). Many people may see teaching as something that anyone with or without formal training can do (Quirke, 2009). Finally, teaching lacks the prestige granted to other professions as teachers cannot claim to hold unchallenged authority over their area of expertise (Brint, 1994). Unlike other professions such as law or medicine, the work of teaching can be legally performed without state certification, outside of large bureaucratic organizations, in the open market. This confluence of the expansion of private education and the teachers' weak professional status sets the stage for an empirical analysis: How do teachers maintain their professional status outside of public education? This paper explores the research question: What are the dynamics of teacher professionalism within a **deregulated field**?

Case Study: Private Education in Ontario

Private Education Growth

Roughly 9 per cent of Canadian families enroll their children in non-public school alternatives; approximately 6.5 per cent exclusively choose private schools, and another 2.4 per cent enroll children in both public and private schools (Davies and Aurini, 2011). In Canada, and Ontario in particular, private school enrolments are on the rise. In 1960, only 1.9 per cent of Ontario children attended private schools; following steady increases since the late 1980s, more than 5 per cent of school children attended by 2010 (Ontario Ministry of Education, 2013; Van Pelt, Allison, and Allison, 2007). Attendance is higher in Toronto where roughly 9 per cent of students attend private schools (Ontario Ministry of Education, 2003). There has been a near doubling of the number of private schools in Ontario in the past two decades, from 560 in 1996 to more than 1040 by 2014 (Ontario Ministry of Education, 2003, 2014). These schools include venerable elite preparatory academies, Montessori schools, a variety of religious schools, as well as small, non-elite secular academies (Davies and Quirke, 2007).

Additionally, Ontario private tutoring companies have experienced substantial expansion. Private tutoring has sometimes been referred to as "shadow education" to denote its imitation of the formal school system (Bray, 2009). Homework support and exam and test preparation are all ways private tutoring has traditionally "shadowed" the formal education system. Tutoring companies tend to be one of two types: local neighbourhood mom-and-pop companies that tend to operate as small independent companies, and chain or franchise locations of a larger learning centre company, like Sylvan or Kumon.

This cottage industry that once consisted of a peppering of lone tutors and test-prep companies has grown into a multi-billion dollar industry worldwide (Aurini, Davies, and Dierkes, 2013). Almost one quarter of Canadian parents with school-age children has hired tutors in the past three years (Canadian Council of Learning, 2007; Hart, 2012). Gathering the most recent figures from just 17 countries, Aurini et al. (2013) conservatively estimate that the worldwide tutoring industry generates at least $41 billion in sales per year. A recent study projects that the tutoring industry will grow to $102.8 billion by 2018 (Crotty, 2012). Between 1996 and 2010 the number of tutoring businesses in Ontario more than doubled from 245 to roughly 570 locations (see Aurini [2012]). While traditional forms of tutoring continue to expand, a new breed of tutoring services has evolved that goes beyond test-prep and homework support. Preschool reading programs, study skills and time management courses are just a few of the many services offered by North American learning centres. Learning centres are franchised operations and in some instances have internationalized (Aurini et al., 2013).

Private Education Legislation

What does the expansion of private education mean for teachers? Ontario's private education sector is deregulated; private education legislation is relatively loose. There are no restrictions[1] on who can operate a private school in the province. Prospective principals must provide a notice of intention to operate and documentation that their premises have been inspected and approved by health, safety, and fire officials, along with a $300 fee. Private schools can legally operate after they have met these requirements, as long as they provide instruction during regular school hours to at least five students[2].

While private secondary schools that wish to grant high school credits[3] must follow the state-mandated curriculum, other private schools and all private tutoring companies can offer any educational programs. Moreover, private schools and learning centres may operate as small businesses, employing anyone they deem suitable. Neither principals nor private school teachers need to be certified by the state, nor do they require formal teaching experience; anyone is free to open a private school. The state does not interfere in staffing practices of private schools and tutoring centres. As such, education services provided outside of public schools are beyond the reach of the state. Teachers or tutors in the private education sector work in the open market and are not granted the protection of state-supported market shelter. In other words, the work of teaching can be performed by non-teachers in the private education sector. Ontario's loose regulation has created an educational free for all; private schools and tutoring companies can hire anyone they deem appropriate.

Data and Methods

Between 2001 and 2006, data were collected through site visits and interviews at Toronto private schools and private tutoring centres in Toronto and Hamilton, Ontario. A sample of schools was drawn from a government registry of Toronto private schools. We excluded schools that are members of the elite Conference of Independent Schools, including venerable preparatory schools such as Toronto's Havergal College and Upper Canada College. We also excluded religious, language, and reform schools. Scholars have levied attention on elite private schools[4] (Maxwell and Maxwell, 1995; Podmore, 1976) and religious schools (Davids, 2003; Pomson, 2002; Van Brummelen, 1993; Zine, 2008). These private schools also tend to have dense networks and affiliations with established associations (for example, Ontario Alliance of Christian Schools, United Jewish Appeal Federation, Conference of Independent Schools). We wanted to explore private schools that did not offer prestige or religious instruction, and were not necessarily affiliated with existing private school networks. Since 1970, the number of non-elite secular Ontario private schools has ballooned compared to the numbers of elite independent schools, which have not experienced such growth (Podmore, 1976; Ontario Ministry of Education, 2000, 2014). At the time of data collection, Toronto had 64 such schools. We conducted interviews and site visits at 45 schools. We interviewed principals at each school. We did not interview teachers, but in many of the small private schools principals also teach as part of their day. We gathered supplemental data from an additional 15 schools, bringing the total number of schools included in the study to 60.

The sampling frame for tutoring businesses and learning centres was generated from the *Yellow Pages*. Businesses that offered specifically supplementary tutoring such as ESL (English as a second language), language instruction (for example, French), music, art, and companies that provide test prep assistance for writing standardized exams (for example, Graduate Management Admission Test, or the Law School Admission Test) were excluded, which permitted key comparisons between tutoring businesses and public schools. From a list of 52 businesses in Toronto and Hamilton, 42 businesses agreed to an interview, yielding a response rate of over 80 per cent. Of these, 29 were independent mom-and-pop tutorial companies and 13 were one of six learning centre brands. Supplemental data were gathered from the websites of 5 of the 10 businesses that declined an interview, for a total of 47 businesses surveyed.

Education businesses were contacted by phone, and an interview with the principal or owner was requested. Interviews lasted between 45 and 120 minutes. Interviewees were asked about their school or business history, teachers, practices and goals, and their perceptions of parental demands and preferences. Pseudonyms were used for all schools and tutoring businesses. Responses were coded according to a variety of categories, including hiring practices and teacher characteristics.

Findings

This study finds that the professional status of private education workers is lower than public sector teachers. Using Ingersoll and Merrill's (2011) criteria for professionalization, teachers' professional status is particularly undermined with respect to (1) credentials; (2) compensation; (3) specialization; and (4) professional development.

Got Credentials? Non-certified Teachers in Private Education

It is very common for Ontario private schools and especially tutoring companies to hire non-certified individuals to perform the work of teachers. In our sample, 85 per cent of private schools hired non-certified[5] staff. None of the independent tutoring businesses and only one of six learning centre brands prefer to hire certified teachers. Most businesses hire university students and a handful of subject specialists who have an undergraduate or graduate degree in math or sciences. The highly standardized and regulated nature of franchises renders teaching credentials unnecessary; tutors must follow a highly prescriptive program and are not permitted to improvise. In the case of independent tutoring businesses, the opposite is true. Since most independent tutoring companies tend to specialize in a narrow range of services such as math or science, tutors' expertise in a subject area trumped certification; having a degree in math might be more valued than a Bachelor's degree in education.

The lack of state-certified teachers in private schools and tutoring companies is not surprising, given the occupational backgrounds of private school principals and tutoring centre owners. Half of private school principals were trained as teachers prior to opening their school; many even taught for years in public schools; some had worked as vice-principals and principals in public schools. Of the other half (who were not certified as teachers), five had worked in business; seven taught in private schools; three were former tutors; with the others drawn from a number of backgrounds: nursing, computer training, the non-profit sector, with one running a daycare, and another teaching at the university level. It was even less common for tutoring and learning centre owners to have formal teaching credentials as teachers. Only 8 of 47 had teaching credentials or experience in an education-related field. The rest hailed from fields such as business or psychology.

"Teachers Can't Be Made, They're Born": Rationale for Hiring Non-certified Teachers

One common reason given for hiring staff that are not certified is the notion that teaching is not a difficult task. Non-certified principals did not seem daunted or intimidated by the technical work associated with teaching or running a school. Many principals, particularly those who had taught previously in private schools or who had worked as tutors, felt that individuals could simply begin teaching without any training, and that they could do a superior job to certified teachers. Principals seemed to feel that if someone is familiar with the curriculum, they are equipped to teach. Many principals considered that opening or running a school did not take special training or skills.

Many principals dismissed teacher credentials as optional; they did not think that certification added to or enhanced teachers' ability to teach. As one private school principal quipped: "If they have a teaching certificate, who cares, sometimes. Because you can have a teachers' certificate and be a terrible teacher" [Kipling Academy]. There was a general sense among both certified and non-certified principals that teaching ability was an innate personality characteristic. As one principal succinctly remarked: "Teachers can't be made, they're born" [Clarkson High]. The notion that no matter how someone is trained, it will not change whether they are a good teacher or not, was frequently expressed (Quirke, 2009).

Principals' views on teacher certification ranged from positive feelings, to indifference, to outright hostility toward certified teachers. Fewer than 10 per cent felt that it is important for prospective staff to have formal teaching qualifications. Yet even limited support for certification is not necessarily borne out in hiring practices. A number of principals did assign some importance to having certified teachers, but this was often accompanied by hiring uncertified teachers, and then encouraging them to get their certification afterwards. When principals do hire certified teachers, they do so with ambivalence. Non-profit private schools (that is governed by a board of directors) were more likely to hire only certified teachers, while for-profit schools (that is owned and operated by a principal) were less likely to do so. Nine per cent of for-profit schools and 29 per cent of non-profit schools employed only credential teachers. Beyond this, there did not seem to be a strong pattern with respect to which schools or principals were most likely to express a desire to employ credentialed teachers. For instance, principals who were themselves certified were not more likely than uncertified teachers to say that they preferred to hire certified teachers.

Principals who did hire certified teachers did so selectively, especially with respect to art and physical education. As one uncertified principal quipped: "How technically competent do you have to be to play baseball? I know the rules to baseball. . . . It's only two periods a week" [Dundas Academy]. There was a sense among even principals who were supportive of certified teachers that certification was nice to have if the positions could be filled easily enough, but not uniformly important. Other principals simply did not discuss issues of certification whatsoever and simply filled positions as they saw fit, pragmatically hiring uncertified individuals without a great deal of deliberation over whether teacher certification is a suitable or desirable characteristic. Principals emphasised that it was important for their teachers to share the philosophy of the school and to be passionate, caring and flexible, rather than having skills such as classroom management or knowledge of children's development.

Principals were emphatic that parents did not think teaching credentials were important. Ultimately, in the private education sector, if clients do not demand it, business owners see little incentive to hire credentialed teachers. As one tutoring business owner said: "In reality I don't think it makes much difference to [parents]. I don't think they're concerned" [TS: 011]. Private school principals report the same thing; parents do not demand teaching credentials. One principal, who was certified as a teacher in Ontario, explained that parents do not care about whether or not he has formal teaching credentials:

People don't care. If what you do works and you're good at what you do, they couldn't care less. I couldn't remember the last time anyone asked me if I even had a university degree. They don't care; all they know is, their kids come here and they do better and they get on to what they want to do [Long Branch High].

The notion that parents tend not to ask about whether teachers are certified to teach was a common theme. When parents do ask, they do so infrequently:

Q: When parents come here, do they ever ask if you're a qualified teacher?

B.U.: I've had, in the past five–six years, I've had maybe three people ask me that. You know why? Because a lot of the students we've had are through word of mouth. We have parents saying "my child was doing this, and now they're doing this and I'm so happy," and that's all they want to know. The parents don't care about anything else. I've had a few parents ask me, and they say "I'm just asking because I'm curious, I actually don't care. If you're able to work with my kid, that's more important to me" . . . they're not the least bit interested in what certificate you have. It doesn't make the least bit of difference [Burlington High].

Principals explained that parents were more concerned that teachers are charismatic, caring, and knowledgeable, rather than formally certified. In one example, a certified principal runs a very small school where she is also the sole classroom teacher. When asked if it matters to parents that she is formally trained as a teacher, she pointed to her status as a parent of two boys, rather than her certification. She explained that parents had a particular relationship with, or trust in her, and that her certification as a teacher was not a deciding factor. Principals explain that parents are often coming to seek out their school precisely because they are having trouble with certified teachers in a public school, suggesting that private educators who are not certified as teachers may be more appealing to parents and students than credentialed teachers.

Certified Teachers as "Miserable" People

Many school principals report that they simply do not want to hire certified teachers. These principals explain that they are "biased against" certified teachers, as state certified teachers are "burnt out," or "miserable." Private school principals and tutoring centre owners report a clear preference for young, un-certified individuals who are passionate or enthusiastic. Certified teachers are seen as too bureaucratic, inflexible, demanding, and too accustomed to a union-mentality workplace. Credentialed teachers are not viewed favourably by tutoring businesses because they are seen to use the tutoring industry as a suitable part-time job before obtaining a full-time position in the public school board. As one principal who herself dropped out of teachers' college remarked, she avoids hiring certified teachers:

We would screen resumes, and if we saw teachers' college, we almost put them aside immediately. It really is as much indoctrination as you can say perhaps goes on in the public system itself. Teachers' college! I think of it like inbreeding. . . . A lot of us have very anti-teachers' college feelings [York Mills Academy].

Another principal explained that he preferred uncertified teachers, because trying to change certified teachers' thinking was "like crawling over a mile of broken bottles" [Bronte High]. Even principals who are teachers' college graduates and have worked in public schools reported very negative views of certified teachers, referring to them as incompetent and unable to cope.

Learning Centre chain franchisers, who sell individual tutoring branches to learning centre managers or franchisees, tended not to favour certified teachers, citing them as lacking the "entrepreneurial spirit" and ambition required to operate a profitable business. As one franchiser noted:

> We have some teachers in the system. Generally we find that teachers lack ambition, I mean commercial ambition, and they don't have a sense of business investment. They're used to an environment whereby your federation or your union guarantees [salaries and benefits]. You don't put in extra effort unless you're paid sort of thing. It's a big paradigm shift for them [Learning Centre Franchiser].

Most owners and franchisers focus on fostering community relationships and keeping customers "happy." Credibility, not credentials, we were told, built a solid rapport with customers. For this, teachers are not seen as ideal to run tutoring businesses. As one entrepreneur stated: "the president of the Royal Bank of Canada did not necessarily start off as a teller!" [Ontario Learning Centre]. Instead, franchises emphasised that the role of the learning centre manager or franchisee is to "manage" not "teach," since they were responsible for all administrative and managerial aspects of running the learning centre business.

What Works in Private Education: Charisma and Passion

Public schools must, by law, hire certified teachers. In contrast, private education organizations can hire staff based on subjective criteria such as personality or life experience. Private schools and tutoring companies are characterized by non-bureaucratic hiring practices. Principals and tutoring business owners emphasise the importance of non-professional qualities, such as charisma, philosophical views, passion or love for teaching, flexibility, and a caring or nurturing attitude. Many principals claim that they make hiring decisions based on a feeling, that they can immediately identify teachers who would fit into their school. One principal related that potential teachers just have to show that they have the same "headspace" as she does. For tutoring companies, credentials were less important than hiring enthusiastic, young, or "cool" instructors. As the franchisee of a budding learning centre stated:

> [Parents] want their kid to be happy, and like coming here. And so parents, who are paying the money, they are going to ask their kids, "do you like it, are you happy?" If the child likes the teacher and is getting the results with the child then whether they're certified or not, or have two heads, it doesn't make any difference. So charisma really matters. And we try to get people who are going to be cool. It's not like school. It's all on a first name basis. They [the students] are customers, and we treat them like customers, and kids really aren't used to getting that kind of treatment, certainly not in the education domain, or any domain for that matter [Simcoe Learning Centre].

Principals who do appear to support teacher certification emphasise the importance of personal qualities, openly admitting that while they do look at teachers' formal training, certification does not guarantee that teachers will teach well. Even principals who claim to prefer to hire certified teachers do so with ambivalence, assigning a great deal of weight to qualities such as "passion," and "liking children":

> A lot depends on his desire, and on his passion, and on his devotion. Because sometimes you can be a very professional person, and just not caring. And our teachers, they take so, they're very involved in the children's life, and they take everything very close to heart [Union Academy].

Qualities not traditionally associated with professional status come to the fore in private education. While principals in this study emphasised how important it was for staff to care for students, in other professional arenas, it is unlikely that doctors or lawyers would be judged primarily on whether they "take everything very close to heart" when dealing with their patients and clients. Yet among private school principals, personal qualities such as being flexible and caring supersede formal certification. In private education organizations, we found hiring criteria to be subjective and idiosyncratic. Hiring decisions are often made based on instinct, a feeling whether someone is a good teacher or not, rather than bureaucratic professional hiring standards, such as years of experience.

Doing It for Love, Not Money: Compensation in the Private Education Sector

Compared with public school teachers, private education workers are less well compensated. Only two principals reported that they could pay salaries comparable to that of public system teachers. Principals were very frank in their admission that they simply were not able to pay teachers what they would earn if they worked in the public system:

> We can't compete with the wages that the government runs teachers, unions pay teachers so in that respect a lot of the people that come to us prefer the smaller environment and they realize that their pay is not as high as they would get if they went into the public school system [Whitby Academy].

As such, wages within the private education sector are much lower than public sector salaries; private educators report that they simply cannot afford to pay public school board rates. For their part, tutoring businesses expressed that certified teachers were not ideal workers because they require higher compensation. Principals in the private sector openly preferred teachers with less experience: "I like to hire younger teachers. . . . It's lower in wages, and two, they are more mouldable, and we do have a system here" [Dundas Academy]. Teachers' low pay in the private sector is justified by principals reporting that teachers do not care about pay and are instead motivated by a sense of altruism. They explained that their teachers were paid low wages, but their love for education work made it worthwhile:

> They're here not for the pay. They're here because they want to do this. Our one high school teacher, she's fantastic, she works another job in the evenings, but she's here doing it because she loves it [Burlington High].

Another principal remarked that her teachers are not driven by money, but instead, the teachers are "people in life who are helpers" who "really want to help these kids" [Runnymede High].

Similarly, tutors and even certified teachers in the tutoring industry are poorly compensated. Tutoring companies and franchises typically hire instructors on a part-time basis with no obligations such as contracts, benefits, or guaranteed hours. This arrangement allows owners to increase or decrease their workforce depending on the number of students they have enrolled in each month. On average, tutors are paid between ($CDN) $12 and $13 per hour, while learning centre managers earn approximately $25,000 to $30,000 per year. Considering the level of responsibility and skill needed to run a centre, and that managers hold at least one, and in many cases, two university degrees, this salary is extremely low. Learning centre managers are responsible for all administrative aspects of operating the centre. They hold meetings with prospective and current parents and students and staff, conduct and evaluate diagnostic tests and track students' progress, often performing tutoring work themselves. Unlike certified public school teachers, tutors are required to work evenings, weekends and the summer months. Overall, the rationale for lower levels of compensation in private education organizations is that private sector teachers do not mind earning lower salaries because they simply love to work with children.

Flexibility over "Tunnel Vision": Specialization in Private Education

One of the hallmarks of professionalization is specialization. Yet this practice is not fostered in private education. At small schools with few resources, principals try to hire teachers with a range of skills, who can fulfill several roles in the school. A sense of professional specialization is largely met with resistance in private schools, as it tends to be seen as tantamount to "tunnel vision" or inflexibility. Many principals actively avoid teachers who have a particular specialization. These public school teachers are seen as inflexible and unable to fit in with the philosophy of their small school:

> As we're small, we have difficulty in keeping teachers. We've always looked for teachers that can do more than one subject. That's the only way this has worked. We don't just want someone that does "Grade 10 Math"—there is no such thing [Castle Frank High].
>
> I'm looking for people [who are] eclectic because in a small private school you can't have people who have tunnel vision. I can't have a science teacher who can only teach chemistry or only wants to teach chemistry and won't or doesn't want to do anything else [Long Branch High].

As such, specialization and expertise are not necessarily valued traits in private schools. Instead, many principals expressed the need for teachers "to wear a lot of hats" [Dupont Day School]. Only three principals said that they wanted teachers to be "specialists" in their subjects, yet these principals did not necessarily hire certified teachers. Principals may want teachers to teach particular subjects, but this appears to be a pragmatic response to a shortfall of resources, rather than an entrenched respect or recognition of teachers' professional expertise.

Similarly, learning centre tutors, who may be certified teachers, are expected to be a jack-of-all-trades in part because of the imperatives of franchising. Franchising tends to expand the offerings in which any particular business might engage. Whether drug stores, business supplies, or gyms, the existence of franchise forms encourages businesses to expand their menu of services in order to meet new market niches. As one interviewee explained, "Your clients out-grow you." To combat this problem, most learning centres offer a wide range of services that span beyond tutoring, to enrichment programs and personal development courses such as "how to get organized" and "public speaking." Similarly, these businesses cater to a wide range of ability levels (that is, remedial to enrichment) and age ranges by offering preschool reading programs all the way up to university preparation courses. Consequently, tutors are expected to teach from a wide menu of services and education needs. Except in the cases of subject specialists, most tutors teach all age levels and programs. Like private schools, the logic that underlies this practice is rooted in the belief that specialization is not necessary in the sphere of private education.

Overall, in the private education sector, there is not very much support for the notion of professional specialization, except for some subject specialists who teach or tutor older students (that is, advanced math and sciences). By and large, businesses prize adaptability and flexibility over traditional professional notions of specialization. While a criminal lawyer would never be expected to take on a real estate client, what Ingersoll (2003) calls "out of field teaching" is the norm in the private education sector. Respect for professional specialties or norms of specialization—already weak in the public sector—is all but absent here. This is demonstrated by the reluctance with which those in positions of power hire teachers who position themselves as having a particular professional specialization.

Off the Radar: Professional Development

The notion that teachers should update or maintain their technical competence and professional expertise through ongoing professional development is not broadly accepted within private education. Providing teachers with professional development opportunities such as workshops was foreign to all but one principal, who was a state-certified teacher. No other principal mentioned professional development for teachers as a priority or even a consideration. It may be that principals did not want to invest resources into part-time staff members who are constantly in flux. To be fair, most schools operate with minimal resources; principals may not have the fiscal latitude to provide in-service professional development workshops. Many schools only employed a handful of teachers; the expense of providing specialized professional development would have been prohibitive. Yet the expense of professional development is not the whole story; teachers' professional development was simply not within principals' purview. Teachers' work was not considered to warrant additional training. Many principals did not appear to see teaching as a complex skill that needed to be continually upgraded. Instead, as discussed above, teaching ability was largely considered innate, tied to personality and passion.

Similarly, tutoring businesses and franchises tended to embrace a crash and burn business model. Most interviewees stated that they had to "feel into" the businesses, and in the case of franchises, franchisees were expected to hit the ground running. Here, the owner of a Canadian learning centre brand explained the difficulty of training franchisees who operate learning centres:

> so we get people with $120,000–$150,000 in liquid assets to invest . . . which usually means their net worth is somewhere between $300,000–$500,000 and that would also include their home, so, they're not adventuresome people who can

afford a long training period. One of our challenges has been to figure out how to train them so they can hit the ground running as efficiently and inexpensively as possible and then support them. So we transfer kind of the learning curve from the board room to the centre but by supporting them it's not as steep of a curve as it could have been [Ontario Learning Centre].

Tutors in independent tutoring businesses and learning centres also do not spend much time on professional development activities. Learning centre tutors are instead versed on the dictates of the program and the method of delivery to create consistency among tutors and between franchise locations. Even body language is strictly controlled. Tutors are coached on how to sit, make hand or arm gestures to students (for example, the importance of outstretching rather than folding arms), and use key phrases at various junctures in the session. Such regulation routinizes the delivery of services leaving little discretion to the individual tutor.

In summary, within Ontario's private education sector, a distinctly non-professional model of teaching appears to be thriving. The majority of private schools and tutoring businesses prefer to hire non-certified teachers. The ability to teach is seen as an innate personality trait, rather than understood as a complex skill requiring formal training. Even though many lack a background in education, they are confidently setting up shop. Private education workers are paid less, and the professional norms of specialization and professional development is not supported or fostered within this sector. While professions such as law

Table 11.2 Professional Characteristics: Full Professionals, Public Sector Teachers as Semi-professionals and Private Sector Teachers as Non-professionals

Criteria	Full Professionals (i.e., physicians)	Public Sector Teachers: Semi-professionals	Private Education: Non-professionals
Credentials	Licence, certification required	Licence, certification required	Certification not required, teachers often uncertified
Compensation	High	Lower than most professions	Lower than public sector teachers
Specialization	High (i.e., paediatrician would not perform brain surgery)	Low (much out-of-field teaching)	Lower than public sector teachers; "flexibility" demanded
Professional development	Expected, ongoing	Moderate, not required	Few opportunities for professional development
Induction	Extensive training for new practitioners	Few effective mentoring programs	Low; absent in private sector
Authority	High, self-governance	Moderate; high inside classroom, but no control over training, curriculum	Lower than public sector
Prestige	High	Low compared to other professions	Lower than public sector

Source: Adapted by the authors from Ingersoll and Merrill (2011).

and medicine enjoy full professional status, teachers can only claim "semi" professional status (Ingersoll and Merrill, 2011). The data presented above suggest that a third model of professional status is emerging whereby teachers in private education can ultimately be characterized as non-professional. It is difficult to judge whether teachers in private settings enjoy less authority as teachers or lower levels of prestige. Overall, however, the characteristics outlined in the above sections suggest an emerging non-professional model of teaching.

At best, the teaching profession is a "weak" profession, enjoying only partial status as a profession. The data presented above document the large proportions of non-teachers performing educational work in Ontario's private education sector. Moreover, teachers' already weak status is further diminished through the organizational practices of private schools and private tutoring centres that privilege charisma and flexibility over professional traits such as credentials and specialization.

Conclusion and Discussion

We find that the professional status of teachers who work in the private education sector is lower than that of teachers who work in the public sector. Using Ingersoll and Merrill's (2011) criteria for professionalization, the professional status of education workers is particularly threatened with respect to (1) credentials; (2) compensation; (3) specialization; and (4) professional development. Credentials are the lynchpin of professionalism. Without certification, it is exceedingly difficult for teachers to maintain other criteria signalling professional status, such as professional experience or specialization. There is a general lack of respect for teacher certification among the school principals and tutoring businesses surveyed. Even the few individuals who do hold positive attitudes toward teacher credentials give equal weight to non-professional qualities such as a nurturing spirit or love for teaching; no one defends teacher certification as a process. In fact, many principals were fervent in their objection to certified teachers. It is difficult to know whether private education owners and principals prefer non-certified teachers because they genuinely believe these workers are of a better quality, or whether perhaps their attractiveness may stem in part from the lower wages uncertified staff may command. Many respondents argued that a teaching credential adds no extra value to their school or tutoring business. We did find that schools that were run as for-profit businesses were more likely than schools run as non-profit organizations (run by boards of governors) to exclusively hire non-certified staff. In other words, schools where the principal did not have to answer to a board of governors were much less likely to have certified teachers on staff. As such, it appears that private education organizations might not be motivated by purely ideological or philosophical reasons to hire non-certified teachers. In the private education sector, there seems to be more to be gained for businesses to employ uncertified teachers and less to be gained with respect to legitimacy by hiring credentialed teachers.

Overall, in emphasising teachers' emotional and personal connections with students, teachers' status is undermined; nurturing teachers are afforded lower status than professional occupations with more rational, instrumental roles (Dillabough, 1999). As this understanding of teaching work as a natural, innate talent takes root, the claim that teachers should be seen as professionals, with particular expertise, credentials, and so forth, is further weakened.

The low pay offered in this sector is justified by the rationale that teachers will work for lesser wages because of their desire to help children. As well, the professional norm of specialization is not respected in the private education sector. With the exception of a handful of subject specialists who have expertise in math and related disciplines, specialization is seen as neither necessary nor advantageous. Professional development is all but absent in the schools and businesses surveyed. It is not considered important, because teaching is not seen as a complex skill that needs to be continually upgraded. Instead, teaching is seen as an innate talent. As one education consultant who serves an up-market of parents and students explained, the professional status and expert authority teachers enjoy is precarious, as parents may think they know more than teachers do. Ultimately, teachers' inability to lay claim to a particular body of expertise—the notion that anyone with some enthusiasm and charisma can teach—undercuts teachers' status as professionals (Brint, 1994).

Overall, criteria or traits that signal professional status are intertwined; when a profession begins to lack certain professional qualities, such as certification, it is difficult for them to maintain an overall sense of professional status. There is a lack of a coherent notion of professional status in the private education sector. Certification may be present without specialization, and vice versa, leaving this sector without a system of coherent, unified professional norms. This study concludes that teachers' professional status is diminished by the practices of private schools and private tutoring centres. The practices of private tutoring and private school owners may not directly affect the day to day work of teachers in the public sector. Nevertheless, the diminished professional status of workers in the private education sector and the proliferation of an education field that is run largely by those without formal training sets the stage for parents and the broader public to question the necessity of many elements traditionally or currently associated with teachers' work, such as credentials, specialization, or compensation, that are hallmarks of professionalism. As such, the lack of a coherent notion of professionalism in private education may bring the potential for downward pressure on public school teachers, prompting them to lose further ground with respect to their own professional stature as public sector workers.

We question whether other semi-professions, such as social work and nursing, who traditionally perform work in the public sector, would experience a similar undermining of their status in the private sector. What we see from our data is that there is a parallel tier of work performed in the private sector by both certified and uncredentialed workers who take on a substantially diminished status: poor compensation, lacking claims to specialization or professional development. We do not see a lower tier of lawyers or doctors working in the private sector who earn lower wages or who are not afforded the full stature of "professional." We make the argument that it is teachers' already weak professional status that relegates their work outside of the shelter of state organizations (and beyond the purview of a professional association or labour unions) to that of a lower-tier within the occupation. Given teachers' weak status as semi-professionals, it appears that an even weaker parallel jurisdiction has emerged that rejects standard professional traits, allowing these organizations to strategically function without "professionals" (see Aurini [2006]; Quirke [2009]). This situation speaks to the potential for far-reaching unintended consequences. As the province of Ontario has left the private education field largely unregulated, this deregulated space has been fertile ground for the creation of a lower tier where education workers have more diminished status, compared to their counterparts in the heavily regulated public sector.

We conclude that the status of workers in the private education sector in Ontario is lower than the middling or "semi-professional" status enjoyed by public sector teachers. The non-professional model of education work that we found to be characteristic of the educational organizations we surveyed was similar among private schools, tutoring companies, and learning centre franchises. We argue that the deregulated nature of this sector diminishes teachers' already weak status as semi-professionals.

Questions for Critical Thought

1. Based on Quirke and Aurini's findings, should private education workers be considered "professionals"?
2. What sets teaching apart from professions like law and medicine in terms of the knowledge base each profession relies on to perform its work?
3. Why do you think that credentialed teachers are not favoured by private education businesses?
4. To what degree is it problematic that the private education sector is virtually free from government regulation? Are students benefitting from this lack of regulation?

Glossary

Credentials Typically a degree or certificate from a reputable post-secondary institution that entitles someone to perform a specific task or type of work, excluding those who lack such certification. Teachers in Ontario publicly funded schools are expected to hold a Bachelor's of Education degree, a credential granted by certain accredited Ontario universities. Teachers are required to be licensed members of the province's professional teaching body, the Ontario College of Teachers. Those who lack these credentials are considered "uncertified" and therefore ineligible to teach in publicly funded schools in Ontario.

Deregulated field A sector or market that lacks government rules or regulations. In Ontario, the private education sector is largely deregulated, as governments do not compel businesses to adhere to rules governing state-run schools. Moreover, teachers' unions and the Ontario College of Teachers, a body that regulates the teaching profession, do not interfere in private education. Governments do not oversee private education organizations such as private schools or private tutoring businesses.

Private tutoring For a fee, individual tutors, private companies, and learning centre franchises may provide remedial help or assistance with attaining academic advantage. Private tutoring may include help for studying specific content in advance of an upcoming exam or may encompass general study skills, covering academic content that may or may not be covered by mainstream public schools. Sometimes referred to as "shadow education," private tutoring generally takes place outside of school hours and does not involve teachers or other school staff. Tutors may be subject specialists or generalists and may or may not have formal credentials.

Semi-profession An occupation that is considered relatively weak, because of its shorter training and mitigated authority. Semi-professions lack the stature enjoyed by "full" professions such as law and medicine. Ingersoll and Merrill (2011) specify that at best, the teaching profession can be considered a semi-profession. Other classic examples of semi-professions include nursing and social work.

Notes

1. One of the principals, an experienced public school teacher, had served several months in prison for assault. He currently heads a small private school that claims to be able to reach "at risk" youth, given the principal's unique life experience. It is legal for him to run the school, despite his having a criminal record.
2. Private schools do not receive funding from the state. A private school is lawfully defined as an "institution in which instruction is provided at any time between the hours of 9 a.m. and 4 p.m. on any school day for five or more pupils who are of or over compulsory school age in any of the subjects of elementary or secondary school study" (Subsection 1(1) of the *Ontario Education Act*, Ontario Ministry of Education, 2015).

3. Private high schools offering high school credits are inspected by the Ministry of Education every two years to ensure compliance with the province's expectations.

4. See Maxwell (1970) and Weinzweig (1970) for analyses of Havergal College and Upper Canada College, respectively.

5. For the purposes of this research, a "certified" teacher is defined as someone who has a Bachelor's of Education degree and is licensed to teach in the province of Ontario, as a member of Ontario's College of Teachers, the province's professional licencing body.

References

Adams, T. "Profession: A useful concept for sociological analysis?" *Canadian Review of Sociology* 47(1) (2010): 49–70.

Aurini, J. "Crafting legitimation projects: An institutional analysis of private education businesses." *Sociological Forum* 21(1) (2006): 83–111.

Aurini, J. "Patterns of loose and tight coupling in a competitive marketplace: The case of learning center franchises." *Sociology of Education* 85(4) (2012): 376–90.

Aurini, J., Davies, S., and Dierkes, J. *Out of the Shadows? An Introduction to Worldwide Supplementary Education*. Bingley: Emerald Press, 2013.

Aurini, J., and Quirke, L. "Does market competition encourage strategic action in the private education sector?" *Canadian Journal of Sociology* 36(3) (2011): 173–97.

Bray, M. *Confronting the Shadow Education System: What Government Policies for What Private Tutoring?* Paris: IIEP Policy Forum, UNESCO Publishing, 2009.

Brint, S. *In An Age of Experts: The Changing Role of Professionals in Politics and Public Life*. Princeton: Princeton, 1994.

Canadian Council of Learning. *Survey of Canadian Attitudes Toward Learning: Results from Elementary and Secondary School Learning*, 2007. Retrieved from: www.ccl-cca.ca/ CCL/Reports/SCAL/2007Archive/

Crotty, J.M. "Global private tutoring will surpass $102.8 billion by 2018." *Forbes Magazine* (30 October 2012). Retrieved 25 April 2014 from: www.forbes.com/sites/jamesmarshallcrotty/2012/10/30/global-private-tutoring-market-will-surpass-102-billion-by-2018/

Davids, L. "Enrollment trends in Canadian Jewish day schools: What and why?" *Journal of Jewish Education* 69(1) (2003): 63–8.

Davies, S., and Aurini, J. "Determinants of school choice in Canada: Understanding which parents choose and why." *Canadian Public Policy* 37(4) (2011): 459–77.

Davies, S., and Quirke, L. "Providing for the priceless student: Ideologies of choice in an emerging educational market." *American Journal of Education* 111(4) (2005): 523–47.

Davies, S., and Quirke, L. "Innovation in educational markets: An organizational analysis of third sector private schools in Toronto." In *School Sector and Student Outcomes* Maureen Hallinan (ed.), (39–71). Notre Dame: Notre Dame Press, 2006.

Davies, S., and Quirke, L. "The impact of sector on school organizations: Institutional and market logics." *Sociology of Education* 80(1) (2007): 66–89.

Davies, S., Quirke, L., and Aurini, J. "The new institutionalism goes to the market: Comparing the logics of private schooling, tutoring and homeschooling." In *The New Institutionalism and the Study of Education*, H. Meyer and B. Rowan (eds.), (103–22). Albany: SUNY Press, 2006.

Dreeben, R. "Teaching and the competence of occupations." In *The Social Organization of Schooling*, L.V. Hedges and B. Schneider (eds.), (51–90). New York: Russell Sage Foundation, 2005.

Dillabough, J. "Gender politics and conceptions of the modern teacher: Women, identity and professionalism." *British Journal of Sociology of Education* 20(3) (1999): 373–92.

Etzioni, A. *The Semi-professions and Their Organization: Teachers, Nurses, Social Workers*. New York: The Free Press, 1969.

Freidson, E. *Professional Powers: A Study of the Institutionalization of Formal Knowledge*. Chicago: University of Chicago, 1986.

Hart, D. *Public Attitudes toward Education in Ontario 2012*. 2012. Retrieved 22 April 2014: www.oise.utoronto.ca/oise/UserFiles/File/OISE%20Survey/18th_OISE_Survey/OISE%20SURVEY%2018.pdf

Ingersoll, R.M. *Who Controls Teacher's Work?* Cambridge: Harvard University Press, 2003.

Ingersoll, R.M., and Merrill, E. "The status of teaching as a profession." In *Schools and Society: A Sociological Approach to Education*, J. Ballantine and J. Spade (eds.), (185–198). Fourth edition. Thousand Oaks: Pine Forge Press/Sage Publications, 2011.

Larson, M.S. *The Rise of Professionalism*. Berkeley: University of California Press, 1977.

Maxwell, M.P. "Social structure, socialization and social class in a Canadian private school for girls." PhD thesis, Cornell University, 1970.

Maxwell, M.P., and Maxwell, J, "The reproduction of class in Canada's elite independent schools." *British Journal of Sociology of Education* 16(3) (1995): 309–26.

Ontario Ministry of Education. *Private School Count and Enrolment by Religious Affiliation*. Toronto: Queen's Printer for Ontario, 2000.

Ontario Ministry of Education. *Private School Enrolment by Level of Instruction, 2002–2003*. Toronto: Queen's Printer for Ontario, 2003.

Ontario Ministry of Education. *Quick Facts: Ontario Schools, 2011–12*. Toronto: Queen's Printer for Ontario, 2013. Retrieved 22 April 2014 from: www.edu.gov.on.ca/eng/general/elemsec/quickfacts/2011-12/quickFacts11_12.pdf

Ontario Ministry of Education. "Private Elementary and Secondary Schools." (2014). Retrieved 22 April 2014 from: www.edu.gov.on.ca/eng/general/elemsec/privsch/result.asp

Ontario Ministry of Education. *Ontario Education Act*. (2015). Retrieved 13 July 2015 from: www.ontario.ca/laws/statute/90e02

Podmore, C. "Private schooling in English Canada." PhD thesis, McMaster University, 1976.

Pomson, A. "Jewish day-school growth in Toronto: Freeing policy and research from the constraints of conventional sociological wisdom." *Canadian Journal of Education* 27(4) (2002): 379–98.

Quirke, L. "Legitimacy through alternate means: Schools without professionals in the private sector." *British Journal of Sociology of Education* 30(5) (2009): 619–32.

Rowan, B. "Comparing teachers' work with work in other occupations: Notes on the professional status of teaching." *Educational Researcher* 23(6) (1994): 4–17.

Sciulli, D. "Continental sociology of professions today: Conceptual contributions." *Current Sociology* 53(6) (2005): 915–42.

Van Brummelen, H. "The effects of government funding on private schools: Appraising the perceptions of long-term principals and teachers in British Columbia's Christian schools." *Canadian Journal of Education/Revue canadienne de l'éducation* 18(1) (1993): 14–28.

Van Pelt, D., Allison, P.A., and Allison, D.J. *Ontario's Private Schools: Who Chooses Them and Why?* Studies in Education Policy. Fraser Institute Occasional Paper, (May 2007): 1–34. Retrieved from: www.societyforqualityeducation.org/reports/OntariosPrivateSchools.pdf

Weinzweig, P.A. "Socialization and subculture in Elite education: A study of a Canadian boys' private school." PhD thesis, University of Toronto, 1970.

Wilkinson, G. "Workforce remodelling and formal knowledge: The erosion of teachers' professional jurisdiction in English schools." *School Leadership and Management* 25(5) (2005): 421–39.

Zine, J. *Canadian Islamic Schools: Unraveling the Politics of Faith, Gender, Knowledge and Identity*. Toronto: University of Toronto Press, 2008.

12

Indigenous Philosophies, Counter-Epistemologies, and Anti-colonial Education
The Case of Indigenous Proverbs and Cultural Stories

George J. Sefa Dei (Nana Adusei Sefa Ateneboah I)

Introduction

Within the field of sociology of education, questions of knowledge and the social, cultural and political contexts of knowledge production are critical areas of debates and discussion. Increasingly, many of the contemporary critical dialogues of the sociology of education are about contestations of knowledge. There are growing critiques for radical social theorists particularly from the Global South and from other **Indigenous** communities calling for the examination of the ways of producing, interrogating, legitimizing, and disseminating knowledge in national and transnational contexts and spaces. For a number of Indigenous scholars we see this as part of the struggle of a counter-visioning of schooling and education that hold some possibilities for working with "**multi-epistemes**" (that is multiple ways of knowing) to understand our complex world. There is a need to develop epistemological diversity or plurality (that is, diverse ways of knowing) in institutions of learning while simultaneously responding to the epistemic violence and the **epistemicide** of colonized bodies in (white) colonial spaces (see also Fanon [1967]; Andreotti, Ahenakew, and Cooper [2011]; Lebakeng [2010]; Cajete [1994], [2000]; Nakata [2007]; Mignolo [2000]). For example, by epistemic violence and epistemicide I refer to processes of schooling and education that marginalizes, devalues, denigrates, erases, or negates Indigenous languages and local people's knowledge systems while privileging the knowledges and languages of dominant groups (for example, English and Eurocentric thought). We can no longer afford not to bring multiple ways of knowing into the academy.

Why should some knowledges count as "valid" while others are discounted, disputed, or rendered invalid? How do we make such determinations? Do we even agree on the parameters of coming to such understanding? And why should we be delegitimizing knowledges that are based on different philosophical groundings that we are used to? These questions can never be deemed simplistic. It is sheer intellectual arrogance to insist that one's way of reading the world is the only legitimate and valid way of coming to understanding our worlds. In my on-going work on **anti-colonial education**, I employ **Indigenous epistemologies** that seek to destabilize, threaten, and reimagine alternatives to colonial thinking and practice. I do this with the hope of contributing to a robust epistemological framework (that is, knowledge prism) that allows for the coexistence of, and conversation between multi-epistemes. Through this work I explore three arguments: (1) that our epistemological frameworks must consider the body of the knowledge producer and the place and context in which knowledge is produced; (2) that the anti-colonial is intimately connected to **decolonization**, and by extension, decolonization cannot happen solely through Western scholarship; and (3) that the complex problems and challenges facing the world today defy universalist solutions but can be responded to or remedied by multi-centric ways of knowing/doing/being.

In writing about counter-epistemologies I acknowledge that the sources and uses of any knowledge are not apolitical. Knowledge use and its application is always politically consequential. We must be aware of the politics, desires, and the power relations and politics that shape all forms of knowledge including the processes of production, validation, interrogation, and dissemination of knowledge. A truly transformative context of epistemological diversity or plurality must destabilize existing power relations. It must challenge dominant Eurocentric knowledge systems and the tendency for such knowledge to devalue other bodies of thought and local communities while masquerading as universal knowledge. There is a particularity to such bodies of knowledge and we must engage the power dynamics of destabilizing hegemonic knowledge systems if we are to create space for multi-centric ways of knowing to exist in Western academies. While we bring humility to knowing, acknowledging, and respecting different and divergent perspectives in seeking to transform our academic communities, we must always be mindful of the tendency to evaluate and offer legitimation to other ways of knowing through dominant paradigms.

Entering the topic from a distinctly African perspective, this paper will argue that Indigenous philosophies and epistemologies constitute legitimate, anti-colonial ways of knowing/doing/being. In engaging the Indigenous through an anti-colonial discursive lens, the paper will survey these questions: What is the role and place of Indigenous educational philosophies (for example, proverbs, sages, meditations, story forms, fables, and tales) in the pursuit of socially transformative education?; How can educators provide anti-colonial education that develop in young learners a strong sense of identity, self and collective respect, agency, and the kind of individual empowerment that is accountable to community empowerment?; and What is the role of local knowledge formations in subverting the colonial hierarchies embedded in conventional schooling? Finally, how do we re-envision schooling and education to espouse at its centre such values as social justice, equity, fairness, resistance, and decolonial responsibility?

As racialized, colonized, and Indigenous bodies, we cannot afford to become "intellectual imposters" and "colonial mimics" within the academy (see also Nyamnjoh [2012]). Instead, we need to be at the forefront pioneering new analytical systems for understanding our communities "steeped in home-grown cultural perspectives" (Yankah, 2004). Our pursuit of anti-colonial education must shed all traces of the intellectual grandstanding that is so heralded in the watered-down decolonial projects of the academy, often presented as "critical education."

Theorizing "Indigenous" and Indigeneity

There have been several contestations as to what Indigenous really means? As noted in Dei (2014c) for someone writing from an African-centred perspective, I also have to contend with academic charges there is no African Indigenous given the vestiges of colonization. In this paper, I bring a broader definition to Indigenous to encompass Aboriginal, African,

Hawaiian, Australian, South American, Caribbean, and other knowledge systems. I do realize the limits in evoking Indigenous that fails to note, understand, and articulate the differences alongside any similarities in ways Indigenous peoples and their knowledges have been colonized. Most cultures can trace their Indigenousness. I see "Indigenous" about primarily the Land, a close relation and association with the Land as a place and sacred site. There are teachings of the Land and Mother Earth, which constitute the source of Indigenous cultural knowings. Borrowing from earlier work I, therefore, conceptualize Indigenous knowledge as knowledge developed upon "long-term occupancy" of a place, that is, the Land (see also Fals Borda [1980]) and accumulated on the basis of experiencing the social and natural worlds. It is knowledge that heralds the interface of society, culture, and Nature. Such knowledge also draws links between the body, mind, soul, and spirit in the "coming to know." Indigenous knowledge can be found in multiple forms, sites, and sources and the plural in speaking of "knowledges" implies this understanding.

The "Indigenous" is about unbroken residence and the knowledge that comes with such a length of time. However, to say "Indigenous" is about Land, place, body, and politics requires some further teasing out. While local knowledge addresses knowledge localized in a place, the question of Land, connections with spirit and metaphysical realms of existence of a place is central to a conception of Indigenous (see also Dei [2011]). One does not lose her or his Indigeneity through forces of colonialism or globalization. To give a concrete example, Africa had its Indigenous knowledge before the advent of colonialism. While colonialism and Euro-modernity has changed this body of knowledge, it has not been lost but has been transformed to suit emerging contexts, situations, and challenges. Indigenous is not simply an identity; it is also about process, politics, and subjectivities. Indigenous peoples possess Indigenous knowledges, but one does not have to be Indigenous to work with such knowledge responsibly. In other words, in terms of the application, Indigenous knowledge is not for the sole use or application of Indigenous peoples.

Indigenous knowledge recognizes all knowledge as local and yet shared. This means such knowledge works with contexts as important sources in coming to know. Also, that knowledge is shared in ways that allows for humans to know about each other in complex and multiple ways. Consequently, although Indigenous knowledge can be local, it is not parochial. Such knowledge is also part of the universal knowledges of the world, suggesting the possibility of universal, human communication. Affirming such knowledge is not about boxing such knowledge into a past, a pristine environment, or some obscure place and corner. It is not about identity-based knowledge or identity claims of knowing. It is rather recognition of the importance of culture, history, politics, and identity intertwined and in coming to know. Knowledge resides in bodies and in cultural memory. To reiterate, our epistemological frameworks need to consider the body of the knowledge producer and the place and context in which knowledge is produced. There is a particular politics of knowing that emerges from histories of colonization, genocide, and violence that sought to obliterate whole groups of their knowledge base and social existence. Such politics of knowing is about reclamation and resistance. It is for this reason that Indigenous knowledges are very much tied to decolonial projects. In effect, there is some urgency in claiming Indigenous voices as part of shared experiences and knowledge across such identities. To be versed in Indigenous knowledges, one must be connected to the land. One must be in touch with the local communities where such knowledges are daily in vogue and expressed. One cannot study Indigenous knowledges from a distance.

The dichotomy of Western science knowledge and Indigenous knowledge is problematic in as much as it claims that there is only one knowledge. There are no "good" and "bad" knowledges. Science is not only about Western knowledge. There is Indigenous science. Local peoples' craftspersonship in metal and stone working, wood carving, sculpture and other art forms, food production and farming technologies, traditional forms of governance and political organization, health, and environmental knowledges constitute science and technology and practise of Indigenous knowledges. These knowledges still constitute the way of life for many Indigenous peoples in rural communities. All such knowledges inform us differently about our worlds. There are multiple knowledges or different types of knowledge systems because human societies see and interpret the world around us differently. Our understandings of society, culture, Nature, and cosmologies and, in particular, the interactions of the physical and metaphysical worlds differ. These interpretations are shaped by the way we make sense of the occurrences around us. Whether in science, mathematics, technology, family life, conceptualizations of the environment, agricultural and food systems, art, or religion, humans bring different understandings shaped by some basic cosmological principles.

Claiming "Indigenous" is a project of decolonization and all projects of decolonization require "Indigeneity." In such context Indigeneity becomes a process and is about identities and subjectivities, as well as about resistance. Such resistance is to colonial imposition of dominant bodies of knowledge and practices. By insisting on their ways of knowing, such resistance is an affirmation of bodies as knowers and a link between identity and knowledge production. In fact, colonized communities never lose their Indigeneity by embracing their Indigenous epistemologies. But there is no grand narrative or metanarrative about Indigeneity. Claims of Indigeneity are about new "relationships" and new "subjectivities" (for example, "Indigene," "non-Indigenous subjects," "colonial settlers," "racialized immigrants").

Proverbs and Cultural Stories as "Indigenous Philosophies"

I will now make a case of Indigenous African **proverbs** as counter-epistemologies for anti-colonial education. It is important to place some questions on the table: How are changing trends in proverb scholarship impacting the way Indigenous proverbs are perceived in the society and in the academy?; and Has paroemiology influenced the status of proverbs in society? Indigenous proverbs have been extensively researched and analysed. Increasingly proverbs have been understood as epistemologies. Proverbs (like cultural stories, oral narratives, and mythologies) have long been part of the Indigenous knowledge systems in many communities. Proverbs help African peoples connect understandings of culture, society, Land, environment, history, tradition as valid sources of knowledge. In presenting proverbs as Indigenous philosophies (and science) I enthuse that African proverbs establish the basis of a peoples' cosmology/worldview or "worldsense" (Oyewumi, 1997), the underpinning of social values system, the method and methodology of coming to understand such knowledges and how we make the bridging of a theory and practice. Proverbs represent a philosophy of life, customary teachings and wise sayings about social action and daily practice. Proverbs have different levels of intellectual sophistication and depth. Proverbs as cultural knowings point to the power and relevance of intercultural communication. The power of proverbs is allowing the young learner to grow mentally, spiritually, and morally into adulthood. The body of epistemology espoused in proverbs connects place, spirit, and body.

Proverbs as "African philosophies" relate to the concept of self and the community, responsibility, respect for oneself, peers, and authority, and mutual interdependence and community building and their place in school curricular, pedagogical, and instructional initiatives to enhance youth learning (see Kudadjie [1996]; Yankah [1989], [1995]; Opoku [1997], [1975]; Ogede [1993]; Kalu [1991]; Pachocinshi [1996]; Abubakre and Reichmuth [1997]; Dei [2014a], [2014b]). See also such excellent accounts of the ways Indigenous communities utilize proverbs, parables, folktales, and mythologies to convey meanings of society, nature, and cultural interactions (see Abrahams [1967], [1968a], [1968b], [1972]; Dorson [1972]; Taylor [1934]; Wolfgang and Dundas [1981]). We also know that Aboriginal traditions focus more on storytelling as conveying powerful meanings similar to those encoded in proverbs, parables, fables, and tales in other Indigenous contexts (Firth, 1926; Johnston, 2011; Chamberlin, 2004; Iseke-Barnes and Brennus, 2011; Eastman and Nerburn, 1993; and Stiffarm, 1998).

Similar to proverbs, Indigenous storytelling is a cultural practice and an act of resistance. Stories convey cultural knowledges, serving as guides, and offer ways to inform younger generations of their histories, cultures, and identities. For Indigenous peoples, storytelling is used as powerful teaching tools (Dion, 2004). Stories as Indigenous knowledge are usually acquired experientially (Struthers and Peden-McAlpine, 2005). Social values transmitted through stories include "loyalty, respect, responsibility, honesty, humility, trust, and sharing" (MacLean and Wason-Ellan, 2006, 9). Indigenous storytelling imparts worldviews such as the interconnected relationship among living and non-living things (Mehl-Madronna, 2010). Atleo (2004) pointed out that beliefs about the universe as connected to other realms formed an essential part of Nuu-chah-nulth origin stories. The salience of the metaphysical as applied to Indigenous stories is expanded by Chamberlin (2011, 127), who stated that in world of creative thought, "we engage on terms that reflect our own meanings and values." In essence, storytelling captures central features of Indigenous identity and can contribute to developing a sense of self and group affiliation. Lanigan (1998) has maintained that by exposing children to storytelling, they develop an awareness of their identity and their connection to the Indigenous community. Mehl-Madronna (2010) conceptualized identity as stories that build on ancestral and collective connections, as well as the relationship to the land. The collective aspect of storytelling is also evident in how the information is passed on and the relationship between the listener and the storyteller. In Indigenous storytelling, the listener is responsible for interpreting the importance of the story (Dion, 2004; Piquemal, 2003). Proverbs and storytelling helps young learners connect their learning at school and in communities.

Through storytelling Aboriginal and Indigenous oral traditions and worldviews centring on the relational aspect of collectivity can enhance learning from and with others. Storytelling as a methodology allows stories to be relayed to renew and reaffirm Indigenous identities, while advancing holistic well-being and an implicit disavowal of hierarchal human relationships. Storytelling draws on collective knowledge building, trust, and mutual understanding. Storytelling serves as healing. For example, the practice of storytelling is also useful for more internal processes, such as addressing emotional pain or trauma. Both the talking circle and the healing circle are Indigenous cultural practices involving participants sharing their stories of trauma or pain to one another in a respectful and supportive environment (see Thomas and Bellefeuille [2006]). Storytelling in the healing circle supports participants' agency, the ability to heal through narration of their experiences, and the development of a relationship of mutual equality between counsellor and patient. Through storytelling as healing there is an interconnection of lived "experience, relationships, spirituality and connectedness, empowerment, and self-awareness" (Thomas and Bellefeuille, 2006, 202).

Storytelling as methodology goes beyond the academic contributions to scholarly literature to encompass the healing opportunities inherent in disclosing one's experience in an environment of compassion, support, and non-judgement. Mehl-Madronna's (2010) work shows the importance of community in the building of positive social relationships and shared connections to storytelling activity and healing. This is a fundamental knowledge base of Indigenous worldviews, and through storytelling, such perspectives are actively reinforced to younger members of the Indigenous community.

Among types of stories there are Creation stories explaining how the world and its inhabitants came into being (see Russell [2000]). Such stories emphasise harmony and balance among human beings and living and non-living things (McGregor, 2009). Creation stories show no disconnect between the world of humans and animals. The characters in these stories illustrate teachings related to strength, resilience, courage, emotions, and altruism. Such values are further developed by the juxtaposition of innate strength with emotional or spiritual will. All creation stories emphasise the significance of the environment, which is the idea that it is Mother Earth that gives life to all other things and therefore deserves everyone's full respect. Then there are the Trickster tales as Indigenous stories. These tales centre on the actions of the trickster character. The trickster character is defined as "a sort of half-human, half-god like character with supernatural powers which he can use at will" (Friesen and Friesen, 2002, 10). While the trickster characters provide entertainment (Friesen and Friesen, 2002), they also "teach culturally appropriate attitudes and values" (Ryan, 1999, 6). In order to teach these lessons, the story usually involves the trickster committing actions that for the most part, are to his and others' detriment. Whether in the Cree's creation myth or in Ananse stories there is the trickster figure—an embodiment of the elements of retribution, amends, companionship, and perhaps redemption. Although most Indigenous communities have different names for the trickster figure, the inherent qualities of the trickster are essentially the same, specifically, the trickster tests boundaries, disregards norms and standards for behaviour (Archibald, 2008). Additionally, Archibald (2008, 5) states, "the trickster seems to learn the lessons the hard way and sometimes not at all. At the same time, the trickster has the ability to do good things for others and is sometimes like a powerful spiritual being and given much respect." The trickster is a type of multidimensional character involving contradictions of good and bad, freedom, and restriction.

The Pedagogic, Instructional, and Communicative Relevance of Proverbs and Cultural Stories for Schooling and Education

African Proverbs

Akan Proverbs, Ghana

1. If you want to know how heavy a bag of salt is ask the one carrying it.
    (Wo pese wuhu nkyene mu duro a bisa dea eso nno.)

    This proverb carries a host of significant messages. It attests to the importance of seeking knowledge from the right source. Those who seek to assist others in their endeavours must first ascertain the nature of assistance required from the beneficiaries. People can speak and attest to their own histories and, if given the chance, can best articulate what they see as happening in their lives and what ought to be done. Working with such a knowledge base is significant to secure buy-in from the purported beneficiaries of development assistance. In a world where the most powerful and dominant have the power to decide the fate of the colonized and subordinate it is important to affirm the power and agency of the colonized. Yet they can design their own futures rather than have their futures designed for them.

2. Rain does not only fall on one house alone.
   (*Nsuo nto ngu baakofoo fie.*)

   This proverb is about community and communities. It is built on an understanding that no one is an island unto herself or himself. That we all live our lives as part of communities and the individual only makes sense in relation to the community they are part of. An individual action has repercussions for the group and community. The proverb is used to teach youth about discipline, gratitude, social and community responsibility, and the importance of living good lives that enrich the individual as well as their families and communities. The success of one is the success of all and vice versa. Individual failure is a collective failure. When an individual commits an offence, it has far-reaching implications for the wider family and community to which they belong.

Igbo Proverbs, Nigeria

3. Stealing a drum is very easy but where to play it is the problem.
   (*Izuru ịgba dị mfe ma ebee ka a ga-anọ kụọ ya.*)

   This is a proverb about character building and probity. Secrets are not kept forever. The truth cannot be hidden for good. Actions have consequences and what is done in secret always comes out in the open. We cannot hide our actions and this is why it is important to live responsibly. The ownership of a property can never be denied. We cannot deny one's hard-earned efforts and take away her or his fame forever.

4. A step taken marks the end of a long journey.
   (*Otu nzo ụkwụ biri ogologo njem.*)

   This proverb teaches about setting goals and achieving them through high determination and hard work. Small steps are important steps. A task is never completed unless one gives it a try. Little by little we can achieve big goals and ambitions. We can know greatness of a person from the initial stages in life. The socialization process that a child undergoes early in life helps lay the foundation on which a solid structure is built. Small steps in life are important as they mark the beginning of life's achievements.

While noting the particular and perhaps unique contexts for which proverbs are spoken, I maintain that African proverbs adequately allow for both an interpolation and an extrapolation of meanings to serve the wider purpose of education generally. Thus, in the context of Canadian education one can point to some continuity with Aboriginal Studies in regards to oral tradition and storytelling contributing to educational studies. These studies have always noted the critical link of culture and pedagogy. Proverbs, like cultural stories, are part of a grounded theory for local knowledge production. Such knowledge can rightly be applied outside of their given contexts. Indigenous peoples have never maintained exclusive "ownership" of knowledge. In connecting Indigenous cultural knowings and educational change in multiple contexts, I am also insisting that teaching and learning need to be culture-based and culturally relevant in order to address the social, economic, spiritual, emotional, psychological, and political realities of learners. Educational research needs to direct more attention to the ways cultural knowledges (including oral traditions, proverbs, and stories) are taught or passed down to young learners within local communities.

Trickster Stories

Story One: Mister Turtle and the Leopard

In Hamilton's recounting of this West African folktale, Old Turtle, ill with a fever, approaches Mr. Leopard's "missus" (1997, 91) and claims that he'll "go ride him like a horse" (1997, 92). Mr. Leopard becomes incensed when this message is relayed to him by his "missus." So Mr. Leopard travels to Turtle's home to confront him. When Turtle denies making the statement, Leopard decides to settle the matter by returning home and talking to Missus Leopard. When Turtle claims he is ill, Mr. Leopard offers, "Come, I'll tote you" (1997, 95). Missus Leopard laughs as she sees her husband return home with a turtle riding his back. Angry and embarrassed at being outwitted, Mr. Leopard whips Old Turtle with a stick.

This is clearly a story of brains over brawn. Mr. Leopard is clearly outwitted by the sheer wit and brilliance of the Turtle. But every action has its consequences as the Turtle learned the hard way. He must suffer the consequences of his actions.

Story Two: Tortoise and the Hare

Tortoise proposes to have a race with Hare. Hare, "ashamed to compete in a race with anyone as slow as Tortoise" (Todd, 1979, 14), reluctantly agrees to participate in the competition. In preparation for the race, Tortoise asks all of his tortoise relatives to wait at particular spots along the route and "be ready to run" (1979, 15). When the race begins, Hare runs slowly so as to not over-exhaust himself in a competition that he is certain he will win. But every so often, Hare stops and asks, "Tortoise, are you there?" (1979, 15) to which Tortoise's strategically positioned relatives waiting along the route would reply, "Yes indeed, I'm here behind you" (1979, 15). Becoming increasingly anxious about Tortoise's remarkable speed, Hare darts to the finish line where he falls down out of exhaustion and dies.

This story is told to teach youth about using knowledge wisely. Knowledge is different from wisdom as the latter can be applied to get one out of difficult situation/ circumstances. It is a story of how to outwit someone with accumulated wisdom. But it also carries knowledge about the ills of sheer competition and striving to win at all cost. In effect, there are powerful social consequences for every human action.

Story Three: The Three Friends: A Tortoise, a Bird, and a Twig—Lessons of Community and Responsibility

> Once upon a time, three friends—a tortoise, a bird, and a twig—were living together in a forest near Life-is-hard village. The bird was always fond of singing and would sing at the slightest opportunity. For the umpteenth time, the tortoise asked the twig to advise the bird to stop singing all the times since such behaviour could put all of them in danger one day. In each case, the bird responded that what it does should not be of concern to anyone because when there is a danger, it is willing to face it alone.
>
> One afternoon, a hunter, who was returning from hunting without game, heard the bird singing. The hunter aimed its gun at the bird and shot it. The bird did not fall anywhere than exactly where the tortoise was lying. Satisfied that he, at least, has something to show his family, the hunter gladly took the tortoise alongside the bird. To make things easier for him to carry, the hunter cut the twig to tie both the bird and the tortoise. Owing to the action of the bird, both the tortoise and the twig were placed in immeasurable danger.

This story has significant instructional and pedagogic lessons for learners. The story speaks to how we are related and connected to each other. There is the power of community and communities (however defined) over the fragmentation of selves as simply individuals, each locked in her/his own subjectivity (see Abraham [2011]). Schooling is about a community of learners and how we maintain a conducive, healthy environment as well as a collective solidarity for learning if everyone recognizes they are part of a community. The story allows learners to understand the "self" as not autonomous but connected to a larger community. Such understanding helps us to act responsibly in the community and environment we live in. Our very survival as people is dependent on how we act in the collective interest of the community, and this is the lesson from this story. No one is an island to himself or herself. Whatever we do or fail to do may have direct implications on others. The political economy of the (Western) academy nurtures this sense of individualism and competition where learners think success simply comes through individual effort and sole concern of a learner's self-interest. There is a deep sense of "me" which constantly interferes with our ability to relate to others as a community of learners. However, this story shows the need for individuals to strive for the collective good of the community rather than the individual, selfish ambitions. It reminds us that when we act only in our interest, we endanger the existence of the whole community. The bird acted in selfishness and, in the process, placed the lives of the twig and the tortoise at risk. The individual is important but she/he is important in so far as they are linked to a group/community they are part of. Success comes through collective efforts matched with individual self-discipline and a commitment to the welfare of all learners. Educational success is both academic and social success, and in either case of success, connecting the individual to the group is very significant.

The moral lesson from this story is that as learners all need to be considerate, mindful of the presence and interest of others; we have to exhibit a conscience and social character that show that we belong to a community of beings. This is the African spirit of *Obuntu*:

I am because we are. The "I" is intertwined with the "We." They are both inseperable and are connected in many ways. If we are connected, then what each one of us does or fails to do matters and must be of concern to all. The failure or success of one learner is the failure and success of all. The tortoise was wise to have warned the bird. The story also reminds us of our responsibilities as members that share the Earth with other cosmological beings. To what extent do we act responsibly to protect others (including animate and inanimate objects) and also ourselves? According to Wangoola (2000, 265), "Humans we are but a weak link in the vast chain of nature, which encompasses many animals, plants, birds, insects, and worms, and indeed inanimate beings such as stones and rocks." Thus, our actions and inactions have direct implications on what happens to nature and the community as a whole. We share the earth with the living, the dead, and even unborn. Thus, we cannot act anyhow for our selfish pleasure without taking into consideration the existence of others. How can we pollute the rivers, denigrate the environment when we are supposed to share with others?

Story Four: Democracy in the Animal Kingdom—Lessons of Power, Location, Subjectivity, and Voice

Democracy was something that used to be cherished and respected in the animal kingdom. In those days, all animals, supposedly, had the same rights to exercise free speech in every public gathering. In one such meeting, the antelope was unfortunately seated beside the lion. Any time the antelope raised its hand to speak to any issue at the meeting, the lion stared angrily at it. Knowing the lion and the danger it presents to any animal that crosses its path, the antelope has no other choice than to place its hand down. After several efforts to speak, albeit with the same reaction from the lion, the antelope realized that unless something was done about its situation, it would leave the meeting without being heard.

With this in mind, in the middle of discussing an important issue on the agenda, the antelope suddenly stood up and moved a motion to end the meeting on the ground that the sitting arrangement does not favour some of the animals. Since all the animals had seen what was going on between the lion and the antelope, they motion was seconded by the elephant. The meeting was adjourned with a majority "Yes" votes from the animals present. Of course, the only "No" vote came from the lion.

This story is about power and voice, the importance of coming to voice and questioning about who has the power to speak and who has the power also to refuse to listen. This is the essence of critical education: to ask tough questions and demand answers. Silence can be complicity but it can also show a willingness to contribute to one's oppressions. However "coming to voice" and "refusing to remain silent" come at a cost and can be read on bodies differently. Thus, context is also equally important. For the antelope, there was no place for it to speak. It was rendered tongueless, speechless, and voiceless. The antelope also noted that the genesis of its problem was where it is located in the meeting. Thus, unless dominant bodies begin to understand the lived experience at the margin, they will never understand the resistance voices of the peripheralized bodies. "Can the subaltern speak?" is a question Gayatri Spivak posed in the late 1980s. She answered the question: "The subaltern cannot speak" (Spivak, 1988). Spivak concluded that the subaltern cannot speak not because they are speechless, voiceless, or tongueless but because the discourse at the centre of learning is so controlled and manipulated that there is no space for the subalterns to voice their conditions and experiences of marginalization. For Spivak these questions must be answered: Who has power and privilege to speak and to speak for whom? What are the various political, social, economic, and psychological conditions within which one is rendered voiceless? Can educators, of the dominant, truly and honestly speak for historically oppressed and silenced racialized, gendered, classed, sexualized, and disabled bodies? Spivak concluded that the degree of oppression was simply so intense and overwhelming that the subalterns cannot simply speak. Although Gayatri Spivak is aware that the subalterns are already speaking in their own enclaves, she is, however, concerned that the subalterns may not be speaking in the sophisticated and technical language that we so often use in the Ivory Tower.

As many have noted, our task, as critical educators, is to join our communities to collectively hear the discontent, disruptive, and discomforting voices of the subaltern. In this era of neo-conservative mobilization and "conservative modernization as the new hegemonic bloc" (Apple and Buras, 2006, 12), in an era of the "new biopolitics of disposability" where certain bodies appear to be easily disposable given the dictates of the global market force (Giroux, 2006), joining communities to hear the subalterns speak or making the violent conditions of the subalterns visible at the centre of knowledge production, validation, and dissemination is significant. It has been noted that the marginalized have always spoken and it is a question of whether they are being heard and by whom that matters.

This story also informs that for certain marginalized bodies the act of speaking up is the only way to ensure their survival and safety. Antelope spoke out knowing the consequences of its action. However, there was an even bigger danger if it had chosen silence over speaking up. Marginalized bodies cannot afford to play victims but must out of rage speak up against their daily marginalization. bell hooks (1995) long ago contended that there was a place for rage in activism. The rage of the oppressed is a propeller that forces them to openly and defiantly challenge injustice and oppression. Rage of the oppressed, contrary to the negative meaning the dominant have of it (see Grier and Cobbs [1968]; hooks [1995]), helps the oppressed not to forget or feel complacent about their conditions of marginalization. Rage is the only place where marginalized bodies are allowed to reclaim their emotional subjectivity (see West [1994]). Without rage, marginalized bodies find ourselves in a state of *nihilism*—a state or condition where the individual accepts, as normal, conditions of "horrifying meaninglessness, hopelessness, and, most importantly, lovelessness" (West, 1994, 23). The *nihilism* of marginalized bodies is a relief to the oppressor because it deflects any accountability and responsibility. *Nihilism* denies marginalized bodies of any agency and resistance power. It makes marginalized bodies play the victim card instead of standing up to their oppressors. Within the context of this story, the antelope spoke out of rage. Rage was the only friend that woke it from inaction and apathy. It is the only emotional experience that unties its tongue. This rage of the antelope can also be interpreted as synonymous with self-love. Rage does not emerge in silence. There are moments when one can choose strategically to be silent and that, in itself, can be powerful. It can speak of an intellectual agency. However being silent when one does not have to and when it comes at a cost is to accept to be defined as being complicit in one's untenable situation.

This rage of the antelope was not the same as the stare of the lion. The lion's is a defence against the status quo; it is a defence against its selfish interests; it is a defence against structural and institutional change. When the lion releases its rage, the effect is counter-productive; its intent is to silence marginalized voices like those of the antelope, and any form of resistance. While the rage of marginalized bodies is born out of self-love, the same cannot be said about the rage of the oppressor. The rage of the oppressor is born out of self-hatred. We need critical education to equip marginalized learners (in particular) to come to voice and to engage in political and intellectual struggles for our self-preservation, self-defence. Reclaiming our oppressed voices is to insist on our ability to design our own futures. "Coming to voice" is also about developing a rage to ask questions about power, privilege, and the colonial and oppressive relations in which we find ourselves. Through voicing and critical reflection over our rage we begin to understand and interpret our material and social existence and work for change.

Discussion

It is important for us to engage Indigenous philosophies from culturally informed contexts. Power, resistance, and community are some common themes that can be found throughout many of the African trickster tales and local proverbs. Trickster characters engage in subversive acts in ways that challenge social hierarchies and dominant, sometimes violent, forces of oppression. Proverbs and stories offer counter-narratives to challenge prevailing thoughts and dominant ideas. Their modes of communication challenge conventional ways of knowledge production, interrogation, and dissemination of ideas. They present different and multiple readings of our world. They show other ways local communities come to understand their social and natural worlds and the interactions among them. In these ways proverbs and cultural stories constitute ways of decolonizing contemporary schooling, education, and knowledge production. Proverbs and cultural stories offer a knowledge base for teaching about anti-racism given the focus on morality, justice, equity, fairness, diversity, and difference in society. These teachings give proverbs and cultural stories a political edge and as such cannot be understood as offering apolitical messages. Decolonization is one of such powerful political messages of proverbs and cultural stories. Community is also central to many of these proverbs and tales, especially in the case of stories involving tricksters who engage in resistance and social action with or for the benefit of a larger collective. Incorporating these tales and proverbs into classroom teaching can open up opportunities for students to engage in decolonizing and anti-oppressive practices as they examine how these trickster figures, for example, refuse normalized social hierarchies through inventive and collaborative approaches. The import of local proverbs and tricksters' creative approaches encourage young people to imagine new possibilities for interacting with the world.

To focus, for a moment, on trickster tales there are some important lessons to be learned. Thinking through the complexities of human beings and their interactions with the world around them, tricksters are represented in contradicting and ambivalent ways. Trickster stories can help students see the multifaceted nature of identity and perspectives. A number of these stories depict the life adventures of complex and imperfect tricksters. Trickster stories and, in particular, the origin tale elements, provide alternative ways of perceiving the natural world that counter Western empiricist approaches. These tales speak to the power of Indigenous storytelling to provide alternative ways of knowing. Collective action is central to overcoming an opposing force. A family sharing stories around a fire is a powerful pedagogic and instructional moment, as are the teachings of the relevance of community and spirituality in peoples' lives. The role of the turtle is a common character in African Indigenous trickster tales. The trickster tale deals with themes of trust and spirituality in intersecting ways. The significance of spirituality in trickster storytelling is found in these stories as they deal with elements of spirituality and religious worship that might warrant exploration as they relate to themes of community-building and resistive practice. Ghanaian Ananse tales suggest their integral role in Asante identity and community formation.

The power of trickster stories to bring people together cannot be underestimated. The wit and cunning ability of the trickster needs an audience to chime in their interpretations of the actions of the trickster. Gender roles are accentuated. Teachings of trickster stories are about life and death, social safety, and gender codes and norms. For example, Aso's central role in Ananse's trickery is particularly significant given the male-centerdness of most of the trickster tales. Aso's role points to the representation of women in Indigenous trickster stories. The trickster embodies contradicting qualities that make his identity as a trickster hero somewhat intangible. Trickster stories are supposed to encourage listeners to embrace their contradictory and fluid identities. They also reveal tricksters who, despite their strength and wit, each possess failings of some kind that result in death or punishment.

As noted elsewhere (Dei, 2014a, 2014b) there is extensive research on Aboriginal storytelling touching on instructional, pedagogic, and communicative implications (see McKeough et al. [2008]; Battiste [1998]; Hallett, Chandler, and Lalonde [2007]; Mehl-Madrona [2010]; Atleo [2009]). Aboriginal storytelling reveals a link with oral culture and knowledge production and particularly the ways young learners can engage cultural stories for the lessons of every life and social action. The same can be said of proverbs as cultural narratives. They present us with multiple ways of knowing and coming to know. Indigenous epistemologies and approaches to oral storytelling and proverbs clearly constitute Indigenous ways of knowing. Indigenous proverbs and trickster tales challenge dominant epistemologies and philosophies by encouraging listeners to re-consider their own assumptions. While many of the African proverbs and trickster tales are centred on lessons of power and resistance, North American trickster stories deal with the significance of multiple identities and ways of knowing. Rather than asserting clearly defined answers and values, these proverbs and tales encourage students to come up with their own interpretations, which will further help them become agents in their own learning. Many of the Indigenous proverbs and trickster tales critique forms of oppression and challenge conventional ways of knowing. Indigenous African proverbs and trickster stories generally employ creative models of social struggle. They point to the important relationship between identity and the body that could be relevant to examine with young learners, especially through references to animals, humans, and other aspects of local culture (Knutson, 2004) and physical health (Wilbert and Simoneau, 1989).

In highlighting the pedagogic, instructional, and educational implications of proverbs and cultural stories, some points are worth reiterating: Educational research findings continue to point to the great incongruence of the educational curricula and teachers' pedagogies with students' Indigenous identity (Kanu, 2011). Teaching can ground students in their identities, cultures, and histories, and because proverbs and cultural stories speak of history, culture, and identity, they offer opportunities for effective teaching. Also, Indigenous proverbs and oral storytelling are predicated on precepts of Indigenous epistemology, including experiential ways of knowing, collectivity, and interconnectedness. Such values are also found in Indigenous stories and proverbs. Battiste (2002) points out that Elders provide the knowledge in which to develop authentic curricula based on the epistemology of Indigenous peoples. Freisen and Freisen (2005, 12) argue Elders "are the people who have the knowledge of traditional ceremonies, medicines, stories, songs, history, genealogy and life experiences." Elders as educators can impact knowledge about communities' cultures and histories, and they can use proverbs and stories as mediums for such instruction and communication.

Bringing Indigenous proverbs and cultural stories into the classroom will require proper care and consideration for educators to familiarize themselves with the precise meaning of these oral narratives and the protocols to follow when introducing stories to students (Archibald, 2008). Proverbs and trickster stories as well as creation stories often contain lessons relating to moral values, character development, learning from one's mistakes, and understanding and respecting the relationship that exists between humans and the physical environment. When these are brought into the classroom, students are exposed to practical examples of the exhibition of character building the enactment of social values. In the classroom setting, the integration of these stories can be included in the Language arts curricula, as well as other subject areas such as History, Social Studies, and Mathematics.

Storytelling and the use of proverbs constitute creative interplay of social and creative skills enacted by both speaker and audience. Storytelling and proverbs involve more than the solitary performance of the narrator; they are an interaction between the audience and listener where both are active participants in creative thinking and problem solving. The nature of storytelling and the evocation of proverbs is that they engage the audience's higher order thinking skills, for stories and proverbs rely on students and the audience to construct mental images from the information transmitted by the storyteller and narrator. Theoretical literature on both proverbs and storytelling continues to suggest that they foster imaginative and problem solving skills for young and adolescent learners. Storytelling and proverbs enhance not only oral expression but also the written component of language development. Apart from learning how to write for one's audience, storytelling and proverbs serve as an effective strategy for teaching children the rudiments and structure of language (Dierking, 2007).

Questions for Critical Thought

1. In what ways do proverbs and cultural stories constitute local ways of knowing and challenge dominant systems of thought?
2. What is Indigenous in a contemporary context of modernity?
3. How can we transform schooling and education through multi-centric ways of knowing?
4. What are some of the challenges, limitations, and cautions in the use of local proverbs and cultural stories as pedagogy and instruction for the contemporary learner?
5. How do we deal with the question of power issues and relations in the claims of Indigenous and Indigenous knowledge?
6. How do we decolonize the school curriculum?

Glossary

Anti-colonial education An approach to theorizing colonial and re-colonial relations and the aftermath and the implications of power/imperial structures on processes of knowledge production, interrogation, validation, and dissemination, as well as claims of Indigeneity and the recourse to resistance, subjective agency, and politics.

Decolonization The historical and on-going process of ridding oneself (that is, body, mind, soul, and spirit) from colonial vestiges of thinking and acting. It is a process of becoming an authentic self that is conscious of one's history, heritage, culture, identity, and social positioning not determined by a colonial force or imperial order.

Epistemicide The devaluation and negation of the knowledge systems, including languages of local and Indigenous peoples, to the extent of their extinction.

Indigenous The term is used in this context to refer to local ways of knowing based on long-term occupancy of the Land or Earth space. It is accumulated knowledge based on observations of society, Nature, and culture interactions on a given Land.

Indigenous epistemologies A body of knowledge and the claims to a knowledge base associated with a people's Indigenousness to a place and the processes of Indigeneity (that is, identity, culture, history, and ways of knowing).

Multi-epistemes Multiple ways of knowing, that is, claims of multiple perspectives as in different and varied bodies of knowledge.

Proverbs The wise sayings of local and Indigenous peoples contained in oral narratives expressed as cultural messages and teachings about everyday experiences, social action, and moral conduct.

Acknowledgements

I would like to acknowledge the assistance of Dr. Kerry-Ann Escayg and Stephanie Cheung of the Ontario Institute for Studies in Education of the University of Toronto (OISE/UT) for the literature work on Indigenous cultural stories. Dr. Paul Adjei, Jadie McDonell, Dr. Isaac Darko, and Harriet Akanmori also shared ideas on African proverbs and their interpretations. I also acknowledge the assistance of the many Ghanaian, Nigerian, Kenyan, and Canadian local research assistants and consultants, students, parents, and Elders who have been central to my research work on Indigenous philosophies (Lateef Layiwola, Joy Odewumi, Chinyere Eze, Provost Hakeem Olato Kunbo Ajose-Adeogun, Tola Olajuwon, Dr. A.O.K. Noah, Samuel Njagi, Grace Makumi, Moodley Phylis, Anane Boamah, Osei Poku, Kate Araba Stevens, Daniel Ampaw, Ebenezer Aggrey, Paa Nii, Alfred Agyarko, and Professor Kola Raheem), and the many students, educators at local universities as well as parents, Elders and cultural custodians. I thank Yumiko Kawano of the Department of Social Justice Education, OISE/UT for assistance in my response to reviewers' comments.

References

Abraham, A. "African and Western knowledge synthesis." Unpublished course paper, SES 1924H Modernization, Development and Education in African Context (Fall, 2011). Department of Sociology and Equity Studies, Ontario Institute for Studies in Education of the University of Toronto (OISE/UT), 2011.

Abrahams, R. "On proverb collecting and proverb collection." *Proverbium* 8 (1967): 181–184.

Abrahams, R. "A rhetoric of everyday life: Traditional conversational genres." *Southern Folklore Quarterly* 32 (1968a): 44–59.

Abrahams, R. "Introductory remarks in a rhetorical theory of folklore." *Journal of American Folklore* 81(32) (1968b):143–58.

Abrahams, R. "Proverbs and proverbial expression." In *Folklore and Folklife*, R. Dorson (ed.), (117–127). Chicago: Chicago University Press, 1972.

Abubakre, R.D., and Reichmuth, S. "Arabic writing between global and local culture: Scholars and poets in Yorubaland." *Research in African Literatures* 28(3) (1997): 183–209.

Apple M.W., and Buras, K.L. *The Subaltern Speak: Curriculum, Power, and Educational Struggles*. New York: Routledge, 2006.

Andreotti, V., Ahenakew, C., and Cooper, G. "Epistemological pluralism: Ethical and pedagogical challenges in higher education." Unpublished paper, 2011.

Archibald, J. *Indigenous Story Work: Educating the Mind, Heart, Body and Spirit*. Vancouver: University of British Columbia Press, 2008.

Atleo, M.R. *Tsawalk: A Nuu-chah-nulth Worldview*. Vancouver: University of British Columbia Press, 2004.

Atleo, M.R. "Understanding Aboriginal learning ideology through storywork with Elders." *The Alberta Journal of Educational Research* 55(4) (2009): 453–67.

Battiste, M. "Enabling the autumn seed: Toward a decolonized approach to Aboriginal knowledge, language, and education." *Canadian Journal of Native Education* 22(1) (1998): 16–27.

Battiste, M. *Indigenous Knowledge and Pedagogy in First Nations Education: A Literature Review with Recommendations*. Ottawa: National Working Group on Education and Indian and Northern Affairs Canada, 2002.

Cajete, G. *Look to the Mountain: An Ecology of Indigenous Education*. Durango: Kivaki Press, 1994.

Cajete. G. *Native Science: Natural Laws of Interdependence*. Santa Fe: Clear Light Publishers, 2000.

Chamberlin, J.E. *If This Is Your Land, Where are Your Stories?: Finding Common Ground*. Toronto: Alfred A. Knopf Canada, 2004.

Chamberlin, J.E. "From hand to mouth: The post-colonial politics of oral and written traditions." In *Reclaiming Indigenous Voice and Vision*, M. Battiste (ed.), (124–41). Vancouver: University of British Columbia Press, 2011.

Dei, G.J.S. "Integrating local cultural resource knowledge as education for young learners." *Canadian and International Education* 40(1) (2011): 21–40.

Dei, G.J.S. "African Indigenous proverbs and the instructional and pedagogic relevance for youth education: Lessons from the Kiembu of Kenya and Igbo of Nigeria." *Journal of Education and Technology* 1(1) (2014a): 1–28.

Dei, G.J.S. "African Indigenous proverbs and the question of youth violence: Making the case for the use of the teachings of Akan proverbs for Canadian youth character and moral education." *Alberta Journal of Educational Research* (2014b). (Accepted-revisions).

Dei, G.J.S. "Indigenizing the school curriculum: The case of the African university." In *African Indigenous Knowledge and the Disciplines*, Gloria Emeagwali and George J. Sefa Dei (eds.). Rotterdam, New York: Sense Publishers, 2014c. (Forthcoming).

Dierking, C. *Teaching Early Writing and Reading Together*. Gainesville: Maupin House Publishing, 2007.

Dion, S. "Retelling to disrupt: Aboriginal people and stories of Canadian history." *Journal of the Canadian Association for Curriculum Studies* 2(1) (2004): 55–76.

Dorson, R. (ed.). *Folklore and Folklife*. Chicago: Chicago University Press, 1972.

Eastman, C.A., and Nerburn, K. (ed.). *The Soul of an Indian: And Other Writings from Ohiyesa (Charles Alexander Eastman)*. Novato: New World Library, 1993.

Fals Borda, O. "Science and the common people." *International Sociology* 2(4) (1980): 329–47.

Fanon, F. *The Wretched of the Earth*. Third edition. (Trans. C. Farrington). London: Penguin, 1967.

Firth, R. "Proverbs in native life, with special reference to those of the Maori, I." *Folklore* 37(2) (1926): 134–53.

Friesen, J.W., and Friesen, V.L. *Aboriginal Education in Canada: A Plea for Integration*. Edmonton: Brush Education, 2002.

Friesen, J.W., and Friesen, V.L. *First Nations in the Twenty-First Century: Contemporary Educational Frontiers*. Edmonton: Brush Education, 2005.

Giroux, H. "Reading Hurricane Katrina: Race, class and the biopolitics of disposability." *College Literature* 33(3) (2006): 171–96.

Grier, W., and Cobbs, P. *Black Rage*. New York: Basic Books, 1968.

Hallett, D., Chandler, M.J., and Lalonde, C.E. "Aboriginal language knowledge and youth suicide." *Cognitive Development* 22(3) (2007): 392–9.

Hamilton, V. "Old Mister Turtle gets a whipping." *A Ring of Tricksters: Animal Tales from*

America, the West Indies, and Africa, (59–71). New York: Blue Sky Press, 1997.

hooks, b. *Killing Rage: Ending Racism*. New York: Henry Holt and Company, 1995.

Iseke-Barnes, J, and Brennus, B. "Learning life lessons from Indigenous storytelling with Tom McCallum." In *Indigenous Philosophies and Critical Education*, G.S. Dei (ed.), (245–61). New York: Peter Lang, 2011.

Johnston, B. *Objibway Heritage*. Toronto: McClelland & Stewart, 2011.

Kalu, Ogbu U. "Gender ideology in Igbo religion: The changing religious role of women in Igboland." *Africa/Istituto Italo-Africano* 46(2) (1991): 184–202.

Lanigan, M.A. "Aboriginal pedagogy: Storytelling." In *As We See … Aboriginal Pedagogy*. L.A. Stiffarm (ed.), (103–120). Saskatoon: University of Saskatchewan Extension Press, 1998.

Mehl-Madrona, L. *Healing the Mind through the Power of Story: The Promise of Narrative Psychology*. Vermont: Bear & Company, 2010.

Opoku, K.A. *Speak to the Winds: Proverbs from Africa*. New York: Northrop, Lee & Shepard, 1975.

Opoku, K.A. *Hearing and Keeping. Akan Proverbs*. Accra: Asempa Publishers, 1997.

Oyewumi, O. *The Invention of Women: Making an African Sense of Western Gender Discourses*. Minneapolis: University of Minnesota Press, 1997.

Pachocinshi, R. *Proverbs of Africa: Human Nature in the Nigerian Oral Tradition: An Exposition and Analysis of 2,600 Proverbs from 64 Peoples*. Continuum International Publishing, 1996.

Piquemal, N. "From native North American oral traditions to Western literacy." *Storytelling in Education* 49(2) (2003): 113–22.

Russell, D. *A People's Dream: Aboriginal Self-Government in Canada*: Vancouver: University of British Columbia Press, 2000.

Ryan, A.J. *The Trickster Shift: Humour and Irony in Contemporary Native Art*. Vancouver: University of British Columbia Press, 1999.

Spivak, G.C. "Can the subaltern speak?" In *Marxism and the Interpretation of Culture*, C. Nelson and L. Grossberg (eds.), (271–313). Champaign: University of Illinois Press, (1988).

Stiffarm, L.A. (ed.). *As We See … Aboriginal Pedagogy*. Saskatoon: University Extension Press, University of Saskatchewan, 1998.

Struthers, R, and Peden-McAlpine, C. "Phenomenological research among Canadian and United States Indigenous populations: Oral traditions and quintessence of time." *Qualitative Health Research* 15(9) (2005): 1364–76.

Taylor, A. "Problems in the study of proverbs." *Journal of American Folklore* 4(183) (1934): 1–21.

Thomas, W., and Bellefeuille, G. "An evidence-based formative evaluation of a cross-cultural Aboriginal mental health program in Canada." *Australian e-Journal for the Advancement of Mental Health* 5(3) (2006): 1–14.

Todd, L. "Tortoise and the Hare, I: Intelligence beats speed." In *Tortoise the Trickster and Other Folktales from Cameroon*, (14–16). New York: Shocken Books, 1979.

Wangoola, P. "Mpambo, the African multiversity: A philosophy to rekindle the African spirit." In *Indigenous Knowledge in the Global Contexts: Multiple Readings of the World*, G. Dei, B. Hall, and D. Rosenberg (eds.), (265–77). Toronto: University of Toronto Press, 2000.

West, C. *Race Matters*. New York: Vintage Books, 1994.

Wilbert, J., and Simoneau, K. (eds.). "A story of armadillo." *Folk literature of the Ayoreo Indians* (359–61). Los Angeles: UCLA Latin American Center Publications, 1989.

Wolfgang, M, and Dundas, A. *The Wisdom of Many: Essays on the Proverb*. New York: Garland Publishing, 1981.

Yankah, K. *The Proverb in the Content of Akan Rhetoric: A Theory Proverb Praxis*. Bern and Frankfurt au Main: Peter Lang, 1989.

Yankah, K. *Speaking for the Chief: Okyeame and the Politics of Akan Oratory*. Bloomington and Indianapolis: Indiana University Press, 1995.

Yankah, K. *Globalization and the African Scholar*. Monograph. Accra: Faculty of Arts, University of Ghana, 2004.

13

Cyberbullying Prevention and Response
Adults' Responsibilities and Interventions

Ryan Broll

Introduction

In late 2006, American teen Megan Meier took her own life after experiencing incessant **cyberbullying**, becoming one of the first high-profile victims of **cyberbullicide**. Since Megan's death, other young people's suicides have also been linked to cyberbullying, and public concerns about cyberbullying and its negative impact on youth have increased accordingly. By the 2012 and 2013 suicides of Canadian teens Amanda Todd and Rehtaeh Parsons—both of which received international media coverage for their notoriety—societal angst had reached a tipping point and a clear narrative had emerged. As the story seemingly so often goes, anonymous cyberbullies or, more often, somebody known to the victim (Wolak, Mitchell, and Finkelhor, 2006) digitally harasses a young person during the school day, in the evenings, and/or on weekends. After enduring the harassment for some period of time, alone, lacking support, and unable to envision a future that does not include incessant cyberbullying, the young person takes his or her own life to escape ongoing torment.

As one columnist concluded, "A number of high-profile incidents in recent years have demonstrated that cyberbullying . . . can lead to grave consequences *if not handled properly*" (Manasan, 2012; emphasis added). The clear assumption in this columnist's statement, which is shared by many commentators and experts, is that more should be done to support young people who are cyberbullied. While traditional bullying, such as the stereotypical physical or verbal aggression often encountered on the school ground, was often considered a school-based problem to be dealt with at school, it is much less clear how cyberbullying ought to be handled. Teachers and school administrators (for example, principals, vice-principals) are much less likely to witness cyberbullying than other forms of bullying, such as a physical altercation on the playground (Hoff and Mitchell, 2009). Furthermore, although amendments to Canadian education acts often require school personnel to take action to address any type of bullying that occurs on or off school property if it affects students at school (for example, see Ontario's *Education Amendment Act* [Keeping Our Kids Safe at School]), some confusion remains about when or if schools can legally respond to cyberbullying. Particularly in the United States, school officials have been reluctant to address cyberbullying for fear of violating students' First Amendment right to free speech (Hinduja and Patchin, 2009). Within schools, therefore, standard approaches to addressing bullying must be re-evaluated when considering cyberbullying. In particular, the distributed nature of cyberspace may necessitate the sharing of responsibility to prevent and respond to cyberbullying (Broll, 2014).

Several American states and the Canadian federal government have proposed or enacted legislation that would make cyberbullying a crime (see Broll and Huey [2015]), but such legislative amendments are slow and inherently reactive. Several groups of adult stakeholders who have an interest or responsibility in protecting youth from harm may be able to provide more immediate and preventative interventions. However, little is currently known about how adults prevent and respond to cyberbullying. The purpose of this chapter is to examine the ways in which three groups of adult stakeholders—teachers and school administrators, police officers, and parents—prevent and respond to cyberbullying. I begin by briefly discussing youth technology use, before turning to a review of what is presently known about cyberbullying: what it is, who it affects, how it impacts them, and what youth are doing about it. I then examine the ways in which adults prevent and respond to cyberbullying. I begin by discussing teachers, school administrators, and police officers, who are important but peripheral actors (Broll, 2014). I then examine the prevention and response efforts of parents, the most important adult stakeholder group (Broll, 2014), and some of the challenges parents encounter in dealing with cyberbullying. I conclude by discussing some of the implications of these findings.

Youth and Social Media

Social media is the collection of websites, programs, and apps that allow users to create and share their own content (boyd, 2014), and it is exceptionally popular among young people. Among teen Internet users, more than 8 in 10 use social media sites or apps, such as Facebook, Twitter, YouTube, Instagram, Vine, Snapchat, and Pinterest (Lenhart et al., 2011). By Grade 11 almost all teens own their own cell phone, usually a smart phone (Steeves, 2014), which provides ubiquitous access to the Internet and social media.

Cell phones and the Internet have afforded youth new opportunities to socialize, but contrary to some adults' beliefs this socializing "is not separate from or in addition to 'real life': rather, all this activity is rooted in and a part of it" (Collier, 2012, 2). In other words, although adults often think of young people's lives as a series of binaries—online versus offline, public versus private, and so forth—youth consider their lives to be much more fluid and may not distinguish between their online and offline identities (Collier, 2012). In general, electronic socializing has been found to positively impact youth. In an often-discussed paper, Wellman and his colleagues (2001) found that the Internet supplements social capital by extending pre-existing relationships into the electronic world. More recent research has similarly found that those who are the most social offline are also the most social online (Quan-Haase, 2008) and that the strongest offline social relationships are also the strongest online social relationships (Ellison, Steinfield, and Lampe, 2007). Among youth, **networked communication** may also increase opportunities for creative expression (Tapscott, 1998), learning and civic participation (Livingstone and Haddon, 2009), and identity experimentation (Davies, 2004).

Bullying in the Digital Age

Although social media, the Internet, cell phones, and other forms of networked communication have led to many positive developments and can benefit youth in a myriad of ways, some scholars have suggested that cyberspace is an unsafe place for young people to socialize (Shade, 2007). Of the risks that youth are exposed to in cyberspace, cyberbullying is believed to be the most common (Palfrey, Boyd, and Sacco, 2009). Although some variation exists, most research finds that cyberbullying—which refers to repeated behaviours performed by one or more people via networked technologies for the purpose of harming a less powerful individual (Tokunaga, 2010)—is most common during middle school (Tokunaga, 2010). Across all grades and ages, though, about one-quarter of young people report experiencing cyberbullying and one-fifth report cyberbullying others (Patchin and Hinduja, 2012). Both males and females experience cyberbullying, but its nature and quality is often gendered: females tend to be cyberbullied because of their appearance and sexual experience, whereas males are often targeted because of their athletic ability (or lack thereof) and their real or perceived sexual orientation (Hoff and Mitchell, 2010).

Even though it is apparent that cyberbullying affects a sizable proportion of young people, it is believed to be less common than more traditional forms of bullying, like verbal, physical, and relational bullying (Wang, Iannotti, and Nansel, 2009). Curiously, though, young people who are cyberbullied report poorer outcomes in some domains than victims of traditional bullying (Wang, Nansel, and Iannotti, 2011), perhaps because cyberbullying can be an incessant form of 24-hour-a-day, seven-day harassment. For example, in comparison with their peers, young people who are cyberbullied demonstrate higher rates of social anxiety (Juvoven and Gross, 2008) and report increased anger, sadness, fear, and a sense of powerlessness (Hoff and Mitchell, 2009). Youth who are cyberbullied also have decreased self-esteem (Katzer, Fetchenhauer, and Belschak, 2009; Patchin and Hinduja, 2010). As previously noted, cyberbullicide has received expansive media attention and, although the relationship is not as simplistic as it is often described, a correlation between cyberbullying and suicidal ideation does seem to exist. Hinduja and Patchin (2010) found that young people who are cyberbullied and those who cyberbully others are both more likely to report contemplating suicide than those youth uninvolved in cyberbullying. Furthermore, youth who have been cyberbullied and those who have cyberbullied others are 2 times and 1.5 times more likely, respectively, to have attempted suicide compared to those youth uninvolved in bullying.

Aside from its negative impact on young peoples' emotional well-being, cyberbullying also adversely impacts youth at school. In comparison to youth who are not involved in bullying, young people who are cyberbullied have poorer grades (Beran and Li, 2007), have higher rates of truancy (Katzer et al., 2009), and are more likely to cheat on tests (Hinduja and Patchin, 2007). Victims of cyberbullying are also more likely to have been suspended and to have brought a weapon to school (Ybarra, Diener-West, and Leaf, 2007). Little is known about the educational outcomes of those who perpetrate cyberbullying. Although findings about the negative outcomes of cyberbullying are instructive, it is important to note that they are drawn from cross-sectional studies; thus, temporal and casual relationships cannot be established.

Young people who are cyberbullied usually do something to address their victimization (Patchin and Hinduja, 2006). Most often, youth attempt to address cyberbullying on their own rather than tell others about their experiences. Smith et al. (2008) found that almost half (43.7 per cent) of respondents in their sample of British secondary school students did not tell anyone they were cyberbullied. Instead, victims of cyberbullying frequently try to prevent further harassment by employing strict privacy controls across their social media accounts and by changing their usernames and passwords to avoid unwanted encounters

(Juvoven and Gross, 2008; Smith et al., 2008). Fifteen per cent to 25 per cent of young people who are cyberbullied actively confront the bully online or offline (Juvoven and Gross, 2008; Patchin and Hinduja, 2006).

Some young people who are cyberbullied do tell others about their experiences. When such conversations arise, youth are most likely to inform a friend that they have been cyberbullied (Smith et al., 2008). Only about 1 in 6 youth who have been cyberbullied tell their parents, and only about 1 in 10 tell a teacher (Smith et al., 2008). Hoff and Mitchell (2009) observed somewhat higher reporting rates, finding that slightly more than one-third of cyberbullied youth told a parent about their experiences and 1 in 6 told a teacher. Even still, the vast majority of youth do not tell an adult when they are cyberbullied. Ultimately, many young people choose not to tell an adult they have been cyberbullied because they believe the harassment will stop on its own (Hoff and Mitchell, 2009). Three additional reasons have been offered to explain why youth may not report cyberbullying to adults. First, many young people believe that it is important to learn how to manage problems encountered in cyberspace on their own (Juvoven and Gross, 2008). According to this perspective, youth believe that seeking help in response to cyberbullying is something that kids do, and they want to be seen as adults (Tokunaga, 2010). Second, some youth fear that adults will restrict their access to technology if they report cyberbullying. Thus, coping with the problem on their own is considered an acceptable risk in exchange for technology-use privileges (Agatston, Kowalski, and Limber, 2012). Third, and specifically in relation to educators, some young people do not tell school officials about cyberbullying because they think that their reports will not be taken seriously; the situation will not be handled confidentially; that nothing will be done; or that reporting will exacerbate their problems (Agatston et al., 2012; Hoff and Mitchell, 2009).

Although many young people do not report cyberbullying to an adult, an important minority do. Furthermore, most anti-bullying advocates encourage young people to tell a trusted adult when they are being bullied or cyberbullied. Unfortunately, though, because young people and adults often perceive of and use technology differently, adults' current responses to cyberbullying (for example, "clamping down on bullies" through new laws and codes of conduct, banning access to technology and social media) are misguided, ineffective, and counterproductive (Shariff, 2008). If adults' responses are ineffective, as Shariff suggests, it is likely that those young people who do report experiencing cyberbullying to an adult will not do so again in the future, and it is unlikely that others will consider reporting a viable option. While a handful of scholars have addressed adults' responsibility to intervene (Hinduja and Patchin, 2009; Shariff, 2008), few have studied adults' actual responses. However, understanding adults' current responses to cyberbullying is essential for improving future responses and better serving the needs of young people affected by cyberbullying.

Method

Data for this study were drawn from in-depth interviews conducted between March 2012 and February 2013 with 34 participants in south-western Ontario, Canada. Following a review of the literature and media accounts, and an examination of responses to traditional bullying, parents, teachers and school administrators, and members of law enforcement were identified as key adult stakeholders involved in cyberbullying prevention and response. Although other groups of adults, such as security teams working for private corporations (for example, Microsoft, Facebook), Internet service providers, and officials with non-governmental organizations, have an important role in addressing cyberbullying, these individuals and groups tend to defer to parents and educators by providing them with suggestions as to how to best address cyberbullying, and they often encourage victims and their families to contact the police when appropriate. Thus, their involvement is secondary to the three groups of adults that I examine in this chapter.

Seven parents of young people who had been involved in cyberbullying were interviewed. In one additional case, the cousin of a young person who had been cyberbullied was interviewed instead of a parent because she had more intimate knowledge of her cousin's experiences than did the victim's parents. In addition, interviews were conducted with 14 educators, including 3 elementary school teachers, 5 secondary school teachers, and 6 school administrators (principal or vice-principal). Lastly, 12 members of law enforcement were interviewed, including 3 patrol officers, 7 school resource officers, and 2 crime prevention officers. Interviews averaged approximately one hour in length and were audio recorded and later transcribed subject to the informed consent of all participants. The interview guide was flexible, but it also served to ensure that all participants were asked similar questions and that the same themes were covered in each interview. For example, all participants were asked what they have done to prevent cyberbullying, what actions they have taken when they became aware of a cyberbullying incident, and whether their responses were limited in any way. Data were analysed using thematic analysis (Braun and Clarke, 2006).

On the Periphery: How Educators and Police Officers Prevent and Respond to Cyberbullying

Teachers, school administrators, and police officers have an important role in preventing and responding to cyberbullying, but they occupy a peripheral position in comparison to parents (Broll, 2014). Nevertheless, parents and educators often call upon police officers for support in dealing with particularly serious cyberbullying incidents (Broll and Huey, 2015). Moreover, crime prevention programs delivered by officers, like the Values, Influences, and Peers (V.I.P.) program for Ontario Grade 6 students regularly include lessons on Internet safety. Young people spend several hours each day in the company of teachers and school administrators, who now often incorporate social media into lesson plans and class activities. However, whereas traditional bullying was considered a school-based problem with teachers and school administrators being primary responsibility for intervening when incidents occurred (Holt and Keyes, 2004), educators are less likely to witness cyberbullying first hand, and many teachers and school administrators lack the resources and expertise to adequately prevent and respond to cyberbullying (Hoff and Mitchell, 2009). Furthermore, school administrators' typical responses to traditional bullying may actually be harmful when addressing cyberbullying. For instance, most schools restrict access to technology during the school day, so suspending cyberbullies may enhance their access to technology and, therefore, their ability to continue to harm others (Madigan, 2010).

The teachers and school administrators interviewed for this study identified similar challenges when it comes to addressing cyberbullying. Most notably, they reported a lack of comfort with network communications and expressed difficulty staying on top of technology trends. Several teachers also expressed feeling uncertain about how to respond when they become aware of cyberbullying. Indeed, it would seem that improved professional development on topics such as youth social media use and cyberbullying is warranted.

According to an elementary school teacher: "Professional development is needed to teach teachers how to approach these topics, how to be sensitive to these issues." School administrators described challenges with disciplining students who engaged in cyberbullying. Although they noted that having a written record (that is a printout of harassing comments) of the bullying is helpful, the administrators also explained that they are still establishing norms for disciplining students. Furthermore, some school administrators felt that their need to be "very nurturing and politically correct" with students undermined opportunities to explain the seriousness of cyberbullies' actions.

Nevertheless, the teachers were committed to doing what they could to teach youth about healthy relationships online and offline. In other words, they saw their role as being primarily one of prevention. Some teachers described making simple statements in class to encourage students to be thoughtful citizens. For example, a Grade 9 teacher explained that she asks her students, "Every day you come into school and you decide whether you're actually going to be nice to other people. . . . So what decisions are you going to make today?" A number of teachers also explained the importance of educating students about safe social media use, when the curriculum allows for it. For example, a veteran school administrator explained that students need to learn that:

> it's about a new education about how you want to communicate and what you communicate. . . . That's what we're supposed to be doing. . . . Remember, it's public and permanent. The privacy thing is kind of an ironic statement—there is no privacy in the cyber world. And how do you navigate and educate people around that?

Although teachers and school administrators expressed uncertainty with technology and are limited by the confines of the curriculum, simple messages and education about safe social media use are important tools in cyberbullying prevention.

While the educators viewed themselves in a mostly preventative position, police officers aim to both prevent cyberbullying and respond swiftly to the most serious incidents. Indeed, governments are increasingly mandating a police response to cyberbullying (see Broll and Huey [2015]), and police officers seem to agree that they ought to have a role in addressing cyberbullying. Hinduja and Patchin (2012) found that 95 per cent of school resource officers (SROs) believe that cyberbullying is a serious problem deserving of a response from law enforcement, and 70 per cent of the officers surveyed reported having investigated a cyberbullying case within the past year. While the police officers interviewed for the present study agreed that they should be involved in cyberbullying prevention and response efforts, contrary to current legislative efforts, they did not agree that cyberbullying should be a criminal offence. Instead, they felt as though current *Criminal Code* offences can be applied to cyberbullying cases that are criminal in nature (for example, harassment, threats) but noted that few cases reach such levels. Indeed, the officers indicated a strong disdain for having to charge youth for "just being mean" to one another. Moreover, the officers believed that most incidents can be resolved informally. As one patrol officer said: "People don't realize it's not like what people see on TV. We try our hardest to keep [young people] out of the courthouse."

To these officers, the best way to keep youth out of the courthouse is to prevent cyberbullying from occurring in the first place. One SRO who provides support in both elementary and secondary schools proudly said: "My goal, my job, is to be the preventative person." Frequently, being the preventative person involves teaching youth how to use networked technologies safely. The officers reported that one of their most common lessons involves teaching young people that their online words and actions have real offline consequences. According to an elementary SRO: "Youth don't understand that if they're going to threaten somebody face-to-face, it's no different than using the computer to threaten them." Some officers described speaking to cyberbullies formally or informally in school administrators' offices, while others noted that teachers sometimes invite them into their classroom to address the whole class after an incident has occurred. In general, however, the officers preferred being called upon early in the school year and before any incidents had taken place. In particular, the SROs and crime prevention officers routinely offered assembly style presentations for students about cyberbullying and safe social media use. Many of these officers also offered presentations for parents to support their efforts to educate their children about cyber safety.

First Responders: How Parents Prevent and Respond to Cyberbullying

Efforts to prevent and respond to cyberbullying are centred on parents (Broll, 2014). Parents are the group of adults to whom cyberbullying is most likely to be reported (Hoff and Mitchell, 2009; Smith et al., 2009) and parents' close relationship with their children makes them the most engaged of all adult stakeholders (Broll, 2014). While teachers, school administrators, and police officers have important roles to play, parents often call upon them for support when they have exhausted all other options. For example, a secondary school vice-principal said: "If I see a parent and they're coming in about [cyberbullying], it's frustrating for me because they've reached a point of exasperation," and a crime prevention officer stated: "If people have called the police, it's probably their last resort." In the pages that follow, I examine how parents attempt to prevent cyberbullying from occurring, what they do once an incident has taken place, and some of the challenges they face when preventing and responding to cyberbullying.

Managing Risks to Prevent Cyberbullying

Parents described a common goal of "preventing the worst" (Beck, 1992). In reference to cyberbullying, preventing the worst usually means ensuring their children do not commit suicide as a result of cyberbullying. Indeed, cyberbullicide was a real fear among the parents interviewed. Many parents felt that by minimizing their children's risk exposure, they would also decrease the likelihood of cyberbullying occurring. Thus, closely monitoring their children's technology use was a favoured risk management strategy among parents. Some parents followed the widely held edict that children should only use technology in common areas of the house, like kitchens or living rooms. For example, the mother of an 11-year-old girl who was physically threatened on Facebook mandates that her children use the family's two laptops only in the kitchen, which is the most frequented room in their house. As this mother simply stated, "My children are not allowed to use laptops in their bedroom." Another mother said that the rules governing technology use changed in her house after her daughter was suspended from school for cyberbullying a classmate. Prior to this incident, her children were permitted to use technology anywhere in the house.

Now, laptop use is limited to the family kitchen and several other restrictions have been implemented:

> We have two laptops and they sit here [in the kitchen], and we monitor when they work on homework. They're allowed 15 minutes for e-mailing their friends . . . and they know that we monitor it at any time. We know their passwords, and we have parental controls on the computers. . . . We've got time constraints, so they can only go on at certain times.

This mother put these restrictions in place to, hopefully, ensure no further incidents transpire. Other parents went further to manage their children's risk of involvement in cyberbullying by employing more invasive surveillance strategies. Sometimes, these surveillance strategies were taught to parents by police officers, as in the case of the mother whose daughter was suspended for cyberbullying her classmate. This mother learned of standard parental monitoring software available within the Microsoft Windows operating system only when an officer who had become involved in her daughter's case demonstrated its use to her. The officer explained that: "laptops actually come with parental controls that you don't even have to buy. It's like right in Microsoft, or whatever." Now, every time this mother logs onto her computer: "it will say, 'Check the parental controls to see . . . .'" Other parents went further still by installing keylogging software on computers their children use. Whereas parental monitoring software usually allows parents to restrict their children's access to certain programs or websites and provides a general overview of their activities (for example, time spent online, websites visited), keylogging software records every keystroke typed, including those that were typed and then deleted. The father of two teenage children casually explained, "We have what is called Net Nanny, and then we also . . . have software where we record every single keystroke. That's not a big deal, really." According to this father, keylogging software is necessary because his children are technologically savvy enough to render moot more benign risk management strategies, which his children apparently disapprove of.

Given the popularity of social media websites among youth (Lenhart et al., 2011), it is not surprising that parents expressed specific anxieties in relation to these platforms and took steps to keep their children safe when using websites like Facebook and Twitter. Parents felt that social media sites represented one of the most likely realms in which cyberbullying could occur and, as such, rather than celebrating social media's positive features parents tended to strictly regulate their children's social media use. Parents of younger children simply and effectively managed the perceived risks of using social media by refusing to allow their children to use these websites. Interestingly, the costs of these restrictions, such as the potential loss of social capital for their children, were not referenced by parents. Other parents required their children to share social media passwords with them so that they could log-in to their children's accounts and view lists of friends and private or direct messages at any time. Of such practices, one mother said: "Then I know what is going on, and if I know what's going on, I can respond and deal with it." Other parents more passively browse their children's social media profiles and accounts in search of problematic content, often by befriending their children on such sites.

Rather than, or sometimes in addition to, using surveillance strategies, some parents also espoused the value of "being friends" with their children. According to parents who identified with this approach, if their children consider them friends, they will be more likely to share negative encounters, such as cyberbullying, with them. A father of two teenage children was a vocal supporter of this risk management approach, and he spoke at length of the benefits of being friends with his children: "You keep all lines of communication open all the time. . . . If that happens, and once they accept you as an equal, then the problem is over." According to this perspective, emotionally supporting children significantly reduces cyber risks.

Lastly, some parents aimed to entirely eliminate the source of the threat by encouraging their children to unplug from technology. One mother described tirelessly working to find a real-world hobby for her child. After countless failures, eventually her daughter took a liking to horseback riding, which has reduced her exposure to technology. Similarly, the mother of twin 11-year-old boys explained that when her children's friends visit her house, computer time is not permitted. Instead, "it's always go outside and play, go outside and play." By encouraging their children to engage in non-technologically mediated activities, parents' felt that they were greatly reducing the opportunities for cyberbullying to occur.

Reducing Harm by Responding to Cyberbullying

Once their children have become involved in cyberbullying, parents' objectives shift from a focus on risk management—preventing the harm from occurring—to a focus on harm reduction. Sometimes, parents' responses involve directly engaging with the bully. Parents' felt that by making their presence visible to cyberbullies, their child would become a less desirable target and the bullying would cease. For example, when one interviewee's daughter was threatened via Facebook, the mother used the social media platform to inform the bully that she monitors her daughter's account, and that the bully's behaviour was unacceptable, and that if future threats were made the police would be contacted. This mother stated that, following this exchange, no further bullying occurred. Similarly, the cousin of a teenage girl who was bullied on Facebook reported that another individual in her family frequently responds to harassing Facebook posts that appear to target her cousin to ensure the bullies know adults are observing their behaviours.

Parents also espoused the perceived value in directly contacting the bully's parents. Interviewees who advocated for this approach trusted the kindness and sensitivity of other parents, believing that once the bully's parents learned what their child was doing, they would intervene and discipline their child. More often than not, this approach seemed to accomplish parents' goal of swiftly stopping bullying targeting their child. For instance, the mother of a teenage girl who was cyberbullied by a male classmate said: "I called the mom right away, and I said, 'Do you know your son said this?' And he was in big trouble." In another instance, the parents of the cyberbully learned about their daughter's behaviour before the parents of the bullied child became aware of the situation. The bully's father contacted the victim's parents to tell them: "We know our daughter is doing it, we don't know how to tackle it. The parents were very understanding and gave us some time to work it out."

In addition to involving other parents when responding to cyberbullying, participants often reported cyberbullying to school authorities. The cousin of a teen girl who was cyberbullied attended the girl's school and said: "Look, this is what's going on, I don't know what to do about it." Indeed, many parents viewed school administrators as a valuable resource capable of sharing their expertise in responding to bullying with parents. Of course, as noted above, many teachers and school administrators are uncertain with their own responses to cyberbullying. Perhaps as a result, some parents reported negative encounters with school administrators that would make them wary of informing members of the school community of future bullying incidents. For example, upon learning that her daughter was cyberbullying a classmate, one mother took her daughter to her school to tell the principal what she had been doing. This interviewee felt that she was "doing the right thing" by asking her child to admit her poor behaviour to school authorities and make reparations for her actions. However, after learning about the cyberbullying, the school principal developed a "personal vendetta" toward the offending student, incessantly calling her to the office and disciplining her for the most trivial of things. In the end, the young girl chose to switch schools and the mother wished that she had never informed the principal about the cyberbullying.

Although all parents wanted the bullying directed toward their child to stop, their wishes varied along a continuum from altruistic to self-centred. For some parents, their goal was simply to minimize the harms directed toward their child, regardless of who else may be hurt. As one father said: "Let your kid bully somebody else, just don't bully mine." In contrast, other parents wished to address the root causes of cyberbullying—a rarity in a society increasingly focused on risk (Beck, 1992). For instance, another father suggested: "Maybe my daughter escapes or my son escapes, but maybe somebody else's daughter or son doesn't. So we wanted to address the whole issue. It's not a cosmetic treatment we're going in for, it's not my children alone."

Parents' Challenges in Preventing and Responding to Cyberbullying

Despite their best intentions and efforts, parents' cyberbullying prevention and response efforts were undermined by two important challenges: balancing their children's safety with their freedom, and their own lack of comfort with social media and networked communications. Many parents visibly struggled to reconcile their competing goals of managing their children's digital risks (that is, keeping their children safe from cyberbullying) and allowing their children to manage their own risks (that is, incrementally increasing their children's privacy and freedom). When one mother, who spoke at length about these competing demands, was asked where her children use computers in her house, she replied: "They're in their rooms, and that's a function of giving them freedom as well as trust." Likewise, the father of a 16-year-old girl suggested that "the idea is not to pry, and many times we respect their privacy." At the same time, these parents questioned whether their strategies were appropriate and effective. As the latter father later remarked, in an exasperated tone: "I don't know. I hope I'm doing it right because, you know, you never know."

Parents' also struggled to manage their children's risks and reduce harms given their own unfamiliarity with the media through which cyberbullying often occurs. This difficulty was noted by the cousin of a teenage girl who was cyberbullied: "If their parents don't understand computers very well, they don't know what's going on, they can't really even talk to her about it." The mother of a 12-year-old girl who cyberbullied a classmate and was cyberbullied herself explained this challenge in more detail:

> We didn't have computers growing up, we had keyboarding. It is, to me, a scary new world. It's great, the computers, but there's so much for kids to get into trouble with on the computer, and I find that kids, when they're younger and immature, they don't see the big picture. They don't realize what they can get into.

Later in the same interview, this mother returned to the challenges of monitoring her daughter online, stating: "It is kind of scary for parents because it's a whole new world of things."

Discussion

Preventing and responding to traditional bullying was widely agreed to be the responsibility of schools, which is where bullying was most likely to occur (Hoff and Mitchell, 2009). The role of educators in preventing and responding to cyberbullying is much less clear. Although amendments to safe schools legislation often require teachers and school administrators to address cyberbullying that occurs off campus but affects students at school, educators rarely directly witness cyberbullying and may be hesitant to overstep their legal authority by punishing cyberbullies (Hinduja and Patchin, 2009). Certainly, cyberbullying occurs in a more distributed medium than traditional bullying and, accordingly, distributed efforts to prevent and respond to cyberbullying may be necessary. Thus, bullying is no longer a problem isolated to schools and teachers and school administrators must rely on others to effectively address cyberbullying.

Previously, parents have been identified as having primary responsibility for preventing and responding to cyberbullying (Broll, 2014). As risk managers, parents engage in reactive and preventative activities to foster a sense of security among their children. In particular, parents use a variety of surveillance techniques, ranging from the passive monitoring of social media accounts to the active use of parental controls and keylogging software, to anticipate problems and address security threats (that is, cyberbullying) before they occur (Johnston and Shearing, 2003; Shearing, 2001). Indeed, proactive parenting—in which parents aim to lessen their anxieties and fears and protect their children by pre-emptively addressing risks—has become synonymous with good parenting (boyd and Hargittai, 2013). Accordingly, parents are expected to formulate rules governing their children's Internet (Lenhart and Madden, 2007) and cell phone (Lenhart et al., 2011) use in order to minimize their children's exposure to risk. When harms do occur, as risk managers parents must strive to minimize losses and mitigate the damage caused by cyberbullying (Johnston and Shearing, 2003). Interestingly, parents' surveillance practices often come at the expense of education—that is, rather than teaching their children how to safely use technology, parents instead used a variety of surveillance strategies to observe their children's behaviour. Education is certainly a more time consuming approach and, in an era of single parent and dual income families, monitoring software may serve as parents' electronic eyes (Lyon, 1994).

To minimize the risk of cyberbullying and harms caused when incidents do occur, many parents were found to restrict their children's technology use to common areas of the house and, sometimes, during predetermined hours of the day. At the same time, parents struggled to balance the need to protect their children with their own desire to afford their children greater autonomy and trust. Thus, many parents walk a fine line between protecting their children and over-protecting their children, in which case they may unwittingly reduce young people's opportunities to learn, explore, socialize, and formulate identities in the digital world (boyd, 2014; Livingstone and Haddon, 2009).

When preventing cyberbullying fails, parents must transition to harm reduction approaches to prevent the "worst" from occurring (Beck, 1992). Parents' most common responses were collaborative (see also Broll [2014]), and many referenced contacting the bully directly, the bully's parents, or administrators at their child's school. Despite these efforts, parents were challenged by their own lack of comfort with new technologies (Ribak, 2001).

Although not referenced by the parents who participated in this study, other frequently cited challenges include adults' and young peoples' contrasting conceptualizations of the social nature of technology (Collier, 2012; Shariff, 2008) and logistical challenges associated with monitoring increasingly portable and miniaturized technologies (Livingstone and Bober, 2005).

This study addresses an important gap in the literature by examining the ways in which parents and other adult stakeholders prevent and respond to cyberbullying. Although it is no doubt important for parents to manage their children's risk of involvement in cyberbullying, parents' efforts should also focus on teaching their children how to use technology safely and appropriately. As Ribak (2001) explains, young people understand technology better than many adults; however, adults understand the social relationships embedded within those technologies far better than youth do. By making young people aware of the social impact of their digital actions, parents, educators, and the police can help to broadly improve security—and reduce risks—in the digital world.

Questions for Critical Thought

1. Both traditional bullying and cyberbullying are defined by three characteristics: (1) the behaviour is repeated; (2) the bully intends to cause harm to his or her target; and (3) there is a power imbalance between the bully and his or her target. How do these characteristics differ in relation to cyberbullying when compared to traditional bullying? Are these conditions important characteristics of cyberbullying, or is a new definition that accounts for the nature of networked communications necessary?
2. Many parents seem to prefer using surveillance software to monitor their children's online activities to teaching their children how to safely use social media. Given parents challenges in managing and responding to cyber risks, do you agree with this strategy? Why or why not?
3. Did your parents talk to you about cyberbullying and safe social media use? If so, what strategies did they use and did you find their approach to be effective?
4. Many teachers educate students about issues outside of, or only loosely related to, the official curriculum. Should schools take on a more active role in teaching young people about safe social media use and cyberbullying? What might such instruction look like? Are there any disadvantages to schools teaching such lessons?

Glossary

Cyberbullicide Suicide that is directly or indirectly related to experiencing cyberbullying.

Cyberbullying Repeated behaviours performed by one or more people via digital media for the purpose of harming a less powerful individual.

Networked communication Communication that takes place over networked technologies, such as the Internet and cell phones.

Social media The collection of websites, programs, and apps that allow users to create and share their own content, such as Facebook, Twitter, YouTube, Instagram, Vine, Snapchat, and Pinterest, among others.

References

Agatston, P., Kowalski, R., and Limber, S. "Youth views on cyber bullying." In *Cyber Bullying Prevention and Response: Expert Perspectives*, J.W. Patchin and S. Hinduja (eds.), (56–71). New York: Routledge, 2012.

Beck, U. *Risk Society: Towards a New Modernity.* Thousand Oaks: Sage, 1992.

Beran, T., and Li, Q. "The relationship between cyber bullying and school bullying." *Journal of Student Wellbeing* 1(2) (2007): 15–22.

boyd, d. *It's Complicated: The Social Lives of Networked Teens.* New Haven: Yale University Press, 2014.

boyd, d., and Hargittai, E. "Connected and concerned: Variation in parents' online safety concerns." *Policy & Internet* 5(3) (2013): 245–69.

Braun, V., and Clarke, V. "Using thematic analysis in psychology." *Qualitative Research in Psychology* 3(2) (2006): 77–101.

Broll, R. "Collaborative responses to cyberbullying: Preventing and responding to cyberbullying through nodes and clusters." *Policing & Society* (2014). (Published online ahead of print).

Broll, R., and Huey, H. "'Just being mean to somebody isn't a police matter': Police perspectives on policing cyberbullying." *Journal of School Violence* 14(2) (2015): 155–76.

Collier, A. "A 'living Internet': Some context for the cyber bullying discussion." In *Cyber Bullying Prevention and Response: Expert Perspectives*, J.W. Patchin and S. Hinduja (eds.), (1–12). New York: Routledge, 2012.

Davies, G. "Negotiating femininities online." *Gender and Education* 16(1) (2004): 35–49.

Ellison, N.B., Steinfield, C., and Lampe, C. "The benefits of Facebook 'friends': Social capital and college students' use of online social network sites." *Journal of Computer-Mediated Communication* 12(4) (2007): 1143–68.

Hinduja, S., and Patchin, J.W. "Offline consequences of online victimization: School violence and delinquency." *Journal of School Violence* 6(3) (2007): 89–112.

Hinduja, S., and Patchin, J.W. *Bullying Beyond the Schoolyard: Preventing and Responding to Cyber Bullying.* Thousand Oaks: Corwin Press, 2009.

Hinduja, S., and Patchin, J.W. "Bullying, cyber bullying, and suicide." *Archives of Suicide Research* 14(3) (2010): 206–21.

Hinduja, S., and Patchin, J.W. "School law enforcement and cyber bullying." In *Cyber Bullying Prevention and Response: Expert Perspectives*, J.W. Patchin and S. Hinduja (eds.), (161–184). New York: Routledge, 2012.

Hoff, D.L., and Mitchell, S.N. "Cyber bullying: Causes, effects, and remedies." *Journal of Educational Administration* 47(5) (2009): 652–65.

Hoff, D.L., and Mitchell, S.N. "Gender and cyber bullying: How do we know what we know?" In *Truths and Myths of Cyber Bullying: International Perspectives on Stakeholder Responsibility and Children's Safety*, S. Shariff and A. H. Churchill (eds.), (51–64). New York: Peter Lang, 2010.

Holt, M., and Keyes, M. "Teachers' attitudes toward bullying." In *Bullying in American Schools: A Social-Ecological Perspective on Prevention and Intervention*, D. Espelage and S. Swearer (eds.), (121–39). Mahwah: Erlbaum, 2004.

Johnston, L., and Shearing, C. *Governing Security: Explorations in Policing and Justice.* New York: Routledge, 2003.

Juvoven, J., and Gross, E.F. "Bullying experiences in cyberspace." *The Journal of School Health* 78 (2008): 496–505.

Katzer, C., Fetchenhauer, D., and Belschak, F. "Cyber bullying: Who are the victims? A comparison of victimization in Internet chatrooms and victimization in school." *Journal of Media Psychology* 21(1) (2009): 25–36.

Lenhart, A., and Madden, M. *Teens, Privacy, and Online Social Networks: How Teens Manage Their Online Identities and Personal Information in the Age of MySpace.* Washington: Pew Research Centre, 2007.

Lenhart, A., Madden, M., Smith, A., Purcell, K., Zickuhr, K., and Rainie, L. *Teens, Kindness and Cruelty on Social Network Sites: How American Teens Navigate the New World of Digital Citizenship.* Washington: Pew Internet and American Life Project, 2011. Retrieved 7 October 2014 from: www.pewinternet.org/2011/11/09/teens-kindness-and-cruelty-on-social-network-sites/

Livingstone, S., and Bober, M. *UK Children Go Online: Listening to Young People's Experiences.* London: London School of Economics and Political Science, 2005.

Livingstone, S., and Haddon, L. "Introduction." In *Kids Online: Opportunities and Risks for Children*, S. Livingstone and L. Haddon (eds.), (1–15). Bristol: The Policy Press, 2009.

Lyon, D. *The Electronic Eye: The Rise of the Surveillance Society*. Cambridge: Polity Press, 1994.

Madigan, L. *Cyberbullying: A Student Perspective*. (2010). Retrieved 16 May 2013 from: www.illinoisattorneygeneral.gov/children/cyberbullying_focus_report0610.pdf

Manasan, A. "What parents can do to stop cyberbullying." CBC News (13 October 2012). Retrieved 18 September 2013 from: www.cbc.ca/news/canada/story/2012/10/12/cyberbullying-strategies-parents-q-a.htmls

Palfrey, J.G., boyd, d., and Sacco, D. *Enhancing Child Safety and Online Technologies: Final Report of the Internet Safety Technical Task Force*. Durham: Carolina Academic Press, 2009.

Patchin, J.W., and Hinduja, S. "Bullies move beyond the schoolyard: A preliminary look at cyber bullying." *Youth Violence and Juvenile Justice* 4(2) (2006): 148–69.

Patchin, J.W., and Hinduja, S. "Cyber bullying and self-esteem." *Journal of School Health* 80(12) (2010): 614–21.

Patchin, J.W., and Hinduja, S. "Cyber bullying: An update and synthesis of the research." In *Cyber bullying prevention and response: Expert Perspectives*, J.W. Patchin and S. Hinduja (eds.), (13–35). New York: Routledge, 2012.

Quan-Haase, A. "University students' local and distant social ties: Using and integrating modes of communication on campus." *Information, Communication and Society* 10(5) (2008): 671–93.

Ribak, R. "Like immigrants: Negotiating power in the face of the home computer." *New Media and Society* 3(2) (2001): 220–38.

Shade, L.R. "Contested spaces: Protecting or inhibiting girls online?" In *Growing Up Online: Young People and Digital Technologies*, S. Weber and S. Dixon (eds.), (227–44). New York: Palgrave Macmillan, 2007.

Shariff, S. *Cyber Bullying: Issues and Solutions for the School, the Classroom, and the Home*. New York: Routledge, 2008.

Shearing, C. "Punishment and the changing face of governance." *Punishment and Society* 3(2) (2001): 203–20.

Smith, P.K., Mahdavi, J., Carvalho, M., Fisher, S., Russell, S., and Tippett, N. "Cyber bullying: Its nature and impact in secondary school pupils." *Journal of Child Psychology and Psychiatry* 49(4) (2008): 376–85.

Steeves, V. *Young Canadians in a Wired World, Phase III: Online Privacy, Online Publicity*. Ottawa: Media Smarts, 2014.

Tapscott, D. *Growing Up Digital: The Rise of the Net Generation*. New York: McGraw-Hill, 1998.

Tokunaga, R.S. "Following you home from school: A critical review and synthesis of research on cyber bullying victimization." *Computers in Human Behaviour* 26(3) (2010): 277–87.

Wang, J., Iannotti, R., and Nansel, T.R. "School bullying among adolescents in the United States: Physical, verbal, relational, and cyber." *Journal of Adolescent Health* 45(4) (2009): 368–75.

Wang, J., Nansel, T.R., and Iannotti, R.J. "Cyber and traditional bullying: Differential association with depression." *Journal of Adolescent Health* 48(4) (2011): 415–17.

Wellman, B., Quan-Haase, A., Witte, J., and Hampton, K. "Does the Internet increase, decrease, or supplement social capital? Social networks, participation, and community commitment." *American Behavioural Scientist* 45(3) (2001): 437–56.

Wolak, J., Mitchell, K., and Finkelhor, D. "Online victimisation of youth: Five years later." (2006). Retrieved 16 May 2013 from: ww.unh.edu/ccrc/pdf/CV138.pdf

Ybarra, M.L., Diener-West, M., and Leaf, P.J. "Examining the overlap in Internet harassment and school bullying: Implications for school intervention." *Journal of Adolescent Health* 41(6, Suppl 1) (2007): S42–S50.

14

To MOOC or Not to MOOC

An Exploration of Their Purpose, Fate, and Future Tensions from the Perspective of Canadian Educators

Delia Dumitrica and Amanda Williams

Introduction

In 2012, the popularity of **Massive Online Open Courses** (**MOOCs**) soared. For example, *The New York Times* dubbed 2012 as the "Year of the MOOC" (Pappano, 2012) and the Global Language Monitor ranked the acronym the sixth most common used word in the English-speaking world (Winnipeg Free Press, 2013).

Key to the present discussion about MOOCs is the seductive promise, aptly captured in *The Globe and Mail*, that this pedagogical innovation "may signal the start of a new, more open university culture that could change the way Canadian knowledge moves and grows around the world" (Bradshaw, 2012, A6). Broad predictive claims such as this while appealing in principle promote a utopian vision of the MOOC phenomenon as a **disruptive innovation**; they also construct this educational opportunity as fairly homogenous in terms of expected purposes and possible futures.

In contrast to offering such a one-dimensional approach to MOOCs, this chapter aims to interrogate totalizing claims about MOOCs as an entirely new and uniform phenomenon. This is accomplished by situating them in a broader historical context and understanding their emergence based on the views of those who are actually supporting and creating MOOCs. More precisely, we draw on a set of 11 in-depth interviews conducted in 2013–2014 with participants who have been involved in MOOC development within Canadian higher education institutions. In the absence of reliable, holistic work on specific countries and their use of MOOCs, the geopolitical focus is important: many Canadian researchers and universities have been at the forefront of online education in general (McAuley et al., 2010) and MOOCs in particular. In fact, according to our estimates, over 30 MOOCs had already been offered in Canada by 2014.

This chapter begins with a brief historical overview of the Canadian distance education and MOOC landscape. Here we illustrate that rather than imagining MOOCs as a radical change in the direction of post-secondary education, they can also be appreciated as something deeply embedded in an existing dialogue about increased **commodification** and democratization within Canada's universities. Next, our empirical findings are presented by reviewing two major questions addressed by our respondents: why are members of the

Canadian post-secondary community involved with MOOCs; and what sort of future is projected for this phenomenon? In doing so, we demonstrate how past tensions continue to frame our participants' views about their practices and their perspectives about the state of post-secondary education today and its ongoing struggles.

Before MOOCs: A Brief Look at the History of Distance Education in Canada

While it is easy to embrace MOOCs as an entirely groundbreaking phenomenon based on media hype, this tends to ignore a very important part of their history (Harasim, 2000; Rodriguez, 2012). Often forgotten is that an array of online educational alternatives exists alongside MOOCs, including online degrees offered by accredited institutions to course packages (that is course outlines, assignments, and rubrics) ready for implementation in different settings. Consequently, it should come as no surprise that the discussion and debates that such other options have provoked about pedagogy, student retention, and business models re-emerge in current views of MOOCs. However, MOOCs remain unique in their desire to be free and accessible to all.

The development of distance education in the North American context seems intrinsically linked to the professionalization of the workforce. As Sumner (2000, 275) notes, the institutionalization of distance education has historically "served the system" by focusing on providing students professional skills rather than "harnessing education to social change." While the success of the Open University in the United Kingdom (1969) increased the prestige of distance learning in higher education, the economic and neo-liberal discursive framing of information and communication technologies (ICTs) in the early 1990s in both Canada and the United States augmented the professional, market-oriented shaping of post-secondary online education (see Sumner [2000] and Gutstein [2004] for a deeper discussion of such trends).

Since the 1970s, the Canadian post-secondary sector has been involved in distance education. The first such initiatives, that is, Athabasca University in Alberta and the Télé-Université project at the University of Québec (now TÉLUQ), are still offering degrees. By the 1980s, Canada had offered its first online graduate courses through the Ontario Institute for Studies in Education (OISE) at the University of Toronto (Harasim, 2000). A decade later, Simon Fraser University launched Virtual-U, one of the first online learning environments (Harasim, 2000).

The shift from distance to online education has been, to a large extent, influenced by the policy framing of the role of ICTs in creating an economic competitive advantage for Canada. Although detailed empirical research on the history of online education in Canada is largely missing, the Canadian government has positioned online education as a means of reducing the "soaring" costs of public service and improving "the availability and quality of education" (Industry Canada, 1994, 9). This policy move to link use of ICTs and education resulted in the allocation of significant financial resources by means of two initiatives: (1) the SchoolNet project (1994–2007), which sought to create an educational network linking schools, museums, and Aboriginal communities; and (2) the TeleLearning Network of Centres of Excellence (TL-NCE) (1995–2002), a non-profit enterprise mandated to develop pedagogical know-how in telelearning. Notwithstanding the local benefits of these projects, the economic impetus behind the government's agenda has had important long-term consequences in terms of promoting a **technological deterministic** approach to technology as a tool for learning and an emphasis on the commercialization of education at all levels (Gutstein, 2004, 301).

From the 2000s onward, however, a new discursive space for challenging the emerging **corporatization** of the education process emerged, associated with grassroots interests in preserving the open character of the Internet. Terms such as *open content, open access*, and *open software* became more and more prominent as a response to the Internet itself becoming increasingly overtaken by commercial interests and state surveillance. The field of education saw the emergence of various initiatives aimed at countering increasingly restrictive copyright regimes by making resources freely available online (for example, the Creative Commons). Yet such open, free resources were also increasingly commodified by the capitalist system: new business models built around open resources emerged not only in the field of programming (for example, Fitzgerald [2006] as well as Learner and Tirole [2001]), but also in the realm of academic publishing (for a good discussion of different open access business models see Fuchs and Sandoval [2013]).

In sum, over the last three decades the groundwork for making MOOCs a possibility in Canada has been established along with underlying concerns about the commodification of education, coupled with a desire to keep educational resources open and accessible in the face of increased financial strain.

The Emergence of MOOCs in Canada

The official history of MOOCs began in 2008, with a course offered by two Canadian researchers at the University of Manitoba (see Figure 14.1). CCK08—Connectivism and Connective Knowledge was developed by George Siemens and Stephen Downes. It was offered to both for-credit students and anyone in the world interested in participating. Dealing with educational issues, the course explored the idea of connectivism as a pedagogical model (Downes, 2012). While CCK08 was not the first of its kind (other courses, mostly in education, were being offered as early as 2007), it is often credited with popularizing the acronym MOOC (Rodriguez, 2012). Along with the University of Manitoba (where CCK08 was offered), the University of Regina was also leading the way to MOOCs: in 2007–8, Alec Couros offered a graduate course in education (Social Media and Open Education—EC&I 831) to both for-credit and non-credit students. The course consisted of recorded presentations

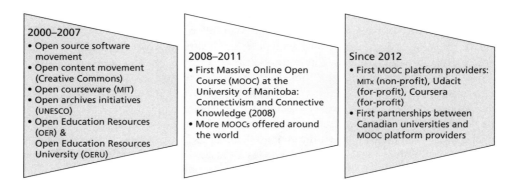

Figure 14.1 The Emergence of Massive Online Open Courses

from various guest speakers (EC&I 831 About, n.d.). Additionally, Personal Learning Environments, Networks and Knowledge (PLENK2010) was offered at Athabasca University at the beginning of the MOOC craze, as a partnership between Stephen Downes, George Siemens, Dave Cormier, and Rita Kop.

Despite these early pioneering efforts, the idea of MOOCs as a distinct format of online education took off with the almost simultaneous emergence of three major MOOC software providers in 2011: MITx, Udacity, and Coursera. All three were, in one way or another, directly connected to American Ivy League universities and benefitted from massive initial investments (Yuan and Powell, 2013). MITx was born out of the online education department at the Massachusetts Institute of Technology, already renowned for their OpenCourseware initiative (first piloted in 2002). Officially launched in 2011, its open platform component was transformed into a non-profit entity renamed edX, owned by MIT and Harvard University (that collectively put in $60 million toward this initiative). At Stanford University, two other MOOC platform providers were forming, this time in a for-profit format: Udacity was launched in 2011 with a $21.1-million investment from venture capitalist firms, while Coursera began in 2012 as a partnership between four universities (Stanford University, Princeton University, University of Michigan, and University of Pennsylvania). Coursera benefitted from an initial investment from venture capitalist firms of $22 million. Yet this historical overview is, in itself, distorted: while these Ivy League enterprises were widely publicized, leading to a flurry of public debates around MOOCs, they were by no means the first to provide online course solutions (for example, Khan Academy, Udemy, Codecademy). To date, they exist alongside many other—yet less visible—MOOC platform providers.

It was the rise of these widely publicized MOOC providers that captured Canadian universities' attention. By the summer of 2012, the University of Toronto had announced a formal partnership with Coursera. A few months later, other agreements followed, accompanied by increased media attention. In May 2013, the Canadian Broadcasting Corporation's (CBC) *The National* ran a story on MOOCs, featuring various professors across Canada who extolled the potential of open courses to make knowledge available to everyone; on their part, specialized publications such as *Academic Matters* or *University Affairs* have also debated at large the pros and cons of MOOCs (see, for example, Charbonneau [2012]; Fullick [2012]; Singh and Adelman [2013]).

To date, the Canadian MOOC landscape seems dominated by two platform providers. Coursera boasts partnerships with University of Toronto (U of T), the University of British Columbia (UBC), McMaster University and the University of Alberta (U of A). The U of A had to quickly switch gears, shelving a prior agreement with Udacity that never materialized (the platform provider seemed to changed focus offering exclusively computer science courses) turning to Coursera to offer its first MOOC—Dino 101. For its part, edX has entered partnerships with McGill University and the U of T.

Although widely popularized, these partnerships are by no means the only MOOC initiatives across Canada. In Vancouver, Dr. Erika Frank, a Canada Research Chair at UBC, has worked on developing NextGenU—a free, online learning platform offering access to medical and health-related education for students in low-income countries. NextGenU was officially launched in 2013, providing courses through collaborations with professional associations and universities in the United States and Canada. Like NextGenU, Edulib is an online platform offering free courses by the École des Hautes Études commerciales de Montréal (HEC Montréal) faculty. In addition, other Canadian scholars have arranged their own MOOCs, relying on open source software and already existing applications. For example, in

April 2013, the University of Prince Edward Island launched a Facebook-delivered MOOC introducing first-year students to the experience of post-secondary education. Moreover, online education pioneer Alec Couros (University of Regina) partnered up with other colleagues in offering an etMOOC: Educational technology and media. Furthermore, in British Columbia, Ashot Masuk at Thompson Rivers University (TRU) led a MOOC focused on art and reconciliation. Such initiatives are less visible but nonetheless represent the wide array of topics, structures, and educators involved with the creation of MOOCs.

Just as the broad overview of distance education presented in the previous section illustrates, the formation of MOOCs remains deeply entrenched in the twin attempts to disrupt traditional organizational structures, making them more open or innovative (a democratic aim) and to incorporate them into the existing course offerings and even tap into their economic potential. Put differently, what seems to have begun as a desire to do something quite innovative quickly became co-opted by the structures and partnership arrangements of larger platforms. In fact, courses such as CCK08, CCK09, CCK11, and PLENK 2010 have been labelled "cMOOCs" because they included smaller classes and were created to foster learner creation and facilitation in online spaces. Students and teachers were positioned as equal "nodes" in this networked learning space, and multiple technologies were deployed (Ebben and Murphy, 2014). In contrast, courses delivered via entities such as Coursera and Udacity are sometimes known as "xMOOCs," as they tend to be professor created, command large audiences, and use the tools provided by the platform to design their courses (Ebben and Murphy, 2014).

MOOCs in Canada: Views from the Ground

As are many other scholars interested in new media, we were intrigued by the consistent exposure of MOOCs in mass media and academic popularizations. Our research project aimed to provide a much needed empirical investigation of MOOCs in Canada, by focusing on the various actors involved in the development of such a course. To our surprise, our participants painted a complex picture of the motivations that inspired their involvement in MOOCs and their view of the future for these courses. Much of the hyped Canadian media attention to MOOCs announced the shaking up of education (Grundy, 2013), juxtaposing the allegedly enthusiastic student crowd welcoming MOOCs (Ellwand, 2013) versus the perpetually disgruntled (and old-fashioned) professors, fearing that they will lose their jobs (Yakabuski, 2013). In contrast, our participants provided a richer assessment of the tensions permeating the future of such online courses. Furthermore, where much of the media portrayals focused primarily on the novelty of MOOCs, engaging primarily with the three Ivy League platforms—Coursera, Udacity, and edX—our participants' accounts situated MOOCs within larger discussions of pedagogical models for online and offline post-secondary education. Though they brought to light the diversity of technological and institutional means available for offering a MOOC, their responses also highlighted the challenges associated with the competing forces of commodification and democratization which characterize the present day post-secondary institutional structure described in the previous sections.

What follows is our participants' discussion regarding the motivations for offering MOOCs and of the future of these endeavours in more detail. The findings come from a non-probability, convenience sample (interviewees were selected because they were readily available), as well as a snowball sample (in which respondents are selected based on the recommendations of previous interview participants). More specifically, our results are drawn from interviews with nine instructors involved in the creation of MOOCs, one librarian, and one teaching assistant (the final two were recommended by previous interviewees). The initial study participants were recruited by looking at various platforms and identifying Canadian courses and via Web searches. Each respondent was asked a series of semi-structured qualitative interview questions by telephone, and each interview was approximately 45 minutes to an hour. The data were coded seeking out latent and explicit themes across the set (Berg, 2007).

In presenting our findings we have identified the general area of study (social sciences and the humanities, applied sciences, and/or health sciences) and the type of institute in which the MOOC was offered, differentiating between "primarily undergraduate" (a university without a substantive graduate program) and "research university" (which provides a wide array of graduate studies). This is similar to the distinction that *Maclean's* magazine uses in its yearly ranking of Canadian universities.

Why MOOC?

Although the acronym may suggest a certain homogeneity when it comes to the courses offered, educators are keenly aware of the fact that no two are the same. It is not only that each class has a specific role within a broader curriculum, but that the instructor teaching it has a certain amount of freedom to tailor it to the learning goals he or she finds most relevant to their discipline. From the perspective of the creators we interviewed, offering a MOOC was driven by a set of different motivations, ranging from personal and political reasons (Interviews 5, 9, 10, 11), to top-down institutional requests by Deans, Provosts, and Chairs (Interviews 2, 3, 4, 6, 8). This is important to note, as the motivations of the creators often shape not only the design, look and feel of the course, but also the means of evaluating its impact. Moreover, it became clear that participants were driven by their position within the educational system and accompanying power dynamics (that is, how easy is it to refuse requests from those in upper administration?), as well as personal beliefs about what can be accomplished with online education.

If our participants were all motivated by one common purpose, it was curiosity. Having read about MOOCs in the media and heard discussions about their "disruptive potential," the faculty members we interviewed wanted to get first-hand experiences regarding what MOOCs could accomplish. This is nicely captured by one of the respondents working in applied sciences at a research university who notes: "I was open to doing this because I wanted to learn more about the technologies required to do an online course" (Interview 8). While an important driver (which challenges the stereotypical image of the technologically inept professor, refusing to adapt to the times), it was also clear that curiosity alone is unlikely to sustain long-term involvement with MOOCs. In fact, as our participants were quick to discover, the development of a MOOC is an incredibly time- and resource-intensive enterprise that seriously impacts not only the instructor's professional, but also personal life. As one interviewee notes MOOCs "take over your life" (Respondent 7, social sciences and humanities, research university). In addition, a support member at a research university suggested the following: "MOOCs are an enormous amount of work . . . [they] draw on skills you do not have" (Respondent 6). According to our respondents some of these costs are likely to decrease significantly upon re-offering the same course.

Curiosity was also closely tied to an interest in improving one's teaching and experimenting with new pedagogical models. In some cases, the faculty members we interviewed had a longstanding interest and/or experience with blended learning, the **inverted classroom** model, or online education. Upon being approached by the upper administration to develop a MOOC (as a consequence of a formal partnership between the university and the MOOC platform provider), some faculty members were asked to adapt a large-scale introductory course in disciplines such as computer science, engineering, statistics, or psychology to a MOOC. In such cases, they saw an opportunity to use MOOCs as a pedagogical sandbox, or a place to play and take risks. This is well captured in the following claims:

> We were developing the materials for the MOOCs, but we were intending to also use them for the campus courses. We wanted to try offering them using the inverted classroom model (Respondent 2, social sciences and humanities, research university).
>
> We wanted to create re-useable objects . . . we created PowerPoints, animations, ideas and themes that would transfer over (Respondent 8, applied sciences, research university).

Yet, for others, the pedagogical motivation had more to do with providing an alternative to the top-down (instructor→student) learning model. Such faculty members saw MOOCs as an opportunity to centre learning around the existing knowledge and needs of the learner (rather than the assimilation of a standardized set of knowledge or competencies) and tended to develop new courses, entirely designed for a MOOC environment. Respondent 5 (social sciences and humanities, research institution) is representative of this position:

> I was thinking it would be something new . . . something that would be accessible and open to a diverse audience . . . centred around one's own knowledge . . . balancing personal knowledge with the material we were using in the course, a lot of it is starting from your own personal assumptions and knowledge and going deeper to explore what and why you think [the way you do about the issue].

As is Respondent 10 (social sciences and humanities, primarily undergraduate institution):

> Ultimately a MOOCs is the ultimate form of blended learning potential . . . how to bring people from remote areas together. . . . I was very interested in MOOC but not interested in the xMOOC idea (that is do your entire university degree on-line through a big company). . . . What I wanted was to open up the possibility of a new form of education.

Not surprisingly, such faculty members were also driven by an ethical commitment to public education. For Respondent 5, active in social sciences and humanities at a research institution, MOOCs were "for things that the general public might benefit from." In discussing the MOOC, this respondent emphasised the opportunity of "widespread public education opportunity" offered by such types of courses. Other participants were driven by the desire to respond to perceived social needs by providing free education where it was most needed. Importantly, they saw such online education as an opportunity for quick responses to current needs. Furthermore, MOOCs were envisioned as a means of public education (free to everyone with a computer and Internet connection and aimed at building critical thinking skills and addressing current social problems) by both faculty members who worked within the context of formal institutional agreements with the three major platform providers and those using open source, in-house tailored platforms. This is strongly linked to some of the discussions associated with new media and democratization highlighted in previous sections.

The personal factors driving faculty members' involvement with MOOCs do not, however, exist in a vacuum. The university's administration, the support staff, the students, the academic publishing industry, the education technology sector (including the platform providers), all have different sets of motivations driving their involvement with MOOCs. Our participants also reflected on what they perceived as the administration's reasons for supporting—or not—the MOOC experiment. Universities, we heard, were in this in order to position themselves as leaders riding the (Ivy League enticed) technological wave. Furthermore, university administrations appear to be interested in understanding how MOOCs can bring in much needed revenue. Last, but not least, universities may perceive this involvement as part of their civic duty task (although, because the cost of developing a MOOC is in the tens of thousands of dollars, this motivation seems less likely). Respondent 2 (social sciences and humanities, research university) encapsulates some of these ideas:

> Why is any university doing this? They don't really know. There is the supposition that there is a business model out there. . . . A lot of universities have that in the back of their mind, a lot of them see it as marketing outreach, or even citizenship, sharing expertise openly and freely with the world, and quite honestly, a third motivation for a lot of them is "Harvard is doing it, Princeton is doing it." When a lot of these Ivy League schools do it, . . . you say . . . "we want to do it too!"

As did Respondent 6, (social sciences and humanities, primarily undergraduate institution):

> When the university [entered] into this, they knew they wanted to be there and they were not sure why . . . there is an element of brand management in this . . . the popular press of higher education really took over this discussion and how MOOCs can change the face of education . . . I think that is unlikely to happen but I think what MOOCs are doing is enabling us to brand manage, improve our reach internationally and rapidly learn about best practices that inform our credit based learning opportunities.

Such statements illustrate the sorts of pressures described by participants that MOOCs present to administrators most of which remain rooted in economic concerns (wanting to "sell themselves" effectively).

In sum, when discussing the goals behind offering MOOCs, many of the tensions highlighted in the previous sections around the commodification and corporatization of universities became apparent. While the pedagogical and democratic potential of MOOCs were certainly goals our respondents were enthusiastic about, the relationship between the ethical commitment to "education for all" that some of them shared and the possible institutional format and goals for MOOCs was often approached in a pragmatic way: the future of MOOCs was seen as dependent on the emergence of a successful business model. This was an interesting and unexpected finding in and of itself, since the semi-guided interview questions did not explicitly ask about the financing of MOOCs, indicating that thinking about higher education in corporate terms has in fact become increasingly normalized.

Imagining the Future of MOOCs

The question of the future of MOOCs further invoked the pragmatic view of post-secondary education as an economic enterprise, as it was met by our participants with two types of responses: (1) further reflections on a potential return on investment for universities within a fairly conventional fee structure; and (2) a proposal for educational reform that required a dramatic shift in the way universities are organized and potentially funded (including the idea of a free and for-credit model). As noted by Respondent 2 (applied sciences, major research university), the prospects for MOOCs in the decades to come "will depend on the business model."

While MOOCs are unlikely to go away anytime soon, our interviews collectively suggest that the real question is: what benefit do such courses offer to higher education institutions? In assessing the responses, our participants advance several possible roles that complement or work within the general structure of universities today:

- MOOCs may become one of many strategies to increase the university's visibility (referring to a form of brand management).
- MOOCs may help reduce teaching costs, either by providing a template that can be adapted easily by different instructors teaching similar courses or by outsourcing speciality classes to other universities and directing your students (and part of their tuition costs) toward them.
- MOOCs may assist with the recruitment of new students, either by allowing them to obtain academic credit in exchange for a cost or by getting the students "hooked" on higher education through a free course, thus enticing them to join a paid degree.
- MOOCs may become experiments for improving best practices for paid online education.

Despite a desire to think about what a viable business model for today's universities and MOOCs could look like, participants did not feel confident predicting which of these scenarios are most likely to happen. But the fact that finding a way to make money was top of mind in situating the future of MOOCs is significant. This likely speaks to some of the present day realities most of those teaching in the university system experience, including the fact that post-secondary education curricula seem to be increasingly directed by corporate administrative concerns such as creating visible and effective international branding, streamlining degrees, treating students as customers, and directing research interests as a response to the economic indicators established by the various levels of government and/or corporate sponsorship (via scholarship or funding opportunities). Factors such as these certainly can contribute to an increasing sense of powerlessness when it comes to decision making by faculty members. This unease was nicely captured by Respondent 2 (applied sciences, research university) who noted: "my big worry is that the cheap, multiple-choice lecture will start to be dominant."

In addition, given the high price of developing a MOOC (both from a technical capacity and human resource perspective), questions of cost versus quality and outcomes remain at the heart of many faculty members' concerns about MOOCs. For example, Respondent 7 (social sciences and humanities, research university) vividly describes a disconnect between instrumental goals and democratic motivations at the heart of debates on the future of higher education:

> What we see is universities are getting much more expensive, the government is not funding education as much, and people are trying to develop relationships with corporate partners, which is scary. Very scary. I think that is more of a bigger conversation about what is happening in our society, where the money is being held. But . . . is there a benefit to the institution that can warrant this expense? I don't know. Not sure about that. Sadly, I don't think there is as much [benefit to the institution] as there is a benefit to the people who are taking it.

As this comment reveals our respondents were able to move beyond the hype of MOOCs simply offering something new and innovative and imagine a future in which such courses become another way in which capital interests become concentrated in the hands of a few.

To some extent, a faculty member's view of the future of MOOCs was also shaped by the institutional and disciplinary contexts within which she/he was located. When adapting an existing course to a MOOC, participants saw the latter as a pedagogical experiment that allows them to understand how to improve these courses:

> Where are MOOCs going? I think one thing that is going on now is this research to figure out how they're working, what they can be used for and how they fit into that picture. . . . Assess various aspects [of MOOCs] to see whether they are meeting the needs of the learners and they are useful resources. And the other thing we are doing is integrating these materials into our on-campus courses. Hopefully, [this will] enhance our on-campus courses (Respondent 3, applied sciences, research university).

"The greatest thing [about MOOCs] is that it has provided us with loads of real data of how students work on-line faster than we would have gotten in any conventional courses. . . . [We can now] fast track what works and what does not for online learning. . . . [It is] a research tool for an institution" (Respondent 6, support staff, research university).

As these quotes suggest, those interviewed consistently sought out ways to connect MOOCs as an experimental space that would ultimately make the paid for credit opportunities even better.

Despite the general tendency to justify the investment in MOOCs associated with traditional cost structures within the post-secondary system, there was also space for a wider democratic and civic engagement dialogue. For example, those who have developed a brand new MOOC spoke about the prospects of **public education** and of popularizing academic research as the most important opening brought along by MOOCs. Respondent 4, working in social sciences and humanities with a major research university, states that "the basic idea that education should be accessible in some form for everyone" was at the core of MOOCs. She reframes the question of the costs as a knowledge mobilization activity (which remains a potential to be explored, given the Social Science and Humanities Research Council's commitment in this area): "It is a great way of knowledge mobilization—now, when I think of my research projects, I think whether there is an outcome to put this into a MOOC." Respondent 5 (social sciences and humanities) and Respondent 8 (applied sciences), both working at research universities, also spoke about preparing a MOOC based on thinking about a wider audience and making the materials more accessible to a larger group of learners to improve a dialogue. However, they recognize the complex problems of access and quality associated with this type of education:

> [MOOCs] are not going to lead to the end of higher education, nor does it mean it won't be disparity anymore. . . . We still need access, and the digital divide is still a problem. What I found with this demographic taking MOOCs—there were very high numbers of people who already have a degree. . . . I think there's definitely a class dynamic there, people with education are the ones getting access to these opportunities. . . . However a number of the folks who took the course commented on how they could not take such a course where they live. . . . They were 200 miles from the local college and they did not offer anything like this. This was their access to a whole other world. . . . It does break down some of those spatial barriers (Respondent 5).

> Trying to create equivalencies with MOOCs are mostly a disappointment. MOOCs are not a substitute but rather an invitation to learn. It does not compete with an accredited engineering degree which is much more intensive in terms of class time and tutorials (Respondent 8).

The struggle between wanting to embrace MOOCs as something different but still concede that they are embedded in a wider social structure in which class, hierarchy, and traditional views of what proper training encompasses still exist are clear in such statements.

The respondents who were most excited about the democratic potential of MOOCs were those working outside of the major educational platforms. This alternative imagining of MOOCs included moving into an educational system that is for credit and for free. The best example of this that we encountered in our interview set is that of NextGenU. In this model, students access online learning objects compiled by an instructional team to support their basic knowledge acquisition. They are then mentored in a face-to-face environment about how to apply this knowledge. All of the skills gained are mapped against a set of competencies determined by the professional association related to the courses theme (that is, a course on emergency medical management would have to meet competencies set out by a professional physician association). A proponent of this model made the following claims about the future of MOOCs:

> Higher education henceforth and for all time will be about DOOHICHEs (democratically open, outstanding hybrid of Internet-aided, computer-aided, and human-aided education) [not MOOCs]. I do not see any other way to do this so that education becomes more freely available. There is global agitation for this. . . . Educating women and men everywhere is so important to raise quality of life (Respondent 9, health sciences, research university).

She also asserts that "it is amazing what you can do when you take money out of the equation." In addition, as another participant notes, the NextGenU model was clearly designed to meet a real need for "health care workers in the developing world . . . however in developed countries, it will be up to universities to decide how they want to use this and integrate what we offer" (Respondent 11, health sciences, research university). She states that could solve some staffing issues for universities without the work force to deliver specific courses but wanting to offer them (this could be for paid or unpaid credit). Despite such ringing endorsements, this model can easily fit a neo-liberal view of the educational system which reduces education to simply serving the needs of a global workforce and nothing more. This concern is reinforced by the claim made by Respondent 11 (health sciences, research university): "[NextGenU] funders want to see proper metrics and clear deliverables when comes to impact on local communities which can be challenging to know how to measure."

The one example in our interviews that seemed to encapsulate the most open and or accessible ideals was found in the RMOOC (described by Respondent 10, social sciences and humanities, primarily undergraduate institution). The "R" was added to the MOOC acronym to represent the central theme of the learning opportunity: reconciliation. This educational experience, built using WordPress, served as an opportunity to chronicle the work of different artists who participated in a residency on the history of residential schools in Canada and the ongoing work of the Truth and Reconciliation Commission. The residency took place in Kamloops, British Columbia, and was affiliated with Thompson Rivers University (TRU). The residency artists and outside participants could watch other artists create (via photos and videos) and contributed to what they were seeing via Twitter, blogs, and/or email dispatches. While the residency ended in September 2013, it remains online as an archive and resource. In speaking about its aims, its creator notes:

> We need to reframe what constitutes pedagogy. What constitutes a course? The learned professor imparting his or her knowledge (this is open to all sorts of critiques) or . . . is it something more? Such as: allowing information to exist . . . and allowing people to participate and bring their own expertise to the table, and allowing them to feel at the end that they have been able to learn something and work at a new level. . . . [This was] not a traditional MOOC for credit. It had no assignments. It was like a fluid, ongoing database but always interactive with participants (Respondent 10, social sciences and humanities, primarily undergraduate institution).

This interviewee suggested hesitancy with "xMOOCs" (courses offered through large platforms), identifying them as problematic and advocating for an "alternative pedagogy." He argues:

> We cannot be blind to the changes that are happening in our institutions economically and pedagogically. We need to make [MOOCs] effective for ourselves so we do not have administrators coming to us and saying you are teaching this course of 10,000 students and it will be computer evaluated (Respondent 10, social sciences and humanities, primarily undergraduate institution).

As this statement reveals despite his democratic aims, the economic pressures currently facing the higher education system still remain a crucial part of his future imaginary surrounding MOOCs.

Based on the array of responses described above, the corporate pressures on education remain difficult to escape even in models that potentially espouse a public (non-instrumental) view of post-secondary education. Though there seems to be some space to challenge existing models of higher education in terms of funding and/or pedagogical approach, even in doing so, it remains difficult to move beyond the need to sell oneself to potential funders thus transforming democratic ideals into visions easily situated within a wider neo-liberal dialogue where universities are still talked about in terms of economic returns as opposed to wider social, moral, or ethical ideals.

Conclusion

The overall goal of this chapter has been twofold. First, it has attempted to offer a historical overview of the development of distance education generally and MOOCs more specifically in Canada. In doing so, it has illustrated the many tensions that emerged historically between efforts to position higher education as something that should be accessible to all and those that see the corporatization of universities as inevitable and even desirable. These dual pressures are nicely articulated by Sumner (2000, 282) who claims the following about online education:

> Distance educators can continue to serve the system, supporting multinational corporations, the military or administration, or simply maintaining the convenient isolation of distance students. Or they can actively begin to serve the lifeworld, empowering students to work together to solve community problems that threaten the basis of the lifeworld itself—such as clean air, fresh water, biodiversity, unadulterated food, health care, education, child/elder care and productive work.

As this quote illustrates, MOOCs carry with them some important historical baggage that cannot easily be discarded with a new acronym and a larger-scale use of online educational tools. Put differently, this chapter argues that it is important to locate the debates about MOOCs within their wider historical context and remember that the corporatization of post-secondary education did not start with these courses and, consequently, will likely not be resolved by them.

The second goal of this chapter has been to highlight how those who are creating and supporting MOOCs talk about their personal motivations and those of wider institutional structures at present and in the future. This empirical view helps indicate how difficult navigating the pressure to resist commodification and corporatization had become for those who want to experiment with MOOCs or challenge the present structure of the Canadian higher education landscape, making it more accessible to a variety of learners from around the world.

Clearly, the articulation of education, technology, and capitalism provides an important frame through which university administrators and faculty members come to make sense of new learning opportunities. In thinking about the future of MOOCs, our participants went back to the question of feasible business models for MOOCs. While things are currently at an incipient stage, our participants did not necessarily see MOOCs as the end of higher education institutions as we know them; yet they warned against the use of online education as a mechanism of legitimizing budget cuts and staff downsizing, leading to the further depreciation of the quality of higher education. Our research shows, however, that when faculty members make decisions on the shape and goals of MOOCs, their discipline, position within the institution, and pedagogical ethos inevitably leave their mark on the MOOCs' format. For researchers interested in MOOCs, it is important to recognize the interdependence between these online courses and the wider context within which they are developed (including their place within the long-term vision of the university, their technological infrastructure, and their educational and pedagogical aims). In other words, there is nothing inevitable about MOOCs becoming a mechanism of corporatization and commodification of higher education; on the other hand, given the current climate in Canadian higher education, it is highly likely that MOOCs will become so, if faculty members do not take an active stand in deciding upon the role, format and goals of MOOCs within their respective disciplines.

Overall, it is hoped that this work has helped illustrate that MOOCs are much more complex than typical media hype would make them appear. In and of themselves, MOOCs are neither the panacea to solving high tuition costs, skill shortages, and gaps in teaching expertise, nor the death knell for traditional bricks and mortar institutions. The specific role MOOCs may or may not take within post-secondary institutions depends, to a great extent, on the ways in which these institutions and their faculty members will come to understand their role in Canadian society. It is also clear that while increased access to high-speed Internet has likely facilitated the capacity to offer MOOCs to so many learners around the world, these courses are not simply emerging as those espousing a simplistic technological deterministic argument would suggest simply because the technology finally permits us to educate in this new manner. Personal, institutional, and wider structural pressures (such as the increased need for a skilled workforce), remain a crucial driver of our interest in MOOCs. Furthermore, given their reliance on technology, the opportunity to bring education to those who need it most (that is, those without the ability to own and use technology) remains, in our opinion, unfulfilled and, in the current format of MOOCs, at best is unfulfillable.

Finally, although it is hard to predict the future of MOOCs, recent developments indicate that concerns around the commodification and corporatization of higher education are far from settled. For example, in May 2013, San José State University was shaken by the public rebuttal of a course produced by edX by its faculty members, worried that professors were being replaced by "cheap online education" (Parry, 2013). Eventually, the university announced it was stopping its for-credit MOOC program with Udacity (Waters, 2013). As well, in September 2013, a Princeton University professor publically announced his concerns over the use of MOOCs to justify cuts to state-university budgets (Parry, 2013). In contrast, in early 2014, Udacity, Georgia Tech, and AT&T, announced they would be offering a Master's degree using MOOCs. Such examples illustrate that although opponents to MOOCs do exist, this may not be enough to stop the overall trend of corporatization that has permeated the North American post-secondary landscape thus far, especially in the context of online education.

Questions for Critical Thought

1. Are MOOCs a disruptive innovation? Why or why not?
2. Based on your own experiences of the education system in Canada, do you feel that higher education has become increasingly commodified or corporatized?
3. What do you see as the future for MOOCs in Canada and elsewhere?
4. Is public education a realistic goal for higher education in Canada? Why or why not?
5. What potential or challenges does the inverted classroom offer to the student learning experience? What about for instructors?

Glossary

Commodification A part of corporatization, this is simply the transformation of goods and services into objects with a specific value in the marketplace (Mosco, 1996, 41). This can include seeking to monetize and measure the educational experience quite generally or monetizing other elements such as teaching, researching, publishing, and networking.

Corporatization Treating all components of education as business transactions as opposed to public goods (that is, students as customers, instructors as service providers, courses as goods, and the pressure to brand an institution).

Disruptive innovation Popularized by Christensen (1997), the term refers to the path that a specific product or service takes to enter a market. At first, the product or service produces small changes but quickly builds momentum, usurping the major established competitors.

Inverted classroom A pedagogical approach that emphasises students accessing course content outside of the classroom (typically via videotaped lectures). Class time is then used to engage in activities that clarify, enhance and apply concepts. Synonyms for this term include backwards classroom, flipped classroom, and reverse teaching. For additional clarification on this concept see Margulieux et al. (2014).

Massive Online Open Courses (MOOCs) This term stands for Massive Open Online Courses. MOOCs are also labelled according to their pedagogical goals: xMOOCs refer to the transformation of traditional courses into online classes, through the use of major educational platforms (such as Coursera, edX, or Udacity), while cMOOCs refer to courses informed by Siemens' (2005) notion of connectivism, which involves smaller classes aimed at fostering learner creation and facilitation in online spaces.

Public education A philosophy of education that sees education as the key to public life, a place where the democratic ideals such as freedom, equality, truth, and diversity are valued, fostered, and taught. As Kezar (2004, 429) notes the results of this can encompass: "educating citizens for democratic engagement, supporting local and regional communities, preserving knowledge and making it available to the community . . . advancing knowledge through research, developing the arts and humanities, broadening access to ensure a diverse democracy, developing the intellectual talents of students, and creating leaders for various areas of the public sector."

Technological determinism A view of technology as causing social and cultural change (that is, having an effect on how societies function). It typically encompasses two major components: technological autonomy and technological imperative. Technological autonomy positions technology as independent of social factors: technology is seen as the result of advancements in scientific knowledge and, as such, as a self-controlling and self-expanding force. In this case, MOOCs are seen as the result of a technological (rather than economic, cultural, or political) development. Technological imperative implies that developments in technology are unstoppable and universal; that is there is a certain inevitability to them. In this case, MOOCs become envisaged as universally applicable and equated with social progress. Technological determinism has been criticized for its failure to consider the role of social factors (for example, economics, politics, legal frameworks, cultural values) in the development of technology (see Wyatt [2008]).

References

Berg, B. *Qualitative Research Methods for the Social Sciences*. Sixth edition. Boston: Pearson, 2007.

Bradshaw, J. "Building open-learning platforms in Canada." *The Globe and Mail* 8 October 2012: A6.

Charbonneau, L. "The massive hype of MOOCs." *University Affairs* 17 July 2012. Retrieved 1 December 2014 from: www .universityaffairs.ca/margin-notes/the-massive-hype-of-moocs/

Christiansen, C. *The Innovator's Dilemma.* Boston: Harvard Business School Press, 1997.

Downes, S. "Creating the Connectivist Course." [Blog post]. 6 January 2012. Retrieved 28 July 2015 from: www.downes.ca/post/57750

Ebben, M., and Murphy, J.S. "Unpacking MOOC scholarly discourse: A review of nascent MOOC scholarship." *Learning, Media and Technology* (Ahead-of-print), (2014): 1–18.

EC&I 831. "About." 1 December 2014. Retrieved 14 May 2014 from: http://eci831.wikispaces.com/About

Ellwand, O. "Roar of approval greets online dinosaur course; U of A offers free lessons; University's Dino 101 first of its kind." *Edmonton Journal* 31 July 2013: A1.

Fitzgerald, B. "The transformation of open source software." MIS *Quarterly* 30(3) (2006): 587–98.

Fuchs, C., and Sandoval, M. "The diamond model of open access publishing: Why policy makers, scholars, universities, libraries, labour unions and the publishing world need to take non-commercial, non-profit open access seriously." *tripleC: Communication, Capitalism & Critique* 13(2) (2013): 428–43.

Fullick, M. "Following the heard, or joining the merry MOOC escapades of higher-ed bloggers." *University Affairs* 31 July 2012. Retrieved 1 December 2014 from: www.universityaffairs.ca/speculative-diction/following-the-herd-or-joining-the-merry-moocscapades-of-higher-ed-bloggers/

Grundy, S. "Online learning shaking up the world of education; digital revolution offers challenges to traditional campus experience." *Times–Colonist* 30 January 2013: A11.

Gutstein, D. "The brief life of the telelearning network." In *Seeking Convergence in Policy and Practice, Communications in the Public Interest*, Marita Mall and Leslie Regan Shade (eds.), (301–18). Ottawa: Canadian Centre for Policy Alternatives, 2004.

Harasim, L. "Shift happens: Online education as a new paradigm in learning." *Internet and Higher Education* 3(1) (2000): 41–61.

Industry Canada. *The Canadian Information Highway. Building Canada's Information and Communication Infrastructure.* Ottawa: Spectrum, Information Technologies and Telecommunications Sector, 1994.

Kezar, A.J. "Obtaining integrity? Reviewing and examining the charter between higher education and society." *The Review of Higher Education* 27(4) (2004): 429–59.

Margulieux, L.E., Bujak, K.R., McCracken, W.M., and Majerich, D. "Hybrid, blended, flipped, and inverted: Defining terms in a two dimensional taxonomy." Paper accepted to the 12th Annual Hawaii International Conference on Education (HICE), Honolulu, Hawaii, 5–9 January 2014. Retrieved 1 December 2014 from: http://c21u.gatech.edu/sites/default/files/HICE%20Conference%20Proceedings_1556_with%20citation%5B4%5D.pdf

McAuley, A., Stewart, B., Siemens, G., and Cormier, D. "In the open: The MOOC model for digital practice." Charlottetown: University of Prince Edward Island, 2010. Retrieved 1 December 2014 from: www.elearnspace.org/Articles/MOOC_Final.pdf

Mosco, V. *The Political Economy of Communication: Rethinking and Renewal.* Volume 13. New York: Sage, 1996.

Pappano, L. "The year of the MOOC." *The New York Times* 2 November 2012: ED26.

Parry, M. "A MOOC star professor defects—at least for now." *Chronicle of Higher Education* 3 September 2013. Retrieved from: http://chronicle.com/article/A-MOOC-Star-Defects-at-Least/141331/

Rodriguez, C.O. "MOOCs and the AI-Stanford like courses: Two successful and distinct course formats for massive open online courses." *European Journal of Open, Distance and E-Learning*, 2012. Retrieved 13 May 2014 from: http://files.eric.ed.gov/fulltext/EJ982976.pdf

Siemens, G. "Connectivism: A learning theory for the digital age." *International Journal of Instructional Technology and Distance Learning* 2(1) (2005): 3–10.

Singh, A., and Adelman, H. "How open courses are changing the modern university." *University Affairs* 16 January 2013. Retrieved 1 December 2014 from: www.universityaffairs.ca/how-open-courses-are-changing-the-modern-university.aspx

Sumner, J. "Serving the system: A critical history of distance education." *Open Learning: The Journal of Open, Distance and e-Learning* 15(3) (2000): 267–85.

Waters, J.K. "What will happen to MOOCs now that Udacity is leaving higher ed?" *Campus Technology* 11 December 2013. Retrieved 1 December 2014 from: http://campustechnology.com/articles/2013/12/11/what-will-happen-to-moocs-now-that-udacity-is-leaving-higher-ed.aspx

Winnipeg Free Press. "2012 vocabulary reflected impending doom." 2 January 2013: A2.

Wyatt, S. *Technological Determinism Is Dead: Long Live Technological Determinism*. Cambridge: MIT Press, 2008.

Yakabuski, K. "Students are cool with MOOCs, so why aren't professors?" *The Globe and Mail* 5 August 2013: A9.

Yuan, L., and Powell, S. "MOOCs and open education: implications for higher education." White paper. Bolton: JISC/CETIS Centre for Educational Technology and Interoperability Standards, 2013. Retrieved 1 December 2014 from: http://publications.cetis.ac.uk/wp-content/uploads/2013/03/MOOCs-and-Open-Education.pdf

Glossary

achievement gaps Disparities in learning school material that emerge over time between various groups such as social strata.

agency The capacity of an individual or a group to make a choice and to act.

anti-colonial education An approach to theorizing colonial and re-colonial relations and the aftermath and the implications of power/imperial structures on processes of knowledge production, interrogation, validation and dissemination, as well as claims of Indigeneity and the recourse to resistance, subjective agency and politics.

anti-racism A perspective that goes beyond multiculturalism by investigating and trying to erase the power relations at the root of ethnic and racial inequalities.

colonialism The policy or practice of taking full or partial control, by force, over another territory, settling that territory with your citizens occupying it with settlers, and exploiting it socially, economically, and politically. British colonialism began in the late 1600s in Canada.

commodification A part of corporatization, this is simply the transformation of goods and services into objects with a specific value in the marketplace. This can include seeking to monetize and measure the educational experience quite generally or monetizing other elements such as teaching, researching, publishing, and networking.

conflict perspectives Unlike the consensus implicit in functionalism, conflict perspectives look at power relations that create inequality and stratification.

corporatization Treating all components of education as business transactions as opposed to public goods (that is, students as customers, instructors as service providers, courses as goods, and the pressure to brand an institution).

correspondence principle The idea that school streams mirror different kinds of workplaces in order to socialize future workers into various positions in stratified workplaces.

credentials Typically a degree or certificate from a reputable post-secondary institution that entitles someone to perform a specific task or type of work, excluding those who lack such certification. Teachers in Ontario publicly funded schools are expected to hold a Bachelor's of Education degree, a credential granted by certain accredited Ontario universities. Teachers are required to be licensed members of the province's professional teaching body, the Ontario College of Teachers. Those who lack these credentials are considered "uncertified" and therefore ineligible to teach in publicly funded schools in Ontario.

credentialism The practice of hiring individuals with higher levels of formal education because of a surplus of such individuals rather than satisfying the demands of a job. A consequence of this is that formal education becomes rewarded less for its knowledge base and abilities and more for its symbolic representation of completing a credential tier.

cultural capital The collection of symbolic elements such as skills, tastes, posture, clothing, mannerisms, material belongings, and credentials that one acquires through being part of a particular social class. Sharing similar forms of cultural capital with others creates a sense of collective identity and group position.

cyberbullicide Suicide that is directly or indirectly related to experiencing cyberbullying.

cyberbullying Repeated behaviours performed by one or more people via digital media for the purpose of harming a less powerful individual.

decolonization The historical and on-going process of ridding oneself (that is body, mind, soul, and spirit) from colonial vestiges of thinking and acting. It is a process of becoming an authentic self that is conscious of one's history, heritage, culture, identity, and social positioning not determined by a colonial force or imperial order.

deregulated field A sector or market that lacks government rules or regulations. In Ontario, the private education sector is largely deregulated, as governments do not compel businesses to adhere to rules governing state-run schools. Moreover, teachers' unions and the Ontario College of Teachers, a body that regulates the teaching profession, do not interfere in private education. Governments do not oversee private education organizations such as private schools or private tutoring businesses.

disruptive innovation The term refers to the path that a specific product or service takes to enter a market. At first, the product or service produces small changes but quickly builds momentum, usurping the major established competitors.

divisions Locker rooms are explicitly and implicitly boundaried by physical and social divisions. The participants described intimidation practices that created separate spaces between different groups of boys. These were evident both physically by some boys being positioned on the fringes or boundaries of the locker room. The assignment of boys to different places, particularly those marginalized in the locker room, was effectively done through verbal taunting and physically posing, taking up space to maintain separations among boys. Locker rooms like many social spaces can be mapped, reflecting power differentials across the inhabitants in these spaces.

elite Generally refers to a group of individuals that are economically, socially, and/or politically privileged in society. If one thinks of social stratification as a hierarchy, the elite occupy the uppermost position of that hierarchy.

epistemicide The devaluation and negation of the knowledge systems, including languages of local and Indigenous peoples, to the extent of their extinction.

ethnographic voyeurism This term is used to indicate the perception that ethnographers gaze upon participants in a voyeuristic manner. It is a term that is devoid of any evidentiary basis but rather heavily connected to stereotypes and assumptions. In this case the schools might, for example, assume boys do not have body image issues but girls typically would have these concerns. Additionally, schools might impose protective restrictions to researchers investigating issues associated with adolescent bodies, suggesting that it is inappropriate to "look" at youths' bodies. The implicit and explicit fear outside of the research community is translated into gatekeeping that restricts and limits access to participants, usually youth, particularly in school settings and often under the age of consent.

feminization of education A criticism sometimes levelled against contemporary schooling that argues schools are failing boys through such things as having a predominantly female teaching staff, having a curriculum geared toward the supposed interests of girls only, and discouraging physicality in the classroom in favour of orderly sitting, raising hands, and so forth.

field of power A social-cultural space upon which individuals interact and compete with one another for success, and on which various cultural practices and symbolic resources serve as forms of capital.

forms of capital Along with economic capital (for example, money), within a society (on a particular field of power), individuals and families have differing amounts of cultural capital (for example, ways of speaking or dressing), symbolic capital (for example, a university degree), and social capital (for example, exclusive social networks); different forms of capital (for example, time and money) can be invested to obtain other forms (for example, a university degree).

functionalism A sociological perspective that looks at the ways in which social institutions and processes work together to serve the needs of a social structure.

gender norms Feminist sociologists argue that gender norms do not emerge biologically, but culturally. Strong cultural expectations about how to be a man or a woman shape how we behave as men and women.

gender stereotypes Over-simplified beliefs about men and women, generally related to behaviour.

habitus An embodied disposition, formed over time in relation to a field, which can structure individual human practices but also generate creative possibilities.

human capital theory The perspective that people intentionally and rationally invest their time, effort, and money into higher education as a means to acquire greater labour market returns. This self-investment is recognized by employers (identifying the worker as being more skilled and productive), who in turn are willing to pay higher wages.

Indian control of Indian education The stated demand of Indigenous peoples to have sovereign control over the educational systems established for their peoples. This demand, put forward in the "Red Paper" by the National Indian Brotherhood in the 1970s, is seen as a cornerstone of policy to close the gap in educational attainment and protect Indigenous cultures.

Indigenous The term is used in this context to refer to local ways of knowing based on long-term occupancy of the Land or Earth space. It is accumulated knowledge based on observations of society, Nature, and culture interactions on a given Land.

Indigenous epistemologies The body of knowledge and the claims to a knowledge base associated with a people's Indigenousness to a place and the processes of Indigeneity (that is, identity, culture, history, and ways of knowing).

Indigenous peoples The peoples descended from the original peoples who occupied North America when Europeans landed. In Canada, this includes First Nations, Inuit, and Métis peoples.

intergenerational transfer of advantage A process whereby the economic advantages and cultural tools for success in a particular society are inherited by children; similar to cultural reproduction.

intersectionality theory The theoretical approach that individuals' lives and opportunities are inextricably linked to the multiple identities that they occupy in relation to their ethno-racial group, gender, and social class. Many using this approach also include additional characteristics such as sexual orientation and (dis)ability in their understanding of the intersections of identity.

inverted classroom A pedagogical approach that emphasises students accessing course content outside of the classroom (typically via video-taped lectures). Class time is then used to engage in activities that clarify, enhance and apply concepts. Synonyms for this term include backwards classroom, flipped classroom, and reverse teaching.

knowledge-based economy A system of consumption and production that is characterized by the production of intellectual goods and services, emphasises technological advancement, and rewards workers for their knowledge and skills.

life course theory A theoretical approach that is used to understand sociological phenomena by focusing on the structure and context of people's lives over time.

linguistic capital The mastery of language and the relative ability to effectively communicate with other people.

masculinities This term is used throughout the chapter to reflect a fluid way of being a man or boy and specifically relies on theories of gender as socially constructed. This term conceptually challenges long standing arguments that conflate sex with gender and problematizes a more restrictive understating of boyhood and manhood as biologically determined. As a term, masculinities reflects the possibilities of competing ways of being boys that are less restrictive and prescriptive than previously thought.

MOOCs This term stands for Massive Open Online Courses. MOOCs are also labelled according to their pedagogical goals: xMOOCs refer to the transformation of traditional courses into online classes, through the use of major educational platforms (such as Coursera, edX, or Udacity), while cMOOCs refer to courses that involve smaller classes aimed at fostering learner creation and facilitation in online spaces.

multiculturalism The existence, acceptance, and promotion of multiple cultural traditions; it is a key aspect of Canada's stance toward diversity.

multi-epistemes Multiple ways of knowing, that is claims of multiple perspectives as in different and varied bodies of knowledge.

National Household Survey (NHS) When the mandatory long form Census was cancelled in 2010 the federal government introduced a voluntary survey as part of the Census. This is called the National Household Survey.

neoliberalism An economic principle that believes in the benefits of small government, fiscal austerity, privatization, and free trade.

networked communication Communication that takes place over networked technologies, such as the Internet and cell phones.

parent engagement Describes parents' involvement in their children's lives inside and outside of schooling. The actions associated with parent engagement range widely and include everything from communicating with the school, volunteering for and attending school functions, and supporting learning at home. These activities are seen to facilitate children's successful movement through the education system. Parent engagement is also seen to improve children's emotional and social well-being and reduce behavioural problems.

private school An educational institution that does not receive any funding from the government. Funding comes from tuition and endowments. In Canada, private schools include well-established, elite schools, private religious schools, and smaller, newly established schools.

private tutoring For a fee, individual tutors, private companies, and learning centre franchises may provide remedial help or assistance with attaining academic advantage. Private tutoring may include help for studying specific content in advance of an upcoming exam or may encompass general study skills, covering academic content that may or may not be covered by mainstream public schools. Sometimes referred to as "shadow education," private tutoring generally takes place outside of school hours and does not involve teachers or other school staff. Tutors may be subject specialists or generalists and may or may not have formal credentials.

proverbs The wise sayings of local and Indigenous peoples contained in oral narratives expressed as cultural messages and teachings about everyday experiences, social action, and moral conduct.

public education A philosophy of education that sees education as the key to public life, a place where the democratic ideals such as freedom, equality, truth, and diversity are valued, fostered, and taught.

racialization The act or process of imbuing a person with a consciousness of race distinctions or of giving a racial character to something or making it serve racist ends.

reactive hypothesis The reactive hypothesis is premised on the assumption that parents become more involved when their child is experiencing behavioural or academic difficulty in school.

residential schools The history of Indigenous-settler relations in Canada is marked by many horrific attempts to assimilate the Indigenous populations. Residential schools refer to school system set up by the Canadian government, run mostly by churches that stated the objective of indoctrinating and assimilating the young people into Christianity and European ways of living. In an apology given on 11 June 2008 by Prime Minister Stephen Harper, he stated:

> These objectives were based on the assumption Aboriginal cultures and spiritual beliefs were inferior and unequal. Indeed, some sought, as it was infamously said: "to kill the Indian in the child." Today, we recognize that this policy of assimilation was wrong, has caused great harm, and has no place in our country. (www .aadnc-aandc.gc.ca/eng/1100100015644/ 1100100015649)

self-perceived education–job mismatch A subjective measure of education–job match that shows how much an individual believes the skills required to perform on the job differ from those acquired in his or her formal education.

semi-profession An occupation that is considered relatively weak, because of its shorter training and mitigated authority. Semi-professions lack the stature enjoyed by "full" professions such as law and medicine.

social capital The actual or potential resources linked to possession of a durable network of relationships of mutual acquaintance or recognition. For example, the wealthy and powerful may use their "old boys' network" or other social capital to maintain advantages for themselves, their social class, and their children.

social media The collection of websites, programs, and apps that allow users to create and share their own content, such as Facebook, Twitter, YouTube, Instagram, Vine, Snapchat, and Pinterest, among others.

social mobility The movement of individuals, families, households, or other categories of people within or between layers or tiers in an open system of social stratification.

socio-economic status A term used by sociologists to refer to economic aspects of social ranking. It is typically measured with a series of related attributes, including family income, poverty level, parent education, parent employment status, and/or parent occupational prestige.

status traits The characteristics that are assigned to individuals and have social significance in a society, such as ethno-racial group, age, gender, and social class.

summer learning A strategic area of study that compares school-year patterns of learning to those in the summer months. These studies allow researchers to examine learning disparities that emerge outside of school, thus allowing them to distinguish family effects from school effects.

surveillance Surveillance in school locker rooms in particular is a common practice among boys. The covert ways these young men, for example, would purposefully and strategically avoid the furtive glances of their peers reveals the level of surveillance. Boys expressed a discomfort in the locker room in which their peers took up space, imposing themselves through a physical as well as verbal dominance in these spaces. Boys monitor the actions of other boys to affirm they are suitably and appropriately masculine. Measures of harassment and bullying are often used to ensure boys conduct themselves as heteronormative boys.

technological determinism A view of technology as causing social and cultural change (that is having an effect on how societies function). Technological determinism has been criticized for its failure to consider the role of social factors (for example, economics, politics, legal frameworks, cultural values) in the development of technology.

treaties Between 1701 and present day, different groups of Indigenous peoples have entered into agreements with the Crown (First the British and after the Federal Government of Canada). These agreements are called "treaties." These speak to a variety of issues including the rights of peoples to use and enjoy lands occupied by Indigenous peoples and the responsibilities of government and Indigenous peoples. Treaties made prior to 1982 are recognized and protected by the Canadian Constitution. Modern treaties after 1982 are legally binding through other means.

underemployment The situation where an individual's employment fails to utilize the level of training or skill that he or she has obtained through formal education, or when there are unmet expectations for monetary returns on investment in formal education.

Index